Teacher Guidebook
Level A

A Reason For Spelling® Teacher Guidebook - Level A
Copyright ©2012 by The Concerned Group, Inc.

ISBN#: 0-936785-26-8
TL#: SPTGA2012

Published by The Concerned Group, Inc.
P.O. Box 1000, Siloam Springs, AR 72761

Publisher: Russ L. Potter, II • Project Director: Kristin Potter
Senior Editor: Bill Morelan • Layout and Design: Mark Decker
Copy Editor: Mary Alice Hill • Story Editor: Tricia Schnell
Proofreaders: Daniel Swatsenberg, Rachel Tucker

Created by MOE Studio, Inc.
Authors: Rebecca Burton, Eva Hill, Leah Knowlton, Kay Sutherland
Black and White Illustrations: James McCullough
Colorization for Student Edition: Mark Decker
Design and Layout: Mark Decker • Project Leader: Greg Sutherland

Printed in the United States on recyclable paper

For more information about *A Reason For Spelling,*® *A Reason For Handwriting,*®
A Reason For Science® and *A Reason For Guided Reading*®
go to: ***www.AReasonFor.com***

Level **A** | Introduction

Contents:

Acknowledgments:

Field Test Participants:

Virginia Allen, East Rockaway, New York • Mrs. Christine Baker, Belleville, Pennsylvania • Judy M. Banks, Carmichael, California • Darya Birch, San Clemente, California • Mari Anne Burns, Baton Rouge, Louisiana • Karen Dafflitto, St. Louis, Missouri • Kristen J. Dorsett, Prescott, Arizona • Ms. Laura Guerrera, East Rockaway, New York • Mrs. Anne Gutierrez, San Antonio, Texas • Jeanette O. Kappel, Winstead, Minnesota • Sharon K. Kobilka, San Antonio, Texas • Connie Kozitza, Winsted, Minnesota • Vivian I. Sawyer, Carmichael, California • Harold W. Souther, San Antonio, Texas • Cleo F. Staples, Auburn, California • Suezy Tucker, Auburn, California • Martha Woodbury, Los Angeles, California

Special thanks to:

Dr. Larry Burton, Dr. Carol Campbell, Dr. Lee Netherton, Melvin Northrup, Phyllis Paytee, Dr. Linda Romig

Placement Tests

In order to evaluate readiness and accurately meet individual student need, a simple placement test is recommended at the beginning of each school year.

Step 1: *Administer the test*

 Say) Number your paper from one to twenty. I will say the word once, use the word in a sentence, then say the word again. Write a word beside each number on your paper.

(Allow ample time and carefully monitor progress.)

Step 2: *Evaluate the corrected test using the following criteria:*

If the student correctly spells 17 to 20 words:
- Assign the student to Level A program
- Encourage the student to work independently
- Select and assign several Other Word Forms to spell and test

If the student correctly spells 8 to 16 words:
- Assign the student to Level A program
- Allow opportunities to work independently
- Offer Challenge Activities

If the student correctly spells 0 to 7 words:
- Assign the student to Level A program, but use regular lessons without Challenge Activities
- Encourage completion of all Phonics Activities

Placement Test Level A

1.	man	The **man** is tall.
2.	red	I like my **red** hat.
3.	not	We did **not** go to the park.
4.	big	This **big** dog barks a lot.
5.	run	They will **run** in the race.
6.	him	This gift is for **him.**
7.	ball	The **ball** is yellow.
8.	top	We hiked to the **top** of the hill.
9.	day	It is a sunny **day.**
10.	ride	I will **ride** my bike in the parade.
11.	go	The green light means **go.**
12.	ten	I have **ten** fingers.
13.	look	**Look** at the funny clown.
14.	boy	The **boy** kicked the ball.
15.	mother	My **mother** is baking bread.
16.	for	The flowers are **for** you.
17.	blue	The sky looks **blue** today.
18.	her	Did you tell **her** about Jesus?
19.	tell	**Tell** your friend to come in.
20.	and	You **and** I will ride at the park.

Level A | Introduction

Day One

Literature Connection - Each week begins with a Scripture verse, followed by a theme story that develops the principles found in that verse. Topic and description are provided to inform the teacher of the story content. Some teachers may choose to use this theme story for the Monday morning devotional. (A CD version of the story is also available.)

Discussion Time *(optional)* - Discussion questions follow each story, giving the teacher the opportunity to evaluate student understanding, and to encourage students to apply the values found in the Scripture to their own lives.

Day One (cont.)

Preview - The test — study — test sequence begins with this pre-test which primarily uses sentences related to the story. Research has shown that immediate correction by the student — under teacher supervision — is one of the best ways to learn to spell. Optional challenge words are marked with a star to help meet enrichment needs.

Say *(bubble graphic)* - Instructions to the students that are to be read aloud by the teacher are marked with the Say symbol for easy identification.

Progress Chart *(chart graphic)* - Students may record their Preview scores for later comparison against their Posttest scores.

Take a Minute *(clock graphic)* - Simple instructions are provided for committing to memory the Scripture verses upon which the stories are based.

Challenge *(star graphic)* - These words are provided for better spellers. Challenge activities are marked with a star for easy identification.

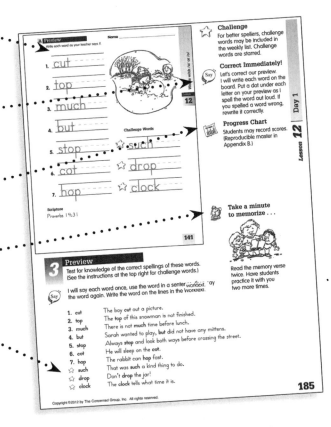

Day One (cont.)

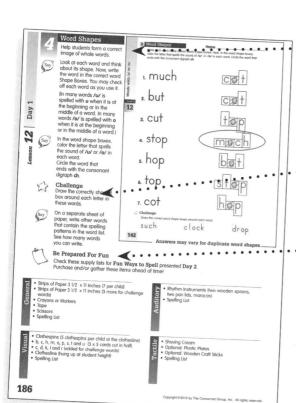

Word Shapes - The use of "Shape Boxes" is a research-based method that helps students form a correct visual image of each spelling word. An additional exercise is provided to enhance student identification of spelling patterns and thus strengthen phonemic awareness.

Challenge *(star graphic)* - These words are provided for better spellers. All challenge activities are marked with a star for easy identification.

Be Prepared for Fun *(list graphic)* - For teacher convenience, a weekly supply list is provided for "Fun Ways to Spell" on Day 1. Supplies for the "General" activity are readily available in most classrooms. Other categories may require minimal extra planning.

Day Two

Hide & Seek - Another research-proven method of spelling instruction, Hide & Seek, is highly effective for dealing with multiple intelligences and varying learning styles.

Other Word Forms *(optional)* - A variety of activities allow students to become familiar with other forms of the week's spelling words.

Fun Ways to Spell - Four options are offered each week. In addition to a "General" activity, "Auditory," "Tactile," and "Visual" options are provided for students with different learning styles. Suggestions are also given for adapting these activities to various classroom settings.

Day Three

Language Arts Activity - Research studies show that meaningful, practical use of spelling words helps students become more familiar with the words they are studying. The weekly Language Arts activity is designed to offer practice in this area.

Take a Minute - Reminders to commit Scripture verses to memory are provided periodically.

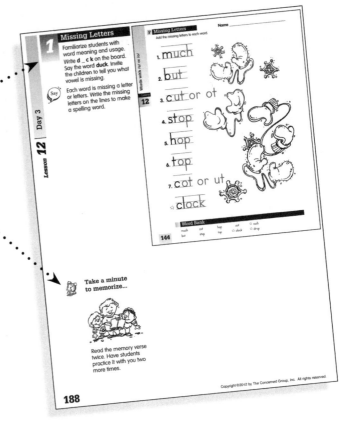

Day Four

Dictation - Students write dictated words to complete sentences. This strengthens their word usage and context skills. Previously taught spelling words are also included in this activity, providing maintenance of spelling skills.

Proofreading - Proofreading allows students to become familiar with the format of standardized tests as they mark misspelled words. Proofreading is also a critical skill that can be incorporated in students' own writing.

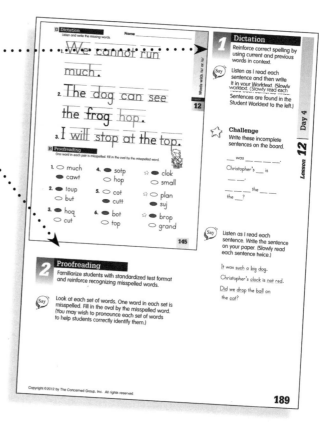

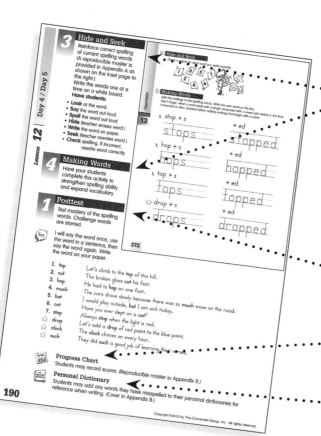

Day Four (cont.)

Hide & Seek/Other Word Forms (optional) - These activities provide additional opportunity for students to practice other forms of their spelling words. (Note: These pages are not in the Student Worktext. A reproducible master for each week is provided in Appendix A.)

Day Five

Posttest - The test — study — test sequence of learning is completed with the posttest. Again, most sentences relate to the theme story.

Progress Chart (chart graphic) - Students may now record their posttest scores to evaluate their weekly progress.

Personal Dictionary (dictionary graphic) - Students may add any words they have misspelled to their personal dictionaries. Each student may refer to his/her custom dictionary while journaling or during other writing activities. (Reproducible cover in Appendix B.)

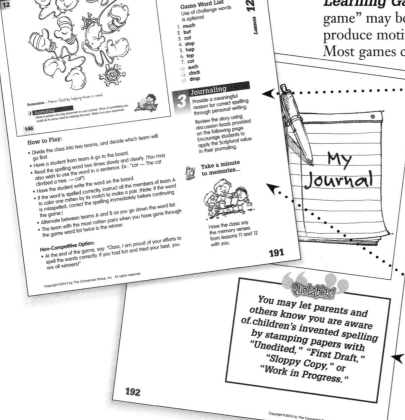

Day Five (cont.)

Learning Game (optional) - The weekly "board game" may be used to reinforce spelling skills and produce motivation and interest in good spelling. Most games can be played multiple times.

Journal Entry - The underlying goal of spelling instruction is to create better writers! This weekly journaling activity allows students to apply their spelling skills in a meaningful way, while encouraging them to make the featured value their own. Guided discussion questions are provided to assist in reviewing the value taught by the story.

Take a Minute - Reminders to commit Scripture verses to memory are provided periodically.

Quotables - Quotes from the comprehensive spelling research provide helpful insights for the teacher.

Introduction

Level A

A Reason For Spelling® emphasizes a balance between spelling skills, application, and student enjoyment. In short, it is designed to be both meaningful and fun! Each level promotes successful classroom practices while incorporating the following research findings:

Research Findings:

Application:

Daily Practice. A daily period of teacher-directed spelling activities based on meaningful content greatly enhances student proficiency in spelling.

Daily lessons in *A Reason For Spelling*® provide systematic development of spelling skills with a focus on Scripture verses and values.

Spelling Lists. The most productive spelling lists feature developmentally-appropriate words of highest frequency in writing.

Through daily lessons, challenge words, and other word forms, *A Reason For Spelling*® focuses on the high frequency words children and adults use in daily writing.

Test — Study — Test. Effective educational programs are built on the learning model of "Test — Study — Test."

A Reason For Spelling® follows a weekly pretest/ posttest format, and also includes a cumulative review for each unit.

Accurate Feedback. Pretest and proofreading results are crucial in helping students identify words that require their special attention.

Regular pretests and proofreading activities in *A Reason For Spelling*® help students identify words requiring their special attention.

Visual Imaging. Learning to spell a word involves forming a correct visual image of the whole word, rather than visualizing syllables or parts.

Every lesson in *A Reason For Spelling*® features word-shape grids to help students form a correct visual image of each spelling word.

Study Procedures. The most effective word-study procedures involve visual, auditory, and tactile modalities.

A Reason For Spelling® uses the "look, say, hide, write, seek, check" method as a primary teaching tool.

Learning Games. Well-designed games motivate student interest and lead to spelling independence.

A Reason For Spelling® includes a wide variety of spelling games at each instructional level.

Self-Correction. Student focus, accomplished through such activities as self-correction of pretests, is an essential strategy for spelling mastery at every grade and ability level.

Teacher directed self-correction of pretests and reviews is encouraged throughout *A Reason For Spelling*®.

Regular Application. Frequent opportunities to use spelling words in everyday writing contribute significantly to the maintenance of spelling ability.

A Reason For Spelling® provides opportunities for journaling in each lesson to promote the use of assigned spelling words in personal writing.

Cohen, Leo A. 1969. *Evaluating Structural Analysis Methods Used in Spelling Books*. Doctoral Thesis, Boston University.

Davis, Zephaniah T. 1987. Upper Grades Spelling Instruction: What Difference Does It Make? *English Journal*, March: 100-101.

Dolch, E.W. 1936. A Basic Sight Vocabulary. *The Elementary School Journal*, Vol. 36: 456-460.

Downing, John, Robert M. Coughlin and Gene Rich. 1986. Children's Invented Spellings in the Classroom. *The Elementary School Journal*, Vol. 86, No. 3, January: 295-303.

Fiderer, Adele. 1995. *Practical Assessments for Literature-Based Reading Classrooms*. New York: Scholastic Professional Books.

Fitzsimmons, Robert J., and Bradley M. Loomer. 1980. *Spelling: The Research Basis*. Iowa City: The University of Iowa.

Gardner, Howard. 1993. *Multiple Intelligences: The Theory in Practice*. New York: Basic-Books.

Gentry, J. Richard. 1997. *My Kid Can't Spell*. Portsmouth, NH: Heinemann Educational Books.

Gentry, J. Richard and Jean Wallace Gillet. 1993. *Teaching Kids to Spell*. Portsmouth, NH: Heinemann Educational Books.

Gentry, J. Richard. 1985. You Can Analyze Developmental Spelling-And Here's How To Do It! *Early Years K-8*, May:1-4.

Goswami, Usha. 1991. Learning about Spelling Sequences: The Role of Onsets and Rimes in Analogies in Reading. *Child Development*, 62, 1110-1123.

Graves, Donald H. 1977. Research Update: Spelling Texts and Structural Analysis Methods. *Language Arts 54* January: 86-90.

Harp, Bill. 1988. When the Principal Asks, "Why Are Your Kids Giving Each Other Spelling Tests?" *Reading Teacher*, Vol. 41, No. 7, March: 702-704.

Hoffman, Stevie and Nancy Knipping. 1988. Spelling Revisited: The Child's Way. *Childhood Education*, June: 284-287.

Horn, Ernest. 1926. *A Basic Writing Vocabulary: 10,000 Frequently Used Words in Writing*. Monograph First Series, No. 4. Iowa City: The University of Iowa.

Horn, Thomas. 1946. *The Effect of the Corrected Test on Learning to Spell*. Master's Thesis, The University of Iowa.

Horsky, Gregory Alexander. 1974. *A Study of the Perception of Letters and Basic Sight Vocabulary Words of Fourth and Fifth Grade Children*. Doctoral Thesis, The University of Iowa.

Lacey, Cheryl. 1994. *Moving On In Spelling*. Jefferson City, Missouri: Scholastic.

Lutz, Elaine. 1986. ERIC/RCS Report: Invented Spelling and Spelling Development. *Language Arts*, Vol. 63, No. 7, November: 742-744.

Marino, Jacqueline L. 1978. *Children's Use of Phonetic, Graphemic, and Morphophonemic Cues in a Spelling Task*. Doctoral Thesis, State University of New York at Albany.

Morris, Darrell, Laurie Nelson and Jan Perney. 1986. Exploring the Concept of 'Spelling Instructional Level' Through the Analysis of Error-Types. *The Elementary School Journal*, Vol. 87, No. 2, 195-197.

Nicholson, Tom and Sumner Schachter. 1979. Spelling Skill and Teaching Practice-Putting Them Back Together Again. *Language Arts*, Vol. 56, No. 7, October: 804-809.

Rothman, Barbara. 1997. *Practical Phonics Strategies to Build Beginning Reading and Writing Skills*. Medina, Washington: Institute for Educational Development.

Scott, Jill E. 1994. Spelling for Readers and Writers. *The Reading Teacher*, Vol. 48, No. 2, October: 188-190.

Simmons, Janice L. 1978. *The Relationship Between an Instructional Level in Spelling and the Instructional Level in Reading Among Elementary School Children*. Doctoral Thesis, University of Northern Colorado.

Templeton, Shane. 1986. Synthesis of Research on the Learning and Teaching of Spelling. *Educational Leadership*, March: 73-78.

Tireman, L.S. 1927. *The Value of Marking Hard Spots in Spelling*. Doctoral Thesis, University of Iowa.

Toch, Thomas. 1992. Nu Waz for Kidz tu Lern Rdn, Rtn. *U.S. News & World Report*, September 14: 75-76.

Wagstaff, Janiel M. *Phonics That Work! New Strategies for the Reading/Writing Classroom*. Jefferson City, Missouri: Scholastic.

Watson, Alan J. 1988. Developmental Spelling: A Word Categorizing Instructional Experiment. *Journal of Educational Research*, Vol. 82, No. 2, November/December: 82-88.

Webster's New American Dictionary. 1995. New York: Merriam-Webster Inc.

Wilde, Sandra. 1990. A Proposal for a New Spelling Curriculum. *The Elementary School Journal*, Vol. 90, No. 3, January: 275-289.

English Second Language (ESL)

Effective teachers are always sensitive to the special spelling challenges faced by ESL students. While it is not practical to provide specific guidelines for every situation where the teacher may encounter students with limited English proficiency, the following general guidelines for two of the most prominent cultural groups (Asian & Hispanic) may prove helpful.

alphabet — Many Asian languages have a significantly different kind of alphabet and students may need considerable practice recognizing English letters and sounds.

vowels — Some Asian languages do not have certain English vowel sounds. Speakers often substitute other sounds. Spanish vowels have a single sound: *a* as in *ball*, *e* as in *eight*, *i* as in *ski*, *o* as in *over*, *u* as in *rule*. The Spanish *a* is spelled *e*, *e* is spelled *i* or *y*, and *i* is often spelled *ai* or *ay*.

ô — The variety of *ô* spellings may cause some problems for Spanish-speaking students.

ü, u̇ — The *u̇* sound does not occur in Spanish, and may cause problems.

ou — This sound is spelled *au* in Spanish.

r — This sound does not exist in Spanish. Many Asian languages do not have words ending with *r*.

b, d, h, j — Spanish and Asian speakers often confuse the sounds of *b / d* and *h / j*.

ge, gi, j — In Spanish, *ge*, *gi*, and *j* most closely resemble the English *h*.

l, f — Many Asian languages do not have these sounds.

k, q — The letter *k* does not exist in Spanish, but the sound *k* is spelled with either *c* or *qu*. The letter *q* always occurs with *ue* or *ui*.

p, g — In most Asian languages, the consonants *p* and *g* do not exist.

v — In Spanish, the letter *v* is pronounced *b*.

w — There are no Spanish-originated words with the letter *w*.

y — In Spanish, *y* is spelled *ll*.

x, z — In Spanish, *x* is never used in the final position. There is no letter or sound for *z*.

ch, sh — The Spanish language does not have the sound *sh*. Spellers often substitute *ch*. Many Asian languages do not contain *sh* or *ch*.

wh, th — The initial *wh* and *th* sounds do not exist in most Spanish and some Asian languages. The Spanish *d*, however, is sometimes pronounced almost like the *th*.

kn — This sound may be difficult for both Spanish and Asian spellers.

s clusters — Spanish clusters that begin with s are always preceded by the vowels *a* or *e*. The most common clusters that will cause problems are *sc*, *sk*, *sl*, *sm*, *sn*, *sp*, *sq*, *st*, and *sw*. Many of these do not occur in Asian languages.

pl, fl, tr, fr, dr — These sounds are used in Spanish, but may not be present in some Asian languages.

ng, nk, nt, nd — Many Asian languages don't have *ng*, *nk*, *nt*, or *nd*. Spanish doesn't include the ng ending.

silent letters — The only silent letter in Spanish is *h*. Silent consonants such as those in *mb*, *lk*, and *gh* do not occur in Spanish or Asian languages.

double consonants — The only double consonants in Spanish are *cc*, *ll*, and *rr*.

ed — In Spanish, the suffix *ed* is pronounced aid. This can be very confusing, especially when the *ed* has the soft *t* sound as in *dropped*.

plurals — Spanish rules for adding plurals are: For words ending in a vowel, add *s*. For words ending in a consonant, add *es*. This may cause confusion both in pronunciation and spelling of English words.

contractions — Only two contractions are used in Spanish: *a el* becomes *al*, and *de el* becomes *del*. Apostrophes do not exist.

syllables — Many Asian languages consist entirely of one and two syllable words. Thus, many longer English words are often confusing.

x

Spelling Generalizations

In the English language, spelling cannot be taught primarily by rules or generalizations. It's a complex language that has evolved from many other languages and therefore contains many irregularities. There are exceptions to almost all spelling rules.

Research, however, indicates that some generalizations are of value in teaching children to spell. These generalizations have few exceptions and apply to a large number of words. Familiarity with these spelling rules can be helpful to many learners. In addition, generalizations that deal with adding suffixes to words can be quite valuable in expanding a student's ability to spell other word forms.

The following generalizations may prove to be helpful:

- The letter *q* is always followed by *u*.

- Every syllable contains a vowel. *Y* can also serve as a vowel.

- Words that end in silent *e*:
  …drop the *e* when adding a suffix beginning with a vowel. (live, living)
  …keep the *e* when adding a suffix beginning with a consonant. (time, timely)

- Words that end in *y*:
  …are not changed when adding suffixes if the *y* is preceded by a vowel. (say, saying)
  …change the *y* to *i* when adding suffixes if the *y* is preceded by a consonant, unless the suffix begins with *i*. (try, tried, trying)

- When *ei* or *ie* are used in a word, the *i* usually comes before the *e* except when they make the /ā/ sound, or follow after a *c*. (believe, eight, ceiling)

- Words ending in one consonant preceded by a single vowel usually double the final consonant when adding a suffix beginning with a vowel. (begin, beginning)

- Words ending with the sounds made by *x*, *s*, *sh*, and *ch* add the suffix *es* to form plurals or change tense. (mix, mixes)

- Proper nouns and most proper adjectives begin with capital letters.

Multiple Intelligences

In recognition of the multiple intelligences theory, *A Reason For Spelling*® provides activities to meet the varied needs of your students. (See "Fun Ways to Spell," and "Hide & Seek.")

Scripture Translation

Since *A Reason For Spelling*® is an elementary level curriculum, the authors have chosen to use a Scripture paraphrase that features simple, easy-to-understand vocabulary.*

Teachers are strongly encouraged to introduce each lesson by reading the "Theme Text" aloud (or have a student read the verse aloud to the class). This helps set the stage for the principles and values students will be focusing on that week.

Scripture verses used in *A Reason For Spelling*® are similar in most translations, allowing teachers to use the Scripture translation their school prefers, without affecting academic content.

Personal Spelling Dictionary

A great way to encourage students' spelling awareness is to help them develop and maintain their own Personal Spelling Dictionary at their desk to refer to when writing. This can be either a spiral-bound or loose-leaf notebook with a few pages designated for each letter of the alphabet. Throughout the school year, encourage students to constantly add words to their Personal Spelling Dictionary, not only from spelling class, but from other classes as well. These should include words a student finds difficult to spell, as well as words of particular interest. (Reproducible cover in Appendix B)

Word Walls

Another excellent method of promoting spelling awareness in your classroom is to create a word wall. This wall (often a large bulletin board) contains commonly used words and words of special interest to your class. The classroom word wall becomes a permanent reference list that students may refer to as they read and write.

Words may be arranged in a variety of ways. Some examples include traditional alphabetical order; groups such as math words, weather words, color words; or alphabetically by the first letter of the targeted vowel schemes. For example:

A	E	I	O	U
gate	eaten	bit	fabulous	fun
tar	dread	like	skeleton	fur
	her	tonight		bubble

Some words could even have picture or context clues added, sample words from word families being studied, or interesting words students want to know how to spell are added throughout the year. Students should be reminded not to simply copy the words from the wall, but to look at the word needed, then write it from memory — or write the word they are having difficulty with, then check it against the word wall.

Games can be played using the word wall as well.
- Rhyming Words: Ask students to find a word that "begins with G and rhymes with rod."

- Sentence Sense: Write the letter l on the board, then say "Look for a word that begins with an l and fits this sentence: I _ _ _ _ Jesus."

- Chant & Clap: Chant the spelling words, clapping for each vowel or consonant.

- Dictate & Write: Dictate a sentence for students to write using words found only on the wall.

- Read My Mind:

I am thinking of one of the words on the wall. It has _____ letters. It begins with _____ .
The vowel is _____. It fits in this sentence: _____.

Flip Folders

The Flip Folder is a great way for students to use the research-based, time-tested "Look — Hide — Write — Seek — Check" method to learn spelling words. They may do this activity on their own or with a partner.

On the front of a standard file folder, make two cuts to create three flaps (see diagram below). On a separate piece of paper, have students make three columns, then write the words they need to study in the first column. Now have students slide the paper into the folder so that the words are under the first flap.

(Say)

- Open Flap 1 and **Look** at the first word.
- Now **Hide** the word by closing the flap.
- Open Flap 2 and **Write** the word in the middle column.
- Open Flaps 1 & 2 and **Seek** the word to . . .
- **Check** your spelling. If the word is misspelled…
- Open Flap 3 and **Write** the word correctly in the third column.

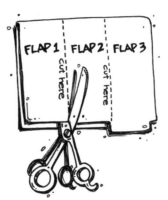
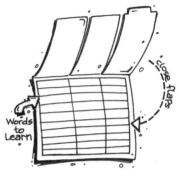

Inventive Spelling/Journaling

The goal of **A Reason For Spelling**® is to create proficient and self-reliant spellers and writers. By combining inventive spelling (through journaling) with formal spelling instruction, an excellent environment is created for students to develop into expert spellers. (A reproducible Journal cover is in Appendix B.)

As children learn to spell, they go through several stages. The move from one stage to another is gradual even though students may spell from more than one stage at one time. Just as a toddler who is talking in complete sentences doesn't suddenly regress to babbling, so students tend to remain relatively stable within and between stages. Recognized stages of spelling development include:

Precognitive Stage: Children use symbols from the alphabet for writing words, but letters are random and do not correspond to sound. (eagle = dfbrt; eighty = acbp)

Semiphonetic Stage: Children understand and consistently represent sounds with letters. Spellings are often abbreviated representing only the initial and/or final sounds. (eagle = e; eighty = a)

Phonetic Stage: Students in this stage spell words like they sound. The speller perceives and represents every sound in a word, though spellings may be unconventional. (eagle = egl; eighty = aty)

Transitional Stage: Students think about how words appear visually. Spelling patterns are apparent. Spellings exhibit customs of English spelling such as vowels in every syllable, correct e-marker and vowel digraph patterns, inflectional endings, and frequent English letter sequences. (eagle = egul; eighty = eightee)

Conventional Stage: This stage develops over years of word study and writing. Correct spelling has different instructional levels. Correct spelling for a group of words that can be spelled by the average third grader would be "third grade level correct" spelling. (eagle = eagle; eighty = eighty)

An effective way to help students transition through the stages is to edit their first drafts, then talk with them about corrections. Discuss why changes are necessary. Encourage students to rewrite journal entries so others can read them easily. Display student work whenever possible. Teach students that invented spelling makes it easier for the writer, but that revision to standard spelling is a courtesy to the reader.

Word Lists

Word lists in *A Reason For Spelling*® are based on frequency of use in student and adult writing; frequency of use in reading materials; spelling difficulty; and grade level familiarity.

Studies used in the development of these lists include: *Dolch Basic Sight Vocabulary* (a list of 220 high frequency words); *The American Heritage Word Frequency Book* (a study of word frequency in print materials for grades three through nine); *Starter Words* (the 190 most frequently used words in children's writing, school materials, and adult print materials); and *A Basic Vocabulary of Elementary School Children.*

These standard references were extensively cross-checked with other respected studies (Gates; Horn; Greene & Loomer; Harris & Jacobson). It is significant to note that very few differences were found among these sources.

For teacher convenience, lesson numbers follow each word, and challenge words are indicated by a star.

about-19	day-13	he's-11☆	mother-24	short-28
above-22☆	did-4	help-2☆	much-12	side-14
add-1☆	dig-4	hen-17	my-16	sit-4
after-23	digit-28☆	her-24	next-2☆	six-26
all-9	do-21	hid-4	nice-14	small-9☆
am-7	dog-3	hide-14	no-16	so-16
an-1	down-19	him-8	none-22☆	some-22
and-7	draw-9☆	his-8	not-3	soon-21☆
are-24	drop-12☆	hit-4	now-19	south-19☆
as-23	each-11☆	hop-12	number-26☆	still-4☆
ask-1☆	eat-11	how-19	odd-3☆	stop-12
at-1	enjoy-22☆	hug-6	of-22	such-12☆
away-13	fall-9	ice-14	off-3	sum-6☆
back-7☆	feet-11	if-8	on-3	take-13
ball-9	few-28	in-8	one-26	talk-9☆
bed-2	finish-8☆	into-8☆	or-24	tall-28
begin-8☆	first-24☆	is-8	orange-27☆	tell-2
best-2☆	five-26	it-4	our-19	ten-17
big-4	for-24	jaw-9	out-19	than-18☆
black-27	four-26	joy-22	pencil-17☆	thank-1☆
blue-27	frog-3☆	just-6☆	penny-17☆	that-23
books-21☆	from-22	kid-4☆	pink-27	the-18
box-3☆	fun-6	kind-14☆	plan-7☆	them-18
boy-22	funny-6☆	know-16☆	play-13	then-17
brown-27	get-2	land-7	pray-13☆	there-18
bug-6	girl-24	law-9	purple-27☆	these-18☆
but-12	glad-7	let-2	put-21	they-18
by-16	go-16	line-14☆	quit-4☆	thick-28☆
call-9	God-3	little-28	ran-1	thin-28☆
came-13☆	going-16☆	long-28	red-2	thing-18
can-1	good-21	look-21	ride-14	think-18☆
cat-1	got-3	Lord-24☆	round-19☆	this-18
cent-17	grade-13☆	love-22	run-6	three-26
circle-24☆	grand-7☆	made-13	said-23	time-14
clock-12☆	green-27	make-13	sand-7	to-21
color-27☆	had-7	man-1	saw-9	tooth-21☆
come-22	hand-7	many-28	school-21	top-12
cot-12	happy-23	may-13	see-11	town-19
count-26☆	has-23	me-11	send-17	try-16
cup-6	hasn't-23☆	mom-3	sentence-17☆	two-26
cut-12	have-23☆	more-28	seven-26	up-6
dad-1	he-11	most-16☆	she-11	us-6

vowel-19☆	boys-22	forgot-4☆
was-23	break-7☆	form-22
wasn't-23☆	bring-27	found-21
we-11	brother-28☆	friend-26☆
we'll-11☆	bubble-5☆	frog-4
well-2	buy-9	full-19
went-17	cake-7	funny-29
when-17	called-23☆	game-7
white-27	came-7	gate-7
why-16	camp-1	gave-7
wide-14	candy-26	give-3
will-8	car-14	gone-4
win-8	card-14	grade-7
with-18	care-15☆	grand-26
write-14☆	child-9☆	grass-29
yellow-27	children-23	great-7☆
yes-2	circle-16	grow-11
you-21	city-17☆	guess-29
your-24	clean-8	gym-3☆
zero-26☆	clock-27	hang-27
	cloud-21☆	hard-14

Level-B

	cold-10	hat-1
	color-16	have-1
above-5	could-19	he's-8
add-1	count-21	head-2
again-2☆	cow-21	hear-19
air-15	crown-21☆	heard-16☆
along-27☆	cry-9	heart-14☆
also-23	dark-14	help-2
always-23	dear-19	here-19
another-28	different-29☆	high-9☆
any-17	digit-3	hold-10
apple-1☆	dinner-29☆	holy-17
arm-14	dish-25	home-10
around-21	does-5	hope-10
ask-1	don't-10☆	horse-22
asked-1☆	done-5	house-21
baby-17	door-22	I'm-9
back-27	dot-4	important-22☆
bake-7	draw-23	index-26☆
balloon-20☆	dress-29	Indian-26
band-26	drop-4	into-3
barn-14	dry-9	its-3
bath-1☆	duck-27	Jesus-8☆
be-8	each-23	job-4☆
bear-15	ear-19	jump-5
because-3☆	east-8	just-5
been-3	easy-17☆	keep-8
before-22☆	end-26	kid-3
begin-3	enjoy-22	kind-26
bell-29	even-8	knew-20☆
below-11☆	ever-2	know-11
bend-26	every-17	large-14☆
beside-15☆	eye-15	last-1
best-2	family-17	late-7
better-29	far-14	left-2
between-8☆	farm-14	leg-2
Bible-9☆	fast-1	letter-29☆
bird-16	father-28☆	light-9
birthday-13☆	find-26	like-15
blind-26	fine-15	line-15
block-27☆	finish-25	live-3
blow-11	fire-15	looked-19☆
boat-10	first-16	Lord-22
books-19	fish-25	lost-4
both-28	flower-21☆	lot-4
bow-21	fly-9	low-11
box-4	food-20	lunch-23☆

map-1
men-2
might-9
milk-27
mitten-29
most-10
mowing-11☆
must-5
name-7
nest-2
never-2☆
new-20
next-2
night-9
noise-22
none-5
noon-20
number-5
obey-7☆
odd-4
often-4
old-10
once-5☆
only-17
orange-22
other-28
over-10☆
own-11
page-7
paint-13
part-14
party-14☆
pay-13
penny-17
people-8
plan-1
plays-13
pond-26
praise-13☆
pray-13
print-3☆
pull-29
purple-16
quit-3
rabbit-29
rain-13
read-8
ready-17
right-9
road-10
roll-10
room-20
round-21
row-11
say-13
second-26☆
sentence-2
set-2
shelf-25☆
shoe-25
shoes-25☆
shop-25
short-25☆
should-25
show-25
shut-25
sick-27
sing-27

sister-3
sleep-8☆
slow-11
small-23
snow-11
snowman-11☆
soft-4
something-27☆
sometimes-5☆
soon-20
sound-21
south-21
stay-13
stayed-13☆
still-29
stood-19☆
store-22
story-17
study-17☆
such-23
sum-5
talk-27
than-1
thank-28
their-15
these-28
thick-28
thin-28
think-28
third-16☆
those-28
thought-28
through-20☆
throw-11
tie-9
today-13
together-28☆
told-10
tomorrow-4☆
too-20
took-19
tooth-20
tow-11
toy-22
train-13
tree-8
truck-27
under-16
until-3☆
use-20
very-17
voice-22☆
vowel-21
walk-23
want-23
wanted-23☆
wash-25
water-16
way-13
we'll-8
were-16
what-5
where-15
which-23
while-15☆
who-20
wish-25

wood-19
word-16
work-16
world-16☆
would-19
write-15
wrote-10☆
yard-14
year-19☆
zoo-20

Level-C

able-27
address-8
afraid-16
ago-20
airport-23
alarm-25
allow-22
alone-20
amount-22
angel-13
angry-17
answer-1
anyhow-22
apart-25
April-27
argue-25
army-25
artist-25
asleep-14
August-21
aunt-9
autumn-21
awake-16
bark-25
began-1
behind-9
belong-9
berry-1
bicycle-19
body-1
boot-31
boss-14
bother-3
bottle-27
bought-21
bread-5
bright-11
broke-5
brook-29
brought-21
bump-9
burn-28
bushes-29
busy-17
butter-8
buzz-2
cactus-2
cage-13
candle-27
careful-15
carry-17
cattle-27
caught-11
cause-21
center-26

certain-14
chair-3
chalk-11
change-3
charge-25
cheek-3
cheese-3
cherry-3
chest-1
chill-1
choose-31
circus-14
classroom-8
clay-4
close-4
cloth-4
clothes-11
clown-22
collar-2
cookie-29
copy-15
corner-23
course-23
cover-15
crash-10
crayon-5
creek-17
crop-2
cross-5
crowd-22
date-16
daughter-21
deaf-2
December-26
deep-17
die-19
dirt-28
dollar-26
doubt-22
drank-9
drew-31
driver-26
drown-22
eagle-27
early-28
earn-28
earth-10
edge-13
eight-16
February-17
felt-2
field-17
fight-19
flag-4
flame-4
flash-4
flew-31
float-20
floor-23
follow-20
football-29
forget-26
fork-15
fort-23
fought-21
fourth-23
fresh-10
Friday-19

front-1
fruit-31
gas-14
gift-1
giraffe-13
glass-4
glove-4
goes-20
gold-20
good-bye-29
grab-5
grandfather-9
grandmother-9
gray-5
ground-22
group-31
half-11
hall-21
hammer-26
handle-27
happen-8
hatch-10
heavy-17
held-1
hello-2
herd-28
honey-17
hood-29
hook-29
horn-23
hour-22
huge-13
hurry-28
husband-9
ink-9
January-13
jar-13
jealous-13
jolly-13
judge-13
jug-13
juice-13
July-13
June-13
kept-15
key-15
kick-10
knee-11
knot-11
ladder-8
lady-16
lamb-2
later-26
lay-16
learn-28
leave-17
less-14
lesson-8
lie-19
life-19
lift-1
list-1
loose-31
loud-22
made-16
mail-16
March-25
mark-25

market-25
marry-17
match-10
meal-17
mean-17
merry-8
metal-27
middle-27
million-8
mirror-26
Monday-9
moon-31
mouse-22
mouth-22
nearby-19
neck-10
needle-27
neighbor-11
neighborhood-29
north-3
notebook-29
November-26
October-15
open-20
order-23
owe-20
pants-2
paper-16
park-25
pass-14
paw-21
person-28
pick-1
place-4
plain-4
plane-16
plant-4
please-4
plow-22
plus-4
pool-31
poor-23
porch-10
pour-23
power-22
prayer-5
price-5
prize-5
proud-5
pulley-29
puppy-1
push-29
queen-15
quick-15
quiet-15
quilt-15
quite-15
race-14
rack-15
rage-13
rake-15
ranch-10
raw-21
really-8
remember-26
return-28
ripe-19

river-26
rode-20
rope-20
rubber-8
ruler-31
rush-10
sack-10
saddle-27
sail-16
salt-21
sandwich-10
sang-9
Saturday-28
save-14
score-23
scrap-7
scratch-7
scream-7
screen-7
scrub-7
search-28
sell-14
September-28
serve-28
sew-20
shade-16
shampoo-31
shark-25
sharp-25
shock-3
shook-29
shout-22
shown-20
shy-19
sidewalk-11
sight-11
sign-19
silver-26
since-14
skate-5
skin-5
skip-5
sleeve-4
slice-4
smart-25
smell-8
smile-19
smooth-31
soap-14
song-21
sore-23
sorry-14
spell-5
spend-5
splash-10
spoke-20
sport-23
spread-7
spring-7
sprinkle-27
squirrel-27
stamp-9
start-25
stiff-2
storm-23
straight-7
strange-7

straw-7
stream-7
street-7
string-7
strong-7
sudden-8
sugar-26
suit-31
summer-26
Sunday-2
sunny-8
supper-8
sweet-14
switch-10
table-16
taught-21
teacher-10
team-17
telephone-20
test-1
thankful-3
thirteen-3
thirty-28
though-11
threw-7
thumb-11
Thursday-3
tight-19
tiny-19
toast-20
track-15
travel-27
truth-31
Tuesday-31
turtle-27
twelve-2
twenty-17
unhappy-8
upon-21
visit-1
wagon-2
wait-16
wall-21
Wednesday-11
weigh-16
west-2
whale-3
wheat-3
whether-3
whip-3
whole-11
wild-19
wind-9
window-2
wing-9
wipe-19
wolf-29
woman-29
wonder-26
wool-29
wore-23
worse-28
wrap-11
young-9

Literature Connection
To increase comprehension and vocabulary development through a value-based story.

Discussion Time
To check understanding of the story and encourage personal value development.

Pretest
To test for knowledge of correct spellings of current spelling words.

Word Shapes
To help students form a correct visual image of whole words and to help students recognize common spelling patterns.

Hide & Seek
To reinforce correct spelling of current spelling words.

Other Word Forms
To strengthen spelling ability and expand vocabulary.

Fun Ways to Spell
To reinforce correct spelling of current words with activities that appeal to varying learning styles.

Dictation
To reinforce using current and previous spelling words in context.

Proofreading
To reinforce recognition of misspelled words, and to familiarize students with standardized test format.

Language Arts Activity
To familiarize students with word meaning and usage.

Posttest
To test mastery of the current spelling words.

Learning Game
To reinforce correct spelling of test words.

Challenge Activities
To provide more advanced spellers with the opportunity to master more difficult words.

Journaling
To provide a meaningful reason for correct spelling through personal writing.

Unit Tests
To test mastery of the correct spelling of the words from each unit.

Unit Challenge Tests
To test more advanced spellers' mastery of the correct spellings of the challenge words from each unit.

Action Game
To provide a fun way to review spelling words from the previous unit.

Certificate
To provide opportunity for parents or guardians to encourage and assess their child's progress.

Parent Letter
To provide the parent or guardian with the spelling word lists for the next unit.

Phonics Units *(Levels A and B only)*
To provide a supplement for promoting phonemic awareness, and a review of basic phonic skills.

Common Spelling Patterns

The following list of sounds and spelling patterns will help you easily identify words with similar patterns.

Sounds	Sample Words	Sounds	Sample Words
a	ask, hat	ō	old, boat, hoe, globe, blow
ā	apron, late, mail, play	ô	talk, cause, draw, soft, thought
ä	father, part, heart	ôr	story, more, ward, four
âr	aware, fair, bear, there	oi	point, boy
b	berry, able, scrub	ou	about, plow
ch	cheese, bunch, latch, nature	p	plan, reply, snap, supply
d	dog, ladder	r	ran, merry, more, write
e	bed, heavy, said	s	say, guess, scent, price, city
ē	she, heat, free, niece, key	sh	ship, cash, mission, machine, special, vacation
f	fish, loaf, off, enough, prophet		
g	give, forgot, shrug	t	ten, put, butter, creased
h	has, anyhow, whole	th	thin, ethnic, with
wh	whine, which	th	them, worthy, smooth
i	dig, gym	u	cup, done, what, young
ī	find, pie, mice, try	ū	human, you, new, tune
îr	clear, deer, pierce, cereal, here	ü	clue, do, soon, fruit
j	just, enjoy, germ, huge, budge	u̇	took, should, push
k	keep, hook, stick, school, can	ûr	earn, stern, first, work, Thursday
l	left, July, haul, fully, tell	v	visit, avoid, arrive
m	meal, calm, climb, common, hymn	w	wash, driveway
		y	young, familiar
n	nice, fun, tunnel, know	z	lazy, jazz, prize, raise, reins, example
ng	along, bringing, thing	zh	measure, erosion
o	not, pond, watch	ə	above, water, animal, gallon, thankful

Warm-Up

Matching Partner Letters

Materials
- 3 x 5 cards or seasonal die-cut shapes

Preparation
Make one set of upper case letter cards and lower case letter cards. Divide the class into two teams.

How to Play:
Give students on **Team A** the upper case letter cards and students on **Team B** the lower case letter cards. Have students find the person on the other team who has their partner letter. You will need to do this more than once, using part of the alphabet for each turn. You may like to time the activity and have students try to find their partners faster each time.

A | **Poetry Connection**

Name _____

The Apples
Apples, crunchy apples, hanging in the tree.
Apples, juicy apples, Jesus made for me.

Down comes an apple with a little stem,
Down, down, down, when I shake the limb.

Apples, crunchy apples hanging in the tree.
Apples, juicy apples, Jesus made for me.

Down come two apples... (continue)

Look at the first letter in each row. Draw a circle around the other letter in the row that is the same.

1. b | a (b) c d
2. g | (g) h i j
3. q | p (q) r s
4. d | b c (d) e
5. p | m n o (p)
6. t | s (t) u v
7. l | j k (l) m
8. h | f g (h) i
9. k | (k) l m n
10. r | (r) s t u
11. n | m (n) o p
12. m | j k l (m)
13. f | d e (f) g
14. j | h i (j) k
15. y | w x (y) z
16. v | u (v) w x
17. w | t u v (w)
18. z | w x y (z)

3

Poetry Connection
Have students follow along as you read the poem. Talk about how this poem might describe writing downstroke letters from top to bottom. Demonstrate downstrokes on the board and guide students to tell which letters have downstrokes. (**a, b, d, h, i, k, l, m, n, p, q, r, t, u, B, D, E, F, H, I, K, L, M, N, P, R, T, Y**)

Activity Page 3

Objective:
To identify matching letters

(Say)

In number one the first letter is **b**. Look in the first row for the other letter just like it. Draw a circle around it. I will say the first letter in each row and you will draw a circle around the letter in the row that is the same.

2

Aa go together.
Aa are partner letters.
Color the apples that have partner letters on them.

1.   2.   3.

A a   F j   K k

4.   5.   6.

X y   E f   Z x

7.   8.   9.

R r   H h   J i

10.   11.   12.

V v   M w   T i

13. N n   14. I t   15. L j

4

---

5 Follow Up

Alphabet Cards

Learning Styles
Kinesthetic and Visual Learners

Materials
• 3 x 5 cards or seasonal die-cut shapes

Preparation
Make one or more sets of lower case letter cards.

How to Play:
Place a set of alphabet cards on a table. These may be used in several ways:
1. Children may stand them up along the chalk tray in alphabetical order.
2. Two children may work together. One may hold up a card and ask the other to name a word that begins with that letter.
3. Two children may work together. One may hold up a card and ask the other to tell what sound that letter makes.

---

4 Activity Page 4

Objective:
To identify uppercase and lowercase partner letters

 Say

Look at the apples at the top of your page. The uppercase and lowercase letters with the same name are partner letters. Describe the differences you see between the uppercase and lowercase forms of the letter **a**. Color the apples that have partner letters on them.

1 Warm-Up

Mail Carrier

Materials
- Box
- Picture cards whose names begin with the letters a, b, c, d, g, p, q, or s, such as apple, ball, cat, duck, girl, pig, queen, sock

Preparation
Put the picture cards in a box.

How to Play:
Deliver the box to a student and ask him/her to select a card. Have the student hold up the card, say the name of the picture, and identify the beginning sound.
Let the student deliver the box to someone else and repeat the activity. Continue until all students have had a turn.

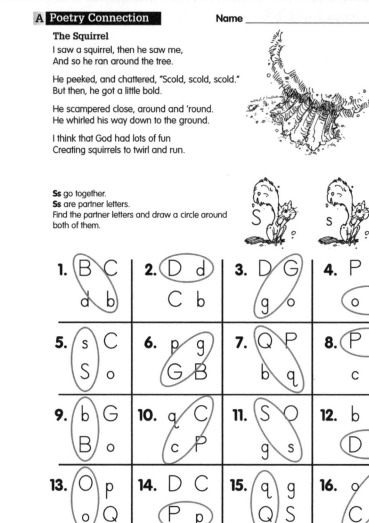

A Poetry Connection

Name _____

Partner Letters

Day 2

The Squirrel

I saw a squirrel, then he saw me,
And so he ran around the tree.

He peeked, and chattered, "Scold, scold, scold."
But then, he got a little bold.

He scampered close, around and 'round.
He whirled his way down to the ground.

I think that God had lots of fun
Creating squirrels to twirl and run.

Ss go together.
Ss are partner letters.
Find the partner letters and draw a circle around both of them.

1. B C d b
2. D d C b
3. D G g o
4. P q o O
5. s C S o
6. p g G B
7. Q P b q
8. P p c D
9. b G B o
10. q C c P
11. S O g s
12. b P D d
13. O p o Q
14. D C P p
15. q g Q S
16. o c C G

5

2 Poetry Connection

Have students follow along as you read the poem. Invite them to find letters that go around and circle them in their poem.

3 Activity Page 5

Objective:
To identify circle letters and their partners

 Say

Look at the squirrels at the top of your page. The uppercase and lowercase letters with the same name are partner letters. Describe the differences you see between the uppercase and lowercase forms of the letter **s**. Find the partner letters in each set and circle them.

Name _____

Follow the dots from **A** to **Z**. What secret animal do you see? Write the first letter of its name on the line at the top of your page.

Alphabetical Order

Day
2

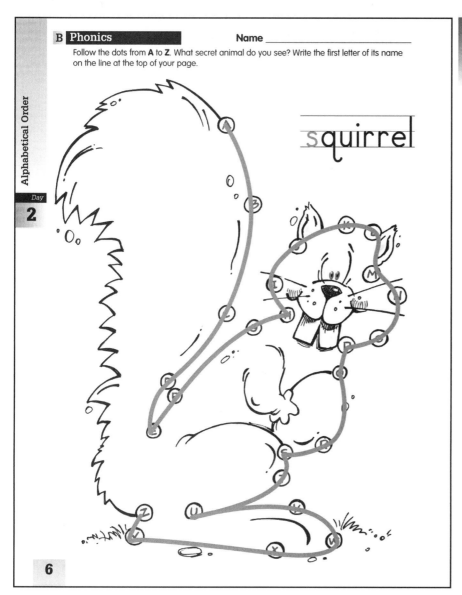

s quirrel

6

Activity Page 6
4

Objective:
To follow alphabetical order

(Say) Find the circled letter **A**. Use your pencil to draw a line from the **A** to the **B** to the **C** and so on to the letter **Z**. Try to guess the secret animal and write the first letter of its name to complete the word at the top of your page.

Follow Up
5

Letter Partner Relay

Learning Styles
Kinesthetic and Visual Learners

Materials
• 4 dry-erase markers or chalk

Preparation
Draw vertical lines to divide the board into four sections. Number the sections from **1** to **4**. Ten feet back from each section, mark a line on the floor. Divide the class into four teams and provide each team with chalk or a marker.

How to Play:
Have each team line up behind the 10-foot line. The first person on each team has chalk or a marker. He will walk up to the board, write **Aa**, walk back, give the chalk or marker to the next person on his team, and go to the end of the line. The second person will walk up, write **Bb**, and so on. Each team will write the entire alphabet through **Zz**. The first team to get to **Zz** and have its alphabet written correctly, is the winner.

Phonics

Lesson **2**

1 Warm-Up

Sound Tray

Materials
- Tray
- Small objects whose names begin with a consonant, such as bell, dish, pencil, quarter, rock, toy duck, penny, book, toy pig, balloon, dime

Preparation
Put small objects on tray.

How to Play:
Invite the students to name each object on the tray with you. Ask a student to hold up two objects from the tray. Have the class tell you whether the objects names begin with the same sound or different sounds. Continue until all students have had a turn.

A Poetry Connection   Name _____

My Balloon
I went to the circus and got something new!
A great big balloon, so round and so blue.

If I should let go, I'd lose it I know,
So I hold the string tightly, and let the wind blow!

Look at the first letter in each row. Draw a circle around each letter in the row that is the same.

1. b   (b) q p (b) (b)
2. p   d (p) (p) b (p)
3. d   q (d) (d) (d) p
4. q   b (q) d (q) (q)
5. d   b (d) (d) p (d)
6. b   (b) (b) d (b) q
7. p   (p) q (p) (p) b
8. q   d (q) p (q) (q)
9. p   (p) b (p) (p) d
10. d   b b (d) (d) (d)
11. q   p (q) p (q) (q)
12. b   (b) (b) d (b) d

7

---

2 Poetry Connection

Have students follow along as you read the poem. Talk about how this poem might describe writing letters that have a circle and stick. Demonstrate by drawing a balloon on a string on the board and guide students to tell which letters include a circle and a stick. (**b, d, p, q**)

3 Activity Page 7

Objective:
To identify the letters **b, d, p, q**

Say In number one the first letter is **b**. Circle each letter in the first row that is just like it. Now, I will say the first letter in each row and you will circle each letter in the row that is the same.

B Phonics

Name _____

Circle the letter for each beginning sound, then write the letter on the line below the picture.

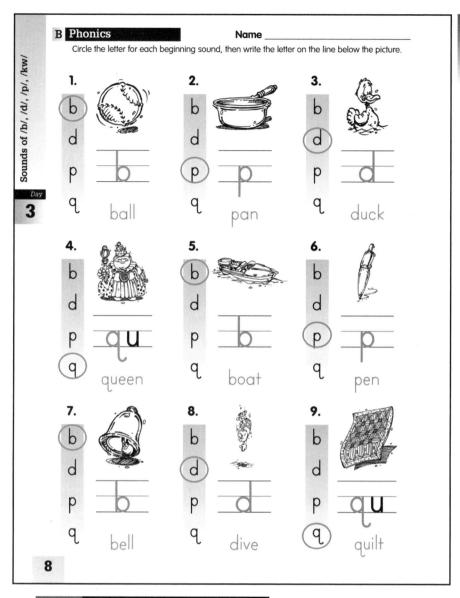

Day
3

Sounds of /b/, /d/, /p/, /kw/

1. b d p q — ball
2. b d p q — pan
3. b d p q — duck
4. b d p q — queen
5. b d p q — boat
6. b d p q — pen
7. b d p q — bell
8. b d p q — dive
9. b d p q — quilt

8

---

4 Activity Page 8

Objective:
To identify the sounds of **/b/, /d/, /p/, /kw/**

Say I will say the name of each picture. Circle the letter for each beginning sound, then write the letter on the line below.

---

5 Follow Up

Around The Room

Learning Styles
Auditory, Kinesthetic, and Visual Learners

Materials
• Self-stick notes

Preparation
Write the letters **b**, **d**, **p**, **q** on the board.

How to Play:
Review the sounds for each letter on the board. Tell the children to find objects in the room that have the same beginning sounds. Have children put a self-stick note to each object they find. Now, have them say the name of each object they tagged, and the sound it begins with. These are some objects that may be found:

books	bins
bear	boy
bell	ball
door	desk
doll	drawer
dime	piano
pencil	paper
paint	picture
queen	quilt
basket	
quarter	
pocket chart	
question mark	
quart jar	
bulletin board	

Phonics

Lesson **3**

7

1 Warm-Up

Going on a Trip

Materials
None

Preparation
None

How to Play:
Tell the students that today they are going on a trip. They may take only things that begin with the sound of **/b/**, **/d/**, **/p/**, or **/kw/**. The first student might say, "I am going on a trip and I'm going to take a ball." The student can name anything that begins with the letter **b**. The next student thinks of a new **b** word to take on the trip. He might say, "I am going on a trip and I'm going to take a **banana**." Each student will try to take a new thing, but the word must begin with **b**. As soon as a student misses by not being able to think of another thing that begins with **b**, start taking things that begin with **d**. Continue until you have used each letter and all students have had a turn.

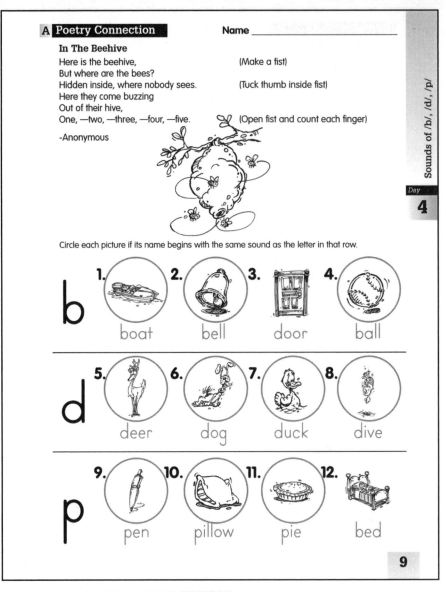

A **Poetry Connection**

Name _____

In The Beehive

Here is the beehive,   (Make a fist)
But where are the bees?
Hidden inside, where nobody sees.   (Tuck thumb inside fist)
Here they come buzzing
Out of their hive,
One, —two, —three, —four, —five.   (Open fist and count each finger)

-Anonymous

Sounds of /b/, /d/, /p/

Day **4**

Circle each picture if its name begins with the same sound as the letter in that row.

b
1. boat 2. bell 3. door 4. ball

d
5. deer 6. dog 7. duck 8. dive

p
9. pen 10. pillow 11. pie 12. bed

9

---

2 Poetry Connection

Have students follow along as you read the poem. Read the poem again while demonstrating the motions. Ask students to do the motions with you. Invite them to circle the number words **one**, **two**, **three**, **four**, and **five** in the last line of the poem.

---

3 Activity Page 9

Objective:
To review the sounds of **/b/**, **/d/**, and **/p/**

 (Say)
I will say the name of each picture. Circle each picture if its name begins with the same sound as the letter in that row.

8

B Phonics

Name _____

Color the honeycomb boxes that have **b**, **d**, **p**, or **q** on them, making a path to help the bees get out of the hive.

Differences of b, d, p, q

Day **4**

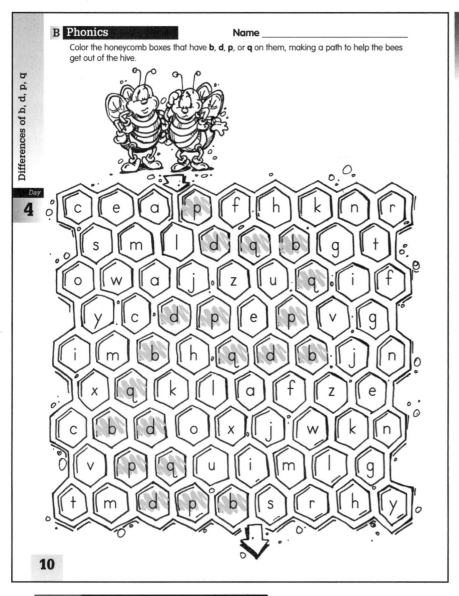

10

---

5 Follow Up

Bean Bag Boxes

Learning Styles
Auditory and
Kinesthetic Learners

Materials
• Four shoe boxes
• Beanbag

Preparation
Using the letters **b**, **d**, **p**, and **q**, label each box with a letter. Line up the four boxes in a row.

How to Play:
Have children take turns tossing a beanbag into a box. They will name the letter on the box that the beanbag lands in and say a word that begins with that letter.

---

4 Activity Page 10

Objective:
To recognize the letters **b**, **d**, **p**, **q**

(Say) Color the honeycomb boxes that have **b**, **d**, **p**, or **q** on them, making a path to help the bees get out of the hive.

1 Warm-Up

Hippity Hop

Materials
None

Preparation
None

How to Play:
Tell the students that you are going to say some words. They should listen carefully for words that begin like **ball**, **dog**, or **pig**. When they hear a word that begins with one of these consonant letters, they should hop like a frog. You may want to use these words:

bed	hen
pen	tin
bat	ball
bunny	sand
book	piano
bark	ladder
dive	bug
moon	bunch
pie	duck
king	dig
dump	cone
dance	dart
home	dare
dark	hook
jar	pink
purple	pat
pot	hold
help	pull
park	play
stop	

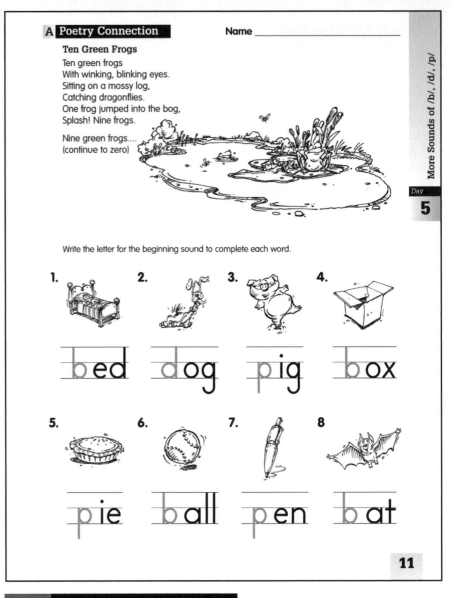

A Poetry Connection

Name _____

Ten Green Frogs

Ten green frogs
With winking, blinking eyes.
Sitting on a mossy log,
Catching dragonflies.
One frog jumped into the bog,
Splash! Nine frogs.

Nine green frogs....
(continue to zero)

Write the letter for the beginning sound to complete each word.

1. b ed
2. d og
3. p ig
4. b ox
5. p ie
6. b all
7. p en
8. b at

11

2 Poetry Connection

Have students follow along as you read the poem. Have ten students come to the front of the room and sit like frogs on a log. Let them do the motions as you read the poem and have one student hop back to his/her seat at the end of each verse until all the frogs are gone.

3 Activity Page 11

Objective:
To review the sounds of **/b/**, **/d/**, and **/p/**
To write the letters **b**, **d**, and **p**

(Say) I will say the name of each picture. Write the letter for the beginning sound to complete each word.

B | **Phonics**

Name _____

Follow the dots from **A** to **Z**. What secret animal do you see? Write the first letter of its name on the line at the top of your page.

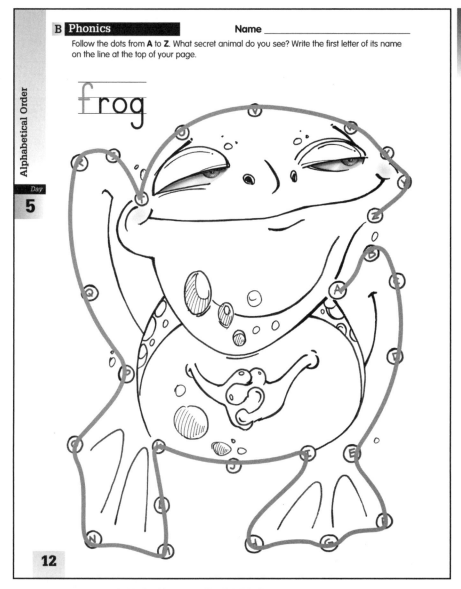

frog

12

Leap Frog

Learning Styles
Auditory and Kinesthetic Learners

Materials
• Two sets of alphabet cards
• Green yarn

Preparation
Outline two large lily pads on the floor at the front of the room with the green yarn. Scatter one set of alphabet cards in each lily pad. Next to each lily pad mark a line on the floor. Ten feet back from each lily pad mark a line on the floor. Divide the class into two teams.

How to Play:
Have each team line up behind the ten foot line. The first person on each team will hop like a frog to the lily pad, find the letter **a**, lay it on the line next to his lily pad then hop back and tag the next team member. The next person will hop to the lily pad and find the **b** to place on the line. Continue until both teams have completed their alphabets.

4 **Activity Page 12**

Objective:
To follow alphabetical order

Say

Find the circled letter **A**. Use your pencil to draw a line from the **A** to the **B** to the **C** and so on to the letter **Z**. Try to guess the secret animal and write the first letter of its name to complete the word at the top of your page.

Warm-Up

Old MacDonald's Farm

Materials
- Drawing paper
- Crayons or markers

Preparation
None

How to Play:
Ask the class to draw pictures whose names contain the sound of **/a/** or **/o/**. Have one student hold up his/her picture and say the name. Sing **Old MacDonald**, using the following format: "Old MacDonald had a farm, E I E I O. And on this farm he had a **fan**, E I E I O. With an **/a/**, **/a/** here, and an **/a/**, **/a/** there . . ." using the picture name and vowel sound in place of an animal and its sound. Continue until all students have had a turn.

The Farmer
The farmer helps us every day.
He gathers the eggs the chickens lay,
He goes to the barn to milk the cows,
Then out to the field where he plows and plows!

He plants the seeds to grow the wheat,
And corn and oats we like to eat.
And when night comes, he kneels to pray,
"Thank you, God, for my busy day."

Sounds of /a/, /o/

Day **6**

Circle each picture if its name contains the same short vowel sound as the letter in that row.

a   1. cat   2. rock   3. ax   4. cub

o   5. egg   6. top   7. cup   8. box

a   9. ant   10. apple   11. ox   12. fan

13

---

2 ## Poetry Connection

Have students follow along as you read the poem. Talk about other things a farmer does.

---

3 ## Activity Page 13

Objective:
To identify the sound of **/a/** and **/o/**

 Say

I will say the name of each picture. Circle each picture if its name contains the same short vowel sound as the letter in that row.

Sounds of Short /a/, /o/

Day 6

Circle the name of each picture.

1. rat (hat) hand
2. box (fox) fog
3. tip tap (top)

4. and an (ant)
5. man (can) cat
6. rip rack (rock)

7. bat bug (box)
8. (map) man wax
9. (log) dog lot

14

Activity Page 14

4

Objective:
To identify the sounds of **/a/** and **/o/**

(Say) I will say the name of each picture. Listen to the sounds you hear. Now, find and circle the word with these sounds.

---

5 **Follow Up**

Short "O" Farm

Learning Styles
Auditory Learners

Materials
None

Preparation
None

How to Play:
Tell the children that the class will be going on a trip to the **Short "O" Farm**, but they need to help you on the visit by choosing words that contain the short **o** sound.
1. To get to the farm, will we ride in a car or a trolley? (**trolley**)
2. Is the farmer's name Bob or Dan? (**Bob**)
3. Will the first animal we see be a cat or a dog? (**dog**)
4. Will we get to sleep in a tent or the loft? (**loft**)
5. At breakfast, will we have hot dogs or pancakes? (**hot dogs**)
6. After breakfast, will we visit the barn or the pond? (**pond**)
7. Should we wear socks or a hat? (**socks**)
8. At the pond, will we see a frog or a snake? (**frog**)
9. To get back to the house, will we run or jog? (**jog**)
10. When we get back, will we be hot or cold? (**hot**)
11. Will we help the farmer feed the hogs or the hens? (**hogs**)
12. After supper, will we sit on the porch or a log? (**log**)

Phonics | Lesson **6**

1 Warm-Up

Guess-the-Letter

Materials
None

Preparation
Write the letters **G**, **g**, **Q**, and **q** on the board. Divide the class into pairs.

How to Play:
Have one student in each pair choose one of the letters and trace its shape on the back of the other student with one finger. That student should try to guess the letter from its shape. Ask pairs to take turns until the four letters have been identified.

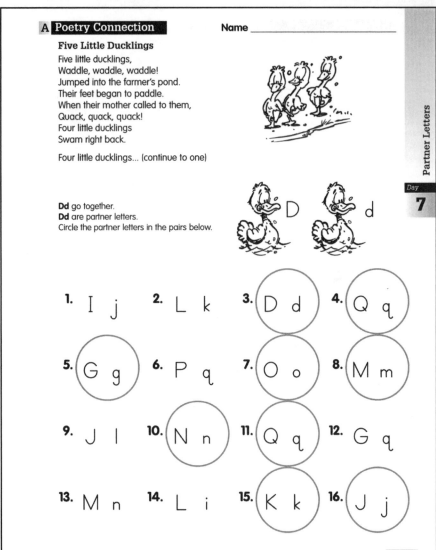

A Poetry Connection   Name _____

Five Little Ducklings
Five little ducklings,
Waddle, waddle, waddle!
Jumped into the farmer's pond.
Their feet began to paddle.
When their mother called to them,
Quack, quack, quack!
Four little ducklings
Swam right back.

Four little ducklings... (continue to one)

Dd go together.
Dd are partner letters.
Circle the partner letters in the pairs below.

1. I j   2. L k   3. D d   4. Q q
5. G g   6. P q   7. O o   8. M m
9. J l   10. N n   11. Q q   12. G q
13. M n   14. L i   15. K k   16. J j

15

Partner Letters
Day 7

2 Poetry Connection

Have students follow along as you read the poem. Have five students come to the front of the room and sit like ducks. As you read the poem again, have one student waddle back to his/her seat at the end of each verse until all the ducks are gone.

3 Activity Page 15

Objective:
To review partner letters

 Look at the ducks at the top of your page. Describe the differences you see between the uppercase and lowercase forms of the letter **d**. Remember, these are called partner letters. Circle the partner letters.

14

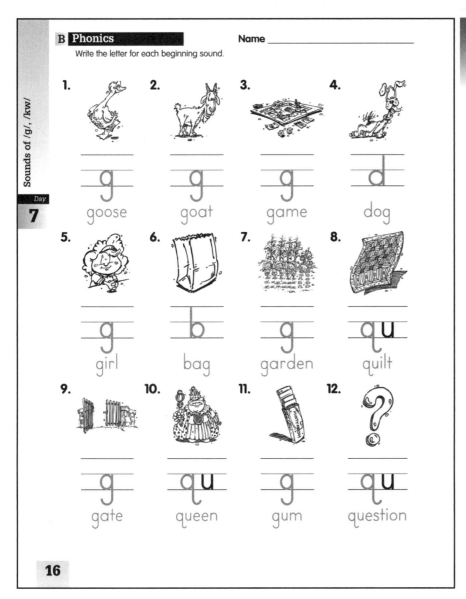

B Phonics

Name _____

Write the letter for each beginning sound.

1. g — goose
2. g — goat
3. g — game
4. d — dog
5. g — girl
6. b — bag
7. g — garden
8. qu — quilt
9. g — gate
10. qu — queen
11. g — gum
12. qu — question

16

---

5 Follow Up

Quack, Quack

Learning Styles
Auditory and
Kinesthetic Learners

Materials
• Blindfold

Preparation
Have the children stand
in a circle.

How to Play:
Designate one child to be
IT and stand in the middle.
IT is blindfolded and says
loudly, "Go, ducks, go." All
of the ducks march around
in a circle until **IT** says, "Stop,
ducks." Everyone stops and
IT points to a child who must
then say "Quack, quack"
and say a word that begins
with the sound of **/g/** or
/kw/. If **IT** guesses who
is speaking, that child
becomes the next **IT** and
the game continues. If **IT**
does not guess correctly,
the game continues until **IT**
is correct.

---

4 Activity Page 16

Objective:
To identify the sounds of **/g/** and **/kw/**
To write the letters **g** and **q**

 Say I will say the name of each picture. Write the letter for its beginning sound on the line below the picture.

Warm-Up

Pet Shop

Materials
None

Preparation
None

How to Play:
Tell the students that today they are going to the pet shop. They may only buy things with the sound of /e/. Invite them to listen carefully to each question and tell you what they can buy.

1. Could I buy a pen or a pig? (**pen**)
2. Could I buy a cat or a hen? (**hen**)
3. Could I buy a bird or an egg? (**egg**)
4. Could I buy a crab or a shell? (**shell**)
5. Could I buy a spider or a web? (**web**)
6. Could I buy a kitty or a bell? (**bell**)
7. Could I buy a nest or a mouse? (**nest**)
8. Could I buy a dog or a bed? (**bed**)

A **Poetry Connection**   Name _____

The Crab
We have a crab in our science lab.
I like him very well.
His tank has water and lots of sand.
He lives inside a shell.

I take him from his tank, sometimes,
So I can watch him walk.
His legs come out, his claws stick out,
His eyes are on a stalk.

He likes to walk along my arm,
And he can climb a tree.
I really like this hermit crab,
And I'm sure he likes me!

Color each shell that has a word with the sound of /e/.

1. ten
2. net
3. tub
4. web
5. beg
6. pet
7. get
8. bed
9. bag

Sound of /e/

Day 8

17

Poetry Connection

2

Have students follow along as you read the poem. Ask the students if any of them have ever had a pet crab. Talk briefly about other pets students have had.

Activity Page 17

3

Objective:
To identify the sound of /e/

(Say)

Color each shell that has a word with the sound of /e/. When you are finished, we will read the words you colored.

B Phonics

Circle the name of each picture.

Name _____

Sound of /e/

Day

8

1. (bed) fed led

2. (jet) pet wet

3. leg (egg) beg

4. ten bent (tent)

5. (nest) not just

6. went man (men)

7. west well (web)

8. tan (ten) tin

9. bill sell (bell)

18

---

5 Follow Up

Bean Bag Boxes

Learning Styles
Auditory and
Kinesthetic Learners

Materials
• Three shoe boxes
• Beanbag

Preparation
Using the letters **o**, **a**, and **e**, label each box with a letter. Line up the three boxes in a row.

How to Play:
Have children take turns tossing a beanbag into a box. They will say the sound of the letter on the box that the beanbag lands in and say a word which has that sound in the middle.

---

4 Activity Page 18

Objective:
To identify the sound of **/e/**

 Say

I will say the name of each picture. Listen to the sounds you hear. Now, find and circle the word with these sounds.

17

1 Warm-Up

Crack the Egg

Materials
• Basket with several plastic eggs that open

Preparation
Write **b**, **c**, or **p** on small slips of paper and put one in each egg.

How to Play:
To play, have a student choose an egg. He/she should open the egg and read the letter on the slip of paper aloud. He/she must then say a word that begins with that letter, and put the paper and egg back in the basket. Continue until everyone has a turn.

A Poetry Connection   Name _____

Baby Chick
I found a little egg on a summer's day,
Out in the barn in a nest of hay.
Peep, peep, peep and peck, peck, peck,
The egg cracked open and out came a neck!
Soon that little chick was up and about.
I'm glad Jesus showed him how to get out.

Look at the word on each egg in the nest. Color the egg if the word begins with the letter **b**.

1. bag
2. bug
3. ball
4. wing
5. bus
6. duck
7. egg
8. boat
9. bat
10. leg
11. nest

19

2 Poetry Connection

Have students follow along as you read the poem. Discuss the fact that God made animals with instincts to know how to do certain things. To help students understand the word **instinct**, discuss other animal behaviors that they are familiar with.

3 Activity Page 19

Objective:
To review the sound of **/b/**

Say

Look at the word on each egg in the nest. Color the egg if the word begins with the letter **b**. When you are finished, we will read the words you colored.

B Phonics

Name _____

Circle the letter for each beginning sound, then write the letter on the line below the picture.

Sounds of /b/, /k/, /p/

Day **9**

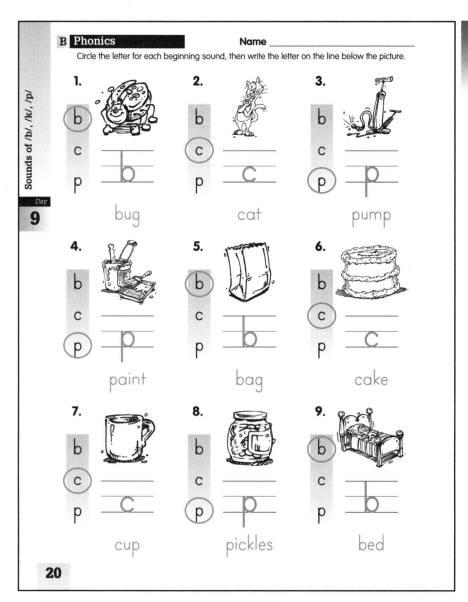

1. b c p — bug
2. b c p — cat
3. b c p — pump
4. b c p — paint
5. b c p — bag
6. b c p — cake
7. b c p — cup
8. b c p — pickles
9. b c p — bed

20

Beginning Basket Review

Learning Styles
Auditory, Kinesthetic, and Visual Learners

Materials
• Basket
• Picture cards of things that begin with **b**, **c**, **d**, **g**, **p**, or **q**

Preparation
Place the picture cards in the basket.

How to Play:
Have a child choose a picture from the basket, say its name, and tell what sound it begins with. Continue until each child has had a turn.

4 **Activity Page 20**

Objective:
To review the sounds of **/b/** and **/p/**
To identify the sound of **/k/**
To write the letters **b**, **c**, and **p**

Say

I will say the name of each picture. Circle the letter for its beginning sound, then write the letter on the line below the picture.

Warm-Up

Giving Gifts

Materials
• A gift bag or
  gift-wrapped box

Preparation
Have students sit in a circle.

How to Play:
Show students the gift bag
or box and ask them what
sound they hear in the
middle of **gift**. Explain that
you will pass the gift around
the circle. When you clap,
the student holding the gift
should name something
with the sound of **/i/** like the
middle of **gift**. Continue until
each student has had
a turn.

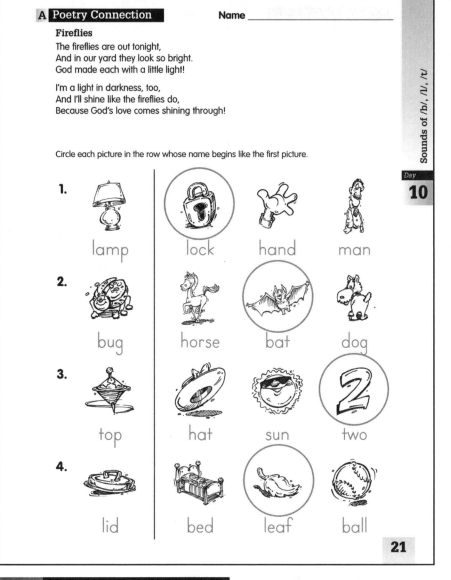

A **Poetry Connection**   Name _____

Fireflies
The fireflies are out tonight,
And in our yard they look so bright.
God made each with a little light!

I'm a light in darkness, too,
And I'll shine like the fireflies do,
Because God's love comes shining through!

Circle each picture in the row whose name begins like the first picture.

1. lamp   lock   hand   man
2. bug   horse   bat   dog
3. top   hat   sun   two
4. lid   bed   leaf   ball

Sounds of /b/, /l/, /t/

Day **10**

21

Poetry Connection

Explain to the students that God gives us many gifts. Have
students follow along as you read the poem. See if they
can tell you what one of God's gifts is to us. Invite students
to read through the poem again and underline each **l** and
t they find.

Activity Page 21

Objective:
To identify the sounds of **/l/** and **/t/**

 I will say the name of the first picture in each row. Now, we
will name the other pictures in the row. Circle each picture
in the row whose name begins like the first picture.

B Phonics

Circle each picture whose name says **i**, as in **lit**.

Name _____

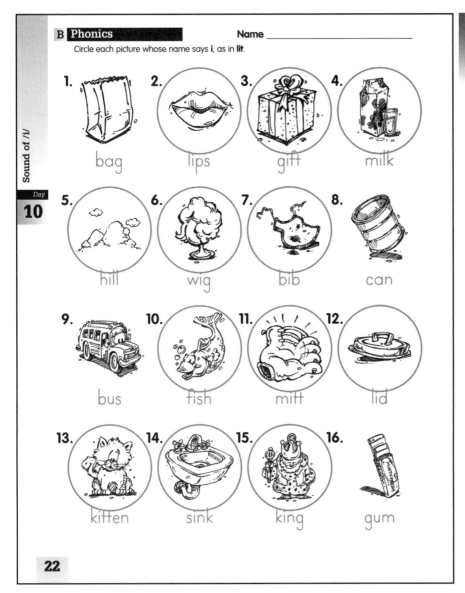

1. bag
2. lips
3. gift
4. milk
5. hill
6. wig
7. bib
8. can
9. bus
10. fish
11. mitt
12. lid
13. kitten
14. sink
15. king
16. gum

 Sound of /i/

 Day 10

22

5 Follow Up

Lighting Lanterns

Learning Styles
Kinesthetic and Visual Learners

Materials
- Camping Lantern (if available)
- Construction paper
- Scissors
- Stapler

Preparation
Using a camping lantern or a lamp, demonstrate how the lantern provides light.

How to Play:
Bring a camping lantern to school. Demonstrate how the lantern provides light. Have the children think of other things that can be lit. Help the children make a lantern by folding a piece of construction paper in half the long way. Show children how to make cuts in the paper about one inch apart starting at the fold and stopping about one inch from the open edge. Have children open their papers, and staple the short ends together. They may then attach a strip of paper for their handle. Children may decorate their lanterns by drawing pictures of things whose name begins with the sound of /l/.

4 Activity Page 22

Objective:
To identify the sound of /i/

Say) I will say the name of each picture. Circle each picture whose name says /i/, as in **lit**.

Warm-Up

Hard Hats

Materials
- Hard hat pattern (Appendix B)
- Old magazines
- Scissors
- Glue

Preparation
Copy a hard hat pattern for each student.

How to Play:
Have students cut out their hard hats. Next have students look through magazines and cut out words or pictures whose names begin with the sound they hear at the beginning of hat. Tell students to glue the cutout pictures onto their hats. Help students cut strips of paper about two inches wide and long enough to go around their heads. They should staple or glue their hats to these strips. Students may wear their finished hats during class.

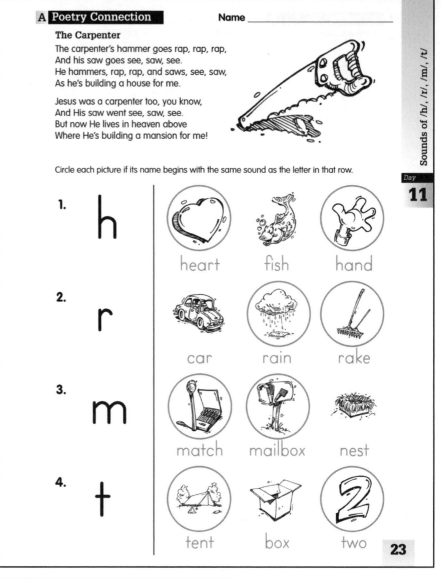

A Poetry Connection   Name _____

The Carpenter
The carpenter's hammer goes rap, rap, rap,
And his saw goes see, saw, see.
He hammers, rap, rap, and saws, see, saw,
As he's building a house for me.

Jesus was a carpenter too, you know,
And His saw went see, saw, see.
But now He lives in heaven above
Where He's building a mansion for me!

Circle each picture if its name begins with the same sound as the letter in that row.

1. h — heart, fish, hand
2. r — car, rain, rake
3. m — match, mailbox, nest
4. t — tent, box, two

23

Poetry Connection

Have students follow along as you read the poem. Ask students why people might wear hard hats while building a house. Read the poem again with a chanting rhythm while the students do motions of rapping and sawing.

Activity Page 23

Objective:
To identify the sounds of **/h/, /r/, /m/,** and **/n/**
To review the sounds of **/l/** and **/t/**

(Say)

I will say the name of each picture. Circle each picture if its name begins with the same sound as the letter in that row.

22

B Phonics

Name _____

Write the letter for each beginning sound on the first line. Write the letter for each ending sound on the second line.

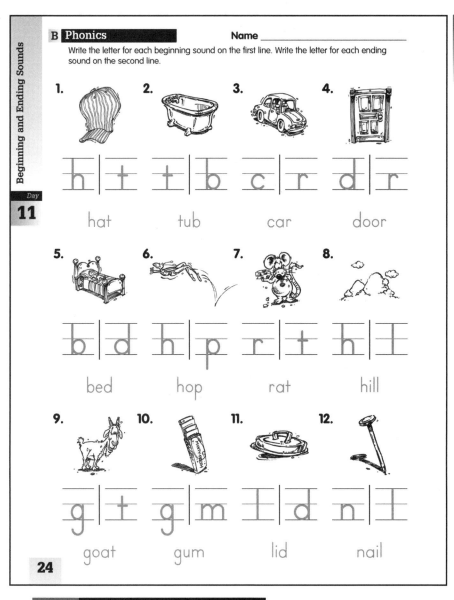

Day **11**

1. `h` `t` — hat
2. `t` `b` — tub
3. `c` `r` — car
4. `d` `r` — door

5. `b` `d` — bed
6. `h` `p` — hop
7. `r` `t` — rat
8. `h` — hill

9. `g` `t` — goat
10. `g` `m` — gum
11. `d` — lid
12. `n` — nail

24

Rap, Rap, Rap

Learning Styles
Auditory and
Kinesthetic Learners

Materials
• Hammer
• Short nails
• Soft wood

Preparation
Start the nails in the wood.
You may like to arrange the
nails in the shape of the
letter **R**.

How to Play:
Explain to the children that
they will be thinking of
words that begin like rap.
When they say a word, they
may come up and **rap, rap,
rap** with the hammer to
drive the nail into the wood.

Phonics | Lesson **11**

---

4 **Activity Page 24**

Objective:
To identify beginning and ending sounds
To write the letters for these sounds

 Say

I will say the name of each picture. Write the letter for each
beginning sound on the first line. Write the letter for each
ending sound on the second line.

23

1 Warm-Up

Musical Mitten

Materials
- A real mitten or a cut-out mitten shape
- Music

Preparation
Have students sit in a circle.

How to Play:
Begin passing the mitten around the circle while the music plays. Stop the music. The person holding the mitten should say a word that begins with the sound of **/m/** like **mitten**. Continue until all the students have had a turn.

A **Poetry Connection**   Name _____

Winter Clothes
I'm wearing a hat, and fluffy ear muffs.
My gloves, and my mittens are pinned to my cuffs.
I've layers of pants, and two sweaters besides.
My three pairs of socks make my feet very wide.
My boots are too tight, like the scarf 'round my throat,
And I don't think my mother can zip up my coat!

Look at each word. Color the space blue if the word begins with **m** like **mitten**. Color the space red if the word begins with **n** like **nose**. Color the other spaces yellow. You will find something that warms you on a cold day.

25

---

2 Poetry Connection

Have students follow along as you read the poem. Invite them to listen for words that describe what the child and his/her winter clothes look like, including words for color and quantity. Use the following example to show how important describing words are:

a mitten	**a big, old, red mitten**
a big mitten	**a big, old, torn, red mitten**
a big, red mitten	

3 Activity Page 25

Objective:
To identify the letters **m** and **n**

Look at each word. Color the space blue if the word begins with the sound of **/m/** like **mitten**. Color the space red if the word begins with the sound of **/n/** like **nose**. Color the other spaces yellow. You will find something that warms you on a cold day.

24

B Phonics　　　　　Name _____

Circle the letter for each beginning sound, then write the letter on the line below the picture.

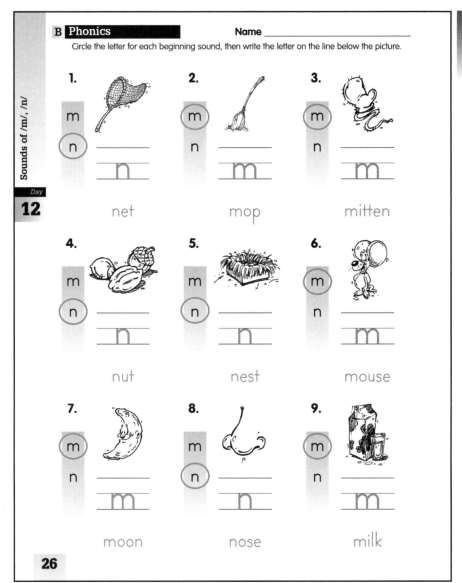

1. m (n) — net
2. (m) n — mop
3. (m) n — mitten
4. m (n) — nut
5. m (n) — nest
6. (m) n — mouse
7. (m) n — moon
8. m (n) — nose
9. (m) n — milk

Sounds of /m/, /n/

Day **12**

26

5 Follow Up

Mitten News

Learning Styles
Kinesthetic and Visual Learners

Materials
- Old newspapers
- Plain paper
- Glue
- Scissors

Preparation
None

How to Play:
Have each child draw, then cut out a large mitten from a sheet of paper. Let them look through the newspapers and find words that begin with the letters **m** or **n**. They may cut out the words and glue them to their mittens to make a collage.

4 Activity Page 26

Objective:
To review the sounds of **/m/** and **/n/**
To write the letters **m** and **n**

Say

I will say the name of each picture. Circle the letter for its beginning sound, then write the letter on the line below the picture.

1 Warm-Up

Fire Truck

Materials
- Mural paper
- Marker

Preparation
On mural paper, draw a long fire truck.

How to Play:
Have students take turns thinking of words that have the sound of **/u/** like **truck**. Print the words on the fire truck.

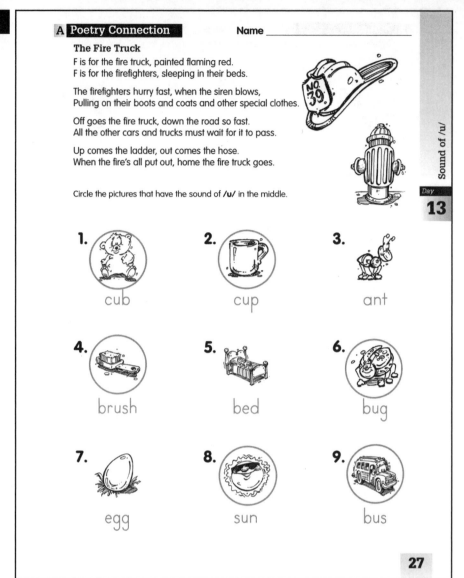

A Poetry Connection   Name _____

The Fire Truck

F is for the fire truck, painted flaming red.
F is for the firefighters, sleeping in their beds.

The firefighters hurry fast, when the siren blows,
Pulling on their boots and coats and other special clothes.

Off goes the fire truck, down the road so fast.
All the other cars and trucks must wait for it to pass.

Up comes the ladder, out comes the hose.
When the fire's all put out, home the fire truck goes.

Circle the pictures that have the sound of /u/ in the middle.

1. cub
2. cup
3. ant
4. brush
5. bed
6. bug
7. egg
8. sun
9. bus

Sound of /u/

Day **13**

27

2 Poetry Connection

Have students follow along as you read the poem. Review fire safety rules and what students should do in case of fire.

3 Activity Page 27

Objective:
To identify the sound of **/u/**

 Say

I will say the name of each picture. Circle the pictures that have the sound of **/u/** in the middle.

B | **Phonics**

Name _____

Write the letter for each beginning sound.

1. f — fish
2. f — fork
3. d — darts
4. f — feet
5. f — fire
6. f — four
7. h — hat
8. f — fence
9. f — fan
10. f — five
11. j — jet
12. f — fox

28

5 Follow Up

Fireman's Ladder

Learning Styles
Auditory, Kinesthetic, and Visual Learners

Materials
None

Preparation
Divide children into two teams. Draw two ladders on the board, but only put one rung on each. Label the ladders **A** and **B**.

How to Play:
Have the first child on **Team A** say a word that begins with **f** like **fire**. Write it on the first rung of **ladder A**. Then a child on **Team B** thinks of a word that begins with **f** like **fire**. Write the word on the first rung of **ladder B**. Continue adding rungs as each team thinks of a word. See which team can make their ladder taller.

4 Activity Page 28

Objective:
To identify the sound of **/f/**
To write the letter **f**

 Say I will say the name of each picture. Write the letter for its beginning sound on the line below the picture.

1 Warm-Up

Letter Partner Relay

Materials
- 4 dry-erase markers or chalk

Preparation
Draw vertical lines to divide the board into four sections. Number the sections from **1** to **4**. Ten feet back from each section, mark a line on the floor. Divide the class into four teams and provide each team with chalk or a marker.

How to Play:
Have each team line up behind the 10-foot line. The first person on each team has chalk or a marker. He will walk up to the board, print **Aa**, walk back, give the chalk or marker to the next person on his team, and go to the end of the line. The second person will walk up, print **Bb**, and so on. Each team will write the entire alphabet through **Zz**. The first team to get to **Zz** and have their alphabet written correctly is the winner.

A **Poetry Connection**

Name _____

Tomorrow
I run the water
In the tub, tub, tub.
I jump right in
And I scrub, scrub, scrub.

My yellow towel
Gets me dry, dry, dry
I'm off to bed,
I won't cry, cry, cry.

I kneel right down
By my bed, bed, bed,
Then jump right in
When my prayers are said.

Can't wait until tomorrow,
No, I can't, can't, can't.
Cousins June and John are coming,
And my uncle and my aunt.

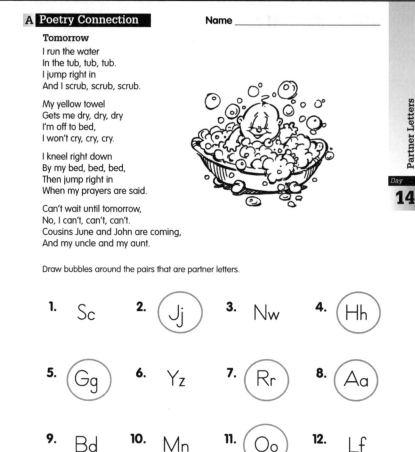

Draw bubbles around the pairs that are partner letters.

1. Sc	2. (Jj)	3. Nw	4. (Hh)
5. (Gg)	6. Yz	7. (Rr)	8. (Aa)
9. Bd	10. Mn	11. (Oo)	12. Lf
13. Db	14. (Qq)	15. (Pp)	16. (Tt)

29

---

2 Poetry Connection

Have students follow along as you read the poem. Discuss things that students like and don't like about baths. Discuss things that might make you want to hurry and finish your bath. Invite students to read through the poem again and circle each **j** and **y** they find.

---

3 Activity Page 29

Objective:
To review partner letters

 Say Draw bubbles around the pairs that are partner letters.

28

B Phonics

Write the letter for each beginning sound.

Name _____

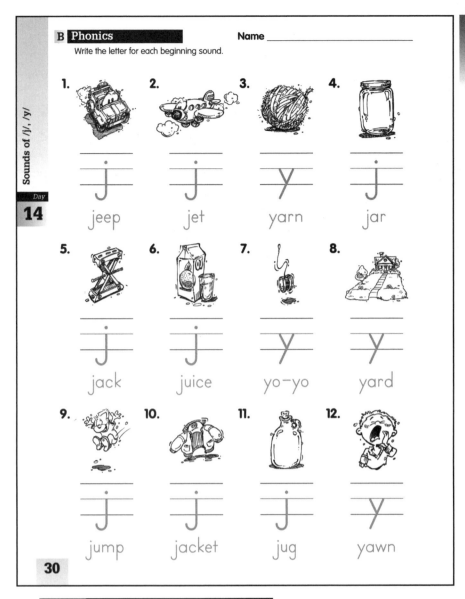

1. j — jeep
2. j — jet
3. y — yarn
4. j — jar
5. j — jack
6. j — juice
7. y — yo-yo
8. y — yard
9. j — jump
10. j — jacket
11. j — jug
12. y — yawn

30

Yellow Duck Pass

Learning Styles
Auditory and Kinesthetic Learners

Materials
- Yellow bath duck
- Music

Preparation
Children should sit in a circle.

How to Play:
Begin passing the yellow duck around the circle while the music plays. Stop the music. The person holding the yellow duck should say a word that begins like **yellow**. Continue until all the children have had a turn.

4 Activity Page 30

Objective:
To identify the sounds of **/j/** and **/y/**
To write the letters **j** and **y**

Say   I will say the name of each picture. Write the letter for its beginning sound on the line below the picture.

Warm-Up

Word Walk

Materials
None

Preparation
Have students line up across the back of the room.

How to Play:
Tell the students that you are going to say some words. Whenever they hear a word that begins with the sound of **/w/**, they should take one step forward. Continue until students reach the front of the room. You may want to use these words:

saw	watermelon
vest	wagon
was	water
wide	zebra
watch	welcome
well	wasp
catch	lemon
wish	well
wade	window
walk	vacuum
vase	wake
word	want

A **Poetry Connection**   Name _____

Sunburn
I built a castle in the sand,
My dad swam in the ocean.
My sister's burned instead of tanned.
She should have used some lotion.

I loved the water and the waves,
But next time I'll be wiser.
I'm sunburned too. My face is red.
Next time I'll wear my visor.

Circle each picture if its name begins with the same sound as the letter in that row.

1. **W**   bird   web   sink

2. **V**   vest   tie   sun

3. **W**   two   net   wagon

4. **V**   sock   van   brush

31

---

2 Poetry Connection

Have the students follow along as you read the poem. Ask if they can think of a time when they knew they should do something, but didn't. Talk about the importance of using sunscreen.

3 Activity Page 31

Objective:
To identify the sounds of **/v/** and **/w/**

Say

I will say the name of each picture. Circle each picture if its name begins with the same sound as the letter in that row.

30

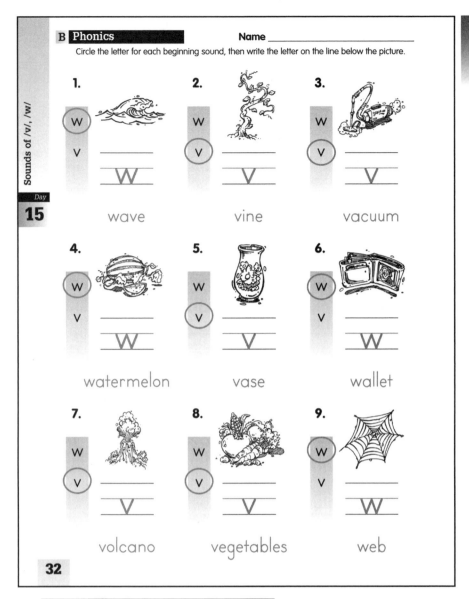

B Phonics

Name _____

Circle the letter for each beginning sound, then write the letter on the line below the picture.

Sounds of /v/, /w/

Day 15

1. (W) V — W — wave

2. W (V) — V — vine

3. W (V) — V — vacuum

4. (W) V — W — watermelon

5. W (V) — V — vase

6. (W) V — W — wallet

7. W (V) — V — volcano

8. W (V) — V — vegetables

9. (W) V — W — web

32

4 Activity Page 32

Objective:
To identify the sounds of **/v/** and **/w/**
To write the letters **v** and **w**

(Say) I will say the name of each picture. Circle the letter for its beginning sound, then write the letter on the line below the picture.

5 Follow Up

Visors

Learning Styles
Kinesthetic and
Visual Learners

Materials
• Visor pattern (Appendix B)
• String
• Hole punch

Preparation
None

How to Play:
Talk about the kinds of hats people wear and the reason each hat works well for the job it was designed for. Tell the children that they will be making visors. Have them draw and color pictures of things that begin with **v**, on their visor. Help them punch holes and tie the strings so the visor will fit their heads. You may want to use these words:

violin	**vase**
valentine	**vine**
vacuum	**vest**
vegetable	**van**
volcano	**vowels**
volleyball	**video**

Phonics

Lesson 16

1 Warm-Up

Singing Songbird

Materials
• Picture of a songbird
• Music

Preparation
Have students sit in a circle.

How to Play:
Begin passing the songbird around the circle while the music plays. Stop the music. The person holding the songbird should say a word that begins with the sound of **/s/** like **song**. Continue until all the students have had a turn.

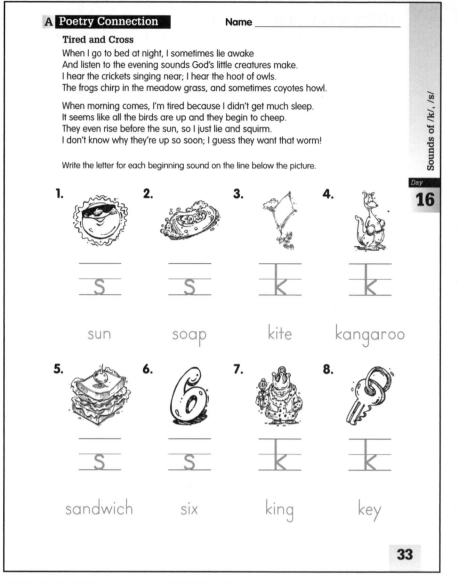

A Poetry Connection   Name _____

Tired and Cross
When I go to bed at night, I sometimes lie awake
And listen to the evening sounds God's little creatures make.
I hear the crickets singing near; I hear the hoot of owls.
The frogs chirp in the meadow grass, and sometimes coyotes howl.

When morning comes, I'm tired because I didn't get much sleep.
It seems like all the birds are up and they begin to cheep.
They even rise before the sun, so I just lie and squirm.
I don't know why they're up so soon; I guess they want that worm!

Write the letter for each beginning sound on the line below the picture.

1. s   sun
2. s   soap
3. k   kite
4. k   kangaroo
5. s   sandwich
6. s   six
7. k   king
8. k   key

Sounds of /k/, /s/

Day 16

33

2 Poetry Connection

Have the students follow along as you read the poem. Read the poem again while they count how many animals were making noises. Invite them to tell about times when they didn't get enough sleep and how they felt the next day. Talk about the importance of getting enough rest.

3 Activity Page 33

Objective:
To identify the sounds of **/k/** and **/s/**
To write the letters **k** and **s**

I will say the name of each picture. Write the letter for its beginning sound on the line below the picture.

32

B Phonics

Name _____

Look at the notes. Beside each note is a picture of something that begins with the sound of /k/ or /s/. Color the note blue if the picture name begins with the sound of /s/ as in **sing**. Color the note red if the picture name begins with the sound of /k/ as in **keep**.

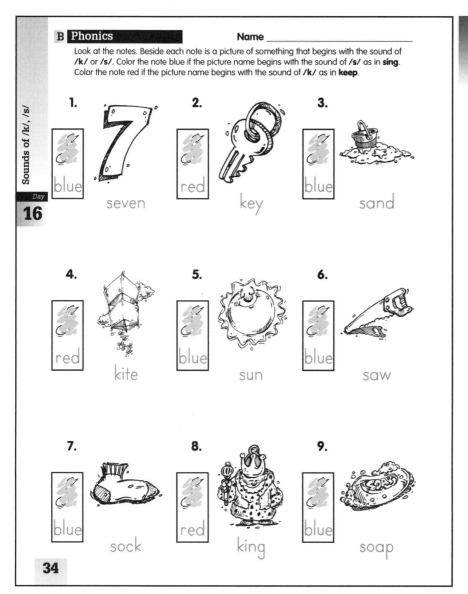

1. blue — seven
2. red — key
3. blue — sand
4. red — kite
5. blue — sun
6. blue — saw
7. blue — sock
8. red — king
9. blue — soap

34

---

5 Follow Up

Kazoo Singers

Learning Styles
Auditory, Kinesthetic, and Visual Learners

Materials
- Kazoos (if kazoos are not available, you may use a piece of wax paper wrapped around a comb, or children may just hum)
- Picture cards whose names begin with consonant sounds including the letters **s** or **k**, such as a sock, king, kite, sled, soap, sun, kitten, and six

Preparation
None

How to Play:
Distribute kazoos to the children. Explain to them that if you hold up a picture whose name begins with /k/, they should hum on their **kazoos**. If the picture begins with /s/, they should remain **silent**.

---

4 Activity Page 34

Objective:
To identify the sounds of /k/ and /s/

Say

Look at the notes. Each note has a picture of something that begins with the sound of /k/ or /s/. Color the note blue if the picture name begins with the sound of /s/ as in **sing**. Color the note red if the picture name begins with the sound of /k/ as in **keep**.

1 Warm-Up

Guess-the-Letter Game

Materials
None

Preparation
Divide the class into pairs. Print the letters **X**, **x**, **Z**, and **z** on the board.

How to Play:
Have one student in each pair choose one of the letters and trace its shape on the back of the other student with one finger. That student should try to guess the letter from its shape. Ask pairs to take turns until the four letters have been identified.

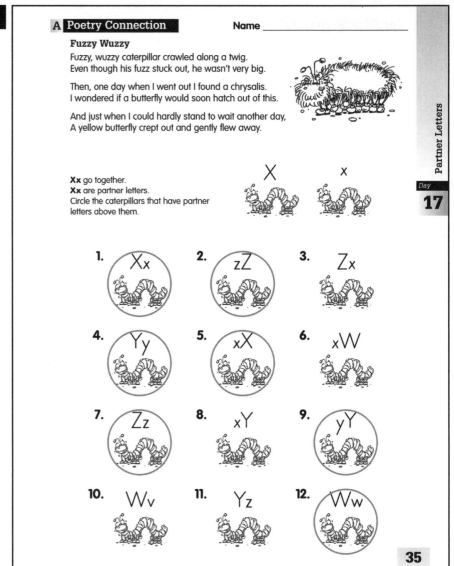

A Poetry Connection   Name _____

Fuzzy Wuzzy
Fuzzy, wuzzy caterpillar crawled along a twig.
Even though his fuzz stuck out, he wasn't very big.

Then, one day when I went out I found a chrysalis.
I wondered if a butterfly would soon hatch out of this.

And just when I could hardly stand to wait another day,
A yellow butterfly crept out and gently flew away.

Xx go together.
Xx are partner letters.
Circle the caterpillars that have partner letters above them.

X   x

1. Xx   2. zZ   3. Zx

4. Yy   5. xX   6. xW

7. Zz   8. xY   9. yY

10. Wv   11. Yz   12. Ww

Partner Letters

Day **17**

35

2 Poetry Connection

Have students follow along as you read the poem. Read the poem again, pausing after each line to let the students tell you which words describe or help them to picture the caterpillar and the butterfly.

3 Activity Page 35

Objective:
To review partner letters

 (Say)

Look at the letters on each caterpillar. Describe the differences you see between the uppercase and lowercase forms of the letter **x**. Remember, these are called partner letters. Complete your page by circling the caterpillars that have partner letters above them.

34

B | Phonics

Name _____

On the butterfly, color each space orange that has a word with the letter **x**. Color each space black that has a word with the letter **z**.

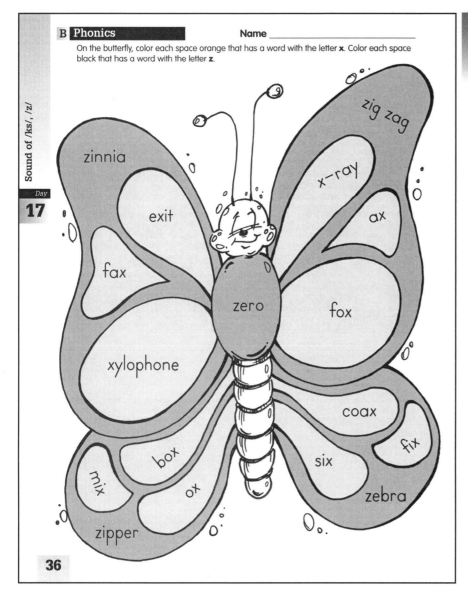

36

---

5 **Follow Up**

Fuzzy Wuzzy Forest

Learning Styles
Auditory Learners

Materials
None

Preparation
None

How to Play:

Tell the children that the class will be going on a nature walk at the **Fuzzy Wuzzy Forest**, but they need to help you by choosing only words that contain the sound of **/ks/** or **/z/**.

1. Did the jacket I wore have a zipper or buttons? (**zipper**)
2. Did I get to walk by Zach or Yolanda? (**Zach**)
3. Did the trail go straight or zigzag? (**zigzag**)
4. Were the flowers we saw violets or zinnias? (**zinnias**)
5. Was the caterpillar Jack found fuzzy or smooth? (**fuzzy**)
6. Was the animal we saw in the pasture a buffalo or an ox? (**ox**)
7. Did the rabbit we saw have one baby or six babies? (**six**)
8. Was the animal that crossed our trail a skunk or a fox? (**fox**)
9. Did we see eight geese or zero? (**zero**)
10. Did we carry our lunches in a box or a bag? (**box**)

---

4 **Activity Page 36**

Objective:
To identify the letters **x** and **z**

Say

On the butterfly, color each space orange that has a word with the letter **x**. Color each space black that has a word with the letter **z**.

Warm-Up

Matching Partner Letters

Materials
• 3 x 5 cards or seasonal die-cut shapes

Preparation
Make one set each of upper case letter cards and lower case letter cards. Divide the class into two teams.

How to Play:
Give students on **Team A** the upper case letter cards and students on **Team B** the lower case letter cards. Have students find the person on the other team who has his/her partner letter. You will need to do this more than once, using part of the alphabet for each turn. You may like to time the activity and have students try to find their partners faster each time.

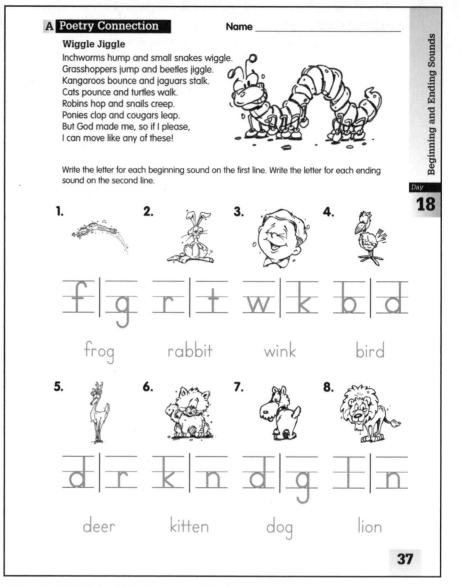

A Poetry Connection

Name _____

Wiggle Jiggle
Inchworms hump and small snakes wiggle.
Grasshoppers jump and beetles jiggle.
Kangaroos bounce and jaguars stalk.
Cats pounce and turtles walk.
Robins hop and snails creep.
Ponies clop and cougars leap.
But God made me, so if I please,
I can move like any of these!

Beginning and Ending Sounds

Day **18**

Write the letter for each beginning sound on the first line. Write the letter for each ending sound on the second line.

1. f | g   frog
2. r | t   rabbit
3. w | k   wink
4. b | d   bird

5. d | r   deer
6. k | n   kitten
7. d | g   dog
8. l | n   lion

37

2 Poetry Connection
Have the students follow along as you read the poem. You may like to read the poem again and let the students imitate the way each animal walks.

3 Activity Page 37

Objective:
To identify beginning and ending sounds

 Say

I will say the name of each picture. Write the letter for each beginning sound on the first line. Write the letter for each ending sound on the second line.

B Phonics

Name _____

Follow the directions above each set of boxes to cross out the letters. Write the remaining letters on the lines to form a word.

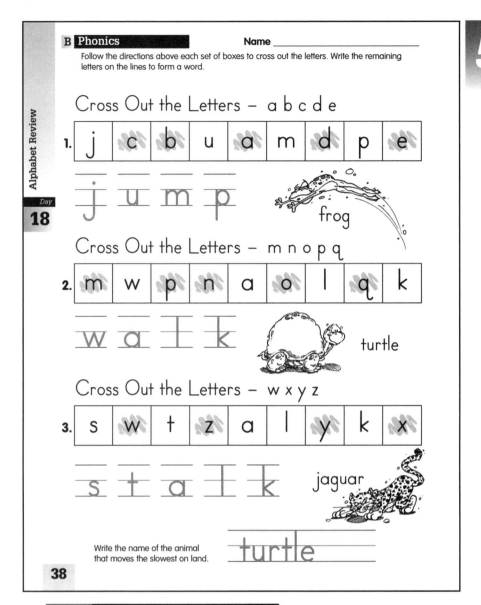

Cross Out the Letters – a b c d e

1. | j | c̶ | b | u | a̶ | m | d̶ | p | e̶ |

j u m p

frog

Cross Out the Letters – m n o p q

2. | m̶ | w | p̶ | n̶ | a | o̶ | l | q̶ | k |

w a l k

turtle

Cross Out the Letters – w x y z

3. | s | w̶ | t | z̶ | a | l | y̶ | k | x̶ |

s t a l k

jaguar

Write the name of the animal that moves the slowest on land.

turtle

---

5 Follow Up

Grandpa's Farm

Learning Styles
Auditory Learners

Materials
None

Preparation
None

How to Play:

Explain to the children that they will be visiting **Grandpa's Farm**. Grandpa has a lot of animals and each one begins with a different letter of the alphabet. The first child might say, "I went to **Grandpa's Farm** and I saw an **alligator**." The child can name any animal that begins with the letter **a**. The next child thinks of an animal that begins with the letter **b**, and so on until you get to **z**.

---

4 Activity Page 38

Objective:

To review the alphabet

 Say

Follow the directions above each set of boxes to cross out the letters. Write the remaining letters on the lines to form a word.

1 Warm-Up

Rhyming Smiles

Materials
• 3 x 5 cards

Preparation
Give each child a 3 x 5 card. Ask the students to draw a smiling face on one side of the card and a frowning face on the other side.

How to Play:
Tell students that you will say pairs of words. If the words rhyme, they should show you the smiling face. If the words do not rhyme, they should hold up the frowning face. You may want to use these word pairs:

ran, man
sail, tail
jump, lamb
barn, yarn
good, wood
fall, fan
car, jar
house, mouse
stop, go
cone, bone
night, light
sun, moon
lock, sock
coat, boat
mail, mile
pan, pane

A Poetry Connection   Name _____

God is Good
God is good to me and you!
And now before the day is through,
I want to thank my God above,
For watching over me with love.

I thank Him for this happy day,
For friends, for food, for work, and play.
I thank Him for my family
And all the things they do for me.

God helps me do the things I should,
To be obedient, kind and good.
He keeps me safe through night and day.
And so, to God, each night I pray.

Rhyming Words

Day 19

Look at each group of words on the windows. If all three words rhyme, color the window. If they do not all rhyme, put an **X** on the window.

39

2 Poetry Connection

Have the students follow along as you read the poem. Ask them to think of other things they can thank God for. You may like to list these on the board or include them in a prayer jar.

3 Activity Page 39

Objective:
To identify rhyming words

(Say)

Look at each group of words on the windows. I will help you say the words. If all three words rhyme, color the window. If they do not all rhyme, put an **X** on the window.

Write the letter for each vowel sound on the line below the picture.

Day 19

Name _____

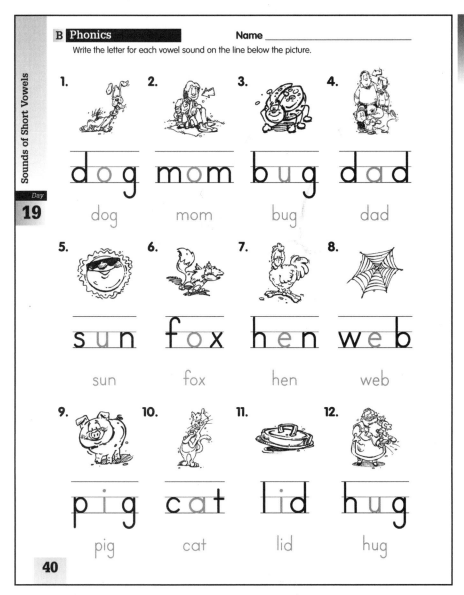

1. d o g
   dog

2. m o m
   mom

3. b u g
   bug

4. d a d
   dad

5. s u n
   sun

6. f o x
   fox

7. h e n
   hen

8. w e b
   web

9. p i g
   pig

10. c a t
    cat

11. l i d
    lid

12. h u g
    hug

40

Follow Up

5

Rhyme Time

Learning Styles
Auditory, Kinesthetic, and Visual Learners

Materials
• Picture cards

Preparation
None

How to Play:
Invite children to work in pairs to play a rhyming game. Give a set of ten picture cards to each pair. Have one child mix the cards and lay them face down in a row. The children should take turns turning over a card. They should say the name of the picture aloud, then try to think of another word that rhymes with it. If they are successful, they get to keep the card. If they cannot think of a rhyme, they should lay the card back down and it becomes the other child's turn. Continue until all the cards are gone.

Activity Page 40

4

Objective:
To review the short vowel sounds
To write the letters **a**, **e**, **i**, **o**, and **u**

(Say) I will say the name of each picture. Write the letter for its vowel sound on the line below the picture.

1 Warm-Up

Sand Castles

Materials
- Sand castle pattern (Appendix B)
- Sand
- Glue

Preparation
None

How to Play:
Give each student a copy of the sand castle pattern. Ask them what sound they hear at the beginning of **castle**. Write the letter **c** on the board. Invite the students to think of other words that begin with the same **c** sound as **castle**. Write these on the board. When they have come up with several words, let them choose one or two to write on their castle, using glue instead of a pencil. Sprinkle sand over the glue to finish the words and set aside to dry.

A Poetry Connection   Name _____

Day At The Beach
Way down by the ocean, way down by the sea,
We spent the whole morning, my mom, dad, and me.

A cool breeze was blowing as we kicked and splashed.
I watched the waves breaking on rocks with a crash.

We looked for bright seashells, we played volleyball.
We built a sand castle—so big, wide, and tall.

Our God made the ocean, and filled up the sea.
Yet wider and deeper is His love for me!

Sound of /o/

Day **20**

Circle the name of each picture.

1.    (log)   dog   lot   tap   pat   (top)   hat   (hot)   hit

4.   5.   6.

ball   bat   (box)   (dog)   dig   dad   top   pit   (pot)

41

---

2 Poetry Connection

Have students follow along as you read the poem. You may wish to have them circle each **o** and **c** they find in the poem. Discuss what students enjoy doing at the beach. Compare the similarities and differences to a swimming pool or lake.

3 Activity Page 41

Objective:
To review the sound of **/o/**

 (Say) I will say the name of each picture. Listen to the sounds you hear. Now, find and circle the word with these sounds.

B Phonics

Name _____

Circle the word that best completes each sentence, then write the word on the line.

1. Bob is very ‾hot‾ . (hot) hop

2. He takes off his ‾socks‾ . (socks) sacks

3. He sits on a ‾rock‾ . rack (rock)

4. He gets in the water with his ‾dog‾ . (dog) dig

5. The sand is ‾soft‾ . sad (soft)

42

5 Follow Up

"O" Oceans

Learning Styles
Kinesthetic and
Visual Learners

Materials
• Old newspapers
• Blue paper
• Glue
• Scissors

Preparation
None

How to Play:
Tell children that the blue paper represents an ocean. Invite them to look through the newspapers to find words with the letter **o** in them. They should draw the shape of a fish or other ocean animal around the word. Next they will cut out the fish and glue it onto their ocean picture.

Phonics

Lesson **20**

4 Activity Page 42

Objective:
To review the sound of **/o/**
To write words with the sound of **/o/**

Say I will read each sentence. Circle the word that best completes each sentence, then write it on the line.

1 Warm-Up

Quack! Quack!

Materials
• Blindfold

Preparation
Have the students stand in a circle.

How to Play:
Designate one student to be **IT** and stand in the middle. **IT** is blindfolded and says loudly, "Go, ducks, go." All of the ducks march around in a circle until **IT** says, "Stop, ducks." Everyone stops and **IT** points to a student who must then say "Quack, quack" and say a word that begins with the sound of **/g/** or **/kw/**. **IT** tries to guess who is speaking, but whether **IT** guesses correctly or not, that student becomes the next **IT** and the game continues.

A **Poetry Connection**   Name _____

The Storm

Rat a tat tat, rat a tat tat,   (children tap on desk with fingers)
Spotting the windowpane.
Oh, how I like to sit indoors
And watch it gently rain.

Boomity boom, boomity boom,   (children clap their hands)
Thunder smashes and crashes.   (lift hands and bring down with fingers
Then the rain comes pouring down   wiggling to show rain pouring)
While the lightning flashes.   (open and close fist to make flashes)

After the storm, I dress up warm
And put on my galoshes.   (pretend to put on boots)
Out in the puddles I jump and slide,   (jump up and down)
While the mud just squishes and squashes.

Day 21

Circle each picture if its name begins with the same sound as the letter in that row.

1. p    pencil   map   peanut

2. qu   queen   quilt   fork

3. g   game   glue   man

43

---

2 Poetry Connection

Have the students follow along as you read the poem. Ask students to name some things that the gentle rain helps. Elicit some words that begin with **g** such as **gardens** and **grass**. Ask how the rain came down in the second verse. Now, ask the students what might get messed up by pouring rain. Elicit words that begin with **p** such as **people, pets, picnics, plants**.

3 Activity Page 43

Objective:
To review the sounds of **/g/**, **/p/**, and **/kw/**

 (Say)   I will say the name of each picture. Circle each picture if its name begins with the same sound as the letter in that row.

B Phonics

Name _____

Write the letter for each beginning sound on the first line. Write the letter for each ending sound on the second line.

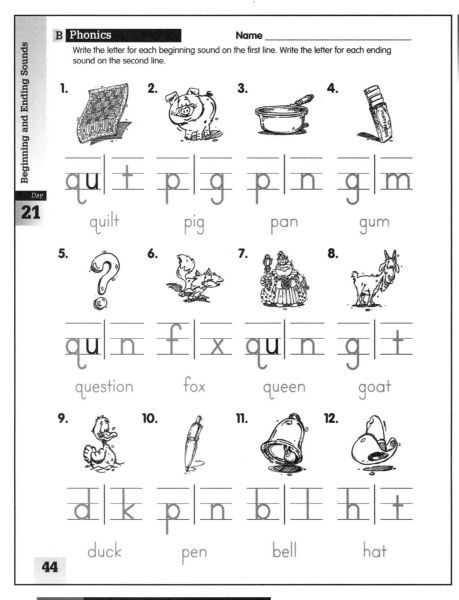

1.	2.	3.	4.
qu | t	p | g	p | n	g | m
quilt	pig	pan	gum

5.	6.	7.	8.
qu | n	f | x	qu | n	g | t
question	fox	queen	goat

9.	10.	11.	12.
d | k	p | n	b | l	h | t
duck	pen	bell	hat

44

 4 **Activity Page 44**

Objective:
To review the sounds of **/g/**, **/p/**, and **/kw/**
To identify beginning and ending sounds
To write the letters **g**, **p**, and **q**

(Say) I will say the name of each picture. Write the letter for each beginning sound on the first line. Write the letter for each ending sound on the second line.

5 **Follow Up**

Gray Clouds

Learning Styles
Kinesthetic and
Visual Learners

Materials
• Finger-paint paper
• White and black
  finger-paints

Preparation
None

How to Play:
Discuss with the children how the sky looks during a rainstorm. Elicit the answer, **gray**. Make a list on the board of other words that begin with the letter **g**. Put large dabs of white and black finger-paint on finger-paint paper for each child. Invite the children to mix the colors with their fingers to make gray. When the gray paint is smeared all over the paper, have children use their index fingers to write some of the words from the board.

1 Warm-Up

Rhythm Bop

Materials
- Rhythm instruments (1 per child)

Preparation
None

How to Play:
Tell the students that you are going to say some words. If the word you say begins with the sound of **/b/** or **/p/** the students should sound their instruments three times. If it does not begin with one of those sounds, they should remain quiet. You may want to use these words:

bike	penny
dog	bed
bus	can
pillow	pig
pie	saw
top	pencil
box	bag
pan	ball
potato	bat
ten	six
pine	goat
butter	bell
purse	

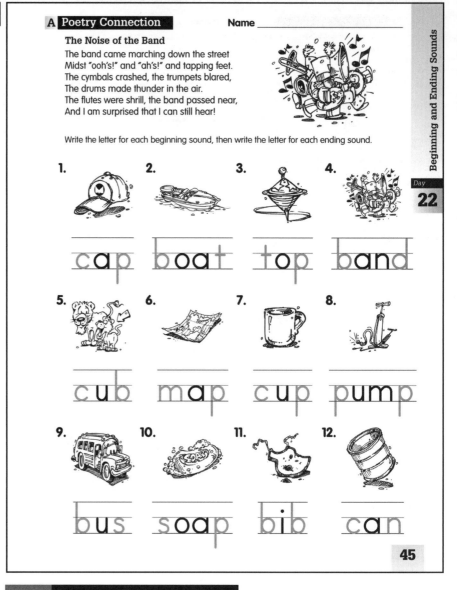

A Poetry Connection   Name _____

The Noise of the Band
The band came marching down the street
Midst "ooh's!" and "ah's!" and tapping feet.
The cymbals crashed, the trumpets blared,
The drums made thunder in the air.
The flutes were shrill, the band passed near,
And I am surprised that I can still hear!

Write the letter for each beginning sound, then write the letter for each ending sound.

1. cap
2. boat
3. top
4. band
5. cub
6. map
7. cup
8. pump
9. bus
10. soap
11. bib
12. can

45

2 Poetry Connection

Have the students follow along as you read the poem. Invite them to circle each **b** and **p** they find. Give each student a rhythm instrument and let them march around the room like a band in a parade.

3 Activity Page 45

Objective:
To review beginning and ending sounds

 Say — I will say the name of each picture. Write the letter for each beginning sound, then write the letter for each ending sound.

44

B Phonics

Name _____

Circle the pictures in each row whose names rhyme.

1. band   bag   hand   bottle

2. goat   game   boat   coat

3. cub   tub   gum   cup

4. jump   desk   stump   pump

Rhyming Words

Day **22**

46

Bean Bag Boxes

Learning Styles
Auditory and
Kinesthetic Learners

Materials
• Two shoe boxes
• Beanbag

Preparation
Using the letters **b** and **p**, label each box with a letter. Line up the two boxes side by side.

How to Play:
Have children take turns tossing a beanbag into a box. They will name the letter on the box that the beanbag lands in and say a word which begins with that sound.

4 **Activity Page 46**

Objective:
To review rhyming words

Say   I will say the name of each picture in the row. Circle the pictures whose names rhyme.

1 Warm-Up

Up and Down

Materials
None

Preparation
None

How to Play:
Tell the students that you are going to say some words. If the word begins with the sound of **d** as in **dog**, they should stand up. The next time you say a word that begins like **dog**, they should sit back down. You may want to use these words:

down	duck
ride	dog
desk	top
door	bed
key	dime
doll	bat
dive	deer
red	toe
dishes	bread
draw	dream

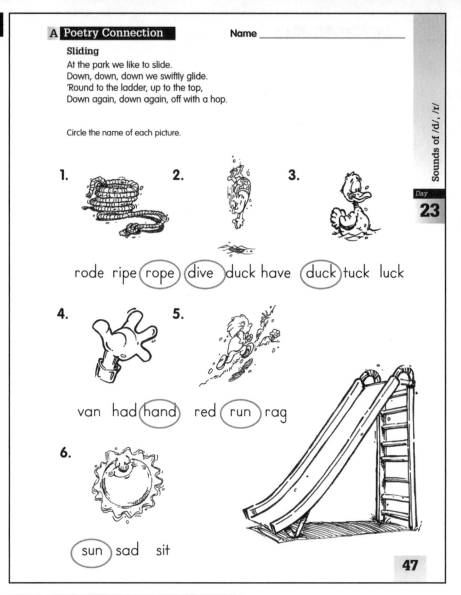

A Poetry Connection

Name _____

Sliding

At the park we like to slide.
Down, down, down we swiftly glide.
'Round to the ladder, up to the top,
Down again, down again, off with a hop.

Circle the name of each picture.

1. rode ripe (rope)

2. (dive) duck have

3. (duck) tuck luck

4. van had (hand)

5. red (run) rag

6. (sun) sad sit

47

---

2 Poetry Connection

Have students follow along as you read the poem. Invite students to tell you about their favorite ride at the park.

---

3 Activity Page 47

Objective:
To review the sounds of **/d/** and **/r/**

(Say) I will say the name of each picture. Listen to the sounds you hear. Now, find and circle the word with these sounds.

46

B Phonics Name _____

Look at the letters that go down the slide. Say each sound, then slide the sounds together to form a word. Now, look at the pictures in the row and circle the one that matches the word.

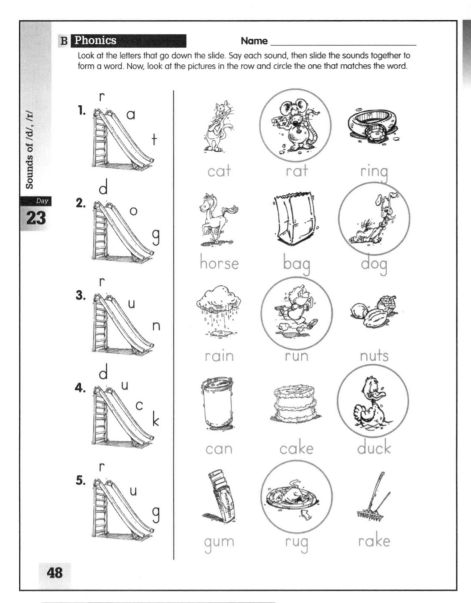

48

Ride the Rocket

Learning Styles
Auditory and Visual Learners

Materials
None

Preparation
None

How to Play:
Tell children to pretend that one of the rides at the park is a play rocket. Invite the children to help you think of ten words that begin with the sound of **r** like **rocket**. Write the words on the rocket. When the list is complete, have the children say each word with you to **count down** to **blast off**!

---

4 Activity Page 48

Objective:
To review the sounds of **/d/** and **/r/**

Look at the letters that go down the slide. Say each sound, then slide the sounds together to form a word. Now, look at the pictures in the row and circle the one that matches the word.

1 Warm-Up

Mail Time

Materials
- Picture cards of a jet, bed, ant, hen, fox, web, cat, can, man, bat, wig, rug, fan, bug, six
- Envelopes

Preparation
Put each picture card in an envelope.

How to Play:
Put each picture in an envelope and "deliver" the mail to various students. Invite a student to open his/her mail, say the name of the picture, and spell the picture name by identifying each sound—beginning, middle, end. Continue until all the students have had a turn.

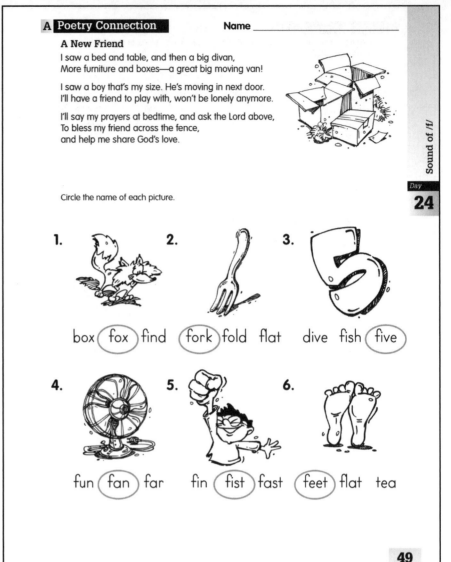

A **Poetry Connection**   Name _____

A New Friend
I saw a bed and table, and then a big divan,
More furniture and boxes—a great big moving van!

I saw a boy that's my size. He's moving in next door.
I'll have a friend to play with, won't be lonely anymore.

I'll say my prayers at bedtime, and ask the Lord above,
To bless my friend across the fence,
and help me share God's love.

Sound of /f/

Day **24**

Circle the name of each picture.

1. box (fox) find
2. (fork) fold flat
3. dive fish (five)
4. fun (fan) far
5. fin (fist) fast
6. (feet) flat tea

49

2 Poetry Connection

Have students follow along as you read the poem. Ask them how the title would fit the poem. Invite the students to tell about a time they moved or had someone new move in close to them.

3 Activity Page 49

Objective:
To review the sound of **/f/**

(Say) I will say the name of each picture. Listen to the sounds you hear. Now, find and circle the word with these sounds.

B Phonics

Name _____

Circle each picture if its name contains the same short vowel sound as the letter in that row.

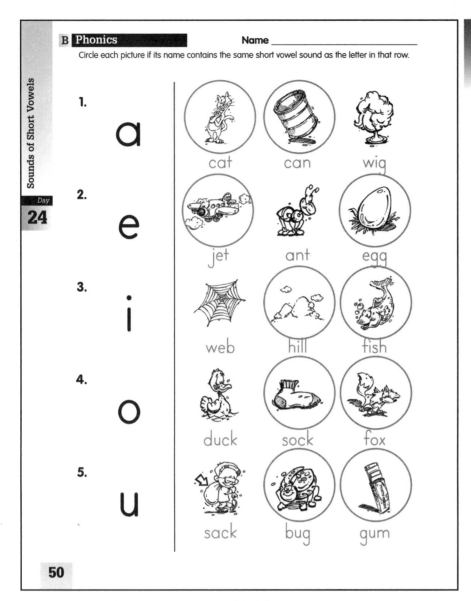

1. a

cat   can   wig

2. e

jet   ant   egg

3. i

web   hill   fish

4. o

duck   sock   fox

5. u

sack   bug   gum

50

Moving Van

Learning Styles
Kinesthetic and Visual Learners

Materials
- Old magazines
- Small box for each group of children

Preparation
Divide the class into groups of 3-4 children.

How to Play:
Tell the children that they are going to help load a moving van. They may only load things that begin with **f** as in **furniture**. Give each group a small box to pack and some magazines. Have them cut pictures of things that begin with **f** and put them in the box.

---

4 **Activity Page 50**

Objective:
To review the sounds of short **/a/**, **/e/**, **/i/**, **/o/**, and **/u/**

(Say) I will say the name of each picture. Circle each picture if its name contains the same short vowel sound as the letter in that row.

1 Warm-Up

Tic-Tac-Toe

Materials
- 3 x 5 cards

Preparation
Make flash cards for several /u/ words such as: **bus, jump, mud, up, cup, gum, bug**, and **duck**. Make flash cards for several short /o/ words such as: **hot, lock, log, sock, mop, box, fox, doll**, and **top**. Mix the cards together. Draw a tic-tac-toe grid on the board. Divide the class into two teams.

How to Play:
Instead of using **X**'s, **Team A** will use **U**'s. Draw a card from the stack of flash cards. Say the word aloud. If it has an /u/ sound, **Team A** may come write a **U** on the grid. If it has an /o/ sound, **Team B** may come put an **O** on the grid. Continue as long as there is interest.

A Poetry Connection

Name _____

To The Top Of The Hill
We set out hiking one fine day. We carried food and water.
We hiked and hiked, the sun shone bright—we couldn't get much hotter!

We climbed the hill with weary steps. We finally reached the top.
So there we sat to eat and rest. It felt so good to stop!

Start at the bottom of the page and write the word that names the picture. Move up to the next set of lines and by changing one letter in the first word you wrote, write the word to go with the second picture. Continue up the hill.

11. top
10. hop
9. hot
8. hog
7. jog
6. jug
5. rug
4. run
3. bun
2. bug
1. hug

51

---

2 Poetry Connection

Have students follow along as you read the poem. Invite them to tell about a time they have gotten hot doing something fun.

3 Activity Page 51

Objective:
To change a letter to form a new word

We will be climbing a hill. To begin, we will start at the bottom of the page and write the word that names the picture. We will move up to the next set of lines and by changing one letter in the first word you wrote, you can write the word to go with the second picture.

B Phonics   Name _____

Circle the pictures that have the sound of /**u**/ in the middle.

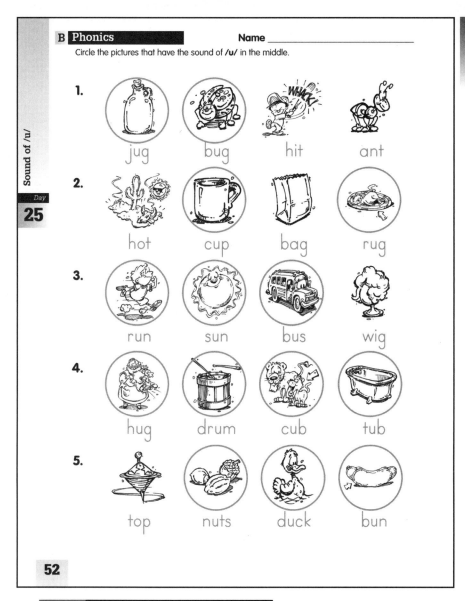

1. jug   bug   hit   ant

2. hot   cup   bag   rug

3. run   sun   bus   wig

4. hug   drum   cub   tub

5. top   nuts   duck   bun

52

Sound of /u/

Day

25

4 ## Activity Page 52

Objective:
To review the sound of /**u**/

(Say) I will say the name of each picture. Circle the pictures that have the sound of /**u**/ in the middle.

---

5 ## Follow Up

Letter Change

Learning Styles
Auditory, Kinesthetic, and Visual Learners

Materials
• 3 x 5 cards

Preparation
Prepare flash cards for several /**u**/ words such as **bus, jump, mud, up, cup, gum, bug**, and **duck**. Prepare flash cards for several /**o**/ words such as **hot, lock, log, sock, mop, box, fox, doll**, and **top**. Mix cards together in a stack. Divide the class into two teams.

How to Play:
Invite **Team A** to draw a card and make a new word by changing one letter. If successful, they can keep the card. If they cannot think of a word, the card goes back in the stack. **Team B** will then draw a card and make a new word by changing one letter. Play continues until no cards are left. The team with the most cards wins.

1 Warm-Up

Giving Gifts

Materials
- A gift bag or gift-wrapped box

Preparation
Have students sit in a circle.

How to Play:
Show students the gift bag or box and ask them what sound they hear in the middle of **gift**. Explain that you will pass the gift around the circle. When you clap, the student holding the gift should name something with the sound of **/i/** like the middle of **gift**. Continue until each student has had a turn.

A Poetry Connection

Name _____

The Little Turtle
This is my little turtle.
I keep him in a box.
He has a bowl to drink from.
He has some climbing rocks.

I like this little turtle
That Jesus made for me.
I'll keep him for a day or two,
But then, I'll set him free.

Write the missing vowel on the line under each picture.

1. pan

2. six

3. bug

4. hot

5. egg

6. pop

7. gum

8. ten

53

---

2 Poetry Connection

Explain to the students that God gives us many gifts. Have students follow along as you read the poem. See if they can tell you what one of God's gifts is to us. Ask if any of the students have ever had a pet turtle. Talk about what would make a good habitat for a turtle.

---

3 Activity Page 53

Objective:
To review short vowel sounds

(Say) You will be listening for the short vowel sound in the middle of each word. I will say the name of each picture. Write the missing vowel on the line under each picture.

B Phonics

Circle the name of each picture.

1. (six) ax mix

2. lad (lid) did

3. mat mix (mitt)

4. sing sank (sink)

5. fan (fin) if

6. fill hide (hill)

7. did bad (bib)

8. fix fast (fist)

9. (pig) dig pie

54

Sound of /i/

Day **26**

Learning Styles
Kinesthetic and Visual Learners

Materials
- Old magazines
- Paper plates (2 per child)
- Turtle pattern (Appendix B)
- Glue
- Crayons
- Scissors

Preparation
Write the letter **t** on the board.

How to Play:
Tell the children that they will be making paper-plate turtles. They may only put pictures that begin with **t** on their **turtle**. Have children look through magazines to find pictures that begin with **t** and glue them on their plates. Children will color the head, tail, and legs of the turtle, then assemble. Staple the two plates with the tops together and the head, tail, and legs between them.

---

4 **Activity Page 54**

Objective:
To review the sound of **/i/**

 Say

I will say the name of each picture. Listen to the sounds you hear. Now, find and circle the word with these sounds.

1 Warm-Up

Railroad Track

Materials
None

Preparation
Divide the class into two teams. Draw two sets of railroad tracks on the board, but only put one railroad tie on each. Label the tracks **A** and **B**.

How to Play:
Have the first student on **Team A** think of something that begins with the sound of **/l/** like **long**. Have him/her tell you the word he/she thought of. Write it on the first railroad tie of **track A**. Then a student on **Team B** thinks of a word that begins with the sound of **/l/** like **long**. Write the word on the first railroad tie of **track B**.
Continue adding railroad ties as each team thinks of a word, to see which team can make their track longer.

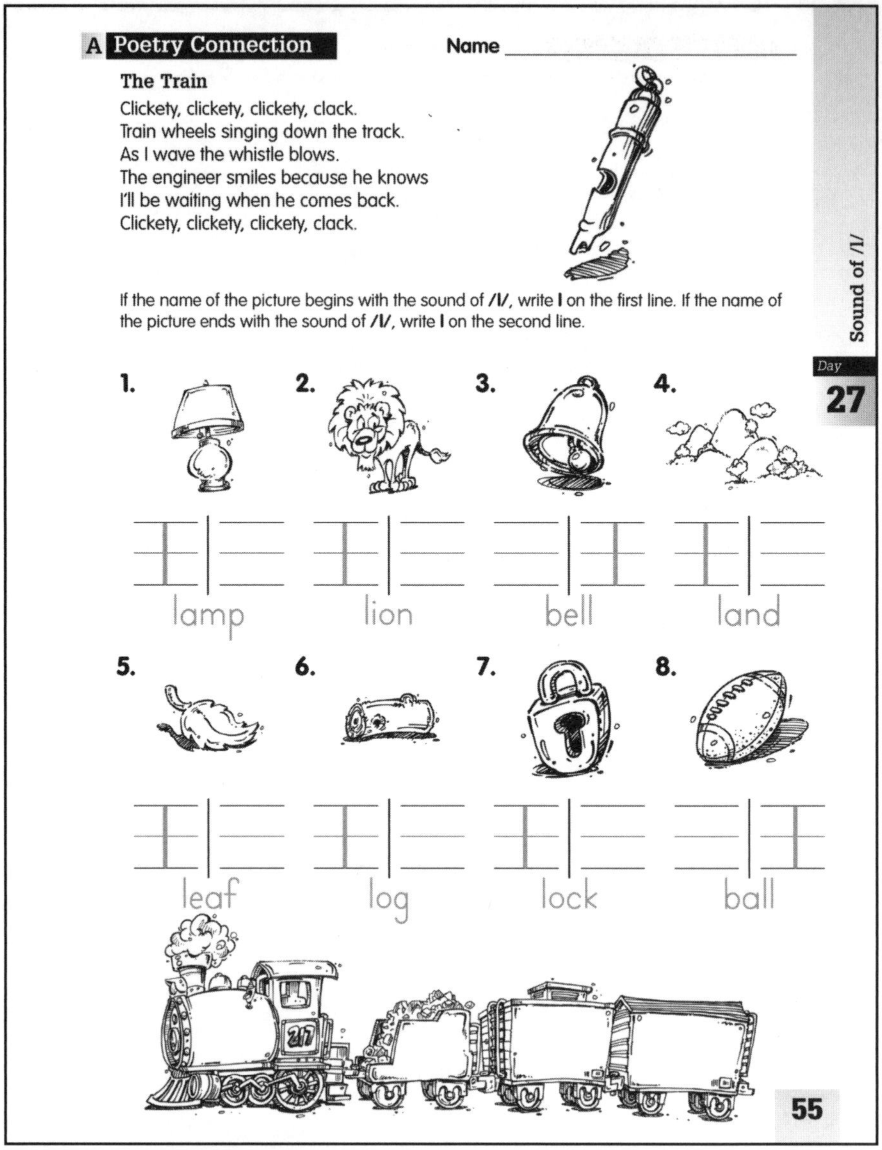
A Poetry Connection
Name
The Train
Clickety, clickety, clickety, clack.
Train wheels singing down the track.
As I wave the whistle blows.
The engineer smiles because he knows
I'll be waiting when he comes back.
Clickety, clickety, clickety, clack.
If the name of the picture begins with the sound of /l/, write l on the first line. If the name of the picture ends with the sound of /l/, write l on the second line.
1. lamp
2. lion
3. bell
4. land
5. leaf
6. log
7. lock
8. ball
27
Sound of /l/
Day 27
55

2 Poetry Connection

Have students follow along as you read the poem. Have them look through the poem and circle each **k** they find. Let them look through the poem again and draw a line under each **l** they find.

3 Activity Page 55

Objective:
To review the sound of **/l/**

Say

I will say the name of each picture. If the name of the picture begins with the sound of **/l/** as in **long**, write **l** on the first line. If the name of the picture ends with the sound of **/l/**, write **l** on the second line.

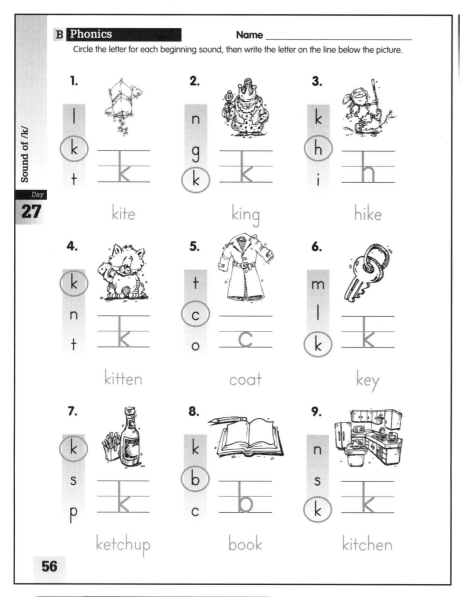

B Phonics

Name _____

Circle the letter for each beginning sound, then write the letter on the line below the picture.

Sound of /k/

Day

27

1.
l
(k)
t

kite

2.
n
g
(k)

king

3.
k
(h)
i

hike

4.
(k)
n
t

kitten

5.
t
(c)
o

coat

6.
m
l
(k)

key

7.
(k)
s
p

ketchup

8.
k
(b)
c

book

9.
n
s
(k)

kitchen

56

---

4 Activity Page 56

Objective:
To review the sound of /k/
To write the letter **k**

 Say

I will say the name of each picture. Circle the letter for its beginning sound, then write the letter on the line below the picture.

---

5 Follow Up

Clickety Clack

Learning Styles
Kinesthetic and
Visual Learners

Materials
None

Preparation
Have students stand in a column to form a **train**. They may put their hands on the shoulders of the student in front of them.

How to Play:
Using the tune to **The Wheels on the Bus**, begin walking around the room singing, "The wheels on the train go clickety clack, clickety clack, clickety clack. The wheels on the train go clickety clack, up and down the track." At the end of the verse, the person in the back says a word that begins or ends with the sound of **/k/**. If correct, he/she may move up to become the engineer as you repeat the activity. You may want to use these words:

kick	black
brick	drink
king	track
bank	stick
think	trunk
back	pink
kite	kitten
blink	key
sink	milk

Phonics

Lesson **27**

55

1 Warm-Up

Noisy "N"

Materials
- Rhythm instruments (1 per child)

Preparation
None

How to Play:
Tell the students that you are going to say some words. If the word begins with the sound of /n/ as in **noise**, the students should play 3 strokes on their instruments. If the word does not begin with the sound of /n/, they should remain silent. You may want to use these words:

net	newspaper
door	nurse
nose	nest
bone	nut
nail	needle
leaf	nine
mop	nap
new	nice
name	neat
pen	not

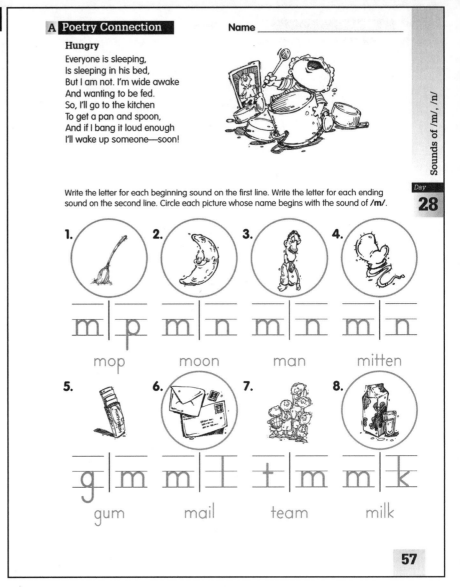

A **Poetry Connection**

Name _____

Hungry

Everyone is sleeping,
Is sleeping in his bed,
But I am not. I'm wide awake
And wanting to be fed.
So, I'll go to the kitchen
To get a pan and spoon,
And if I bang it loud enough
I'll wake up someone—soon!

Day 28

Write the letter for each beginning sound on the first line. Write the letter for each ending sound on the second line. Circle each picture whose name begins with the sound of /m/.

1. m | p   mop
2. m | n   moon
3. m | n   man
4. m | n   mitten
5. g | m   gum
6. m | l   mail
7. t | m   team
8. m | k   milk

57

2 Poetry Connection

Have students follow along as you read the poem. Ask if any of them have ever been the first person to wake up in their house. How does it feel to be awake when no one else is?

3 Activity Page 57

Objective:
To review the sounds of /m/ and /n/

 Say

I will say the name of each picture. Write the letter for each beginning sound on the first line. Write the letter for each ending sound on the second line. Circle each picture whose name begins with the sound of /m/.

B Phonics

Circle the name of each picture.

Name _____

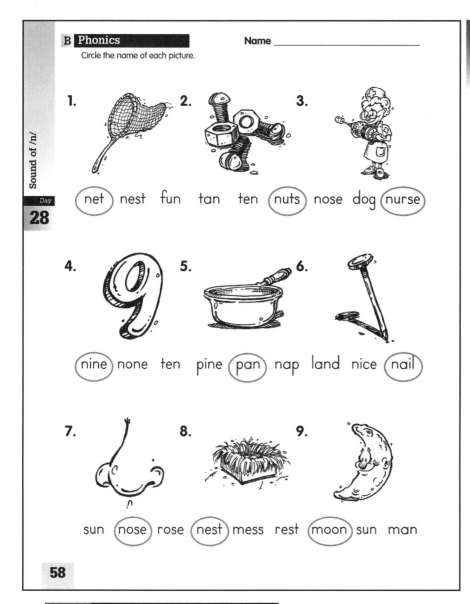

1. (net) nest fun

2. tan ten (nuts)

3. nose dog (nurse)

4. (nine) none ten

5. pine (pan) nap

6. land nice (nail)

7. sun (nose) rose

8. (nest) mess rest

9. (moon) sun man

58

---

4 Activity Page 58

Objective:
To review the sound of **/n/**

(Say) I will say the name of each picture. Listen to the sounds you hear. Now, find and circle the word with these sounds.

---

5 Follow Up
Pan Writing

Learning Styles
Kinesthetic and
Visual Learners

Materials
• Large flat pans (disposable aluminum cake pans work well)
• Salt or cornmeal
• Flash cards with words that begin with **m** or **n**

Preparation
Spread a layer of salt or cornmeal in the aluminum pans.

How to Play:
Tell children that they will try to write some words from memory. They will look at a word card, spell the word softly, turn the card over and write the word in the salt or cornmeal. They may then check their word with the word card. They may erase by moving the side of their hands over the word. They should continue the activity until they have written all the words.

Warm-Up

"X" Marks the Box

Materials
- A small box with the letter **X** on it
- 3 x 5 cards (1 per child)
- Crayons or pencils

Preparation
Make two or three word cards of each of the following words: **wax, ox, fax, mix, six, fix, fox, coax, ax, box, exit, x-ray**. Make enough word cards so there is one per child. Have students sit in a circle.

How to Play:
Show students the box and ask them what sound they hear at the end of **box**. Explain that they will pass the box around the circle. When you clap, the student holding the box should take a word card from the box, but not let anyone see his/her word. When each student has a card, stand in the center of the circle. Tell the students that you will say one of the words and the two or three students who have that word should try to trade places without you getting their chairs. Continue until each student has had a turn.

A **Poetry Connection**   Name _____

Window Boxes
I planted pansies in a box and added several purple phlox.
Then daisies, mums, and daffodils with countless merry, yellow frills.

I added bright petunias bold, some zinnias, and marigolds.
And now my flower box is done, so I will set it in the sun!

Look at each group of words on the window boxes. If all three words rhyme, color the flowers in that box.

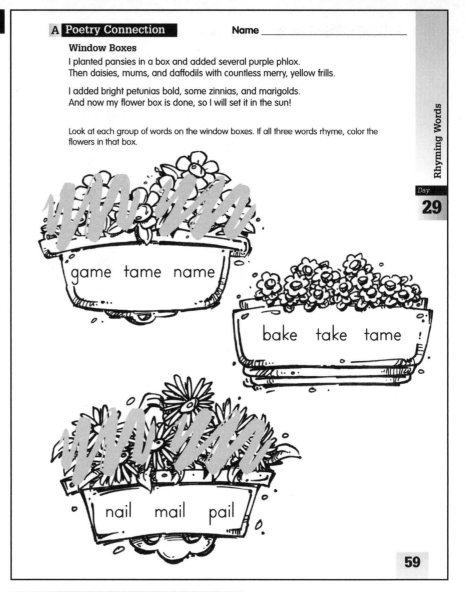

game   tame   name

bake   take   tame

nail   mail   pail

59

---

2 Poetry Connection

Have students follow along as you read the poem. You may like to have some pictures of the flowers mentioned in the poem. Talk about the many varieties and colors of flowers God made for us to enjoy. Ask the students what God sends to help the flowers grow. (**sun, rain**)

3 Activity Page 59

Objective:
To identify rhyming words

 Say

Look at each group of words on the window boxes. I will help you say the words. If all three words rhyme, color the flowers.

B Phonics Name _____

Circle the letter for each ending sound. Place an **X** on the picture if the name of the picture ends with the sound of /**ks**/.

Sound of /ks/

Day **29**

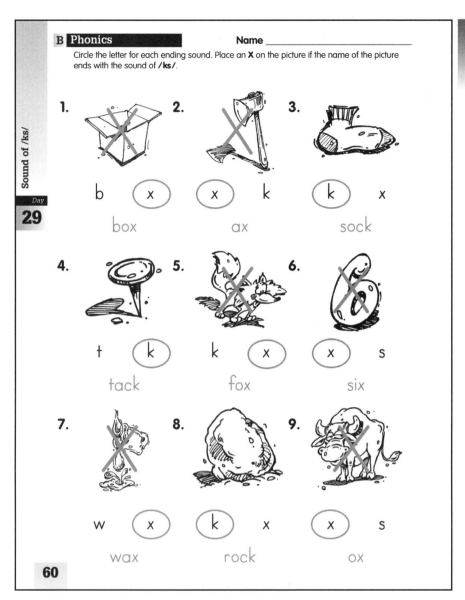

1. b ⊙x
box

2. ⊙x k
ax

3. ⊙k x
sock

4. t ⊙k
tack

5. k ⊙x
fox

6. ⊙x s
six

7. w ⊙x
wax

8. ⊙k x
rock

9. ⊙x s
ox

60

5 Follow Up

Bean Bag Boxes

Learning Styles
Auditory and
Kinesthetic Learners

Materials
• Two shoe boxes
• Beanbag

Preparation
Using the words **Long a** and **Short a**, label each box. Line up the two boxes side by side.

How to Play:
Have children take turns tossing a beanbag into a box. They will say the sound of the letter on the box that the beanbag lands in and say a word which contains that sound.

4 Activity Page 60

Objective:
To review the sound of /**ks**/

 Say

I will say the name of each picture. Circle the letter for its ending sound. Place an **X** on the picture if the name of the picture ends with the sound of /**ks**/.

Warm-Up

Word Walk

Materials
None

Preparation
Have students line up across the back of the room.

How to Play:
Tell the students that you are going to say some words. Whenever they hear a word that begins with the sound of **/w/**, they should take one step forward. Continue until students reach the front of the room. You may want to use these words:

saw	watermelon
vest	wagon
was	water
wide	zebra
watch	welcome
well	wasp
catch	lemon
wish	well
walk	window
wade	vacuum
vase	wake
word	want

A **Poetry Connection**   Name _____

My New Kite
I have a new kite. I want to try it.
I've asked my friend to help me fly it.

But, if this wind keeps up so strong,
I'm sure my kite won't last for long!

Circle each picture that begins with the sound of **/w/**.

1. wind
2. man
3. wood
4. worm
5. web
6. moon
7. violin
8. wagon
9. walk

Sound of /w/

Day **30**

61

Poetry Connection
2
Have students follow along as you read the poem. Invite them to talk about things that happen on a windy day.

Activity Page 61
3
Objective:
To review the sound of **/w/**

 Say

I will say the name of the picture on each kite. Circle each picture if the name of the picture begins with the sound of **/w/**.

B Phonics

Name _____

Hidden on this page is a picture of something that needs wind. Color the space blue if the words begin with **w**. Color the space red if the words begin with **v**. Color the space yellow if the words begin with **y**.

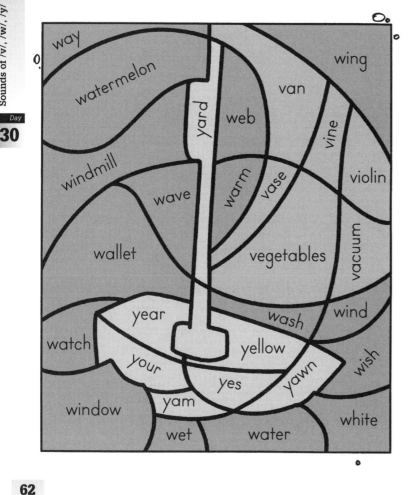

62

5 Follow Up

Whistle While You Work

Learning Styles
Auditory and Kinesthetic Learners

Materials
None

Preparation
None

How to Play:
Explain to the children that it takes wind (air) to whistle. Tell them that you will say some words. If the word you say begins with the sound of **/w/**, they should **whistle**. If the word begins with another sound, they should remain silent. Encourage those who can't whistle to use this chance to practice. You may want to use these words:

wagon	**vegetables**
watermelon	**yard**
windmill	**wave**
wing	**yawn**
vase	**watch**
window	**yak**
van	**water**
yarn	**wind**
wash	**yes**
vine	**violin**
wallet	**wide**
wish	**vacuum**
yellow	**web**
yo-yo	**wet**
wild	

4 Activity Page 62

Objective:
To review the letters **v**, **w**, and **y**

 Say

Hidden on this page is a picture of something else that needs wind. Color the space blue if the word begins with the sound of **/w/**. Color the space red if the word begins with the sound of **/v/**. Color the space yellow if the word begins with the sound of **/y/**.

Lesson **31** | Phonics

1 Warm-Up

Jump and Sit

Materials
None

Preparation
None

How to Play:
Tell the students that you are going to say some words. If the word you say begins with the sound of **/j/**, they should jump up. If two words in a row begin with the sound of **/j/**, jump again. If the word you say begins with the sound of **/s/**, they should sit down. If two words in a row begin with the sound of **/s/**, remain seated. You may want to use these words:

jog	seal
joke	song
jelly	jacket
soap	Jesus
stop	jab
jam	sun
jump	star
jeep	sound
jet	job
sell	jar
sit	

A Poetry Connection   Name _____

Exercise

God made me so I could run and hop and skip and jump,
He made my muscles strong and fit, He made my heart to pump.

I'm glad that I can exercise, and keep my body strong.
God is so loving and so wise! I'll praise Him all day long.

Read the words in the word bank. Say each letter in the word, then look in the puzzle to find that same word. Circle each word you find.

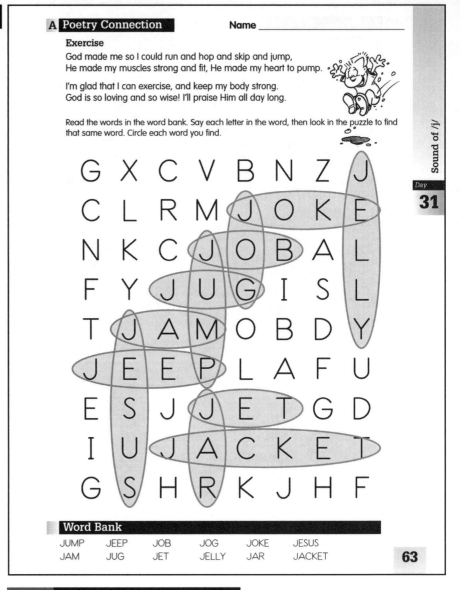

Word Bank

JUMP	JEEP	JOB	JOG	JOKE	JESUS
JAM	JUG	JET	JELLY	JAR	JACKET

63

Day **31**
Sound of /j/

---

2 Poetry Connection

Have students follow along as you read the poem. Talk about how it feels to sit all day and never get up to run and play.

3 Activity Page 63

Objective:
To review the sound of /j/

(This may be the first time students have done a word find puzzle.)

 (Say) Let's read a word from the word bank. Say each letter in the word, then look in the puzzle to find that same word. Circle each word you find.

62

B Phonics

Name _____

Circle the name of each picture.

1.

cane (cone) come

2.

nose (hose) hive

3.

tune   tug   (tube)

4.

cute   (cube)   cub

5.

ran   (rain)   rake

6.

(glue)   gate   gift

64

5 Follow Up

Simon Says

Learning Styles
Auditory and
Kinesthetic Learners

Materials
None

Preparation
None

How to Play:
Play **Simon Says** using directions that begin with the letter **s**, such as:

Skip to me and back
Slide to the side
Spin around two times
Stand on one foot for seven seconds
Spin around on one foot
Stomp your feet six times
Pretend to **skate** across the ice

4 Activity Page 64

Objective:
To identify words with long vowel sounds

Say

I will say the name of each picture. Listen to the sounds you hear. Now, find and circle the word with these sounds.

Warm-Up

Zestful Zinnias

Materials
- Plastic cups (1 per child)
- Potting soil
- Zinnia seeds

Preparation
Write the letter **z** on the board and have the students practice saying the sound.

How to Play:
Invite the students to help plant zinnias. Show the students the package of zinnia seeds. Let each student put some potting soil in his/her cup. Show them how to plant a few seeds in their soil. Help them remember to water their seeds as needed.

Every Time

Every time I see a little creature crawl,
Every time I see a pretty snowflake fall,
I know God planned the world carefully.
He made everything extraordinarily.

Every time I see a shady maple tree,
Every time I see fish swimming in the sea,
I will thank the Lord for His creation.
Everything He made is a sensation.

Every time I see the lightning light the sky,
Every time I see a hummingbird zoom by,
I will thank the Father for His perfect plan,
And remember that He holds me in His hand.

Sounds of /y/, /z/

Day **32**

Circle each picture if its name begins with the same sound as the letter in that row.

1. y — yawn, camel, yard
2. z — bowl, zoo, zig-zag
3. y — penny, yarn, yo-yo

65

---

2 Poetry Connection

Have students follow along as you read the poem. Talk about the seasons and things that are the same and different each season.

3 Activity Page 65

Objective:
To review the sounds of **/y/** and **/z/**

(Say) I will say the name of each picture. Circle each picture if its name begins with the same sound as the letter in that row.

B Phonics

Name _____

Decide what letter is missing in each word and write it in the box to complete the puzzle.
Now, copy each letter in order on the lines at the bottom to find the secret word.

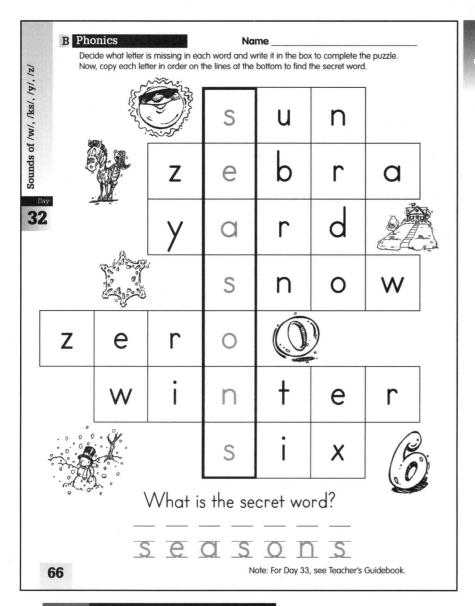

s	u	n	

z	e	b	r	a

y	a	r	d

s	n	o	w

z	e	r	o

w	i	n	t	e	r

s	i	x

What is the secret word?

_s_ _e_ _a_ _s_ _o_ _n_ _s_

Note: For Day 33, see Teacher's Guidebook.

66

---

5 **Follow Up**

Shaving Cream Snow

Learning Styles
Kinesthetic and
Visual Learners

Materials
• Shaving cream
• Paper towels

Preparation
None

How to Play:
Squirt a blob of shaving
cream "snow" on each
child's desk. Invite the
children to smear the "snow"
all over and use their index
fingers to practice writing the
alphabet. Discuss how this
"snow" is the same and how
it is different from real snow.
(When finished, the desks
will be clean and the room
will smell great!)

Lesson 32 | **Phonics**

---

4 **Activity Page 66**

Objective:
To review words with **w**, **x**, **y**, and **z**

 Say

I will say the name of each picture. Decide what letter is
missing and write it in the box to complete the puzzle.
Now, copy each letter in order on the lines at the bottom to
find the secret word.

1 Warm-Up

Capital Letter Relay

Materials
• 4 dry-erase markers or chalk

Preparation
Draw vertical lines to divide the board into four sections. Number the sections from **1** to **4**. Ten feet back from each section, mark a line on the floor. Divide the class into four teams and provide each team with chalk or a marker.

How to Play:
Have each team line up behind the 10-foot line. The first person on each team has chalk or a marker. He will walk up to the board, print **A**, walk back, give the chalk or marker to the next person on his team, and go to the end of the line. The second person will walk up, print **B**, and so on. Each team will write the entire alphabet through **Z**. The first team to get to **Z** and have their uppercase alphabet written correctly, is the winner.

A ▌Poetry Connection

Name _____

The Months of the Year
January lies white and bare.
February breathes crispy air.
March winds chase away the snow
So April's first shy flowers can grow.
May opens blossoms on the trees.
June stirs summer's gentle breeze.
July ripens melons, peaches.
August calls with sandy beaches.
September smells of apple pies.
October, pumpkin, corn, and spice.
November's prayers of thanks we lift.
December celebrates God's gift
Of Jesus—to a world God knew
Would need His love the whole year through!

Look at the picnic items on your page. Write the beginning letter for each month on the line, remembering to use capital letters. Now, color each picnic item, cut it out, and paste it on another sheet of paper to complete the picture.

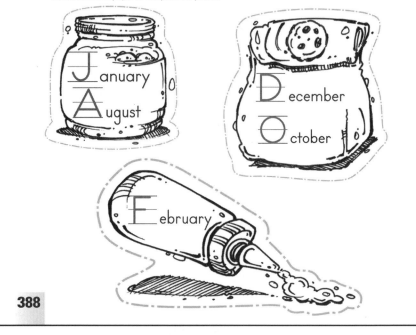

388

2 Poetry Connection

(Use the reproducible master in Appendix B to do this activity.) Have students follow along as you read the poem. Help the students recall what the weather is like during each season, then discuss which months are in that season.

3 Activity Page 388, 389

Objective:

To review the use of capital letters

 Say

Look at the picnic items on your page. Write the beginning letter for each month on the line, remembering to use capital letters. Now, color each picnic item, cut it out, and paste it on another sheet of paper to complete the picture.

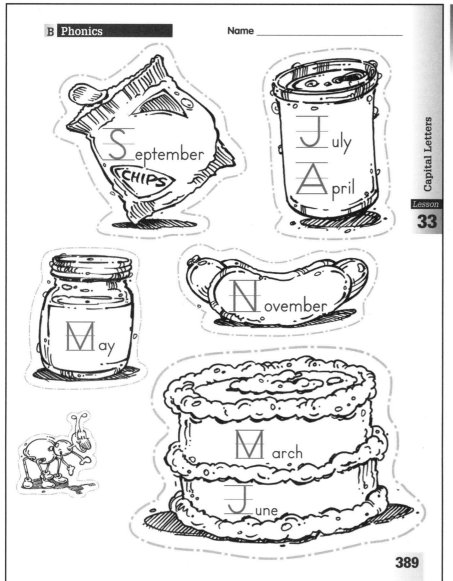

Capital Letters

Lesson **33**

389

Class Picnic
Use the reproducible master in Appendix B to do this activity.

Learning Styles
Kinesthetic and Visual Learners

Materials
- Grocery store ads or seed catalogs
- Scissors
- Paper plates
- Glue
- Pencils

Preparation
None

How to Play:
Have the children look through grocery ads or seed catalogs to find foods they would like to have for a picnic. Have the children cut out those foods, including the brand names, and glue them onto their plates. Now, have the children circle the upper case letters found in the brand names.

1 Warm-Up

Matching Partner Letters

Materials
• 3 x 5 cards or seasonal die-cut shapes

Preparation
Make one set each of upper case letter cards and lower case letter cards. Divide the class into two teams.

How to Play:
Give students on **Team A** the upper case letter cards and students on **Team B** the lower case letter cards. Have students find the person on the other team who has their partner letter. You will need to do this more than once, using part of the alphabet for each turn. You may like to time the activity and have students try to find their partners faster each time.

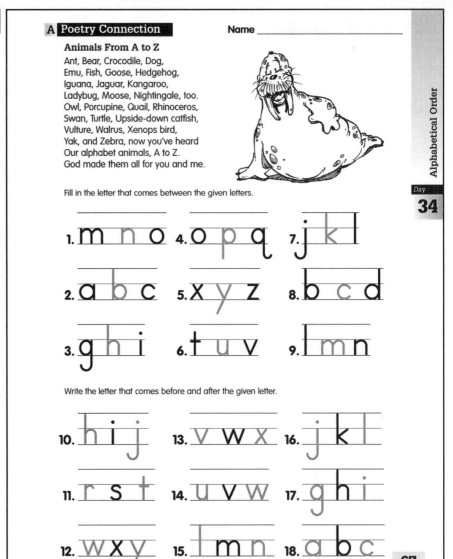

A Poetry Connection   Name _____

Animals From A to Z
Ant, Bear, Crocodile, Dog,
Emu, Fish, Goose, Hedgehog,
Iguana, Jaguar, Kangaroo,
Ladybug, Moose, Nightingale, too.
Owl, Porcupine, Quail, Rhinoceros,
Swan, Turtle, Upside-down catfish,
Vulture, Walrus, Xenops bird,
Yak, and Zebra, now you've heard
Our alphabet animals, A to Z.
God made them all for you and me.

Alphabetical Order

Day **34**

Fill in the letter that comes between the given letters.

1. m n o   4. o p q   7. j k
2. a b c   5. x y z   8. b c d
3. g h i   6. t u v   9. l m n

Write the letter that comes before and after the given letter.

10. h i j   13. v w x   16. j k l
11. r s t   14. u v w   17. g h i
12. w x y   15. l m n   18. a b c

67

2 Poetry Connection

Have students follow along as you read the poem. Have them look through the poem and circle the first letter of each animal name from **A** to **Z**. Invite them to think of other animals that begin with each letter.

3 Activity Page 67

Objective:
To review the alphabet and alphabetical order

 (Say)

On the top section of your page, fill in the letter that comes between the given letters. On the bottom section, write the letter that comes before and after the given letter.

B Phonics

Name _____

Follow the dots from **A** to **Z**. What secret animal do you see? Write the first letter of its name on the line at the top of your page.

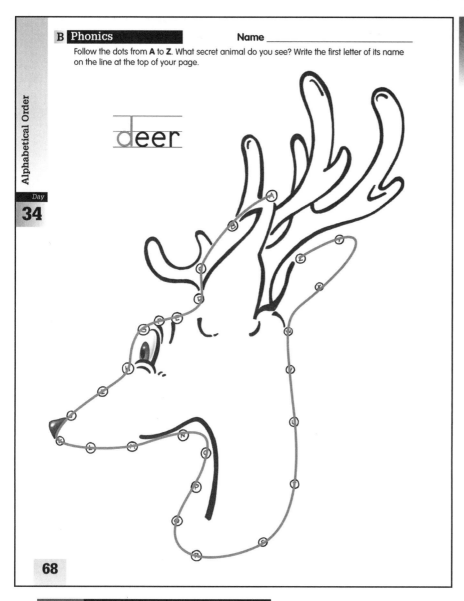

deer

68

---

4 **Activity Page 68**

Objective:
To review alphabetical order

(Say)

Find the circled letter **A**. Use your pencil to draw a line from the **A** to the **B** to the **C** and so on to the letter **Z**. Guess the secret animal and write the first letter of its name to complete the word at the top of your page.

---

5 **Follow Up**

Alphabet Cards

Learning Styles
Kinesthetic and
Visual Learners

Materials
• 3 x 5 cards or seasonal die-cut shapes

Preparation
Make one or more sets of lower case letter cards. Divide the class into two teams.

How to Play:
Place a set of alphabet cards on a table. These may be used in several ways:
1. Children may stand them up along the chalk tray in alphabetical order.
2. Two children may work together. One may hold up a card and ask the other to name a word that begins with that letter.
3. Two children may work together. One may hold up a card and ask the other to tell what sound that letter makes.

Phonics

Lesson **34**

Daily Lesson Plans

Letter

Provide the parent or guardian with the spelling word lists for the next unit.

Say

Show your parents or guardian this letter that tells them what your spelling words will be for the next unit. Ask them to put it in a special place where you will remember to practice them together.

Dear Parent,

We are about to begin our first spelling unit containing four weekly lessons. A set of seven words plus three challenge words will be studied each week. All the words will be reviewed in the fifth week.

Values based on the Scriptures listed below will be taught in each lesson.

Lesson 1	Lesson 2	Lesson 3	Lesson 4
an	get	dog	big
man	let	God	dig
ran	bed	on	it
can	red	off	sit
cat	tell	got	hit
at	well	not	did
dad	yes	mom	hid
☆ thank	☆ help	☆ frog	☆ kid
☆ add	☆ best	☆ box	☆ still
☆ ask	☆ next	☆ odd	☆ quit
Psalm 136:1	Psalm 71:8	Prov. 16:9	Prov. 12:22

Have each student remove this letter from his or her Worktext prior to beginning Lesson 1.

Learning to be Thankful

Beth learns to thank God for loving her no matter how she acts or feels.

"We're home, kids." Mrs. Hill turned the battered pickup into the driveway. "I want you both to run straight upstairs and get your pajamas on. It's way past your bedtime."

"O.K. Mom." Beth lifted her head from the cool glass of the window. *"I don't like visiting Grandpa in the hospital,"* she thought with a sigh. *"He looks so pale and he doesn't talk much. Mom says he'll get well sooner if he knows how much we love and miss him, but it's such a long ride to the hospital and I'm so sleepy!"*

"Luke, did you hear me?" Mom glanced around to the back seat. "Is he already asleep, Beth?"

"Uh-huh," Beth mumbled.

The garage door hummed open, and Mrs. Hill pulled the pickup in beside the car. "Be sure to take your soccer ball and shin guards into the house with you, Beth," Mom warned. "Daddy needs the pickup tomorrow and you have practice right after school."

Beth started stuffing things into her backpack as Mrs. Hill walked around the pickup to help Luke. "And don't forget your spelling book there on the floor," Mom prodded, picking up the droopy little boy.

"I can't carry it all, Mom!" Beth frowned. "Can't you get it?"

"Luke is all I can carry, Sweetheart. You'll have to come back out and get it yourself."

"I'm too tired," Beth whined. "I can't . . ." But Mom was already walking toward the house, Luke's head resting softly on her shoulder. "She always has time to help Luke," Beth grumbled, picking up the book. "He's not the only one that's tired! He doesn't even have to get up and go to school."

Later that night, as Beth snuggled between the warm flannel sheets, Mom peeked in to say good night. "Love you, Bethy. See you in the morning." Beth rolled over and didn't answer.

It seemed she had just fallen asleep when Daddy was gently shaking her shoulder. "Time to get up, Beth," he said. "Mom put clothes out for you, and breakfast is almost ready. You have 15 minutes."

Beth rubbed her eyes and crawled slowly out of bed. She was still so sleepy! A neatly-pressed jumper lay across the foot of her bed. "Mom!" she shouted from the door of her room, "Do I have to wear a dress?"

"Your jeans are in the dryer, but they're not dry yet," Mom answered from the kitchen. "I thought you liked that dress." Without a word, Beth grumpily pulled the jumper over her head, and clomped down the stairs and into the kitchen.

"Here Sweetheart," Mrs. Hill set a pan back on the stove. "Let me do your hair before Luke and Daddy come in."

"Are we still out of granola?" Beth glared at the oatmeal in the pan.

"I'm afraid so," Mom nodded. "I didn't have time to go to the store yesterday, because I had to feed Grandpa and Grandma's horses."

"OUCH!" Beth winced as Mom pulled her blond hair back into a pony tail. "I want short hair like Luke's. No one ever pulls the little hairs at the back of his neck every morning!"

"It was your choice, Bethy." Mom fastened the bright blue bow. "You said you wanted it long so we wouldn't have to use the blow dryer to style it every morning."

"I changed my mind," mumbled Beth.

Beth was still tired and grumpy when Mrs. Hill dropped her off at school 30 minutes later. As she entered the classroom, her best friend Katelynn called to her from across the room. "Come see the baby snapping turtle Tony found in his pond yesterday!"

Beth shook her head and walked directly to her desk. She ignored the hurt look on Katelynn's face and surprise on Tony's as she plopped her backpack down and pulled out her spelling book. Katelynn started toward her, but was stopped by the sound of the bell.

"Everyone to your seats, please." Miss Grant opened her roll book and looked around the room. "Katelynn, please choose someone to help you pass out the spelling books." Katelynn grabbed the bright tub full of worktexts and walked to where Beth was sitting with her head on her desk. "Want to help me pass these out, Beth?"

"Get someone else," Beth frowned. "I don't feel like it."

Katelynn looked surprised, then motioned for Tony to help. "What's wrong with Beth?" Tony whispered, handing Christopher his worktext.

"Got me," Katelynn shrugged.

Miss Grant began the day's lesson with Psalm 136:1. "Oh, give thanks to the Lord, for He is good," Miss Grant said the verse aloud as she wrote it on the board. "Raise you hand if you'd like to share with the class what you think that means. Kristin?"

"We should say thank-you when we pray," Kristin said.

"What do you think, Matthew?"

Matthew smiled. "I need to thank God for my new mountain bike!"

"I'm thankful for my house," Christopher added.

"Rosa, do you want to add something to our list?"

"I need to thank Him for

73

Day 1

Lesson 1

my Grandpa Joe," said Rosa. "He just put a door on our treehouse yesterday so we can sleep up there!"

"Grandpa used to help me build neat stuff in his workshop," Beth thought with a frown. *"Now he's in the hospital and very sick, and I'm sure not thankful for that!"* Out loud she said, "Miss Grant, my grandpa is very sick. And some kids will never get a bike or a treehouse. And some families don't even have houses. What do they have to thank God for?"

Miss Grant looked thoughtful. "Let's think about Beth's question while we do our journaling page today," she suggested, turning to the board. "In your spelling worktext, it says: Dear God, Thanks for (blank). Love, (blank). I'd like you to put words in the first blank, and your name in the second."

The children began to open their worktexts and get out their pencils. "Want to use my soccer pencil, Beth?" Katelynn whispered across the aisle.

Beth's eyebrows went up in surprise. Katelynn never let anyone borrow her special soccer pencil! "Sure!" Beth reached across the aisle and her eyes met Katelynn's. Then Katelynn gave her a big smile. *"I can't believe Katelynn is being so nice to me,"* Beth thought, *"especially after I've been so grumpy all morning!"*

Suddenly she knew the answer to her own question! *"I should thank God for being so good and loving me no matter how I act or feel,"* Beth realized, *"just like my friend, Katelynn."* Then she filled in the blanks as she whispered softly, "Dear God, thank you for your love, and thank you for Katelynn."

2 Discussion Time

Check understanding of the story and development of personal values.

- Why did Beth feel grumpy and tired?
- When was the last time you acted grumpy and tired? Why?
- Do you think God loves you when you feel that way?
- What are you thankful for?
- Have you stopped to thank God for loving you no matter how you feel or act?

74

A Preview

Name _____

Write each word as your teacher says it.

1. man
2. at
3. can
4. ran
5. dad
6. cat
7. an

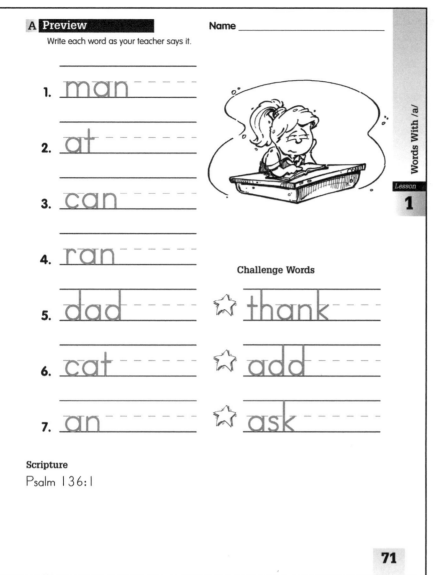

Challenge Words

☆ thank
☆ add
☆ ask

Scripture
Psalm 136:1

71

Words With /a/

Lesson **1**

Challenge

For better spellers, challenge words may be included in the weekly list. Challenge words are starred.

Correct Immediately!

Say Let's correct our preview. I will write each word on the board. Put a dot under each letter on your preview as I spell the word out loud. If you spelled a word wrong, rewrite it correctly.

Progress Chart

Students may record scores. (Reproducible master in Appendix B.)

Day 1

Lesson 1

Take a minute to memorize . . .

Read the memory verse twice. Have students practice it with you two more times.

---

3 Preview

Test for knowledge of the correct spellings of these words. (See the instructions at the top right for challenge words.)

 Say I will say each word once, use the word in a sentence, then say the word again. Write the word on the lines in the Worktext.

1. man	A **man** drove the truck.
2. at	Beth visited her Grandpa **at** the hospital.
3. can	God **can** help you.
4. ran	The horse **ran** very fast.
5. dad	Beth's **dad** said it was time to get up.
6. cat	The **cat** is purring.
7. an	I want **an** apple.
☆ thank	Beth will **thank** God for Katelynn.
☆ add	Mother will **add** some milk.
☆ ask	Beth will **ask** for help.

4 Word Shapes

Help students form a correct image of whole words.

 Say Look at each word and think about its shape. Now, write the word in the correct word Shape Boxes. You may check off each word as you use it.

(In many words **/a/** is spelled with **a**, and it is often spelled this way when it is at the beginning or in the middle of a word.)

 Say In the word shape boxes, color the letter that spells the sound of **/a/** in each word. Circle the words that begin with the sound of **/a/**.

Challenge

Draw the correctly shaped box around each letter in these words.

 Say On a separate sheet of paper, write other words that contain the spelling patterns in the word list. See how many words you can write.

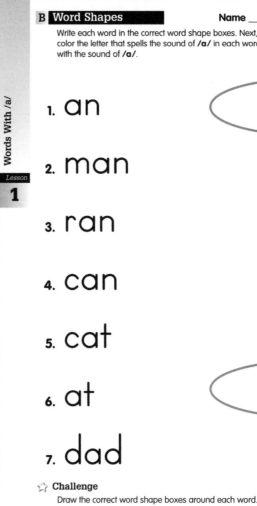

B Word Shapes   Name _____

Write each word in the correct word shape boxes. Next, in the word shape boxes, color the letter that spells the sound of /a/ in each word. Circle the words that begin with the sound of /a/.

Words With /a/ — Lesson 1

1. an
2. man
3. ran
4. can
5. cat
6. at
7. dad

☆ **Challenge**
Draw the correct word shape boxes around each word.

thank   add   ask

72

Answers may vary for duplicate word shapes.

Be Prepared For Fun

Check these supply lists for **Fun Ways to Spell** presented **Day 2**. Purchase and/or gather these items ahead of time!

General
- Crayons
- 3 x 5 Cards cut in thirds (19 pieces per child)
- 3 x 5 Cards cut in thirds (11 more pieces for challenge words)
- Glue
- Construction Paper (about 3 pieces per child)
- Spelling List

Auditory
- Spelling List

Visual
- Sidewalk Chalk
- Spelling List

Tactile
- Damp Sand (in plastic storage box with lid)
- Spelling List

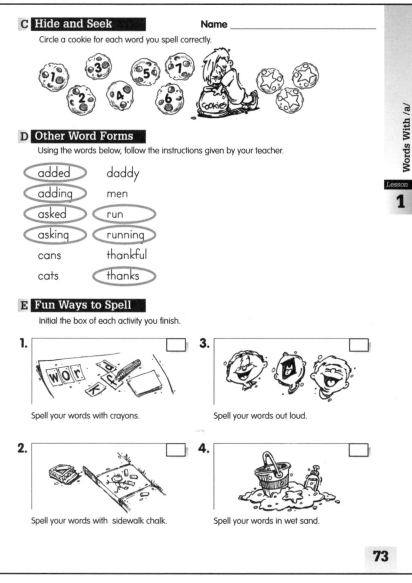

C Hide and Seek

Circle a cookie for each word you spell correctly.

D Other Word Forms

Using the words below, follow the instructions given by your teacher.

(added)	daddy
(adding)	men
(asked)	(run)
(asking)	(running)
cans	thankful
cats	(thanks)

E Fun Ways to Spell

Initial the box of each activity you finish.

1. [ ]
Spell your words with crayons.

2. [ ]
Spell your words with sidewalk chalk.

3. [ ]
Spell your words out loud.

4. [ ]
Spell your words in wet sand.

Words With /a/

Lesson 1

73

---

1 Hide and Seek

Reinforce spelling by using multiple styles of learning.

On a white board, Teacher writes each word — one at a time. **Have students:**

- **Look** at the word.
- **Say** the word out loud.
- **Spell** the word out loud.
- **Hide** (teacher erases word.)
- **Write** the word on their paper.
- **Seek** (teacher rewrites word.)
- **Check** spelling. If incorrect, repeat above steps.

Day 2

Lesson 1

2 Other Word Forms

This activity is optional. Have students find and circle the Other Word Forms that show action.

3 Fun Ways to Spell

Four activities are provided. Use one, two, three, or all of the activities. Have students initial the box for each activity they complete.

Options:

- assign activities to students according to their learning styles
- set up the activities in learning centers for students to do throughout the day
- divide students into four groups and assign one activity per group
- do one activity per day

General

To spell your words with crayons…
- Write each letter of your spelling word on a card.
- Glue the cards on a sheet of paper in the right order to spell your words.
- Check your spelling.

Auditory

To spell your words out loud…
- Have your classmate read a spelling word.
- Say a sentence with that spelling word to your classmate.
- Spell the spelling word you used in that sentence to your classmate.
- Ask your classmate to check your spelling.
- Do this with each word on your word list.

Visual

To spell your words with sidewalk chalk…
- Write each of your words on the sidewalk (ball court or playground).
- Check your spelling.

Tactile

To spell your words in damp sand…
- Use your finger to write a spelling word in the damp sand.
- Check your spelling.
- Smooth the sand with your finger and write another word.

77

Word Scramble

Familiarize students with word meaning and usage.

Write the letters **nda** on the board. Help the students understand that the scrambled letters **nda** spell the word **and** when they are arranged correctly. Guide the students in ordering the letters to spell **and**.

Say) Unscramble the letters to make a spelling word. Write the word on the line.

F Word Scramble

Name _____

Unscramble the letters to make a spelling word. Write the word on the line.

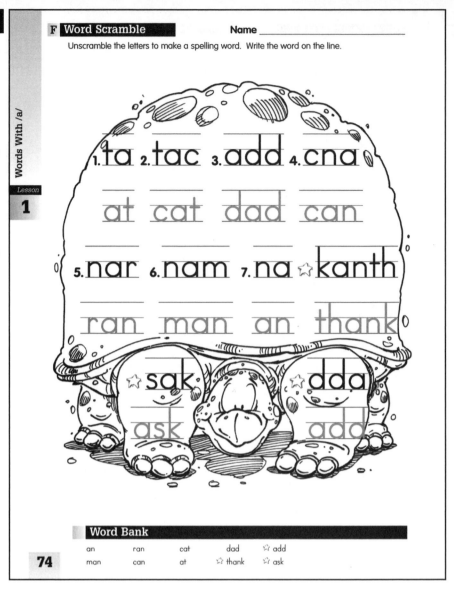

1. ta   2. tac   3. add   4. cna

at   cat   dad   can

5. nar   6. nam   7. na   ☆ kanth

ran   man   an   thank

☆ sak   ☆ dda

ask   add

Word Bank

an	ran	cat	dad	☆ add
man	can	at	☆ thank	☆ ask

74

Take a minute to memorize...

Read the memory verse twice. Have students practice it with you two more times.

G Dictation

Listen and write the missing words.

Name _____

1. That man is my dad.

2. Apples can be red.

3. My cat ran away.

H Proofreading

One word in each pair is misspelled. Fill in the oval by the misspelled word.

1. ● aan
   ○ man

2. ○ ran
   ● bab

3. ● mna
   ○ at

4. ● kan
   ○ an

5. ○ dad
   ● kat

6. ● att
   ○ can

☆ ● thak
   ○ ran

☆ ○ cat
   ● aks

☆ ● abb
   ○ ask

75

---

1 Dictation

Reinforce correct spelling by using current and previous words in context.

(Say) Listen as I read each sentence and then write it in your Worktext. (Slowly read each sentence twice. Sentences are found in the Student Worktext to the left.)

☆ **Challenge**

Write these incomplete sentences on the board.

The ___ said ___ you.

You ___ ___ these numbers.

Tommy will ___ his ___.

(Say) Listen as I read each sentence. Write the sentence on your paper. (Slowly read each sentence twice.)

The <u>man</u> said <u>thank</u> you.

You <u>can</u> <u>add</u> these numbers.

Tommy will <u>ask</u> his <u>dad</u>.

Day 4

Lesson 1

---

2 Proofreading

Familiarize students with standardized test format and reinforce recognizing misspelled words.

(Say) Look at each set of words. One word in each set is misspelled. Fill in the oval by the misspelled word. (You may wish to pronounce each set of words to help students correctly identify them.)

79

3 Hide and Seek

Reinforce correct spelling of current spelling words. (A reproducible master is provided in Appendix A as shown on the inset page to the right.)

Write the words one at a time on a white board. **Have students:**

- **Look** at the word.
- **Say** the word out loud.
- **Spell** the word out loud.
- **Hide** (teacher erases word.)
- **Write** the word on paper.
- **Seek** (teacher rewrites word.)
- **Check** spelling. If incorrect, rewrite word correctly.

4 Making Words

Have your students complete this activity to strengthen spelling ability and expand vocabulary.

1 Posttest

Test mastery of the spelling words. Challenge words are starred.

 I will say the word once, use the word in a sentence, then say the word again. Write the word on your paper.

Hide and Seek

Check a paper for each word you spell correctly.

Making Words

Add the endings to the spelling words. Write the new word on the line.

1. can + s
   cans

☆ thank + s
   thanks

2. dad + s
   dads

☆ add + ed
   added

3. cat + s
   cats

☆ ask + ed
   asked

☆ ask + s
   asks

☆ thank + ed
   thanked

Appendix

Lesson **1**

363

1. cat	The girl held a Persian **cat**.
2. an	The chicken laid **an** egg this morning.
3. man	Adam was the first **man**.
4. dad	My **dad** will be home at 5:30.
5. ran	The boys and girls **ran** around the playground.
6. can	Mom bought a **can** of soup.
7. at	Grandpa was **at** the hospital.
☆ add	We can **add** five plus two.
☆ thank	We should remember to say **thank**-you.
☆ ask	They can **ask** the policeman for directions.

Progress Chart

Students may record scores. (Reproducible master in Appendix B.)

Personal Dictionary

Students may add any words they have misspelled to their personal dictionaries for reference when writing. (Cover in Appendix B.)

I Game

Name _____

Beth left her spelling book in the truck. Lead the way by moving one space each time you or your team spells a word correctly from this week's word list.

Remember : God is good. He loves us even when we're not lovable.

J Journaling

In your journal, finish this thank-you letter to God.
Dear God, Thanks for _____.
Love, _____ (Remember to sign your name!)

76

---

2 Game

Reinforce spelling skills and provide motivation and interest.

Materials

- game page (from student text)
- flat buttons, dry beans, pennies, or game discs (1 per child)
- game word list

Game Word List

Use of challenge words is optional.

1. **an**
2. **man**
3. **ran**
4. **can**
5. **cat**
6. **at**
7. **dad**
☆ **thank**
☆ **add**
☆ **ask**

3 Journaling

Provide a meaningful reason for correct spelling through personal writing.

Review the story using discussion leads provided on the following page. Encourage students to apply the Scriptural value in their journaling.

 Take a minute to memorize...

Read the memory verse to the class twice. Have the class practice it with you two more times.

How to Play:

- Divide the class into two teams, and decide which team will go first.
- Have each student place his/her game piece on Start.
- Have a student from team A go to the board.
- Read the spelling word two times slowly and clearly. (You may also wish to use the word in a sentence. Ex.: "cat — The cat climbed a tree. — cat")
- Have the student write the word on the board.
- If the word is spelled correctly, instruct all the members of team A to move their game pieces forward one space on the game board. (Note: If the word is misspelled, correct the spelling immediately before continuing the game.)
- Alternate between teams A and B as you go down the word list.
- The team to reach the truck first is the winner.

Non-Competitive Option:

At the end of the game, say: "Class, I am proud of your efforts to spell the words correctly. If you had fun and tried your best, you are all winners!"

Journaling (continued)

- How did Beth feel when she came to school? (grumpy and tired)
- Who helped Beth decide she should be thankful? (Miss Grant by talking about the Scripture and Katelynn because she was kind to Beth even though Beth was grumpy and tired.)
- Our text says "Oh, give thanks to the Lord, for He is good." Why was Beth feeling thankful by the end of the story? (Beth realized that even when she wasn't lovable Katelynn was still her friend.)
- Think of some things you are thankful for.
- Finish a thank-you letter to God in your journal today.

"A baby learns to talk by talking. A child learns to spell by spelling."*

*Wilde, Sandra. 1990. A Proposal for a New Spelling Curriculum. The Elementary School Journal, Vol. 90, No. 3, January: 275-289.

The Gloves

Matthew learns to praise God for all the things He does for us, and for not getting mad at us when we make mistakes.

"Leave your glove on the ground 'til the ball is in it," Matthew encouraged. "That way you won't miss those grounders."

"Okay!" Alex smiled as he threw the ball back to his older brother.

"I can't believe that he's only five — he's almost better than I am!" thought Matthew as he tossed the ball back across the yard. "Great catch, Alex!"

"Time to eat, boys," Mom called from the front porch. Both boys dropped their gloves as they ran up the front steps and raced into the house.

"Thanks for helping me, Matthew," Alex said, scooting his chair up to the table. "That was fun!"

"Dad, you should see Alex catch a grounder." Matthew helped himself to steaming mashed potatoes. "He's really getting good!"

"Well, you've really helped him a lot, Matthew," Dad smiled. "You're a good teacher."

Later that night, as the boys were getting ready for bed, Mom called from the kitchen. "Matthew! Alex! Don't forget to bring your gloves in off the front steps."

"I'll get them," Alex offered. "I'm all ready for bed." Alex trotted off as Matthew finished brushing his teeth.

Soon Mom came in for the boys' bedtime story. The three of them sat on Matthew's bed. "'All day long I'll praise and honor You, O God, for all that you have done for me,'" Mom read the Scripture aloud. "How do you think you could do that, boys?" They looked at her blankly, so she continued. "Well, what has God done for you, Matthew?" Matthew scratched his head. "Oh,

food, clothes, our house . . . and toys!"

"I thought Dad earned money and bought you all those things. What do you think, Alex?" Mom prodded, encouraging the boys to think deeper.

Just then, two-year-old Emily toddled into the room and tried to crawl up on the bed. "Phew! I've gotta go change a diaper," Mom laughed, picking up Emily and heading for the door. "Crawl in your beds, and I'll be right back."

"Barrooom!" Bright light flashed across Matthew's plaid sheets followed by a loud roar of thunder!

Matthew sat bolt upright in bed! "How long have I been sleeping?" he wondered, suddenly wide-eyed and alert. He could hear Emily crying down the hall as another flash of lightning was followed by a loud "boom!" Quickly he turned to check on Alex, who was sleeping quietly in the twin bed next to him.

"How can that little guy sleep through this storm?" Matthew thought. He heard the floor boards creak as Mom hurried to his little sister's crib in the next room. He listened as Mom murmured softly, and Em's cries slowly diminished.

"Barrooom!" Another bright flash lit the room, and this time Matthew saw Alex squirm and heard him make a little moaning sound. "I don't want him to wake up and cry like he did in the last storm," thought Matthew. He quietly crawled from between his sheets, then under the quilt at the foot of Alex's bed. "And I kinda like being close to someone during those really loud booms — even if he is only five!"

"Are you okay, Matthew?" Mom

whispered, passing by on the way back to her room.

"Yeah Mom. I just thought Alex might be scared if he woke up in this storm."

"Thank you, Matthew," Mom smiled. "You're always so kind to Alex. I'm very proud of you!"

It seemed only moments later sunlight was streaming in the windows. Matthew stretched and rubbed his eyes.

"Whatcha doin' in my bed, Matthew?" Alex asked sitting up.

"I came over here to protect you in the big storm, Buddy." Matthew yawned and crawled out from under the patchwork quilt. "You never even woke up, did you?"

"Nope. I'm hungry. Let's go eat, then see how full the creek is!" Alex walked over to the window to see if the creek was out of its banks. "Oh no!" he moaned. There on the front steps lay two soaked leather ballgloves — right where he had forgotten them the night before! What would Matthew say? What would Mom do when Matthew told on him?

"What's wrong, Alex?" Matthew walked up behind his younger brother. He pulled the curtain to one side and looked out. "Oh no! My glove! You didn't get them, Alex. I can't believe you forgot! You said you'd bring them both in! Mom will be really upset! You know how she wants us to take good care of our stuff."

"I'm only five!" Tears began to fill Alex eyes. "I was on my way to get them when I saw Emily moving all the little picture-things around the computer with the mouse. I had to stop her before she made a big mess." Alex looked down at the floor. "Then I just forgot. I'm sorry."

"They'll dry." Matthew patted Alex on the shoulder. "Let's just take care of this ourselves before Mom sees them and decides to take your glove away to teach you a lesson."

Alex ran down the porch steps and grabbed the two soggy gloves. He couldn't believe Matthew

Lesson **2** | **Day 1**

wasn't trying to get him in trouble with Mom. "Thanks Matthew," he said as he came back in.

"That's okay," Matthew smiled. "We've got to hurry now or we'll be late for school!"

The day passed quickly, and soon it was time for evening worship. Dad held Emily on his lap as Mom began. "Our verse last night was, 'All day long I'll praise and honor You, O God, for all that you have done for me.'" She paused. "When I came back in from changing Em last night, you boys were sound asleep. I guess you wore yourselves out playing catch yesterday. Anyway, you said that you were thankful to God for food, clothes, and a house."

"Yeah, God gave us you and Dad to pay for all those things!" smiled Matthew.

"What else has God done for you?" Mom paused again. "Does God ever teach you things?"

"I don't think so." Matthew looked puzzled. "How can someone teach you something when you can't even see them?"

"How about through other people?" Dad prompted. "Does God ever use people to help you learn things?"

"Miss Grant teaches us Scripture verses," Matthew nodded.

"And Matthew teaches me how to catch grounders," added Alex.

"Does God ever keep you safe?" Mom handed Emily back the stuffed toy she'd just dropped.

"Miss Grant says we have our own guardian angel," suggested Matthew.

"That's true, Matthew," said Mom. "Who slept on your bed in the storm last night, Alex?"

"Matthew did!" Alex gave his brother a big smile.

"Does God get mad when we mess up?" Matthew turned to look at Dad.

"God sure has good reason to sometimes," Dad smiled. "But God loves us, and is patient and understanding when we make mistakes."

"Like you were this morning, Matthew, when I forgot your glove," explained Alex.

"Glove?" Mom looked over at Matthew and raised an eyebrow.

Matthew grinned sheepishly as Dad continued, "Let's see what we've learned. Scripture says, 'All day long I'll praise and honor You, O God, for all that you have done for me.' So we can praise God for our food, clothes, and other material things. But God also sends people to teach us things, to help us feel safe. And God doesn't get mad at us when we make mistakes." Dad looked around at the family. "I think we have a lot to praise God for! Let's bow our heads and say thank-you right now. Matthew, you go first."

"Dear God, thank you for Dad, for Mom, for Miss Grant, and for my guardian angel. Amen."

"Dear God," Alex prayed next. "Thank you for taking such good care of me. And thank you for sending Matthew to help."

And Matthew smiled and thought, *"I can't believe he's only five!"*

Discussion Time

2

Check understanding of the story and development of personal values.

- Why was Alex thankful for his big brother?
- What kind things had Matthew done for his little brother Alex?
- What has God done for you?
- Have you thanked Him?
- Who helps God take care of you?
- Have you thanked God's helpers for what they do for you?

A Preview

Write each word as your teacher says it.

Name _____

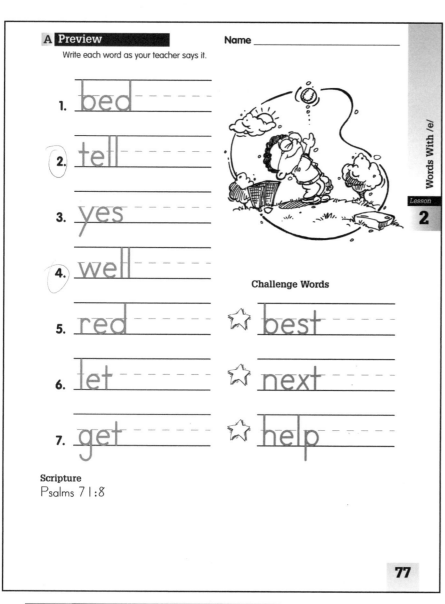

1. bed
2. tell
3. yes
4. well
5. red
6. let
7. get

Challenge Words

☆ best
☆ next
☆ help

Words With /e/

Lesson 2

Scripture
Psalms 71:8

77

Challenge

For better spellers, challenge words may be included in the weekly list. Challenge words are starred.

Correct Immediately!

Say Let's correct our preview. I will write each word on the board. Put a dot under each letter on your preview as I spell the word out loud. If you spelled a word wrong, rewrite it correctly.

Progress Chart

Students may record scores. (Reproducible master in Appendix B.)

Misspelled words may be added to students' personal dictionaries for reference when writing (Reproducible cover in Appendix B).

Take a minute to memorize . . .

Read the memory verse twice. Have students practice it with you two more times.

---

3 Preview

Test for knowledge of the correct spellings of these words. (See the instructions at the top right for challenge words.)

 Say I will say each word once, use the word in a sentence, then say the word again. Write the word on the lines in the Worktext.

1. bed   Mom sat on the edge of Matthew's **bed.**
2. tell   It is important to always **tell** the truth.
3. yes   Matthew said, "**Yes,** I'll go back to sleep."
4. well   We get our water from a deep **well.**
5. red   She likes the **red** roses.
6. let   I will **let** you play with this new toy truck.
7. get   Alex offered to **get** the gloves.
☆ best   This is the **best** birthday I've ever had!
☆ next   It will be your turn **next.**
☆ help   Matthew will **help** Alex learn to catch the ball.

85

Help students form a correct image of whole words.

 Say Look at each word and think about its shape. Now, write the word in the correct word Shape Boxes. You may check off each word as you use it.

(In many words **/e/** is spelled with **e**, and it is often spelled this way in the middle of a word. A double consonant is one consonant sound spelled with the same two consonant letters. Often double consonants follow short vowel sounds.)

 Say In the word shape boxes, color the letter that spells the sound of **/e/** in each word. Circle the words that have double consonants.

☆ **Challenge**
Draw the correctly shaped box around each letter in these words.

 Say On a separate sheet of paper, write other words that contain the spelling patterns in the word list. See how many words you can write.

Day 1

Lesson 2

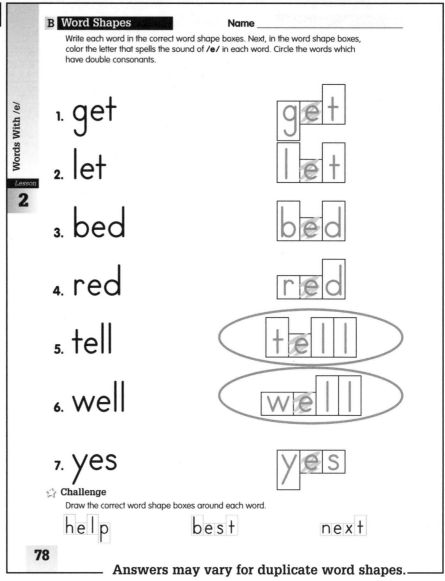

B **Word Shapes** — Name _____

Write each word in the correct word shape boxes. Next, in the word shape boxes, color the letter that spells the sound of /e/ in each word. Circle the words which have double consonants.

Words With /e/ — Lesson **2**

1. get
2. let
3. bed
4. red
5. tell
6. well
7. yes

☆ **Challenge**
Draw the correct word shape boxes around each word.

help   best   next

78

Answers may vary for duplicate word shapes.

 Be Prepared For Fun
Check these supply lists for **Fun Ways to Spell** presented **Day 2.**
Purchase and/or gather these items ahead of time!

General
- Strips of Paper 3 1/2 x 11 Inches (7 per child)
- Strips of Paper 3 1/2 x 11 Inches (3 more for challenge words)
- Crayons or Markers
- Tape
- Scissors
- Spelling List

Auditory
- Rhythm Instruments (two wooden spoons, two pan lids, maracas)
- Spelling List

Visual
- Clothespins (5 clothespins per child at the clothesline)
- b, d, e, g, l, l, r, s, t, w and y (written on 3 x 5 cards cut in half)
- h, n, p and x (added for challenge words)
- Clothesline (hung at student height)
- Spelling List

Tactile
- Shaving Cream
- Optional: Plastic Plates
- Optional: Wooden Craft Sticks
- Spelling List

86

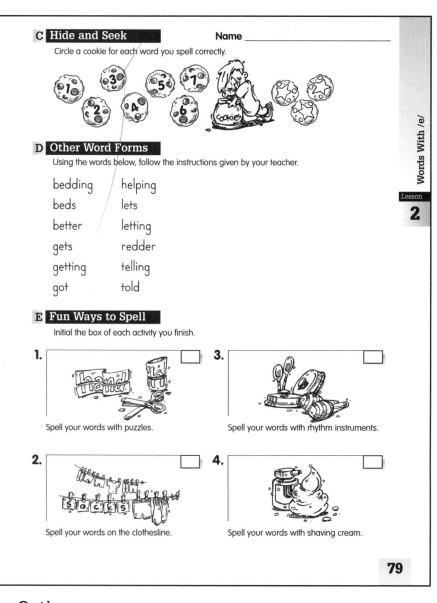

C Hide and Seek

Name _____

Circle a cookie for each word you spell correctly.

D Other Word Forms

Using the words below, follow the instructions given by your teacher.

bedding	helping
beds	lets
better	letting
gets	redder
getting	telling
got	told

E Fun Ways to Spell

Initial the box of each activity you finish.

1. ☐ Spell your words with puzzles.

2. ☐ Spell your words on the clothesline.

3. ☐ Spell your words with rhythm instruments.

4. ☐ Spell your words with shaving cream.

79

---

1 **Hide and Seek**

Reinforce spelling by using multiple styles of learning.

On a white board, Teacher writes each word — one at a time. **Have students:**

- **Look** at the word.
- **Say** the word out loud.
- **Spell** the word out loud.
- **Hide** (teacher erases word.)
- **Write** the word on their paper.
- **Seek** (teacher rewrites word.)
- **Check** spelling. If incorrect, repeat above steps.

2 **Other Word Forms**

This activity is optional. Have students dictate original sentences to you using these Other Word Forms. Write them on the board.

told   **helping**
beds

3 **Fun Ways to Spell**

Four activities are provided. Use one, two, three, or all of the activities. Have students initial the box for each activity they complete.

Day 2 | Lesson 2

Options:

- assign activities to students according to their learning styles
- set up the activities in learning centers for students to do throughout the day
- divide students into four groups and assign one activity per group
- do one activity per day

General

To Spell your words with puzzles…
- Write each word on a strip of paper in big, tall letters.
- Cut your word in half lengthwise.
- Tape the ends of each strip together to make circles.
- Mix the circles together.
- Match the circles again to make your spelling words.

Auditory

To spell your words with rhythm instruments…
- Look at a word on your spelling list.
- Close your eyes.
- Play your rhythm instruments softly while you whisper the spelling of the word.
- Open your eyes and check your spelling.

Visual

To spell your words on the clothesline…
- Choose the letter cards you need to spell a word on your list.
- Clothespin the cards to the clothesline in the right order to spell the word.
- Check your spelling.
- Remove the letter cards from the clothesline and spell the next word on your list.

Tactile

To spell your words with shaving cream…
- Spread a glob of shaving cream across your desk (or on a plastic plate).
- Use your finger (or a wooden craft stick) to write a spelling word in the shaving cream.
- Check your spelling.
- Smear the word out with your finger and write another word.

87

1 ABC Order

Familiarize students with word meaning and usage. Write the words **dog**, **can**, and **fix** on the board. Help the students understand that each word begins with a different letter. Write the letters **d**, **c**, and **f**. Ask the students which letter comes first in the alphabet. Ask which letter comes next. Elicit the response that the letters would come **c**, **d**, **f**. Then write the words in ABC order as **can**, **dog**, and **fix**.

Say — Write the words from each group in ABC order.

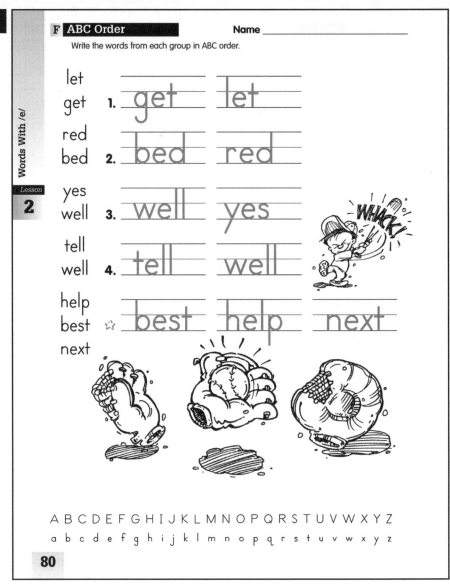

F ABC Order   Name _____

Write the words from each group in ABC order.

Words With /e/

Lesson **2**

let
get   1. get   let

red
bed   2. bed   red

yes
well   3. well   yes

tell
well   4. tell   well

help
best   ☆   best   help   next
next

A B C D E F G H I J K L M N O P Q R S T U V W X Y Z
a b c d e f g h i j k l m n o p q r s t u v w x y z

80

Take a minute to memorize...

Read the memory verse twice. Have students practice it with you two more times.

G Dictation
Listen and write the missing words.

Name _____

1. Dad will get it.

2. The man in bed is not well.

3. Tell your dad we said, "Yes."

H Proofreading
One word in each pair is misspelled. Fill in the oval by the misspelled word.

1. ○ red
   ● tel

2. ● git
   ○ ran

3. ○ yes
   ● reb

4. ○ well
   ● lett

5. ● yse
   ○ can

6. ○ let
   ● beb

☆ ○ help
   ● besk

☆ ● neks
   ○ ask

☆ ● hep
   ○ bed

81

1 Dictation

Reinforce correct spelling by using current and previous words in context.

 Listen as I read each sentence and then write it in your Worktext. (Slowly read each sentence twice. Sentences are found in the Student Worktext to the left.)

☆ **Challenge**
Write these incomplete sentences on the board.

___ ___ ___ carry the ___ ___.

My ___ will do his ___.

Beth ___ to be ___ in line.

 Listen as I read each sentence. Write the sentence on your paper. (Slowly read each sentence twice.)

I can help carry the red bed.

My dad will do his best.

Beth ran to be next in line.

Day 4 | Lesson 2

2 Proofreading

Familiarize students with standardized test format and reinforce recognizing misspelled words.

 Look at each set of words. One word in each set is misspelled. Fill in the oval by the misspelled word. (You may wish to pronounce each set of words to help students correctly identify them.)

3 Hide and Seek

Reinforce correct spelling of current spelling words. (A reproducible master is provided in Appendix A as shown on the inset page to the right.)

Write the words one at a time on a white board.

Have students:

- **Look** at the word.
- **Say** the word out loud.
- **Spell** the word out loud.
- **Hide** (teacher erases word.)
- **Write** the word on paper.
- **Seek** (teacher rewrites word.)
- **Check** spelling. If incorrect, rewrite word correctly.

4 Code

Have your students complete this activity to strengthen spelling ability and expand vocabulary.

1 Posttest

Test mastery of the spelling words. Challenge words are starred.

Say I will say the word once, use the word in a sentence, then say the word again. Write the word on your paper.

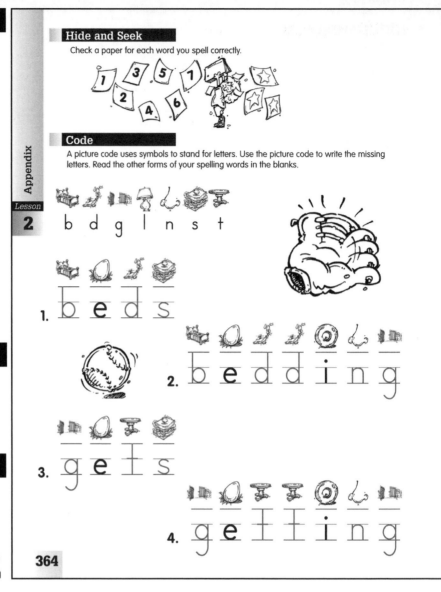

Appendix
Lesson 2

Hide and Seek
Check a paper for each word you spell correctly.

Code
A picture code uses symbols to stand for letters. Use the picture code to write the missing letters. Read the other forms of your spelling words in the blanks.

b d g l n s t

1. b e d s
2. b e d d i n g
3. g e t s
4. g e t t i n g

364

1.	tell	Matthew didn't **tell** Mom that Alex forgot the gloves.
2.	bed	Did you make your **bed** this morning?
3.	well	Emily didn't sleep very **well**.
4.	let	Tony will **let** the turtle go.
5.	yes	Mother said, "**Yes**, you may have some more juice."
6.	get	The children will **get** new shoes.
7.	red	The ball is **red**.
☆	next	Beth is **next** in line.
☆	help	The girl will **help** her mother.
☆	best	Always try to do your **best**.

Progress Chart
Students may record scores. (Reproducible master in Appendix B.)

Personal Dictionary
Students may add any words they have misspelled to their personal dictionaries for reference when writing. (Cover in Appendix B.)

90

I Game

Name _____

God gives us people to love and help us. God gave Alex his big brother Matthew to play ball with him and to encourage him. Circle one softball for each word you or your team spells correctly from this week's word list.

Remember : Never stop praising God for all He has done for you.

J Journaling

Write this sentence in your journal.
God sent _____ to help me today.
Fill in the blank with the name of a helper you know.

82

---

2 Game

Reinforce spelling skills and provide motivation and interest.

Materials

* game page (from student text)
* pencils or crayons (1 per child)
* game word list

Game Word List

Use of challenge words is optional.

1. **get**
2. **let**
3. **bed**
4. **red**
5. **tell**
6. **well**
7. **yes**
☆ **help**
☆ **best**
☆ **next**

3 Journaling

Provide a meaningful reason for correct spelling through personal writing.

Review the story using discussion leads provided on the following page. Encourage students to apply the Scriptural value in their journaling.

 Take a minute to memorize...

Read the memory verse to the class twice. Have the class practice it with you two more times.

How to Play:

* Divide the class into two teams, and decide which team will go first.
* Have a student from team A go to the board.
* Read the spelling word two times slowly and clearly. (You may also wish to use the word in a sentence. Ex.: "cat — The cat climbed a tree. — cat")
* Have the student write the word on the board.
* If the word is spelled correctly, instruct all the members of team A to circle one softball. (Note: If the word is misspelled, correct the spelling immediately before continuing the game.)
* Alternate between teams A and B as you go down the word list.
* The team with the most softballs circled when you have gone through the game word list twice is the winner.

Non-Competitive Option:

At the end of the game, say: "Class, I am proud of your efforts to spell the words correctly. If you had fun and tried your best, you are all winners!"

Journaling (continued)

(Say)

- In our story Matthew realized that he had a wonderful little brother even if he was only five and Alex thanked God for sending Matthew to help take care of him all day long.

- Who are some people you can praise God for every day? (mother, father, grandma, grandpa, aunt, uncle, teacher, police, farmers . . .)

- Write the name of one of God's helpers in your journal today.

> **"A major need for inventive spellers is to have someone answer their questions and correct their mistakes."***

*Lutz, Elaine. 1986. ERIC/RCS Report: Invented Spelling and Spelling Development. Language Arts, Vol. 63, No. 7, November: 742-744.

Doggie Directions

Beth's family experiences God's direction when they decide to get a dog.

"Mom, we really want a dog," Beth pleaded from the back seat of the car.

"What kind of dog were you thinking about, Beth?" Mrs. Hill glanced over her shoulder as she slowed for a stop sign.

"A big one!" added Luke. "One that can run and play with us outside."

"No, no," Beth shook her head. "A little one that can come in the house and even sleep with me."

"Dogs cost a lot of money, kids."

"Really?" Beth was surprised. "How come?"

"First, you have to pay for the puppy. Sometimes he has to have shots. Good dog food is expensive, not to mention bones and toys. Then we'd also need a fence and a dog house for him to sleep in."

"Is that all?" Beth said.

"Well, there are also collars, leashes, food bowls, yearly vaccinations, heartworm medicine, visits to the vet if he gets sick — plus boarding fees whenever we go out of town."

"Why do you keep saying 'he,' Mom?" Beth frowned. "I want a girl dog so she can have lots of puppies."

"That would cost even more money, Bethy." Mom stopped the car in front of the school. "Now hurry or you'll be late. See you this afternoon, Sweetheart."

"Bye, Beth," Luke called after her.

That night after supper, Beth sprawled on the living room rug looking at a book. Luke plopped down beside her. "What are you looking at, Beth?"

"Miss Grant helped me find a book in the school library today about dogs. It has all the kinds of dogs there are. See? It's called *All About Dogs*. Look at this one. Isn't she cute?"

"She's not very cute." Luke argued. "I like this one. He is handsome and big and could really protect us!"

"Which do you like better, Mom?" asked Beth, as Mom joined the two children on the floor. "This cute little doggie or this great big beast?"

Mom smiled. "Oh, I don't know. The Pekingese has beautiful hair, but the Great Dane is so dignified and — HUGE. Let's read what the book says about them both."

Just then Daddy walked in waving a magazine. "I bought *Doggie World* on my lunch break today. There are several ads for puppies in the back listed by breed. Anyone interested?"

"Wow! Do they have Great Danes, Daddy?" Luke hopped to his feet.

"Or Pekingese?" added Beth.

Daddy scooped Luke into his lap. "Let's see . . . they sure do! There are 10 listings for Great Dane Breeders and lots of Pekingese, too." Mr. Hill started flipping through the pages. "Let's see if any of them are close to us."

"Here's what it says about Great Danes." Mom looked back at the book. "'Every line is cleanly chiseled, coupling magnificent size and supple grace.' In other words they look good. 'They are very gentle and loving companions,' it says, 'but guard a home as alertly today as they did in the South African gold mines 100 years ago.' I guess they just look like they could eat you for supper!" she added with a smile.

"Say, there are some breeders just over in Fayetteville," Daddy interrupted. "We could go over and talk to them after we visit Grandpa in the hospital tomorrow."

"Read what it says about the Pekingese, Mom," Beth insisted.

"Let's see . . . 'Once the sacred dog of China, the ancient ancestors of the Pekingese were honored dogs of the imperial palace in Peking.' Maybe that's why Pekingese starts with Peking," Mrs. Hill mused aloud. "'When the British army stormed Peking in 1860, the Chinese killed their sacred dogs so they wouldn't be taken by the foreign devils. Later, the British found some live dogs hiding behind the palace drapes, and one was given to Queen Victoria — who named him Looty.'"

"Daddy," Beth learned over her mother's shoulder for a closer look at the royal dogs. "How much would a Pekingese cost?"

"I don't know, Honey." Mr. Hill stood Luke back on his feet. "But I do know it's 7:30 and time for two kids to get ready for bed. Mom and I will do some more research, and all of us need to pray about this during the next few days."

"I'd like to read a verse to you," Miss Grant opened her Bible the next day in handwriting class. "It's Proverbs 16:9. King Solomon, the wisest man who ever lived, gave us this advice: 'We should make plans — counting on God to direct us.' What sort of plans are children in charge of making?"

There was a long silence. "I think that grown-ups make most of the plans," said Tommy.

"Teachers make plans for us," added Matthew, "and so does whoever takes care of us at home — babysitters, moms, grandmas, and dads."

"But we get to make plans about the games we play," said Katelynn.

"Or whose house we want to go to when we play," said Tony.

"Or forts we build," said James.

"I can decide how to spend my birthday money," Stephen added.

"So," Miss Grant smiled. "Even children get to make some plans themselves! But why don't you get to make all the plans for your life right now?"

Matthew scratched his head. "Well, maybe we don't know how yet."

"Sometimes parents don't know what plans to make either," Beth looked up at Miss Grant. "Our family is thinking about getting a dog. Mom thinks they might cost too much. Luke wants a Great Dane. I think I'd like a Pekingese. Dad says we have to pray an' think some more."

"Who does our text say we can count on to direct us?" questioned Miss Grant.

"God," said Kristin.

"Doesn't the verse say we should make plans?" asked Beth. "We're going tonight to look at puppies. I'm not sure how God is going to direct us though. How can God make everyone in our family happy?"

"God always has a plan, Beth," Miss Grant smiled. "You'll have to let us know how it works out. Okay children, let's take out our handwriting books and turn to lesson 3, day 1. On Friday we'll be writing today's text on a border sheet. Today we're going to practice just the capital and lowercase c." Miss Grant pointed to the board. "They are look-alikes, but aren't identical twins."

That evening, on the drive home from Fayetteville, Luke and Beth were very excited.

"Can we get the Great Dane, Daddy? Please? Oh please?" begged Luke.

"I loved the Pekingese puppy, Daddy," Beth pleaded from her seat in back beside Luke.

"Both those dogs were over $300 kids. I'm afraid that's a little too much for our budget right now." Daddy frowned slightly. "I think we may have to wait and save the money we'll need to buy a dog and all the things it needs. Keep on praying. I'm sure God has a plan for us."

Mr. Hill picked Beth up from school the next day and brought her home on his way to a meeting in Hartford. When they pulled into the driveway they were greeted by an exuberant Luke. "Look who has been at our house all day, Beth!" Behind him romped a medium-sized dog. "I named him Eagle. Isn't he handsome? He played outside with me all day!"

Beth looked at the dog. He was muddy. His tail was crooked. And he was a he! Then Eagle came over to Beth and nuzzled her hand with his cold wet nose.

"He likes you, Bethy," Luke said. Beth squatted down to look at the dog more closely. He rested his head on her knee and looked up with big brown eyes.

Daddy knelt beside Beth. "I'm afraid this is a she, Luke ol' buddy," Mr. Hill laughed.

"Can we keep him . . . I mean her, Daddy?" Luke pleaded.

"Well, we don't know who she belongs to . . . or where she has been . . . or if she is sick." Mr. Hill paused. "But so far the price is right!" he chuckled. "I'll check around, and if no one has claimed her by this weekend, I don't see why we can't keep her. She seems like a very nice dog."

Friday afternoon Beth came in the house with her handwriting border sheet clutched tightly. Eagle shoved her wet nose into Beth's hand and wagged her whole body in greeting. "No one has called about Eagle yet, Mom." Beth looked hopeful. "Does that mean we get to keep her?"

"We sure can," Mrs. Hill beamed.

Beth smiled as she walked to the refrigerator and hung up her border sheet. Eagle followed close behind and leaned against Beth's leg — wagging her crooked tail. Mom read the words that were neatly printed on the border sheet. "We should make plans — counting on God to direct us. Proverbs 16:9."

"You weren't in my plans, Eagle." Beth reached down to gently scratch behind her dog's long ears. "But I'm sure glad God directed us to you!"

Discussion Time

2

Check understanding of the story and development of personal values.

- What surprising way did God direct the Hill family in finding a dog?
- How do you think Luke will feel about having a girl dog?
- How do you think Beth will feel about not getting a Pekingese?
- Do you think Mom and Dad will be happy with Eagle?
- What were the last plans you made all by yourself?
- God loves to help you make plans. He has great ideas! Ask Him to direct you!

94

A Preview

Write each word as your teacher says it.

Name _____

1. on
2. not
3. God
4. mom
5. off
6. dog
7. got

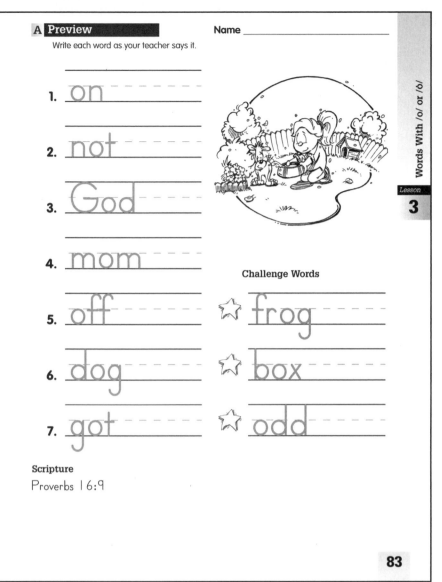

Challenge Words

☆ frog
☆ box
☆ odd

Scripture
Proverbs 16:9

83

Challenge

For better spellers, challenge words may be included in the weekly list. Challenge words are starred.

Correct Immediately!

Say Let's correct our preview. I will write each word on the board. Put a dot under each letter on your preview as I spell the word out loud. If you spelled a word wrong, rewrite it correctly.

Progress Chart

Students may record scores. (Reproducible master in Appendix B.)

Take a minute to memorize . . .

Have students say the memory verse with you once.

---

3 ## Preview

Test for knowledge of the correct spellings of these words. (See the instructions at the top right for challenge words.)

 Say I will say each word once, use the word in a sentence, then say the word again. Write the word on the lines in the Worktext.

1. on — Beth hung her border sheet **on** the refrigerator.
2. not — A Pekingese is **not** a big dog.
3. God — **God** will help us know what to do.
4. mom — Beth's **mom** took her to school.
5. off — The vase fell **off** the table.
6. dog — Eagle was a nice **dog**.
7. got — Beth and Luke **got** a dog of their own.
☆ frog — The **frog** jumped into the pond.
☆ box — The **box** is full of books.
☆ odd — Five is an **odd** number.

Word Shapes

4 Help students form a correct image of whole words.

(Say) Look at each word and think about its shape. Now, write the word in the correct word Shape Boxes. You may check off each word as you use it.

(In many words /ô/ or /o/ is spelled with **o**, and it is often spelled this way when it is at the beginning or in the middle of a word.)

(Say) In the word shape boxes, color the letter that spells the sound of /ô/ or /o/ in each word.

Challenge
Draw the correctly shaped box around each letter in these words.

(Say) On a separate sheet of paper, write other words that contain the spelling patterns in the word list. See how many words you can write.

Write each word in the correct word shape boxes. Next, in the word shape boxes, color the letter that spells the sound of /o/ or /ô/ in each word.

1. dog

2. God

3. on

4. off

5. got

6. not

7. mom

☆ **Challenge**
Draw the correct word shape boxes around each word.

frog   box   odd

84

Answers may vary for duplicate word shapes.

Be Prepared For Fun

Check these supply lists for **Fun Ways to Spell** presented **Day 2**. Purchase and/or gather these items ahead of time!

General
- Crayons
- Piece of Paper
- Spelling List

Auditory
- Box to Store Letters
- d, f, f, g, G, m, m, n, o and t (written on seasonal shapes like leaves or pumpkins)
- b, d, r and x (added for challenge words)
- Spelling List

Visual
- Eraser
- Dark Construction Paper
- Spelling List

Tactile
- Finger Paint
- Plastic Plate or Glossy Paper
- Spelling List

96

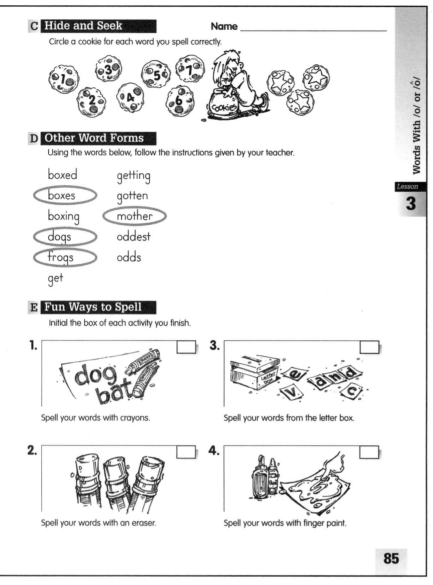

C Hide and Seek

Name _____

Circle a cookie for each word you spell correctly.

(cookies numbered 1–7)

cookies

D Other Word Forms

Using the words below, follow the instructions given by your teacher.

boxed   getting

(boxes)   gotten

boxing   (mother)

(dogs)   oddest

(frogs)   odds

get

E Fun Ways to Spell

Initial the box of each activity you finish.

1. dog bat ☐
   Spell your words with crayons.

2. ☐
   Spell your words with an eraser.

3. ☐
   Spell your words from the letter box.

4. ☐
   Spell your words with finger paint.

85

Hide and Seek

1

Reinforce spelling by using multiple styles of learning.

On a white board, Teacher writes each word — one at a time. **Have students:**

• **Look** at the word.
• **Say** the word out loud.
• **Spell** the word out loud.
• **Hide** (teacher erases word.)
• **Write** the word on their paper.
• **Seek** (teacher rewrites word.)
• **Check** spelling. If incorrect, repeat above steps.

Other Word Forms

2

This activity is optional. Have students find and circle the Other Word Forms that name a person, place, or thing.

Fun Ways to Spell

3

Four activities are provided. Use one, two, three, or all of the activities. Have students initial the box for each activity they complete.

Options:

• assign activities to students according to their learning styles
• set up the activities in learning centers for students to do throughout the day
• divide students into four groups and assign one activity per group
• do one activity per day

rhythm instruments

General

To spell your words with crayons…
• Write each letter of your spelling word in fat, thick letters.
• Check your spelling.

Auditory

To spell your words from the letter box…
• Spell a word from your list by putting the letters in the right order.
• Check your spelling.
• Spell your word out loud.

Visual

To spell your words with an eraser…
• Turn your pencil upside down.
• Use the eraser to write your words on a sheet of dark construction paper.
• Check your spelling.

Tactile

To spell your words with finger paint…
• Smear paint across your plate.
• Use a finger to write a spelling word in paint.
• Check your spelling.
• Smear the word out with your finger and write another word.

1 | Word Scramble

Familiarize students with word meaning and usage.

Write the letters **rde** on the board. Help the students understand that the scrambled letters **rde** spell the word **red** when they are arranged correctly. Guide the students in ordering the letters to spell **red**.

Say: Unscramble the letters to make a spelling word. Write the word on the line.

F Word Scramble   Name _____

Unscramble the letters to make a spelling word. Write the word on the line.

Words With /o/ or /ô/

Lesson **3**

1. dGo — God
2. no — on
3. omm — mom
4. tgo — got
5. ton — not
6. gdo — dog
7. fof — off
☆ xbo — box
☆ dod — odd
box
☆ gorf — frog
odd
frog

Word Bank

| dog | on | got | mom | ☆ box |
| God | off | not | ☆ frog | ☆ odd |

86

Take a minute to memorize...

Read the memory verse twice. Have students practice it with you two more times.

Lesson **3** | Day 3

98

G Dictation

Listen and write the missing words.

Name _____

1. My dog got on the bed.

2. We got a cat.

3. My mom can get off work.

H Proofreading

One word in each pair is misspelled. Fill in the oval by the misspelled word.

1. ● dag
   ○ God

2. ● onn
   ○ off

3. ● gto
   ○ mom

4. ● nat
   ○ off

5. ○ on
   ● Gdo

6. ● oof
   ○ got

☆ ● forg
   ○ odd

☆ ○ next
   ● boks

☆ ● od
   ○ not

87

Dictation

Reinforce correct spelling by using current and previous words in context.

(Say) Listen as I read each sentence and then write it in your Worktext. (Slowly read each sentence twice. Sentences are found in the Student Worktext to the left.)

 Challenge

Write these incomplete sentences on the board.

Daniel's big ___ jumped the ___.

What is in the ___ ___?

___ ___ ___ ___ plant.

Day 4

Lesson **3**

(Say) Listen as I read each sentence. Write the sentence on your paper. (Slowly read each sentence twice.)

Daniel's big frog jumped the best.

What is in the red box?

Mom got an odd plant.

Proofreading

Familiarize students with standardized test format and reinforce recognizing misspelled words.

(Say) Look at each set of words. One word in each set is misspelled. Fill in the oval by the misspelled word. (You may wish to pronounce each set of words to help students correctly identify them.)

3 Hide and Seek

Reinforce correct spelling of current spelling words. (A reproducible master is provided in Appendix A as shown on the inset page to the right.)

Write the words one at a time on a white board.

Have students:

- **Look** at the word.
- **Say** the word out loud.
- **Spell** the word out loud.
- **Hide** (teacher erases word.)
- **Write** the word on paper.
- **Seek** (teacher rewrites word.)
- **Check** spelling. If incorrect, rewrite word correctly.

4 Word Find

Have your students complete this activity to strengthen spelling ability and expand vocabulary.

1 Posttest

Test mastery of the spelling words. Challenge words are starred.

Say | I will say the word once, use the word in a sentence, then say the word again. Write the word on your paper.

1. not   Luke did **not** want a little dog.
2. on   Beth sprawled **on** the rug and looked at a dog book.
3. mom   Beth's **mom** said that dogs could cost a lot of money.
4. God   **God** cares about you.
5. dog   Beth wanted a little **dog**.
6. got   Eagle **got** a new home.
7. off   Please turn the light **off**.
☆ frog   The **frog** with sticky toes is a tree frog.
☆ odd   That is an **odd** looking dog.
☆ box   The cereal **box** is empty.

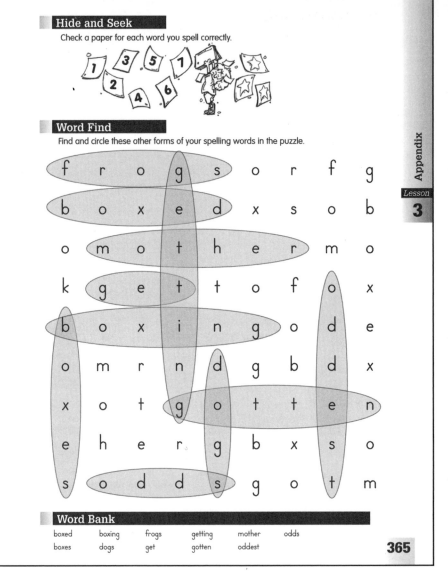

Hide and Seek

Check a paper for each word you spell correctly.

Word Find

Find and circle these other forms of your spelling words in the puzzle.

```
f  r  o  g  s  o  r  f  g
b  o  x  e  d  x  s  o  b
o  m  o  t  h  e  r  m  o
k  g  e  t  t  o  f  o  x
b  o  x  i  n  g  o  d  e
o  m  r  n  d  g  b  d  x
x  o  t  g  o  t  t  e  n
e  h  e  r  g  b  x  s  o
s  o  d  d  s  g  o  t  m
```

Word Bank

boxed	boxing	frogs	getting	mother	odds
boxes	dogs	get	gotten	oddest	

Appendix — Lesson 3

365

Progress Chart

Students may record scores. (Reproducible master in Appendix B.)

Personal Dictionary

Students may add any words they have misspelled to their personal dictionaries for reference when writing. (Cover in Appendix B.)

100

I Game

Name _____

Cross out each **a**, **k**, and **s** with a big **X** to find the hidden spelling words. Using one crayon, softly color the boxes you did not mark so you can see your spelling words better.

a	K	s	G	o	d	a	K	s
K	s	a	K	f	r	o	g	K
o	n	a	K	a	a	n	o	t
s	a	o	f	f	K	s	a	K
a	K	s	a	b	o	x	K	s
K	s	a	K	s	a	K	s	a
s	a	k	a	a	K	s	a	K
g	o	t	s	a	d	o	g	K
a	K	s	a	K	s	a	K	s
o	d	d	K	m	o	m	s	a

Remember : Always let God direct you in your plans.

J Journaling

Write this sentence in your journal.
_____ **can help me make plans.**
Fill in the blank with the name of someone you like to plan things with.

88

How to Play:

- Have each student mark through each letter **a** found on the grid with a big **X**.
- Have each student mark through each letter **k** found on the grid with a big **X**.
- Have each student mark through each letter **s** found on the grid with a big **X**.
- Tell the students that the boxes without **X**'s contain their spelling words.
- Have the students color softly over the boxes without **X**'s so they can see their spelling words more clearly.
- Have the students follow along as you read and spell each word as it appears on the grid.

2 Game

Reinforce spelling skills and provide motivation and interest.

Materials

- game page (from student text)
- pencils (1 per child)
- crayons or colored pencils (1 per child)

3 Journaling

Provide a meaningful reason for correct spelling through personal writing.

Review the story using discussion leads provided on the following page. Encourage students to apply the Scriptural value in their journaling.

 Take a minute to memorize...

Have the class say the memory verse with you once.

101

Journaling (continued)

 Say

- How did God direct the Hill family in their plans to buy a dog? (He helped them all fall in love with a stray dog that needed a home.)

- What did each person in the Hill family like about Eagle? (Mom and Dad liked the price tag — free. Beth was happy Eagle was a loving attentive girl even though she was bigger than a Pekingese. Luke liked the way Eagle romped and played with him and didn't really care that the dog ended up not being a boy.)

- Have you ever asked God to direct your plans?

- Who are some people that help you decide what to do? (parents, teachers, preachers, babysitters . . .)

- In your journal, write the name of someone who helps you make plans.

"When young writers are free to concentrate on what they want to say rather than mechanics, their thoughts can flow more freely."*

*Wilde, Sandra. 1990. A Proposal for a New Spelling Curriculum. The Elementary School Journal, Vol. 90, No. 3, January: 275-289.

Soccer Solution

Stephen finds out that it's not always easy to keep your promises.

"Stephen! Hey, Stephen Wilson!" Tony ran breathlessly up to Stephen on the playground. "What soccer team are you on this year? Do you know yet?"

"Yep, the First National Flyers." Stephen dropped down from the jungle gym. "We have our first practice this Wednesday right after school."

"Too bad you're not on the Blue Lasers." Tony bent over to pick up a shiny stone. "We have the coach whose team won the tournament last year."

"Yeah, but the Lasers' coach is really hard on his boys." Stephen shook his head. "And he yells a lot, too! That's probably why his team won the last few years."

"I'm not very good at soccer, so I'll probably get yelled at a lot!" Tony tossed the rock at a nearby tree. "Do you think you could practice with me? Your papa always works with you and teaches you good moves." He paused. "You probably don't want to help a player from another team though."

"Even if you're not on my team, you're still my friend," Stephen shrugged. "My dad would work with both of us, I'm sure. What are you doing after school?"

"Nothing." Tony kicked at a blade of grass. "Mama has to work late so Grandma Miller is coming over to stay with me until she gets off work. When does your papa get home?"

"A little after five. Maybe you could come over and practice with us until supper."

"Great!" Tony looked up as the school bell rang. "Could you have your mama call Grandma Miller? She says it isn't right to run over to the neighbors all the time without being invited."

"Sure." Stephen said as the boys headed inside. "I'll ask Mom when she picks me up after school."

"Hey, Tony!" Stephen entered the classroom, his arms full of books. "How'd your first practice go last night?"

"Great, man!" Tony beamed. "Our coach had us kick the ball around a line of cones just like your papa showed us Monday night. I was 'sensational' because I'd already practiced it with you!" Tony looked up from his seat. "I like your papa. When can we practice with him again?"

"How about Sunday afternoon?" Stephen asked as he threaded his way toward his desk. "This isn't the weekend that you go to your dad's place, is it?"

"Uh, no." Tony looked down, suddenly quiet.

"Then I'll ask my dad, and have my mom give yours a call."

"Sounds fun!" Tony brightened, then looked at the papers on his desk. "I better get busy now, though. My spelling isn't done yet. I still have to do my journaling!"

Sunday afternoon, Tony plopped down on the grass beside Stephen and his dad.

"Thanks a lot for your help, Mr. Wilson. With your coaching, maybe someday I'll be as good a goalie as Stephen!"

"No way!" puffed Stephen. Both boys were covered with sweat after an hour of intense soccer drills.

"You're really becoming a sensational soccer player, Tony," Mr. Wilson encouraged. "Your coach might

not want all that energy locked in a goalie box, though. He may make you the striker. That's the person who kicks the ball to start the game. Strikers do the most running." Mr. Wilson stood and stretched. "Just keep drilling every day after school, even when I can't practice with you." He headed toward the house. "Wouldn't hurt to run a few laps each day either," he called back over his shoulder. "Helps strengthen your legs."

"Sure is nice of your papa to help me, Stephen." Tony looked down at the crack in the Wilson's driveway. "Mine isn't around very much any more — even on the weekends he's supposed to be."

"I'll share mine with you!" Stephen threw an arm around his friend. "I heard Dad tell Mom how quickly you learn. He says you have… ah, 'a natural talent for soccer'… whatever that means."

"Is that a promise, Stephen?"

"Is what a promise?"

"That you'll share your papa with me?"

"Sure!" Stephen grinned. "That's what friends are for!"

Mr. Wilson continued to help both boys improve during the pre-season. When the real games started, the Wilson's often sat with Tony's mama and Grandma Miller to watch Tony play, and to cheer for his team.

"That was a great pass you made, Tony!" Mr. Wilson said, after the third game of the season. "You really had that forward faked out. Pretty fancy footwork, pal." He patted Tony on the shoulder as Stephen joined them. "Come over tomorrow, and we'll work on some drills to improve your left-foot kicks. Who do you play next week?"

"The First National Flyers — Stephen's team." Tony tried not to look at Mr. Wilson's face.

"Okay." Mr. Wilson and Stephen headed toward their car. "We'll see ya tomorrow, Tony!"

"Dad, do you have to keep helping Tony so

103

much?" Stephen climbed into the back seat of the car.

"I thought you liked practicing your goalie strategy against him," Dad pulled out of the parking lot, and headed towards home.

"Yeah, but he's the star striker of the Blue Lasers!" Stephen complained. "He's all over that field — and we have to play them next week. It might not hurt to let him get a little rusty, don't you think?"

"What do you think, Son?"

"I think we have done more than enough for that show-off." Stephen grouched. "You've taught him how to be a super-duper-sensational soccer player! He's got his own dad. Why can't he help him?"

"Hummm." Dad pulled into the driveway, and without waiting for an answer, Stephen darted into the house and up to his room. This promise was turning out to be more than he bargained for.

In Spelling class the next morning, Miss Grant read what she called a "Literature Connection Story" from Scripture. It was about a father, two brothers, and a promise.

"There was a man who had two sons. He went to the first and said, 'Son, go and work today in the vineyard.' 'I will not,' he answered, but later he changed his mind and went. Then the father went to the other son and said the same thing. He answered, 'I will, sir,' but he did not go. Which of the two sons did what his father wanted?"

"So what do you think, class?" Miss Grant closed the Bible. "Which son kept his promise?"

"Neither one did what he said he'd do." Katelynn seemed puzzled.

"Well, is it a good idea to say you'll do something — then not do it?" Miss Grant looked around. "Tommy?"

"Not really." Tommy shook his head.

"Which son made the

wiser choice?" Miss Grant continued. "Thank you for raising your hand, Kristin."

"The son who said 'no' but decided to do what his Father asked after all," Kristin suggested.

"But the other son said 'yes.' Wasn't that a good thing to say? What do you think, Stephen?"

"Sure it was good, but then he didn't do what he promised!" Stephen's forehead wrinkled. "So really it was worse than the first son because at least the first guy ended up making a good choice in the end."

"So what have we learned about promises?"

"It's good to say 'no' if you think you can't keep a promise," Beth offered.

"Well, I guess that's true," Miss Grant smiled, "but I'm not sure that's why Jesus told this story."

"It's best to make good promises, then keep them?" asked Matthew.

"Yes," said Miss Grant. "And I think we could write that on the board along with our text for this week. Proverbs 12:22 says, 'God delights in those who keep their promises.' You'll be putting that one on your border sheet this Friday in handwriting class. It is a good one to remember."

"Not so easy to do, though," Stephen looked thoughtfully at the words on the board. "Not easy at all."

Dad was surprised when both Stephen and Tony ran out to meet him as he pulled up to the garage. "Hurry up, Dad. I need you to help me practice before our game tonight," Stephen urged. "The Blue Lasers have this super-sensational striker who gets more goals than any other player. I need all the help you can give me!"

"Not talking about you is he, Tony?" Mr. Wilson grinned and patted Tony on the back.

"If it wasn't for the help you and Stephen gave me, I wouldn't be the Blue Lasers' striker." Tony smiled. "Of course, The First National Flyers have Stephen, Sir. He's the best goalie in the league. Everybody says so. I might not be able to get any goals against him!"

"Well, let's get busy and practice, boys," Mr. Wilson grabbed the soccer ball. "Sounds like you both have quite a reputation to keep up!"

2 Discussion Time

Check understanding of the story and development of personal values.

- Do you think the score of Tony and Stephen's soccer game that night was close? Why?
- Why do you think it was hard for Stephen to keep his promise and get his dad to help Tony?
- Have you ever made a promise that was hard to keep?
- When God "delights" (is really happy) in a choice you make, how does it make you feel?

104

Name _____

Words With /i/

Lesson **4**

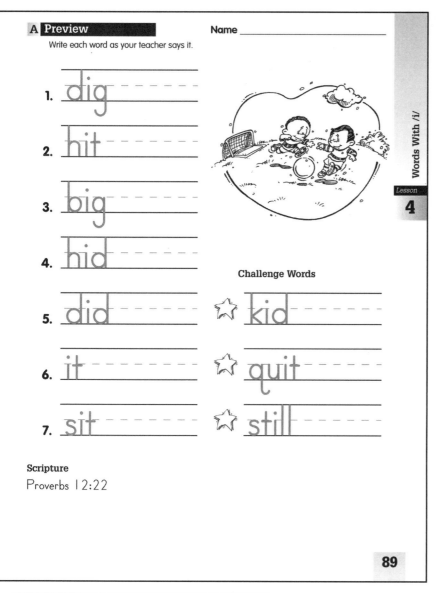

1. dig

2. hit

3. big

4. hid

Challenge Words

5. did   kid

6. it   ☆ quit

7. sit   ☆ still

Scripture
Proverbs 12:22

89

Challenge

For better spellers, challenge words may be included in the weekly list. Challenge words are starred.

Correct Immediately!

Say

Let's correct our preview. I will write each word on the board. Put a dot under each letter on your preview as I spell the word out loud. If you spelled a word wrong, rewrite it correctly.

Progress Chart

Students may record scores. (Reproducible master in Appendix B.)

Day 1

Lesson **4**

Take a minute to memorize . . .

Read the memory verse twice. Have students practice it with you two more times.

---

3 **Preview**

Test for knowledge of the correct spellings of these words. (See the instructions at the top right for challenge words.)

Say

I will say each word once, use the word in a sentence, then say the word again. Write the word on the lines in the Worktext.

1. dig   A hoe is a tool used to **dig** in the garden.
2. hit   The boy **hit** the baseball.
3. big   That is a very **big** dog.
4. hid   My kitten **hid** in the box.
5. did   What **did** you do with the soccer ball?
6. it   Is **it** almost time for the game to start?
7. sit   We will **sit** quietly at our desks.
☆ kid   A baby goat is called a **kid.**
☆ quit   Stephen wanted his dad to **quit** helping Tony.
☆ still   The light is **still** on.

4 Word Shapes

Help students form a correct image of whole words.

 Say

Look at each word and think about its shape. Now, write the word in the correct word Shape Boxes. You may check off each word as you use it.

(In many words /i/ is spelled with **i**, and it is often spelled this way when it is at the beginning or in the middle of a word.)

 Say

In the word shape boxes, color the letter that spells the sound of /i/ in each word.
Circle the word that begins with the sound of /i/.

☆ Challenge

Draw the correctly shaped box around each letter in these words.

 Say

On a separate sheet of paper, write other words that contain the spelling patterns in the word list. See how many words you can write.

Be Prepared For Fun

Check these supply lists for **Fun Ways to Spell** presented **Day 2**. Purchase and/or gather these items ahead of time!

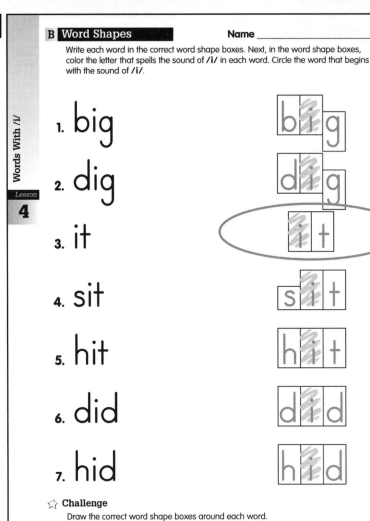

B Word Shapes — Name _____

Write each word in the correct word shape boxes. Next, in the word shape boxes, color the letter that spells the sound of /i/ in each word. Circle the word that begins with the sound of /i/.

Words With /i/ — Lesson **4**

1. big
2. dig
3. it
4. sit
5. hit
6. did
7. hid

☆ **Challenge**
Draw the correct word shape boxes around each word.

kid   still   quit

90

Answers may vary for duplicate word shapes.

General
• 3 x 5 Cards (7 per child)
• 3 x 5 Cards (3 more for challenge words)
• Scissors
• Spelling List

Auditory
• Spelling List

Visual
• Dry Bar of Soap (sample size works well)
• Hand Mirror
• Strong Paper Towel or Washcloth (dry)
• Spelling List

Tactile
• Play Dough
• Spelling List

106

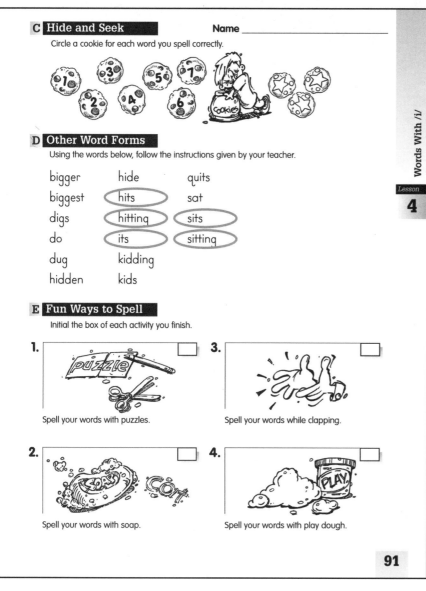

C Hide and Seek

Name _____

Circle a cookie for each word you spell correctly.

D Other Word Forms

Using the words below, follow the instructions given by your teacher.

bigger	hide	quits
biggest	hits	sat
digs	hitting	sits
do	its	sitting
dug	kidding	
hidden	kids	

E Fun Ways to Spell

Initial the box of each activity you finish.

1. □
Spell your words with puzzles.

2. □
Spell your words with soap.

3. □
Spell your words while clapping.

4. □
Spell your words with play dough.

91

1 Hide and Seek

Reinforce spelling by using multiple styles of learning.

On a white board, Teacher writes each word — one at a time. **Have students:**

- **Look** at the word.
- **Say** the word out loud.
- **Spell** the word out loud.
- **Hide** (teacher erases word.)
- **Write** the word on their paper.
- **Seek** (teacher rewrites word.)
- **Check** spelling. If incorrect, repeat above steps.

2 Other Word Forms

This activity is optional. Have students find and circle the Other Word Forms that rhyme with each other.

3 Fun Ways to Spell

Four activities are provided. Use one, two, three, or all of the activities. Have students initial the box for each activity they complete.

Options:

- assign activities to students according to their learning styles
- set up the activities in learning centers for students to do throughout the day
- divide students into four groups and assign one activity per group
- do one activity per day

General

To spell your words with puzzles…
- Write each word on a card.
- Cut each card squiggly, diagonal, or zigzag to make a puzzle.
- Mix your puzzle pieces.
- Put the puzzles together.
- Check your spelling.

Auditory

To spell your words while clapping…
- Look at a word on your spelling list.
- Close your eyes.
- Clap your hands softly while you whisper the spelling of the word.
- Open your eyes and check your spelling.

Visual

To spell your words with soap…
- Write a word on a hand mirror with a dry bar of soap.
- Check your spelling.
- Wipe the word off the mirror with a dry towel or washcloth.
- Write another word.

Tactile

To spell your words with play dough…
- Roll pieces of play dough into ropes.
- Use the ropes to make the letters of each word.
- Put them in the right order to spell each word.
- Check your spelling.

Word Find

1 **Word Find**

Familiarize students with word meaning and usage.

Say) Read each word in the Word Bank. Say each letter in the word, then look in the puzzle to find that same word. Circle each word you find. Write the secret word that is not in the puzzle on the lines underneath the puzzle.

F **Word Find**

Find and circle 9 words.

Name _____

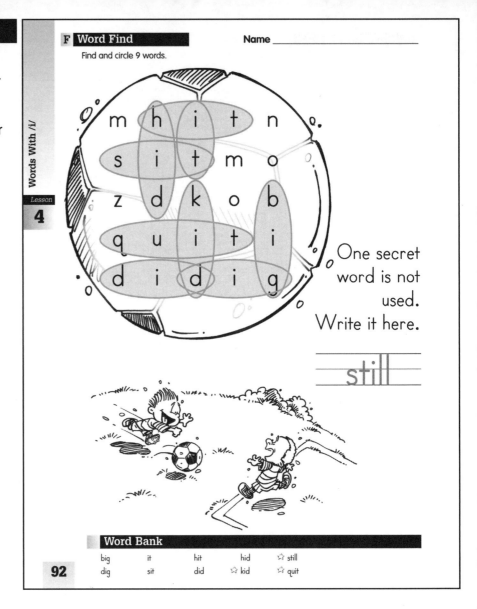

One secret word is not used. Write it here.

still

Word Bank

big	it	hit	hid	☆ still
dig	sit	did	☆ kid	☆ quit

92

Take a minute to memorize...

Read the memory verse twice. Have students practice it with you two more times.

108

G Dictation

Listen and write the missing words.

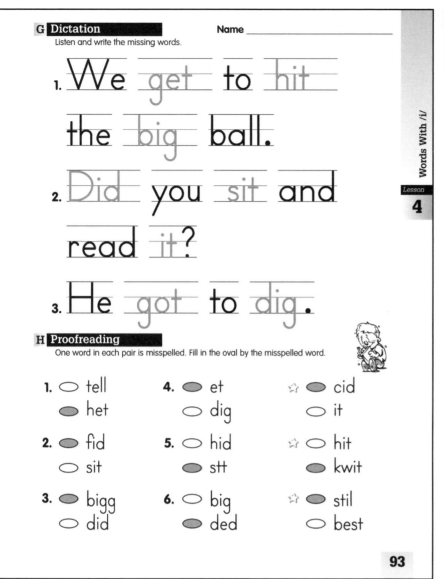

1. We get to hit the big ball.

2. Did you sit and read it?

3. He got to dig.

H Proofreading

One word in each pair is misspelled. Fill in the oval by the misspelled word.

1. ○ tell
   ⬤ het

2. ⬤ fid
   ○ sit

3. ⬤ bigg
   ○ did

4. ⬤ et
   ○ dig

5. ○ hid
   ⬤ stt

6. ○ big
   ⬤ ded

☆ ⬤ cid
   ○ it

☆ ○ hit
   ⬤ kwit

☆ ⬤ stil
   ○ best

93

---

1 Dictation

Reinforce correct spelling by using current and previous words in context.

Say

Listen as I read each sentence and then write it in your Worktext. (Slowly read each sentence twice. Sentences are found in the Student Worktext to the left.)

☆ Challenge

Write these incomplete sentences on the board.

The mother goat ___ to her ___.

Tony ___ sit ___ on the ___.

___ said the ___ ___ his job.

Say

Listen as I read each sentence. Write the sentence on your paper. (Slowly read each sentence twice.)

The mother goat <u>ran</u> to her <u>kid</u>.

Tony <u>can</u> sit <u>still</u> on the <u>box</u>.

<u>Dad</u> said the <u>man</u> <u>quit</u> his job.

---

2 Proofreading

Familiarize students with standardized test format and reinforce recognizing misspelled words.

Say

Look at each set of words. One word in each set is misspelled. Fill in the oval by the misspelled word. (You may wish to pronounce each set of words to help students correctly identify them.)

109

3 Hide and Seek

Reinforce correct spelling of current spelling words. (A reproducible master is provided in Appendix A as shown on the inset page to the right.)

Write the words one at a time on a white board.

Have students:

- **Look** at the word.
- **Say** the word out loud.
- **Spell** the word out loud.
- **Hide** (teacher erases word.)
- **Write** the word on paper.
- **Seek** (teacher rewrites word.)
- **Check** spelling. If incorrect, rewrite word correctly.

4 Scrambled Words

Have your students complete this activity to strengthen spelling ability and expand vocabulary.

1 Posttest

Test mastery of the spelling words. Challenge words are starred.

 Say I will say the word once, use the word in a sentence, then say the word again. Write the word on your paper.

1.	hid	The squirrel **hid** an acorn in the ground.
2.	big	There is a **big** tree in our backyard.
3.	hit	He can **hit** a home run.
4.	dig	The dog will **dig** a hole.
5.	it	Sometimes **it** is hard to keep a promise.
6.	sit	I will **sit** by my friend.
7.	did	Stephen **did** a good thing.
☆	quit	The man **quit** mowing when it started to rain.
☆	kid	Sometimes we call a child a "**kid**."
☆	still	You might see a bird come to the feeder if you hold very **still**.

 Progress Chart
Students may record scores. (Reproducible master in Appendix B.)

 Personal Dictionary
Students may add any words they have misspelled to their personal dictionaries for reference when writing. (Cover in Appendix B.)

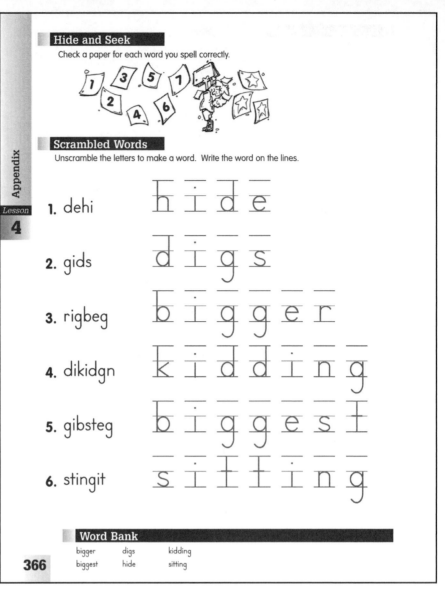

Appendix · **Lesson 4**

Hide and Seek
Check a paper for each word you spell correctly.

Scrambled Words
Unscramble the letters to make a word. Write the word on the lines.

1. dehi — h i d e
2. gids — d i g s
3. rigbeg — b i g g e r
4. dikidgn — k i d d i n g
5. gibsteg — b i g g e s t
6. stingit — s i t t i n g

Word Bank

bigger	digs	kidding
biggest	hide	sitting

366

110

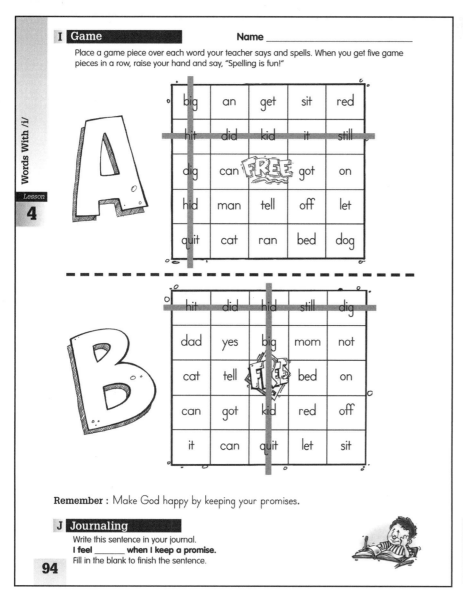

I Game

Name _____

Place a game piece over each word your teacher says and spells. When you get five game pieces in a row, raise your hand and say, "Spelling is fun!"

A

big	an	get	sit	red
hit	did	kid	it	still
dig	can	FREE	got	on
hid	man	tell	off	let
quit	cat	ran	bed	dog

B

hit	did	hid	still	dig
dad	yes	big	mom	not
cat	tell	FREE	bed	on
can	got	kid	red	off
it	can	quit	let	sit

Remember : Make God happy by keeping your promises.

J Journaling

Write this sentence in your journal.
I feel _____ when I keep a promise.
Fill in the blank to finish the sentence.

94

2 Game

Reinforce spelling skills and provide motivation and interest.

Materials

- game page (from student text)
- flat buttons, dry beans, pennies, or game discs (10 per child)
- game word list
- word cards (each word from the game word list written on a card)

Game Word List

This list contains regular and challenge words.

1. **big**
2. **kid**
3. **dig**
4. **still**
5. **quit**
6. **hit**
7. **sit**
☆ **it**
☆ **did**
☆ **hid**

3 Journaling

Provide a meaningful reason for correct spelling through personal writing.

Review the story using discussion leads provided on the following page. Encourage students to apply the Scriptural value in their journaling.

Take a minute to memorize...

Read the memory verse to the class twice. Have the class practice it with you two more times.

How to Play:

- Fold the word cards (see **Materials**) in half, and place them in a container.
- Ask your students to fold the game page in half along the dotted line.
- Have half the class use game card A, and the other half card B.
- Instructions for the students: "Cover the word **FREE** in the center of your card. (pause) I will draw a word from the container, read it aloud, then I will spell it. When you find that word on your card, put a game piece over it. When you have five game pieces in a row (up and down, across, or diagonally), raise your hand and say 'Spelling is FUN!' "
- Play as many times as you like. (As you return the word cards to the container and mix them up, remind the students to clear their game cards.)
- For variety, after playing several games, have the students turn their papers over and use the other game card.

Lesson **4** | Day 5

Say

- Do you think Stephen ever expected Tony to become such a good striker? (no) Why? (because Tony was not a good soccer player until Stephen's dad started helping him.)
- Why was it hard for Stephen to keep his promise and share his Dad with Tony? (Tony was a good striker and Stephen's team was going to play against Tony's in the next game. Stephen didn't want his Dad to help Tony get any better.)
- What are some promises you have made?
- How do you feel when you keep your promises? (You may want to make a list of responses on the board.)
- In your journal, write how you feel when you've kept a promise.

"Invented spelling is not a failure to spell the conventional way but a step on the road to reaching it."*

*Wilde, Sandra. 1992. You kan red this! Portsmouth, NH: Heinemann.

112

Compose a Song?

Matthew learns that finding new ways to praise God can be fun.

"Are we having choir again?" Matthew folded his arms in disgust.

"Three days this week, instead of just two," Miss Grant said cheerfully. "You know, the Christmas program is not that far away and our class has never practiced with the rest of the kids."

"I'm sick of choir," moaned Beth, "Mrs. Espinoza never lets us sit down!"

"She makes us stand there for the whole class," Stephen added, joining the group gathered around Miss Grant's desk. "Even when we aren't singing!"

"Now think about this a minute," Miss Grant said. "I know you like the songs she picks because I hear you singing little parts, and whistling, and humming them all day long."

"I guess so," sighed Kristin. "But why can't we sit and learn the songs?"

"We already know the songs," Beth added. "So why do we keep going over and over them?"

"Mrs. Espinoza just needs to make sure you all know where to stand and when to come in." Miss Grant smiled and skillfully changed the subject. "You also need a chance to practice in your costumes before next week. Aren't you all supposed to dress up as shepherds?"

"My mom is having one made for me!" Daniel jumped up and down with excitement. "It has a big cloth for my head and a coat made out of real sheep's wool. She also bought me a real shepherd's staff with a crook on the end, and some leather sandals, too!"

"That sounds special, Daniel." Miss Grant looked around the room.

"My mom is making mine and Lisa's," Tommy said. "She got our material yesterday. We even helped pick it out. My dad cut me a stick in the woods. He says he's going to make me a shepherd's rod."

"You mean like in the Twenty-third Psalm?" Miss Grant asked. "'Thy rod and thy staff they comfort me?'"

"Yep!" Tommy laughed.

"I'm just wearing a bathrobe." Tony shrugged. "But I do have some cool sandals, and Grandma Miller is making the head-thingy and belt for me."

"I'm sure that will look very nice, Tony." Miss Grant stood and walked around her desk. "You kids need to head for the choir room now, or you'll be late. Line up at the door, and I'll walk over with you."

"Mom, have you gotten a costume for me yet?" Matthew leaned forward in the back seat of the Suburban. "The other kids were talking about theirs today."

"Not yet, but I'm close. I almost finished the robe today while Emily took her nap. I used some material I had stashed away. I also dug out those fisherman's sandals you wore last summer, and I thought we might stop by the store to pick out some material for a belt, and maybe a sash to throw over your shoulder." Mrs. Shilling stopped at the corner, then turned left toward town. "Alex, you can wear the costume Matthew wore last year with a new head cloth, and carry that cane we have in the garage. I think you've grown too much to wear your summer sandals," she laughed, "so you can just be a barefoot shepherd."

"I can't wait to dress up," Alex wiggled with excitement. "This is my first time. Won't it be fun to wear costumes, Matthew? Everyone has to wear them to choir on Friday."

Matthew smiled at his little brother's enthusiasm. "Mom, can we listen to this soundtrack of our program while we drive?" He passed a CD over the front seat. "Mrs. Espinoza wants us to be real familiar with all the parts so we won't make mistakes."

"Sure," Mom popped the CD into the radio. "Did Mrs. Espinoza make one of these for everyone in the school?"

"Yeah, if we brought her the CD."

"And just where did you get this CD, young man?" Mom laughed and raised an eyebrow.

"It's okay, Mom." Matthew smiled. "Dad gave it to me." Then he joined Alex in singing as the CD began to play.

"Who can remember the text we're learning this week?" Miss Grant walked to the board to begin spelling class.

"'Compose new songs of praise to God. Psalm 33:3,'" said Matthew and Stephen together.

"Good job, boys!" Miss Grant smiled at the class. "This morning I'd like to tell you a little more about that text. David was a shepherd. His job was to watch the sheep, to take them to cool places to rest, and to defend them from wild animals who might hurt them — like lions, or bears, or wolves. When the summer got hot and the fields in the valley were dry, David would take the sheep to green pastures high up in the hills. But because there were no fences to keep the sheep in one place, David had to spend a lot of time just sitting and watching."

"Now David was also a great musician. While he sat and watched the sheep, he would take out his small harp and sing. Sometimes he probably sang the songs he had learned in church or at home. But God also gave him a gift for thinking up new words, and then creating new tunes to go along with them. David was so good at composing new songs that King Saul asked him to come play for him in the palace! The words to many of

113

David's songs are found in Scripture in the book we call Psalms. Have any of you ever thought of a new song?"

"I have, in piano lessons," said Beth. "But they didn't praise God."

"Anyone else ever made up a new song?"

"I have," said Katelynn. "Beth, Tony, and I have the same piano teacher."

"What do you think David meant when he sang of composing or thinking up new praise songs to God?" asked Miss Grant. "Should we all write a song today to show Mrs. Espinoza?"

"I don't think I could do that even if I wanted to," Stephen grinned.

"My mom helped a lot with the one I had to do for my piano lesson," said Tony.

"So why did David write this verse?" Miss Grant waited as the children thought this over. "Think about it and we'll talk about it again later."

Friday morning the choir looked like a whole herd of shepherds — with no sheep!

"Daniel," Tommy whispered. "Can I touch your real sheep-wool coat?"

"Sure." Daniel leaned over. "Isn't it soft? Mom had them leave it the natural color that shepherds would have worn on the hills of Bethlehem." He giggled softly. "Look at Katelynn and Beth. You can't see their hair at all. They could be boys!"

"Quiet everyone!" Mrs. Espinoza raised her arms. "Keep your eyes on me so you'll know when to come in. Mr. Jones, you can start the tape now."

As the majestic sounds of "Joy to the World" filled the room, Matthew looked around at the happy, excited faces of his classmates. Some he hardly recognized in their costumes. "I didn't compose this song," he thought, standing tall and proud in his shepherd's costume, "but I sure do like

the way it sounds when the whole school sings it together. It's awesome!"

Wednesday night finally arrived. After the Christmas program was over, Matthew and Alex were met by two very proud parents, and an excited little sister. "I twy hat," said Emily.

As Matthew bent over to place the head cloth on Emily's head, his mom wrapped her arms around him. "Son, you boys really practiced hard. I could tell. That was a wonderful program."

"Baby Jesus," Emily pointed to the manger scene. "See. See."

Stephen's mom walked up and knelt down in front of Alex and Matthew. "You guys did a lovely job tonight? When's your next program?"

The boys grinned and shrugged their shoulders. "Whenever Mrs. Espinoza says."

"She sure plans some neat programs!" Mrs. Wilson continued. "You all looked like you were having a good time up there tonight, too!"

"We were!" Matthew smiled. Then as Stephen walked up, his head cloth sagging over one eye, a thought suddenly popped into his head. "Stephen," Matthew blurted out, "I think I know the answer to Miss Grant's question . . . what it means to 'compose new songs of praise to God.' Remember how we were all complaining the other morning about choir? Well, tonight we sure had fun, and everybody liked our program. Maybe that's what David meant. We need to find new ways to praise God . . . just like we did tonight in Mrs. Espinoza's choir!"

Discussion Time

2 Check understanding of the story and development of personal values.

- Why were the first graders unhappy about practicing for the Christmas program at the beginning of the story?
- Why did Matthew feel like praising God after the Christmas program?
- What caused Matthew to change his mind about the choir songs?
- God loves to hear us sing praises to Him! What are some praise songs you know?

A Test-Words

Write each word as your teacher says it.

Name _____

1. an
2. dad
3. get
4. yes
5. dog
6. not
7. big
8. hid

Review

Lesson
5

☆ **Test-Challenge Words**

On a sheet of paper, write each challenge word as your teacher says it.

Scripture

Psalm 33:3

95

 Test-Challenge Words

On a separate sheet of paper, challenge words may be tested using the sentences below.

 Personal Dictionary

After the tests in the review unit are graded, students may add any words they have misspelled to their personal dictionaries.

 Take a minute to memorize...

Read the memory verse to the class twice. Have the class practice it with you two more times.

---

3 **Test-Words**

Test for knowledge of the correct spellings of these words. (See the instructions at the top right for challenge words.)

 Say

I will say each word once, use the word in a sentence, then say the word again. Write the word on the lines in your Worktext.

1. an — This is **an** orange tree.
2. dad — Matthew got the CD from his **dad**.
3. get — We all **get** to wear shepherd costumes.
4. yes — Mother said, "**Yes**, you may listen to the CD."
5. dog — The **dog** dug a hole under the fence.
6. not — The first graders did **not** want to practice again.
7. big — Daniel had a **big** cloth to wear on his head like a shepherd.
8. hid — Emily **hid** under Matthew's shepherd costume.
☆ thank — Matthew will **thank** his mom for making the shepherd's robe.
☆ help — Matthew will **help** Alex learn the Christmas songs.
☆ frog — We could hear a **frog** croaking outside.
☆ kid — Sometimes people call a child a "**kid**."

1 Game

Materials
- game page (from student text)
- pencils or crayons (1 per child)
- game word list

Game Word List
Use of challenge words is optional.

1. **an**
2. **dad**
3. **get**
4. **yes**
5. **dog**
6. **not**
7. **big**
8. **hid**
☆ **thank**
☆ **help**
☆ **frog**
☆ **kid**

B Game   Name _____

In the story from lesson 3, Beth and Luke counted on God to help them and their parents decide which dog would be best for their family. God sent Eagle. Circle one bowl of dog food for each review word you or your team spells correctly.

96

How to Play:

- Divide the class into two teams, and decide which team will go first.
- Have a student from team A go to the board.
- Read the spelling word two times slowly and clearly. (You may also wish to use the word in a sentence. Ex.: "cat — The cat climbed a tree. — cat")
- Have the student write the word on the board.
- If the word is spelled correctly, instruct all the members of team A to circle one dog food bowl. (Note: If the word is misspelled, correct the spelling immediately before continuing the game.)
- Alternate between teams A and B as you go down the word list.
- The team with the most dog food bowls circled when you have gone through the game word list twice is the winner.

Non-Competitive Option:

At the end of the game, say: "Class, I am proud of your efforts to spell the words correctly. If you had fun and tried your best, you are all winners!"

C **Test-Sentences**

Name _____

The underlined word in each sentence is misspelled. Write the sentences on the lines below, spelling each underlined word correctly.

<u>Cen</u> you sing songs?

1. 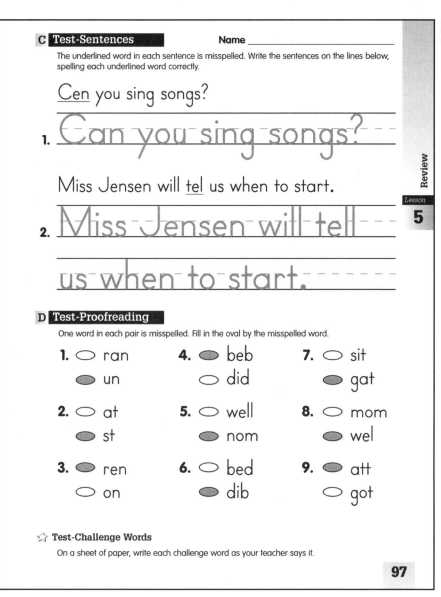 Can you sing songs?

Miss Jensen will <u>tel</u> us when to start.

2. Miss Jensen will tell us when to start.

D **Test-Proofreading**

One word in each pair is misspelled. Fill in the oval by the misspelled word.

1. ○ ran	**4.** ◉ beb	**7.** ○ sit	
◉ un	○ did	◉ gat	
2. ○ at	**5.** ○ well	**8.** ○ mom	
◉ st	◉ nom	◉ wel	
3. ◉ ren	**6.** ○ bed	**9.** ◉ att	
○ on	◉ dib	○ got	

☆ **Test-Challenge Words**

On a sheet of paper, write each challenge word as your teacher says it.

97

Say Read each sentence carefully. The underlined word in each sentence is misspelled. Write the sentences on the lines in your worktext, spelling each underlined word correctly.

Test-Proofreading

2

Familiarize students with standardized test format and reinforce recognition of misspelled words.

Say Look at each set of words. One word in each set is misspelled. Fill in the oval by the misspelled word.

(You may wish to pronounce each pair of words to help students correctly identify them.)

Test-Challenge Words

On a separate sheet of paper, challenge words may be tested using the sentences below.

 Say I will say the word once, use the word in a sentence, then say the word again. Write the word on your paper.

☆	**add**	Matthew's mom will **add** a scarf to his costume.
☆	**best**	Matthew and Alex sang their very **best** in the program.
☆	**box**	Daniel's new leather sandals came in a blue **box**.
☆	**still**	The children stood **still** and quiet, waiting to go on stage.

1 Game

Materials
- game page (from student text)
- flat buttons, dry beans, pennies, or game discs (1 per child)
- game word list

Game Word List
Use of challenge words is optional.

1. can
2. tell
3. ran
4. at
5. on
6. did
7. well
8. bed
9. sit
10. mom
11. got
☆ add
☆ best
☆ box
☆ still

E Game   Name _____

Matthew learned that he could praise God by singing in Miss Espinoza's choir. Show Matthew to his place on stage. Move one space each time you or your team spells a review word correctly.

Review

Lesson **5**

Start

98

How to Play:

- Divide the class into two teams, and decide which team will go first.
- Have each student place his/her game piece on Start.
- Have a student from team A go to the board.
- Read the spelling word two times slowly and clearly. (You may also wish to use the word in a sentence. Ex.: "cat — The cat climbed a tree. — cat")
- Have the student write the word on the board.
- If the word is spelled correctly, instruct the members of team A to move their game pieces forward one space on the game board. (Note: If the word is misspelled, correct the spelling immediately before continuing the game.)
- Alternate between teams A and B as you go down the word list.
- The team to reach Matthew's place on stage first is the winner.

Non-Competitive Option:
At the end of the game, say: "Class, I am proud of your efforts to spell the words correctly. If you had fun and tried your best, you are all winners!"

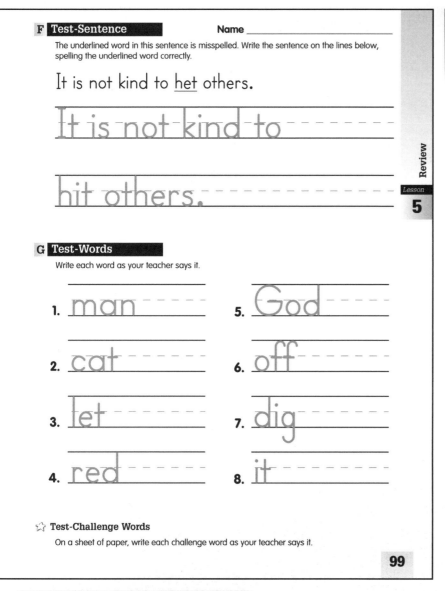

F **Test-Sentence**   Name _____

The underlined word in this sentence is misspelled. Write the sentence on the lines below, spelling the underlined word correctly.

It is not kind to <u>het</u> others.

It is not kind to

hit others.

G **Test-Words**

Write each word as your teacher says it.

1. man   5. God

2. cat   6. off

3. let   7. dig

4. red   8. it

☆ **Test-Challenge Words**

On a sheet of paper, write each challenge word as your teacher says it.

99

Test-Sentence

1 Reinforce recognizing misspelled words.

 Say Read this sentence carefully. The underlined word is misspelled. Write the sentence on the lines in your Worktext, spelling the underlined word correctly.

Personal Dictionary

Remind students to add any words they have misspelled to their personal dictionaries.

Test-Words

2 Test for knowledge of the correct spellings of these words. (Challenge words may be tested on a separate piece of paper. Challenge words are starred.)

 Say I will say each word once, use the word in a sentence, then say the word again. Write the word on the lines in your Worktext.

1. man   The Scriptures tell us about a **man** named David.
2. cat   The **cat** purrs when you pet its fur.
3. let   Beth complained, "Miss Jensen will never **let** us sit."
4. red   My costume is **red** and blue.
5. God   Can you find a new way to praise **God**?
6. off   Please turn the CD **off** now.
7. dig   We will **dig** a hole to plant this rosebush.
8. it   I think **it** was a very nice program.
☆ ask   Let's **ask** Miss Espinoza if we can sit down.
☆ next   Stephen stood **next** to Matthew in the choir.
☆ odd   Emily looked **odd** in the big shepherd's headcloth.
☆ quit   Matthew did not want to **quit** singing.

119

3 Writing Assessment

Assess student's spelling, grammar, and composition skills through personal writing.

Say
- Were the first graders excited about choir at the beginning of the story? (No) Why? (They didn't want to stand while they practiced. They thought they knew all the songs already.)
- What new way did Matthew discover to praise God? (singing in choir)
- What are some new ways you can think of to praise God? (smile, telling stories, saying a poem, writing a letter, talking about Him, praying . . .)
- Think of your favorite way to praise God and write about it in your worktext.

H Writing Assessment
Finish this sentence.

Name _____

I like praising God when _____

_____

_____

_____

Remember : Watch for new ways to praise God every day.

100

A rubric for scoring is provided in Appendix B.

4 Action Game

Reinforce spelling skills and provide motivation and interest.

Materials
- any kind of book (one less than the number of students in the class)
- one **A Reason For Spelling®** book
- small prizes (erasers, pencils, stickers)

How to Play:

Place the books and the **A Reason For Spelling®** book in a circle around a table. Play music as the students march around the table. When you stop the music, each student must touch the book beside him. Have the student touching the **A Reason For Spelling®** book spell a word from this review unit.

If he spells it incorrectly, have him march again; if he spells it correctly, give him a prize and have him return to his desk. Remove one book each time a student drops out and continue the game until every student has spelled a word correctly.

Spelling Is Fun!

ABC's

This certificate is awarded to

_____

for practicing the following words, by doing fun
spelling activities, and playing great spelling games!

Date _____

an	get	dog	big
man	let	God	dig
ran	bed	on	it
can	red	off	sit
cat	tell	got	hit
at	well	not	did
dad	yes	mom	hid
☆ thank	☆ help	☆ frog	☆ kid
☆ add	☆ best	☆ box	☆ still
☆ ask	☆ next	☆ odd	☆ quit

5 Certificate

Provide an opportunity for parents or guardians to encourage and assess their child's progress.

(Say)
- Write your name on the first line.
- Now I will write the date on the board for you to copy on the next line.
- Follow along as I read the certificate out loud.
- Be sure to show your parents or guardian all the words you've practiced spelling.

Take a minute to memorize...

Have the class say the memory verses from lessons 1 and 2 with you.

Day 5

Review **5**

Quotables!

*"Spelling is a gradual process
that develops through trial
and error, and the best way to
teach spelling is to
give students freedom
to take risks in their writing."**

*Scott, Jill E. 1994. Spelling for Readers and Writers. The Reading Teacher, Vol. 48, No. 2, October: 188-190.

6 Letter

Provide the parent or guardian with the spelling word lists for the next unit.

 Say Show your parents or guardian this letter that tells them what your spelling words will be for the next unit. Ask them to put it in a special place where you will remember to practice them together.

Review **5** | **Day 5**

Dear Parent,

We are about to begin a new spelling unit containing four weekly lessons. A set of seven words plus three challenge words will be studied each week. All the words will be reviewed in the fifth week.

Values based on the Scriptures listed below will be taught in each lesson.

Lesson 6	Lesson 7	Lesson 8	Lesson 9
up	had	in	all
cup	glad	win	ball
bug	am	will	fall
hug	and	if	call
fun	land	him	saw
run	sand	is	law
us	hand	his	jaw
☆ just	☆ plan	☆ finish	☆ small
☆ funny	☆ back	☆ begin	☆ talk
☆ sum	☆ grand	☆ into	☆ draw
Psalm 24:1	Prov. 17:14	Prov. 13:20	Psalm 143:10

A Very Different Earth

Rosa learns the importance of taking good care of God's earth and everything in it.

THE EARTH BELONGS TO GOD! EVERYTHING IN ALL THE WORLD IS HIS! PSALM 24:1. The large capital letters printed neatly across the board caught the children's attention as they arrived on Monday morning.

"Wow! Our room sure looks different!" Stephen pointed to the words on the board. "What does that say, Miss Grant?"

"Where did all these plants come from?" Kristin stood by several tall green plants over by the window and touched a large leaf with one finger. "Are we going to keep them?"

"It's like our own private jungle!" Rosa giggled as she joined Kristin.

A bulletin board was covered with pictures of unusual creatures. One was a strange-looking bird with almost no wings. Another looked sort of like a cow, except it had long, stiff hairs sticking up all over its face. There was even a sea animal that seemed to have some kind of beak. James was staring at a picture of an animal with Zebra stripes on its front end, and brown hair like a horse on its back end. "What do you call this animal, Miss Grant?" he joked. "A zorse?"

A table at the front of the classroom was covered with a dark, blue cloth. A pile of brightly-colored books were stacked on one end, and an electric fan at the other. In between were tubs and bags and boxes full of interesting-looking things.

"Are we going to plant something in this dirt, Miss Grant?" Matthew and Beth poked their fingers into a large tub of soil.

"What's this piece of someone's yard doing in here?" Tommy examined a similar tub containing a large clump of earth with grass growing in it.

Miss Grant just smiled as the children explored the changes in their classroom. When it was time for school to start, she called the excited children to their desks.

"Now, let's see if I can answer some of your questions," Miss Grant began. "You've all learned a great many things since you were little babies. One thing you've learned is that when you have something, you must take care of it." She nodded toward Rosa's waving hand. "Rosa, do you have an example?"

"Yes, when my brother and sister and I wanted to get our dogs, Daddy said we had to be sure we always fed and watered them. He said that since Barkley and Digby were our pets that it was our job to take good care of them!"

"That's a very good example, Rosa. We are going to use these things . . ." Miss Grant waved her hand about the room, ". . . to learn how to take good care of our home, the Earth!"

The rest of the day passed in a whirl. The children learned how the earth can "erode" or wash away as they watched what happened when Christopher poured water on the dirt in the big tubs. (At least most of the water went in the tubs.)

Then Miss Grant held up two jars. One looked like clean water, the other looked all muddy. "Which one would you like to take a drink from, Tony?" she asked.

"That one." Tony pointed to the clear one. But when Miss Grant opened the jar and held it near his nose, Tony backed away quickly. "Phew weee, that stinks!" Miss Grant laughed, then showed how water sometimes has bad things in it and can't be used — even if it looks clean. The children also learned how litter in the water or on land affects the earth.

Miss Grant asked another question. "Why is it important to keep our air clean?"

"Because everybody has to breathe!" Beth was quick to answer.

"My aunt told me there are some places the air is so dirty it makes people have headaches and feel sick." Kristin frowned. "That's awful!"

"That's why we need to learn all this stuff . . ." Tommy sounded determined, ". . . so we can fix things when we get big!"

Later Miss Grant showed a video about the many ways trees and plants are helpful to us. They learned how the leaves help keep our air clean and pure. They talked about places where huge areas of trees are being cut and burned.

"But, Miss Grant, what does all this have to do with the zorse and all those other weird animals?" James' face wrinkled in a questioning frown.

"There are many more people on this earth every year. As more people need homes, more forests, grasslands, and other places where animals live are turned into places for people to live. What do you think happens to animals when their homes disappear, James?"

"Well, maybe they move . . . or maybe they just die," James said sadly.

"That's right, James. Your zorse was really called a quagga. The quagga, the passenger pigeon, the dodo, and all the other animals pictured on the bulletin board are 'extinct.' That means that they have died. All of them." Miss Grant looked serious. "There are no more of that kind of animal left on the earth anywhere."

"What can we do to help take care of our earth, Miss Grant?" asked Rosa.

"That's a good question, Rosa. Let's all think about this, then come to school tomorrow with some ideas on how we can help," Miss Grant suggested.

Tuesday morning began with a lively discussion. By 9:30 the children had decided that they were going to clean up Mason Springs Park. Plans were laid for the next day, and excitement mounted.

"Remember, now," Miss Grant admonished as the children prepared to go home. "Wear work clothes tomorrow and some kind of work gloves. Don't forget to bring a sack lunch. There's a 50 percent chance of rain for tomorrow, and if it rains we'll have to wait for a better day. Any questions?"

"Miss Grant, can we pray for good weather?" Kristin asked.

"We certainly can!" Miss Grant smiled. The children bowed their heads as their teacher asked for the blessing of a clear day.

Wednesday dawned cool and clear. Some children's parents helped drive the class to Mason Springs Park. As the children spilled enthusiastically out of the cars, the sun began to shine brightly, and a perfect day began. They filled trash bags with litter. Some gathered fallen limbs and sticks, while others moved rocks to out-of-the-way piles. Even the parents helped by repairing broken swings and playground equipment. Everyone worked hard, and everyone had a great time!

When the clean-up crew gathered around picnic tables to eat their sack lunches at noon, Mason Springs Park looked much better. Rosa sat between her teacher and Sarah, swinging her legs back and forth. "Miss Grant," she spoke her thoughts out loud. "What if everyone learned?"

"Learned what, Rosa?" Miss Grant looked up from unwrapping her sandwich.

"Learned that 'when you have something, you must take care of it.'" Rosa repeated what Miss Grant had told the class. "Wouldn't our Earth look a lot different then?"

"Very different, Rosa." Miss Grant gave her a quick hug. "Very different indeed."

2 Discussion Time

Check understanding of the story and development of personal values.

- What does extinct mean?
- Can you name some animals that have become extinct?
- What can happen to the earth (the air, the water, and the land) if we don't take care of it?
- Think of some ways that you can help take care of the earth God gave us.

A Preview

Write each word as your teacher says it.

Name _____

1. cup
2. bug
3. up
4. us
5. hug
6. fun
7. run

Challenge Words

☆ funny
☆ sum
☆ just

Scripture
Psalm 24:1

103

Challenge
For better spellers, challenge words may be included in the weekly list. Challenge words are starred.

Correct Immediately!
Say Let's correct our preview. I will write each word on the board. Put a dot under each letter on your preview as I spell the word out loud. If you spelled a word wrong, rewrite it correctly.

Progress Chart
Students may record scores. (Reproducible master in Appendix B.)

Take a minute to memorize . . .

Read the memory verse twice. Have students practice it with you two more times.

3 Preview

Test for knowledge of the correct spellings of these words. (See the instructions at the top right for challenge words.)

 Say I will say each word once, use the word in a sentence, then say the word again. Write the word on the lines in the Worktext.

1. cup — Would you like a **cup** of water?
2. bug — The lady **bug** is a very helpful insect.
3. up — The first graders cleaned **up** Mason Springs Park.
4. us — God wants **us** to take good care of the earth he gave to us.
5. hug — Give your mom a big **hug**.
6. fun — Cleaning up the park was **fun** work.
7. run — The horse can **run** very fast.
☆ funny — The quagga was a **funny** looking animal.
☆ sum — The **sum** of two plus two is four.
☆ just — It is **just** about time for class to start.

125

4 Word Shapes

Help students form a correct image of whole words.

(Say) Look at each word and think about its shape. Now, write the word in the correct word Shape Boxes. You may check off each word as you use it.

Note: The word shape boxes are no longer directly across from the word.

(In many words /u/ is spelled with **u**, and it is often spelled this way when it is at the beginning or in the middle of a word.)

(Say) In the word shape boxes, color the letter that spells the sound of /**u**/ in each word. Circle the words that begin with the sound of /**u**/.

Challenge
Draw the correctly shaped box around each letter in these words.

(Say) On a separate sheet of paper, write other words that contain the spelling patterns in the word list. See how many words you can write.

B **Word Shapes**   Name _____

Write each word in the correct word shape boxes. Next, in the word shape boxes, color the letter that spells the sound of /u/ in each word. Circle the words that begin with the sound of /u/.

Words With /u/   Lesson **6**

1. up
2. cup
3. bug
4. hug
5. fun
6. run
7. us

☆ **Challenge**
Draw the correct word shape boxes around each word.

just   funny   sum

104

Answers may vary for duplicate word shapes.

Be Prepared For Fun

Check these supply lists for **Fun Ways to Spell** presented **Day 2**.
Purchase and/or gather these items ahead of time!

General
- Crayons
- 3 x 5 Cards cut in thirds (19 pieces per child)
- 3 x 5 Cards cut in thirds (12 more pieces for challenge words)
- Construction Paper (about 3 pieces per child)
- Spelling List

Auditory
- Spelling List

Visual
- Chalk or Whiteboard Marker
- Chalkboard or Whiteboard (could be individual boards for each child)
- Spelling List

Tactile
- Damp Sand (in plastic storage box with lid)
- Spelling List

126

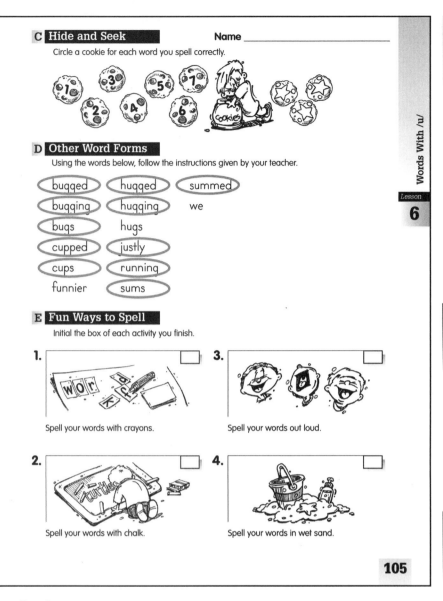

C | Hide and Seek   Name _____

Circle a cookie for each word you spell correctly.

D | Other Word Forms

Using the words below, follow the instructions given by your teacher.

bugged   hugged   summed

bugging   hugging   we

bugs   hugs

cupped   justly

cups   running

funnier   sums

E | Fun Ways to Spell

Initial the box of each activity you finish.

1. Spell your words with crayons.

3. Spell your words out loud.

2. Spell your words with chalk.

4. Spell your words in wet sand.

105

1 | Hide and Seek

Reinforce spelling by using multiple styles of learning.

On a white board, Teacher writes each word — one at a time. **Have students:**

- **Look** at the word.
- **Say** the word out loud.
- **Spell** the word out loud.
- **Hide** (teacher erases word.)
- **Write** the word on their paper.
- **Seek** (teacher rewrites word.)
- **Check** spelling. If incorrect, repeat above steps.

2 | Other Word Forms

This activity is optional. Have students find and circle the Other Word Forms that show action.

3 | Fun Ways to Spell

Four activities are provided. Use one, two, three, or all of the activities. Have students initial the box for each activity they complete.

Options:

- assign activities to students according to their learning styles
- set up the activities in learning centers for students to do throughout the day
- divide students into four groups and assign one activity per group
- do one activity per day

General

To spell your words with crayons…
- Write each letter of your spelling word on a card.
- Glue the cards on a sheet of paper in the right order to spell your words.
- Check your spelling.

Auditory

To spell your words out loud…
- Have your classmate read a spelling word.
- Say a sentence with that spelling word to your classmate.
- Spell the spelling word you used in that sentence to your classmate.
- Ask your classmate to check your spelling.
- Do this with each word on your word list.

Visual

To spell your words with chalk…
- Put your spelling list on your desk.
- Look at a word then walk to the chalkboard (or whiteboard).
- Write your spelling word on the chalkboard (or whiteboard).
- Return to your desk.
- Check your spelling.

Tactile

To spell your words in damp sand…
- Use your finger to write a spelling word in the damp sand.
- Check your spelling.
- Smooth the sand with your finger and write another word.

127

Sentence Fun

1

Familiarize students with word meaning and usage.

Say Using words from the Word Bank, write the spelling word that best completes each sentence.

Challenge

Read these incomplete sentences to your better spellers. Have them write the challenge word that best completes each sentence.

- We added the numbers to find the ___. (sum)
- There is ___ a little salad left. (just)
- The clown looks very ___. (funny)

F Sentence Fun

Write the missing word in each sentence.

Name _____

1. I ran ___up___ the hill.

2. My mom will ___hug___ me.

3. Milk is in my ___cup___.

4. Tom had a ___bug___ in his jar.

5. We had ___fun___ at the park.

6. God wants ___us___ to care

   for the earth.

7. Tell him to ___run___ home.

Word Bank

up	bug	fun	us
cup	hug	run	

106

Take a minute to memorize...

Read the memory verse twice. Have students practice it with you two more times.

128

G Dictation

Listen and write the missing words.

Name _____

1. It is fun to run at the park.

2. My mom and dad gave me a big hug.

3. This bug can fly up.

H Proofreading

One word in each pair is misspelled. Fill in the oval by the misspelled word.

1. ○ up
   ● bg

2. ● hyg
   ○ run

3. ● fvn
   ○ cup

4. ○ bug
   ● rin

5. ○ hug
   ● uus

6. ● yop
   ○ fun

☆ ● gus
   ○ kid

☆ ○ frog
   ● funy

☆ ○ box
   ● som

Words With /u/

Lesson **6**

107

Dictation

1

Reinforce correct spelling by using current and previous words in context.

(Say) Listen as I read each sentence and then write it in your Worktext. (Slowly read each sentence twice. Sentences are found in the Student Worktext to the left.)

Challenge

Write these incomplete sentences on the board.

Grandma ___ gave me ___ ___ ___.

The ___ clown ___ ___ the seesaw.

___ me the ___ of five plus five.

(Say) Listen as I read each sentence. Write the sentence on your paper. (Slowly read each sentence twice.)

Grandma just gave me a big hug.

The funny clown got on the seesaw.

Tell me the sum of five plus five.

---

2 ## Proofreading

Familiarize students with standardized test format and reinforce recognizing misspelled words.

(Say) Look at each set of words. One word in each set is misspelled. Fill in the oval by the misspelled word. (You may wish to pronounce each set of words to help students correctly identify them.)

129

3 Hide and Seek

Reinforce correct spelling of current spelling words. (A reproducible master is provided in Appendix A as shown on the inset page to the right.)

Write the words one at a time on a white board.

Have students:

- **Look** at the word.
- **Say** the word out loud.
- **Spell** the word out loud.
- **Hide** (teacher erases word.)
- **Write** the word on paper.
- **Seek** (teacher rewrites word.)
- **Check** spelling. If incorrect, rewrite word correctly.

4 Making Words

Have your students complete this activity to strengthen spelling ability and expand vocabulary.

1 Posttest

Test mastery of the spelling words. Challenge words are starred.

 (Say)

I will say the word once, use the word in a sentence, then say the word again. Write the word on your paper.

Hide and Seek

Check a paper for each word you spell correctly.

Making Words

Add the endings to the spelling words. Write the new word on the line.

1. hug + s

   hugs

2. bug + s

   bugs

3. cup + s

   cups

4. sum + s

   sums

5. hug + g + ed

   hugged

6. bug + g + ed

   bugged

☆ cup + p + ed

   cupped

☆ sum + m + ed

   summed

367

1.	us	It is up to **us** to keep our neighborhood clean.
2.	hug	The boy gave his dad a tight **hug.**
3.	cup	Mother added a **cup** of sugar to the cookie dough.
4.	bug	The lightning **bug** blinked on and off.
5.	run	The boy will **run** the race.
6.	up	Always pick **up** your things and put them away neatly.
7.	fun	It is **fun** taking care of our earth.
☆	sum	What is the **sum** of three and six?
☆	funny	That was a **funny** story.
☆	just	There are **just** enough cookies for everyone.

 Progress Chart

Students may record scores. (Reproducible master in Appendix B.)

 Personal Dictionary

Students may add any words they have misspelled to their personal dictionaries for reference when writing. (Cover in Appendix B.)

130

I Game

Name _____

Cross out each **i**, **d**, and **w** with a big **X** to find the hidden spelling words. Using one crayon, softly color the boxes you did not mark so you can see your spelling words better.

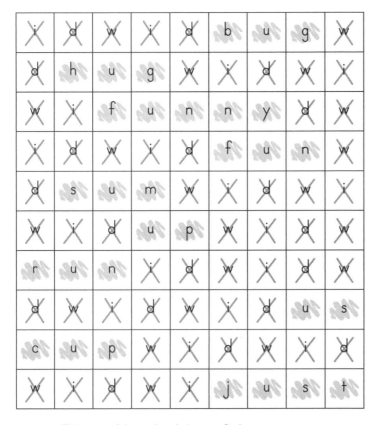

Remember : Take care of the earth—it belongs to God.

J Journaling

Draw a picture in your journal of Mason Springs Park before, during, or after Miss Grant's class clean-up day. Label your picture.

108

2 Game

Reinforce spelling skills and provide motivation and interest.

Materials

- game page (from student text)
- pencils (1 per child)
- crayons or colored pencils (1 per child)

3 Journaling

Provide a meaningful reason for correct spelling through personal writing.

Review the story using discussion leads provided on the following page. Encourage students to apply the Scriptural value in their journaling.

Take a minute to memorize...

Read the memory verse to the class twice. Have the class practice it with you two more times.

How to Play:

- Have each student mark through each letter **d** found on the grid with a big **X**.
- Have each student mark through each letter **i** found on the grid with a big **X**.
- Have each student mark through each letter **w** found on the grid with a big **X**.
- Tell the students that the boxes without **X**'s contain their spelling words.
- Have the students color softly over the boxes without **X**'s so they can see their spelling words more clearly.
- Have the students follow along as you read and spell each word as it appears on the grid.

131

Journaling (continued)

 Say

- Miss Grant's class learned that "when you have something, you must take care of it." Why should we take care of the Earth? (God made it for us to enjoy and care for. If we don't take care of it, the water, air, and food can become unhealthy for people to use. We could lose more of the animals God created.)

- Can we depend on our parents and other adults to take care of the Earth? (No. We all need to work together to keep our planet in good shape.)

- Rosa and her classmates helped to take care of their neighborhood by cleaning up Mason Springs Park. Imagine how the park looked. Draw a picture in your journal of Mason Springs Park before, during, or after the clean-up day, then label your picture.

Quotables!

"Inventive spelling refers to young children's attempts to use their best judgment about spelling."

*Lutz, Elaine. 1986. ERIC/RCS Report: Invented Spelling and Spelling Development. Language Arts, Vol. 63, No. 7, November: 742-744.

Piggy Bank Pardon

Kristin learns a lesson about getting along with her sister.

The moment she opened her eyes, Kristin knew it was not going to be a good day! She was still so-o-o-o sleepy, but Cathy was awake and jabbering non-stop. Sometimes it was just not fun to share a room with your little sister!

Kristin rolled over and covered her head with her yellow blanket. It didn't help much. Cathy sat happily in the middle of her unmade bed and played with her stuffed animals. She spoke in a high, soft voice pretending to be Lucy the stuffed lamb. Then she answered in a lower, louder voice pretending to be Rufus the stuffed dog. Rufus sure seemed to have a lot to say! Kristin sighed and turned over.

"Hey, Kristin!" Cathy used her rough Rufus voice. "Look, it's raining today."

Kristin opened her eyes to peer out the window. Rain dripped down the glass like tears. "Oh, great!" Kristin stared at the gloomy morning sky. "We can't do anything outside today." She turned angrily toward Cathy. "Why can't you ever be quiet and let me sleep late on the weekend?"

Kristin's twin, Christopher, stuck his head around the door of the girls' room. "Hey, you two! It's time to eat." Cathy bounded out of the room right behind him. Kristin slowly dragged herself out of bed grumbling. She stuck her feet in her slippers and headed for the door, pulling her robe on as she went. As she passed Cathy's dresser, the arm she was stuffing into her sleeve thumped solidly against something. Kristin gasped as her sister's precious little pink piggy bank went flying toward the wall. CRASH!

Kristin was still staring in shock at the piggy bank pieces when Cathy burst through the door. "What was that noise . . . Oh no! My piggy bank!" she yelled, "You broke Penelope!" Mom stepped into the room.

"What's all the racket, girls?" She stopped short when she saw the pink pieces scattered on the carpet by the wall. "Oh dear. What happened?"

"Kristin broke Penelope on purpose!" Cathy glared at Kristin.

"I did not!" Kristin defended herself. "It was an accident, Mom."

"She's mad at me 'cause I woke up and she didn't want to," Cathy insisted angrily, "So she broke Penelope!"

"I didn't mean to break your silly piggy bank! You left it too near the edge of your dresser," Kristin argued. "I just bumped it a little."

"I did not! She was right where I always keep her." Cathy knelt on the rug and gently touched a small piece of Penelope the piggy bank. "And now she's ruined!" Tears welled up as Cathy stared down. One piggy eye with long, painted lashes stared back.

"That's enough, girls." Mom herded them out the door. "Daddy and the boys are waiting for breakfast. We'll discuss this later."

The sisters glared at each other throughout breakfast. Christopher was enthusiastically explaining his school project, and Mom and Dad were asking him questions and giving advice.

"May I have some more scrambled eggs, please?" Kristin held her plate out.

"That's the last of them," Dad said, scooping a small, golden mound onto Kristin's plate.

"I want more scrambled eggs, too," Cathy pouted. "Kristin always gets what she wants."

"I didn't know you wanted more, Cathy." Dad calmly poured himself some apple juice. "There are a few more biscuits if you'd like some."

Mom wiped two-year-old Cory's face and lifted him out of his high chair. "Dad and I need to do some household things on the computer this morning. Since Christopher has a school project to finish, I'd like you to keep an eye on Cory this morning, Kristin." Mom was busy cleaning Cory's high chair tray, and didn't see the frown on Kristin's face. It was amazing how big a mess Cory could create. It seemed like he could find a way to make a big mess anywhere, anytime.

"What about Penelope?" Cathy questioned.

"Kristin will clean up the pieces right after breakfast," Mom said over her shoulder as she headed down the hall to change Cory.

"Kristin will clean up the mess. Kristin will watch Cory all morning," Kristin complained to herself as she picked up the piggy bank pieces after getting dressed. "Why doesn't Cathy ever have to do anything around here? I didn't mean to break her dumb bank. Why do I have to clean it all up?"

Later as Kristin tried to entertain Cory with stacks of blocks, Cathy came into the living room and began playing with some dolls. Kristin spotted a doll with a purple dress and long brown hair. "Hey, Cathy! You can't play with my doll!" she said sternly. "You didn't even ask! Go put her away right now, and don't you touch any of my stuff!"

"But I don't have a doll like this," Cathy objected. "I need her to be Mrs. Brady for my doll family."

"If you didn't spend your money on stupid things like that old piggy bank you could get your own doll."

"Penelope wasn't stupid. She was beautiful, 'til you broke her!" Cathy's voice rose.

"And why do you always have to name everything?

133

Lucy, Rufus, Penelope, Mrs. Brady," Kristin mocked in a sing-song voice.

"You're mean, Kristin!" Cathy cried, running from the room. "I wish you weren't my sister!"

Later that evening Mom sat on the couch with an arm around each girl. The fireplace flames made dancing shadows around the room as Mom talked with the girls. "And Scripture tells us in Proverbs 17:14 that 'It is hard to stop a quarrel once it starts, so don't let it begin.' That's good advice for all of us," Mom finished.

The rain still beat softly on the roof as the girls silently got ready for bed. After the lights were out, and everyone was settled for the night, Kristin lay awake thinking about Cathy. She thought about playing dolls together, building a stable for their toy horses out of books, telling each other goofy made-up stories. Kristin remembered the huge smile on Cathy's face as she learned to ride Kristin's old bicycle. She smiled as she thought about how Cathy could come up with names for almost anything! She remembered how proud Cathy had been when she chose the little pink piggy bank and had named it Penelope.

"Cathy?" she whispered across the darkened room.

"Uh-huh," Cathy replied in a sleepy voice.

"I'm really sorry that I broke Penelope. It really was an accident, you know," Kristin sat up and spoke softly into the dark. "Will you forgive me?"

"Uh-huh." Cathy said. "And I'm sorry I got mad, too. I'm glad you're my big sister, Kristin."

"I'll buy you another piggy bank just like her," Kristin offered. "They still have some at the store, and I have enough money saved up. Okay?"

"Okay," Cathy agreed with a yawn. "But I can pay some with my allowance, too."

She paused, then spoke softly as she drifted back to sleep.

"Maybe we'll get a purple one

this time… and name it Priscilla…"

"Right!" Kristin flopped back onto her bed with a smothered giggle. *Leave it to my little sister to think of something like that!* she thought. *"Priscilla, the purple piggy bank!"*

2 Discussion Time

Check understanding of the story and development of personal values.

- Did Kristin break Penelope on purpose?
- How could Kristin or Cathy have stopped the quarrel from starting?
- If Kristin had said she was very sorry right away, do you think the sisters would have quarreled all day?
- How do you think Kristin felt while she was picking up the pieces of the piggy bank?
- How do you think she felt after she told Cathy she was sorry?
- How can you keep a quarrel with someone else from starting?

134

A Preview

Write each word as your teacher says it.

Name _____

1. glad
2. and
3. land
4. am
5. had
6. hand
7. sand

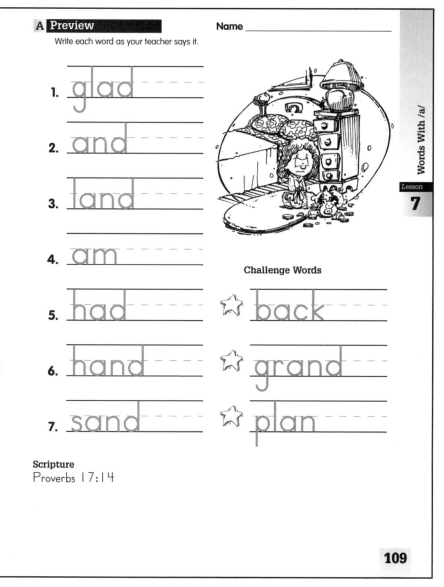

Challenge Words

 back
 grand
 plan

Scripture
Proverbs 17:14

109

 Challenge

For better spellers, challenge words may be included in the weekly list. Challenge words are starred.

Correct Immediately!

Let's correct our preview. I will write each word on the board. Put a dot under each letter on your preview as I spell the word out loud. If you spelled a word wrong, rewrite it correctly.

Progress Chart

Students may record scores. (Reproducible master in Appendix B.)

Take a minute to memorize . . .

Read the memory verse twice. Have students practice it with you two more times.

3 Preview

Test for knowledge of the correct spellings of these words. (See the instructions at the top right for challenge words.)

 I will say each word once, use the word in a sentence, then say the word again. Write the word on the lines in the Worktext.

1. glad — Are you **glad** it's raining?
2. and — Mom talked with Kristin **and** Cathy about their argument.
3. land — The **land** around this pond is very muddy.
4. am — Kristin said, "I **am** sorry I broke Penelope."
5. had — Kristin **had** a bad day.
6. hand — My **hand** won't fit in this glove anymore.
7. sand — The children played in the **sand**.
☆ back — Kristin wanted to go **back** to sleep.
☆ grand — They built a **grand** sand castle.
☆ plan — Miss Grant will **plan** a program.

135

4 Word Shapes

Help students form a correct image of whole words.

 (Say) Look at each word and think about its shape. Now, write the word in the correct word Shape Boxes. You may check off each word as you use it.

(In many words /a/ is spelled with **a**, and it is often spelled this way when it is at the beginning or in the middle of a word.)

 (Say) In the word shape boxes, color the letter that spells the sound of /a/ in each word.
Circle the words that begin with the sound of /a/.

★ Challenge

Draw the correctly shaped box around each letter in these words.

 (Say) On a separate sheet of paper, write other words that contain the spelling patterns in the word list. See how many words you can write.

Lesson **7** | Day 1

Words With /a/

Lesson **7**

B Word Shapes   Name _____

Write each word in the correct word shape boxes. Next, in the word shape boxes, color the letter that spells the sound of /a/ in each word. Circle the words that begin with the sound of /a/.

1. had
2. glad
3. am
4. and
5. land
6. sand
7. hand

☆ **Challenge**
Draw the correct word shape boxes around each word.

p l a n   b a c k   g r a n d

110

Answers may vary for duplicate word shapes.

Be Prepared For Fun

Check these supply lists for **Fun Ways to Spell** presented **Day 2**.
Purchase and/or gather these items ahead of time!

General
- Strips of Paper 3 1/2 x 11 Inches (7 per child)
- Strips of Paper 3 1/2 x 11 Inches (3 more for challenge words)
- Crayons or Markers
- Tape
- Scissors
- Spelling List

Auditory
- Rhythm Instruments (two wooden spoons, two pan lids, maracas)
- Spelling List

Visual
- Clothespins (5 clothespins per child at the clothesline)
- a, d, g, h, l, m, n and s (written on 3 x 5 cards cut in half)
- b, c, k, p and r (added for challenge words)
- Clothesline (hung at student height)
- Spelling List

Tactile
- Shaving Cream
- Optional: Plastic Plates
- Optional: Wooden Craft Sticks
- Spelling List

136

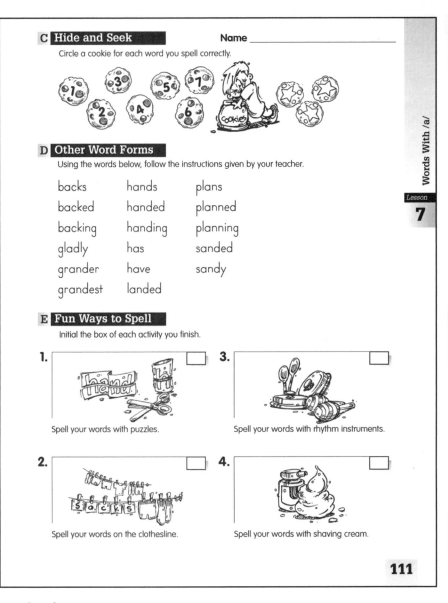

C Hide and Seek

Name _____

Circle a cookie for each word you spell correctly.

D Other Word Forms

Using the words below, follow the instructions given by your teacher.

backs	hands	plans
backed	handed	planned
backing	handing	planning
gladly	has	sanded
grander	have	sandy
grandest	landed	

E Fun Ways to Spell

Initial the box of each activity you finish.

1. ☐
Spell your words with puzzles.

3. ☐
Spell your words with rhythm instruments.

2. ☐
Spell your words on the clothesline.

4. ☐
Spell your words with shaving cream.

111

---

1 **Hide and Seek**

Reinforce spelling by using multiple styles of learning.

On a white board, Teacher writes each word — one at a time. **Have students:**

- **Look** at the word.
- **Say** the word out loud.
- **Spell** the word out loud.
- **Hide** (teacher erases word.)
- **Write** the word on their paper.
- **Seek** (teacher rewrites word.)
- **Check** spelling. If incorrect, repeat above steps.

Day 2

Lesson 7

2 **Other Word Forms**

This activity is optional. Have students dictate original sentences to you using these Other Word Forms. Write them on the board.

landed   sandy
have

3 **Fun Ways to Spell**

Four activities are provided. Use one, two, three, or all of the activities. Have students initial the box for each activity they complete.

Options:

- assign activities to students according to their learning styles
- set up the activities in learning centers for students to do throughout the day
- divide students into four groups and assign one activity per group
- do one activity per day

General
To Spell your words with puzzles…
- Write each word on a strip of paper in big, tall letters.
- Cut your word in half lengthwise.
- Tape the ends of each strip together to make circles.
- Mix the circles together.
- Match the circles again to make your spelling words.

Auditory
To spell your words with rhythm instruments…
- Look at a word on your spelling list.
- Close your eyes.
- Play your rhythm instruments softly while you whisper the spelling of the word.
- Open your eyes and check your spelling.

Visual
To spell your words on the clothesline…
- Choose the letter cards you need to spell a word on your list.
- Clothespin the cards to the clothesline in the right order to spell the word.
- Check your spelling.
- Remove the letter cards from the clothesline and spell the next word on your list.

Tactile
To spell your words with shaving cream…
- Spread a glob of shaving cream across your desk (or on a plastic plate).
- Use your finger (or a wooden craft stick) to write a spelling word in the shaving cream.
- Check your spelling.
- Smear the word out with your finger and write another word.

137

Sentence Fun

Familiarize students with word meaning and usage.

Say) To find the hidden picture, color the spaces purple that have spelling words in them. Color the spaces red that have challenge words.

F **Hidden Picture**

Name _____

To find the hidden picture, color the spaces purple that have spelling words in them.
Color the spaces red that have challenge words.

ant
play
lad
day
am
and
an
hand
ax
sand
land
glad
land
sad
hand
had
on
most
and
at
grand
plan
back

Word Bank

112

had	am	land	hand	☆ back
glad	and	sand	☆ plan	☆ grand

Take a minute to memorize...

Read the memory verse twice. Have students practice it with you two more times.

G Dictation
Listen and write the missing words.

Name _____

1. I am glad we had a big dog.

2. The sand felt good on my hand.

3. I saw the big jet land.

H Proofreading
One word in each pair is misspelled. Fill in the oval by the misspelled word.

1. ○ had
   ● adn

2. ● sanb
   ○ land

3. ○ glad
   ● hanb

4. ● ladn
   ○ and

5. ● glab
   ○ sand

6. ○ hand
   ● ama

☆ ● qlan
   ○ quit

☆ ○ just
   ● bak

☆ ● granb
   ○ funny

113

1 Dictation

Reinforce correct spelling by using current and previous words in context.

(Say) Listen as I read each sentence and then write it in your Worktext. (Slowly read each sentence twice. Sentences are found in the Student Worktext to the left.)

Challenge
Write these incomplete sentences on the board.

Kristin ___ ___ ___ the party.

The ___ ___ in the ___ of the ___.

___ ___ ___ ___ slam.

(Say) Listen as I read each sentence. Write the sentence on your paper. (Slowly read each sentence twice.)

Kristin did help plan the party.

The dog hid in the back of the truck.

Dad hit a grand slam.

Words With /a/

Lesson 7

Day 4

Lesson 7

2 Proofreading

Familiarize students with standardized test format and reinforce recognizing misspelled words.

(Say) Look at each set of words. One word in each set is misspelled. Fill in the oval by the misspelled word. (You may wish to pronounce each set of words to help students correctly identify them.)

139

3 Hide and Seek

Reinforce correct spelling of current spelling words. (A reproducible master is provided in Appendix A as shown on the inset page to the right.)

Write the words one at a time on a white board.

Have students:

• **Look** at the word.
• **Say** the word out loud.
• **Spell** the word out loud.
• **Hide** (teacher erases word.)
• **Write** the word on paper.
• **Seek** (teacher rewrites word.)
• **Check** spelling. If incorrect, rewrite word correctly.

4 Code

Have your students complete this activity to strengthen spelling ability and expand vocabulary.

1 Posttest

Test mastery of the spelling words. Challenge words are starred.

(Say) I will say the word once, use the word in a sentence, then say the word again. Write the word on your paper.

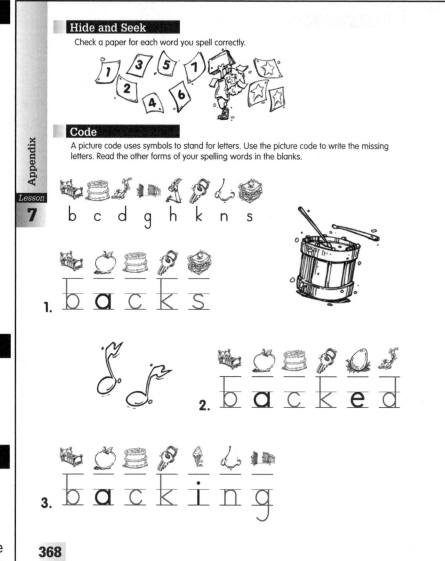

Appendix | Lesson 7

Hide and Seek
Check a paper for each word you spell correctly.

Code
A picture code uses symbols to stand for letters. Use the picture code to write the missing letters. Read the other forms of your spelling words in the blanks.

b c d g h k n s

1. b a c k s
2. b a c k e d
3. b a c k i n g

368

1.	and	Kristin **and** Cathy were quarreling.
2.	land	The plane will **land** in ten minutes.
3.	sand	It is fun to play in the **sand.**
4.	glad	Kristin was **glad** that Cathy forgave her.
5.	hand	Please **hand** me that doll.
6.	had	Cathy **had** named her piggy bank Penelope.
7.	am	I **am** happy to see you.
☆	grand	This park is a **grand** place to play!
☆	plan	Mom will help me **plan** a party.
☆	back	No one could put Penelope **back** together again.

Progress Chart
Students may record scores. (Reproducible master in Appendix B.)

Personal Dictionary
Students may add any words they have misspelled to their personal dictionaries for reference when writing. (Cover in Appendix B.)

140

I Game

Name _____

Kristin and Cathy learned that it's hard to stop a quarrel once it starts. Kristin asked Cathy to forgive her for breaking her bank and helped her buy a new one. Color one penny for each word you or your team spells correctly from this week's word list.

Remember: Don't quarrel. Arguments are easy to start but hard to stop.

J Journaling

Copy and finish this sentence in your journal.
I can keep from quarreling by...

114

---

2 Game

Reinforce spelling skills and provide motivation and interest.

Materials

- game page (from student text)
- brown crayons (1 per child)
- game word list

Game Word List

Use of challenge words is optional.

1. had
2. glad
3. am
4. and
5. land
6. sand
7. hand
☆ plan
☆ back
☆ grand

3 Journaling

Provide a meaningful reason for correct spelling through personal writing.

Review the story using discussion leads provided on the following page. Encourage students to apply the Scriptural value in their journaling.

Take a minute to memorize...

Have the class say the memory verses from lessons 6 and 7 with you.

How to Play:

- Divide the class into two teams, and decide which team will go first.
- Have a student from team A go to the board.
- Read the spelling word two times slowly and clearly. (You may also wish to use the word in a sentence. Ex.: "cat — The cat climbed a tree. — cat")
- Have the student write the word on the board.
- If the word is spelled correctly, instruct all the members of team A to color one penny. (Note: If the word is misspelled, correct the spelling immediately before continuing the game.)
- Alternate between teams A and B as you go down the word list.
- The team with the most pennies colored when you have gone through the game word list twice is the winner.

Non-Competitive Option:

At the end of the game, say: "Class, I am proud of your efforts to spell the words correctly. If you had fun and tried your best, you are all winners!"

Lesson **7** | Day 5

(Say)

• What things did Kristin and Cathy quarrel about? (Getting up, the broken piggy bank, who got the last of the scrambled eggs, Kristin's doll)

• Do you ever quarrel with your brother or sister or maybe a friend? What kind of things might you quarrel about? (Perhaps who goes first, who is to blame for something, etc.)

• Why is it hard to stop a quarrel once it starts? (The people quarreling get angry with each other and then whatever one person does, it bothers the other person. It's hard to say you're sorry.)

• How can you keep a quarrel from starting? (Not getting angry or arguing about something even if you think you're right, etc.)

• Write your ideas in your journal.

"When students invent spellings, they are thinking and learning about words."*

*Scott, Jill E. 1994. Spelling for Readers and Writers. The Reading Teacher, Vol. 48, No. 2, October: 188-190.

Some Good Advice

Katelynn learns the importance of choosing friends wisely.

"Dad will pick you up at three o'clock, girls." Mom said as Katelynn and Jennifer stepped out of the car. "Don't forget your inhaler, Katelynn." Mrs. Hatasaki handed the small metal aerosol bottle to her daughter. Katelynn stuffed it in the pocket of her coat as she walked toward her classroom. She was tired of the episodes of wheezing and the feeling of not being able to get enough air during each asthma attack.

"Come on Katelynn. Get a ball," Beth shouted later as the bell rang for recess. "Let's play four square today!"

"Okay," Katelynn answered.

As she was reaching into the box for the ball, Miss Grant came up behind her quietly. "Katelynn, why don't you go with the third graders to the gym today," she suggested. "I'm afraid if you run around outside in the cold you'll have another attack like you did yesterday."

"But Miss Grant, I want to play with my friends." Katelynn blurted out. "Beth, Sarah, Kristin, and me were going to play four square."

"Kristin and I," Miss Grant corrected. "And our class has the gym this afternoon, so you can play then."

Katelynn walked down the hall toward the gym. "I hate this asthma," she thought. It wasn't so bad at home. Mom knew just what to do and how to control, or even avoid, the attacks. But Miss Grant was just learning about asthma, and often protected Katelynn from things that wouldn't hurt her. It wasn't that cold today. Yesterday, she'd been trying to get their four-square ball back from Daniel when the wheezing started. She hadn't held her breath long enough after using the inhaler because she was out of breath from chasing Daniel. Mom said if she didn't get a full dose of the medication it wouldn't work as fast. It had taken her longer than usual to get the attack under control — and that had really scared Miss Grant.

Katelynn walked into the gym and leaned against the wall. "Hi, Katelynn." Mr. Valentino said. "Miss Grant said you might come in here with us today. Feel free to join any of the games."

"Uh, thanks." Katelynn didn't move from her place by the wall. She watched the bigger girls line up to jump rope. Some kids were playing four square, but didn't need another player. Mr. Valentino was helping the rest of the class form teams for basketball. She watched the girls jumping rope. Maybe they'd let her just twirl and never take a turn jumping. But they'd wonder why, and she didn't really feel like explaining about how she was born with severe asthma and could die if she didn't control it properly. All the kids in her own class already knew.

Two of the girls were standing near by. "Where'd you get the new jean jacket, Sandra?" Katelynn heard one ask.

"Oh, at the mall last night. And you should see my new computer game! You have to kill all the aliens on the space ship before they slice you up and take over the whole Earth."

"Cool!" The other girl nodded. "Did you go in the arcade and play that new Karate game I told you about?"

"No, Mom bought me this jacket, three shirts, and the computer game." Sandra frowned. "And then she said she wasn't spending another dime on me! Can you believe it?"

Katelynn was distracted by two boys fighting over the ball, and Mr. Valentino's shrill whistle. When she looked back at Sandra and her friend, they were huddled with a third girl and giggling. Then all three of them looked her direction and burst into laughter. "I wish I was with my own class," Katelynn thought.

The next day at recess Katelynn stood against the wall again watching the third graders. "Hey, Katelynn, want to play with us today?" Sandra laughed. "You can at least twirl the jump rope. That ol' wall can stand up by itself." The other girls laughed.

Katelynn noticed Sandra's shoes were not scuffed and her jeans were just right — not too long, not too short. Her shirt looked brand new, and the ribbon in her hair matched her outfit perfectly.

"You can take Elizabeth's place." Sandra pointed to the girl she'd been talking to yesterday. It looked like she had on new clothes, too. These girls must be rich.

"Sure, I'll twirl." Katelynn joined the group. No one said much to her the rest of recess, but at least it was better than standing against the wall. Katelynn wondered how they knew she could only twirl and not jump rope.

By the end of the week Katelynn was tired of twirling rope every recess. There were only three kids in the four-square grid, and it sure looked like more fun. As she headed across the gym to talk to them she overheard Sandra. "Did you see what that little first-grader Sarah wore to school this morning? I wouldn't wear it to have a mud fight in! I wonder where her mom was when she got dressed this morning?" Sandra paused as Katelynn walked by. "Hey, aren't you gonna twirl today?"

"Uh, sure." Katelynn stopped. "If you want me too." She was flattered to be included in Elizabeth's and Sandra's game. *"They must be the most popular girls in class,"* Katelynn thought as she picked up her end of the rope.

"How many aliens did you kill after I left last night?" Elizabeth waited impatiently for her turn to jump.

"Not enough to save the planet," Sandra shrugged. "But give me time, and I'll soon be slicing them to pieces!"

143

Soon school was out, and Katelynn and Beth ran out to the parking lot to meet Mrs. Hill. "I can't believe your mom let me come to the mall with you today," Katelynn said.

"Isn't it great?" Beth slid into the back seat.

"And no Luke tagging along to bug us either!" Katelynn fastened her seat belt. "Can you believe those old clothes Sarah wore today?"

"You know their family can't afford new clothes." Beth turned to look at Katelynn. "Someone probably gave Sarah their hand-me-downs. She's still a nice person though."

"They probably meant for her to wear them for playing in the dirt!" Katelynn shot back.

I wonder what's wrong with Katelynn? This doesn't sound like her," Beth thought.

"Hey," Katelynn changed the subject. "You think your mom will let us play at the arcade while she shops?"

"No, she'd never leave us there by ourselves . . . but she might go with us for a while. I'll ask." Beth leaned forward. "Mom, can we go to the arcade?"

"No, I don't think so, Beth," Mom said thoughtfully. "Our family doesn't go to arcades. First, most of the games are about killing or destroying. Second, it costs a lot if you play very long. Third, I think there are a lot more fun things we can do on our girls-night-out."

"Okay," Beth replied. "Can we look at patterns and material for my doll? I want you to make her a soccer outfit just like my uniform."

"Sure," Mom said. "Sounds fun!"

Later that evening, as they passed a computer store, Katelynn stopped. "Hey, can I look in here real quick, Mrs. Hill?"

Mrs. Hill nodded and the girls darted back to the game section. "Oh, I've been wanting to see this!" Katelynn picked up a box from the shelf. "Do you have a demo of this game we can take a look at?"

"Right this way." The clerk went to a computer with a large screen. "These invaders are trying to take over earth. Aim the lasers and shoot them down before they cut you to pieces." As the clerk walked away, Katelynn sat and looked intently at the screen. Mrs. Hill came up and watched for a moment.

"Katelynn," she said, "We have a family rule about not playing games that kill or destroy, whether it costs money in an arcade or not. Does your mom let you play this game?"

"I don't know. She's never seen it."

"Then how did you know about it?" asked Beth.

"Oh, some kids at school."

"Who?" Beth wanted to know. "I don't know anyone with this game."

"Sandra and Elizabeth talk about it all the time at recess." Katelynn moved the mouse rapidly for another shot.

"Are Sandra and Elizabeth new in your class, girls?" asked Mrs. Hill.

"No, they're third graders." Katelynn destroyed another invader.

Beth looked intently at Katelynn. "Is that why you wanted to go to the arcade?" Katelynn nodded. "And did they say nasty things about Sarah's clothes, too?" Beth probed.

"Mmmm Hmm," said Katelynn.

"I was beginning to wonder about you," Beth said. "Now I understand."

"I'm not sure I do." Mrs. Hill looked a little confused. "You can tell me all about it on the way home in the car." She turned and headed out of the store. "Let's go look at the patterns and material before it gets too late."

Monday morning, Miss Grant began spelling class. "Our text for this week comes from Proverbs 13:20. King Solomon says, 'Be with wise men and become wise. Be with evil men and become evil.' Solomon was best friends with God when he first became king, and God blessed him with a double portion of wisdom. Kings and queens came from all over the world to learn from Israel's wise king. But Solomon started spending time with women who didn't love God. Through their influence he led all Israel into sin. Later Solomon was sorry and chose to follow the God of heaven again, but most of his people didn't make that same choice. Israel lost much of its power and influence." Miss Grant paused. "Do you think it's still important to 'be with wise men and become wise' as Solomon suggests?"

"I don't know anyone who doesn't love God here at school." Sarah scratched her head.

"My dad says anything that's more important to you than your friendship with God can lead to sin," suggested Stephen. "Even something like winning a soccer game."

Katelynn looked over at Beth with a knowing smile, then her hand shot up. "Katelynn," said Miss Grant. "Tell us what you think."

"Beth and her mom and I were talking on the way home from the mall last night. Mrs. Hill told us if you spend time with people who are not making good choices, you'll soon be making bad choices, too — just to impress them or to keep them liking you."

"So, class," Miss Grant concluded, "Do you think choosing good friends is still important?"

"Only if you want to be wise!" Matthew said. "That's what Solomon said, and he was one of the wisest men who ever lived!"

2 Discussion Time

Check understanding of the story and development of personal values.

- Do you think Katelynn usually makes fun of Sarah's clothes?
- Why does Katelynn want to learn how to play the arcade game that Sandra and Elizabeth play?
- Why was Katelynn starting to act like some of the big girls in third grade?
- Was that a good choice to make? Why?
- Why is it important to choose your friends carefully?
- It is important to be a good friend. Are you a wise friend that others should choose to be with like Solomon suggests?

A Preview

Write each word as your teacher says it.

Name _____

1. win
2. will
3. if
4. his
5. in
6. him
7. is

Challenge Words

☆ into
☆ finish
☆ begin

Scripture
Proverbs 13:20

115

Challenge

For better spellers, challenge words may be included in the weekly list. Challenge words are starred.

Correct Immediately!

Let's correct our preview. I will write each word on the board. Put a dot under each letter on your preview as I spell the word out loud. If you spelled a word wrong, rewrite it correctly.

Progress Chart

Students may record scores. (Reproducible master in Appendix B.)

Take a minute to memorize . . .

Have the class say the memory verses from lessons 1, 2, and 3 with you.

3 Preview

Test for knowledge of the correct spellings of these words. (See the instructions at the top right for challenge words.)

I will say each word once, use the word in a sentence, then say the word again. Write the word on the lines in the Worktext.

1. win — The girls wanted to **win**.
2. will — Katelynn **will** have to play indoors.
3. if — The glass will break **if** you drop it.
4. his — That is **his** picture.
5. in — Katelynn played **in** the gym.
6. him — Mother will give **him** some food.
7. is — It **is** very cold today.
☆ into — Katelynn went **into** the mall with Beth.
☆ finish — We will **finish** this test soon.
☆ begin — Is it time to **begin** recess?

Word Shapes

4

Help students form a correct image of whole words.

Say Look at each word and think about its shape. Now, write the word in the correct word Shape Boxes. You may check off each word as you use it.

(In many words /i/ is spelled with **i**, and it is often spelled this way when it is at the beginning or in the middle of a word.)

Say In the word shape boxes, color the letter that spells the sound of /i/ in each word. Circle the words that begin with the sound of /i/.

Challenge

Draw the correctly shaped box around each letter in these words.

Say On a separate sheet of paper, write other words that contain the spelling patterns in the word list. See how many words you can write.

B Word Shapes   Name _____

Write each word in the correct word shape boxes. Next, in the word shape boxes, color the letter that spells the sound of /i/ in each word. Circle the words that begin with the sound of /i/.

Words With /i/

Lesson 8

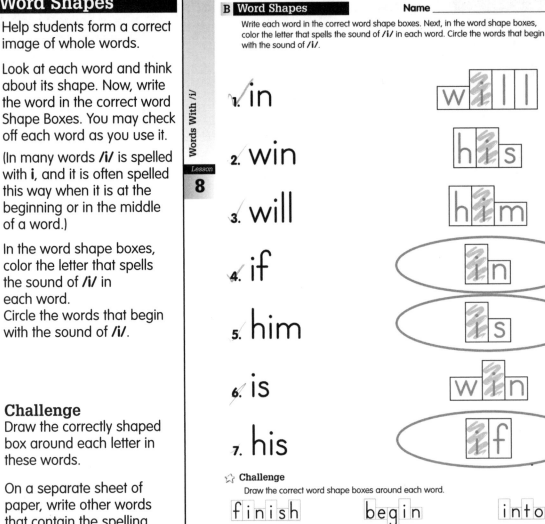

1. ✓ in
2. ✓ win
3. ✓ will
4. ✓ if
5. him
6. ✓ is
7. his

☆ **Challenge**
Draw the correct word shape boxes around each word.

finish   begin   into

116

Answers may vary for duplicate word shapes.

Be Prepared For Fun

Check these supply lists for **Fun Ways to Spell** presented **Day 2**. Purchase and/or gather these items ahead of time!

General
- Crayons
- Piece of Paper
- Spelling List

Auditory
- Box to Store Letters
- f, h, i, l, l, m, n, s and w (written on seasonal shapes like a fir tree or star)
- b, e, g, i, o and t (added for challenge words)
- Spelling List

Visual
- Eraser
- Dark Construction Paper
- Spelling List

Tactile
- Finger Paint
- Plastic Plate or Glossy Paper
- Spelling List

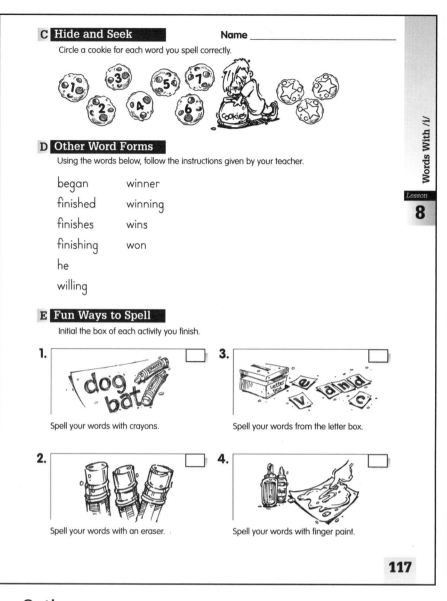

C Hide and Seek

Name _____

Circle a cookie for each word you spell correctly.

D Other Word Forms

Using the words below, follow the instructions given by your teacher.

began   winner

finished   winning

finishes   wins

finishing   won

he

willing

E Fun Ways to Spell

Initial the box of each activity you finish.

1. ☐
Spell your words with crayons.

2. ☐
Spell your words with an eraser.

3. ☐
Spell your words from the letter box.

4. ☐
Spell your words with finger paint.

117

Hide and Seek

1

Reinforce spelling by using multiple styles of learning.

On a white board, Teacher writes each word — one at a time. **Have students:**

- **Look** at the word.
- **Say** the word out loud.
- **Spell** the word out loud.
- **Hide** (teacher erases word.)
- **Write** the word on their paper.
- **Seek** (teacher rewrites word.)
- **Check** spelling. If incorrect, repeat above steps.

Other Word Forms

2

This activity is optional. Have students find the Other Word Form that best completes these sentences.

He __ the race. (won)
I __ reading the book. (finished)

Fun Ways to Spell

3

Four activities are provided. Use one, two, three, or all of the activities. Have students initial the box for each activity they complete.

Options:

- assign activities to students according to their learning styles
- set up the activities in learning centers for students to do throughout the day
- divide students into four groups and assign one activity per group
- do one activity per day

General

To spell your words with crayons…
- Write each letter of your spelling word in fat, thick letters.
- Check your spelling.

Auditory

To spell your words from the letter box…
- Spell a word from your list by putting the letters in the right order.
- Check your spelling.
- Spell your word out loud.

Visual

To spell your words with an eraser…
- Turn your pencil upside down.
- Use the eraser to write your words on a sheet of dark construction paper.
- Check your spelling.

Tactile

To spell your words with finger paint…
- Smear paint across your plate.
- Use a finger to write a spelling word in paint.
- Check your spelling.
- Smear the word out with your finger and write another word.

147

1 Missing Letters

Familiarize students with word meaning and usage.

Write **b_ g** on the board. Say the word **bug**. Invite the children to tell you what vowel is missing.

Each word is missing a letter or letters. Write the missing letters on the lines to make a spelling word.

F Missing Letters

Add the missing letters to each word.

Words With /i/

Lesson **8**

1. h im or is

2. w ill

3. i s

4. h is or im

5. i f

6. i n

7. w in

☆ f in ish

Word Bank

118

in	will	him	his	☆ begin
win	if	is	☆ finish	☆ into

 Take a minute to memorize...

Read the memory verse twice. Have students practice it with you two more times.

G Dictation

Name _____

Listen and write the missing words.

1. Get him his cup.

2. Dad will let him in the house.

3. God is glad I am kind.

H Proofreading

One word in each pair is misspelled. Fill in the oval by the misspelled word.

1. ● wehn
   ○ in

2. ○ if
   ● wil

3. ● hiz
   ○ win

4. ○ him
   ● eff

5. ● ien
   ○ will

6. ● heim
   ○ is

☆ ● finesh
   ○ thank

☆ ○ into
   ● begn

☆ ○ sum
   ● nto

119

---

1 Dictation

Reinforce correct spelling by using current and previous words in context.

 Say Listen as I read each sentence and then write it in your Worktext. (Slowly read each sentence twice. Sentences are found in the Student Worktext to the left.)

 Challenge
Write these incomplete sentences on the board.

Stephen ___ ___ to the ___ line to ___.

Miss Grant ___ ___ ___ to ___ the game.

She put the ___ ___ the ___.

 Say Listen as I read each sentence. Write the sentence on your paper. (Slowly read each sentence twice.)

Stephen <u>will</u> <u>run</u> to the <u>finish</u> line to <u>win</u>.

Miss Grant <u>can</u> <u>ask</u> <u>him</u> to <u>begin</u> the game.

She put the <u>cup</u> <u>into</u> the <u>box</u>.

---

2 Proofreading

Familiarize students with standardized test format and reinforce recognizing misspelled words.

 Say Look at each set of words. One word in each set is misspelled. Fill in the oval by the misspelled word. (You may wish to pronounce each set of words to help students correctly identify them.)

3 Hide and Seek

Reinforce correct spelling of current spelling words. (A reproducible master is provided in Appendix A as shown on the inset page to the right.)

Write the words one at a time on a white board.

Have students:

- **Look** at the word.
- **Say** the word out loud.
- **Spell** the word out loud.
- **Hide** (teacher erases word.)
- **Write** the word on paper.
- **Seek** (teacher rewrites word.)
- **Check** spelling. If incorrect, rewrite word correctly.

4 Word Find

Have your students complete this activity to strengthen spelling ability and expand vocabulary.

1 Posttest

Test mastery of the spelling words. Challenge words are starred.

 Say I will say the word once, use the word in a sentence, then say the word again. Write the word on your paper.

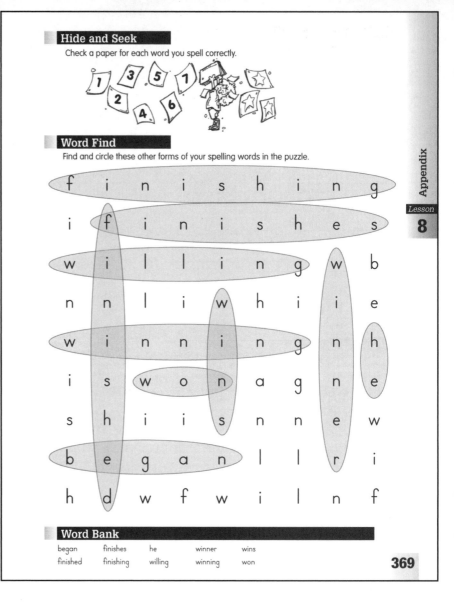

Hide and Seek
Check a paper for each word you spell correctly.

Word Find
Find and circle these other forms of your spelling words in the puzzle.

| f i n i s h i n g |
| i f i n i s h e s |
| w i l l i n g w b |
| n n l i w h i i e |
| w i n n i n g n h |
| i s w o n a g n e |
| s h i i s n n e w |
| b e g a n l l r i |
| h d w f w i l n f |

Word Bank

| began | finishes | he | winner | wins |
| finished | finishing | willing | winning | won |

1. **will** — Katelynn **will** twirl the jump rope.
2. **if** — Katelynn will have trouble breathing **if** she runs too much.
3. **win** — It is more important to do your best than to **win.**
4. **is** — It **is** important to choose our friends wisely.
5. **his** — He always keeps **his** desk very neat.
6. **in** — Katelynn had her medicine **in** case she had trouble with her asthma.
7. **him** — Dad will give **him** an allowance.
☆ **into** — The caterpillar turned **into** a butterfly.
☆ **begin** — We will **begin** reading a story.
☆ **finish** — He will **finish** his lunch.

 Progress Chart
Students may record scores. (Reproducible master in Appendix B.)

 Personal Dictionary
Students may add any words they have misspelled to their personal dictionaries for reference when writing. (Cover in Appendix B.)

150

I Game

Words With /i/

Lesson 8

Name _____

Cross out each **c**, **p**, and **u** with a big **X** to find the hidden spelling words. Using one crayon, softly color the boxes you did not mark so you can see your spelling words better.

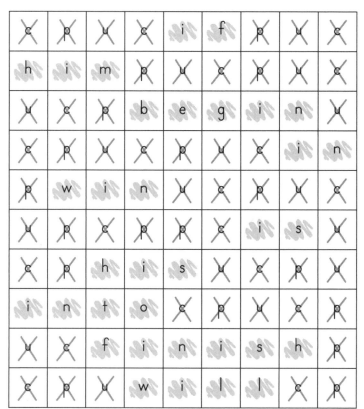

				i	f			
h	i	m						
			b	e	g	i	n	
							i	n
	w	i	n					
						i	s	
		h	i	s				
i	n	t	o					
		f	i	n	i	s	h	
			w	i	l	l		

Remember : Choose good friends who love God.

J Journaling

Copy and finish this sentence in your journal.
I am being a good friend when I...

120

How to Play:

- Have each student mark through each letter **c** found on the grid with a big **X**.
- Have each student mark through each letter **p** found on the grid with a big **X**.
- Have each student mark through each letter **u** found on the grid with a big **X**.
- Tell the students that the boxes without **X**'s contain their spelling words.
- Have the students color softly over the boxes without **X**'s so they can see their spelling words more clearly.
- Have the students follow along as you read and spell each word as it appears on the grid.

2 Game

Reinforce spelling skills and provide motivation and interest.

Materials

- game page (from student text)
- pencils (1 per child)
- crayons or colored pencils (1 per child)

Day 5

Lesson 8

3 Journaling

Provide a meaningful reason for correct spelling through personal writing.

Review the story using discussion leads provided on the following page. Encourage students to apply the Scriptural value in their journaling.

Take a minute to memorize...

Have the class say the memory verses from lessons 6, 7, and 8 with you.

151

Journaling (continued)

Say

- King Solomon said that we become like the people we choose to spend time with. Who was Katelynn around at recess every day? (Sandra and Elizabeth from the third grade class)

- What makes you think they were not good friends for Katelynn to choose? (They never asked Katelynn if she wanted a turn jumping rope. They just let her twirl the rope. They didn't try to get to know Katelynn and find out what she liked to do. They didn't say nice things about Sarah's clothes.)

- Was Katelynn starting to act like her new friends? (yes)

- Who noticed the change in Katelynn? (Her friend Beth and Beth's mom.)

- It is important to choose good friends and to be a good friend.

- Write in your journal about how to be a good friend.

Quotables!

"Spelling is more than rote memorization and drill."*

*Read, Charles, and Richard Hodges. 1982. "Spelling." In Encyclopedia of Educational Research, edited by H. Mitzel. 5th ed. New York: Macmillan.

Surprise from God!

Katelynn asks for God's help in making a difficult choice.

"**B**eth, Sandra invited me to her birthday party tomorrow. What should I do?" Katelynn showed Beth the brightly printed invitation.

"What did you tell her?"

"Well, I told her that I'd have to ask my mom. But I'm not sure I want to go." Katelynn sat down in the empty desk next to Beth's. "Remember what your mom said on the way home from the mall about trying to impress people by doing things we shouldn't do? And then Miss Grant told us about that King What's-his-name . . ."

"Solomon?" offered Beth.

"Yeah." Katelynn nodded. "He made a big mess of his kingdom by choosing the wrong friends. And now I'm not sure I really want to become better friends with Sandra."

"Maybe you could be a good friend to her, and teach her to make good choices," said Beth.

"I don't think she'd listen to me." Katelynn looked down. "She's in third grade."

"Tell your mom to say no!"

"But Sandra and her best friend Elizabeth are the only ones who talk to me at recess. Miss Grant always makes me go to the gym with the third graders because of my asthma!"

"Well . . . what could happen at a birthday party?" Beth shrugged. "Sandra's mom will be there won't she?"

Katelynn frowned. "Sandra's mom lets her do anything she wants. I don't think she'll be much help."

"We can always pray."

"Yes, but I wish King What's-his-name was still around to give me some advice," said Katelynn. "I don't know how God talks to little kids when they need an answer fast."

"Maybe your mom will know what to do. Miss Grant says sometimes God speaks to us through our parents." Beth took out a worktext. "Right now, though, we'd better finish our spelling words."

Soon school was over. Katelynn ran out to the car and plopped down in the front seat next to her mom. "Where is your sister?" Mom asked.

"Jen's class isn't out yet. Mr. Konupcik was still talking to them when I walked by." Katelynn paused. "Mom, Sandra wants to know if I can come to her birthday party tomorrow." She handed her mother the birthday invitation.

"Sandra SaintClair?" Mom raised her eyebrows. "The SaintClairs live over on Stoneridge Court next to the DeVores. Isn't she a fourth grader?"

"No, third."

"Why did she invite you?" Mom prodded.

"Well, Miss Grant has been making me go to the gym with the third graders for first recess. She says it's been too cold for me to go outside because of my asthma."

"Why would she say that?" Mom wondered aloud. "It hasn't been very cold yet. She seemed to understand when I explained the limitations of your asthma at registration."

"Oh, I was chasing that little creep Daniel DeVore who stole our four-square ball," Katelynn explained. "I'd just grabbed his coat when an episode started."

"And you didn't have your medication in your coat pocket," finished Mom.

"Yes, I did. It's just that I was breathing so hard I couldn't hold my breath after I inhaled the mist and didn't get a very good dose . . . so the episode lasted longer than usual. I think it scared Miss Grant."

"It was because you ran so hard," Mom pointed out, "not because you were outside in the cold."

"I know," Katelynn said. "But I get tired of explaining everything to everybody. Miss Grant was just trying to help."

"Is Sandra a nice girl?"

"She's the only one who talks to me at recess," said Katelynn. "I twirl the rope for her and her friend Elizabeth to jump rope."

"I see," said Mom. "Do you ever play anything else?"

"No, they like me to twirl the rope."

Mom turned to look closely at Katelynn. "Do you want to go to the party, Katelynn?"

"Not really, but I don't want them to think I don't like them. They're the only friends I have to play with at recess every morning."

"Hi, everyone!" Jennifer jumped in back and threw her stuff down beside her.

"Well, it's your choice," Mom said to Katelynn. "You can go to the party if you want to." She turned to look in the back seat. "Hi, Jen. Did you have a good day?"

"Dear Jesus," Katelynn prayed quietly in her mind. *"How do I decide what to do now?"*

As soon as they got home, Katelynn went into the kitchen to get a glass of orange juice. Opening the refrigerator door, she noticed her handwriting border sheet hanging there. "Be with wise men and become wise. Be with evil men and become evil. Proverbs 13:20," she read softly. *"Well,"* she thought to herself, *"wise King What's-his-name may be dead, but he's still giving advice! I think he's telling me I can't spend any more time with Sandra. I've got to tell her no. And I can't go to her party, even if I have to 'hold up the wall' all winter."*

Sandra was waiting for

153

Katelynn in the hall the next morning. "Are you coming to my birthday party, or what?"

"No, but thank you for asking me," Katelynn continued walking down the hall.

Sandra ran to catch up to her. "What happened? Did your mom say no?"

Katelynn swallowed. "It was my choice," she said.

"Oh, so you think you're too good for us, Lady Kaydee?" Sandra made an angry face. Suddenly the first bell rang, saving Katelynn from the uncomfortable conversation.

All morning long, she worried about first recess. Sandra was mad! She'd get the whole third grade class to be mean to her. "I hope I made the right choice," thought Katelynn.

As the children lined up for recess Katelynn was almost frantic. For the first time in her life she wished she could have an asthma episode! "Right about now would be just fine!" she mumbled into the collar of her coat. Just then, Miss Grant came up behind her.

"What did you say, Katelynn?" Miss Grant smiled down at her.

"Oh . . . uh, nothing important." She looked up sheepishly.

"Well, you can join us outside today if you'd like." Miss Grant placed a hand on Katelynn's shoulder as they walked down the hall. "Your mom called last night and helped me understand your asthma a little better. I'm sorry I overreacted to your last episode. It's just that I would feel terrible if something happened to you."

Katelynn was thrilled. She grabbed the four-square ball and danced out onto the playground. "Thank you, God," she said looking up at the sky. "Thank you for helping me do your will."

Then she rushed toward her friends. "Beth! Sarah! Kristin!" she yelled. "Let's play four square!"

2 Discussion Time

Check understanding of the story and development of personal values.

- What big choice did Katelynn have to make?
- Do you have hard choices to make like Katelynn?
- How did God help Katelynn?
- Did you know God loves to help us when we ask?
- Do you remember to pray when you need help?

154

A Preview

Write each word as your teacher says it.

Name _____

1. ball
2. law
3. all
4. jaw
5. call
6. fall
7. saw

Challenge Words

☆ small

☆ draw

☆ talk

Scripture
Psalm 143:10

121

 Challenge

For better spellers, challenge words may be included in the weekly list. Challenge words are starred.

 Correct Immediately!

Say — Let's correct our preview. I will write each word on the board. Put a dot under each letter on your preview as I spell the word out loud. If you spelled a word wrong, rewrite it correctly.

Progress Chart

Students may record scores. (Reproducible master in Appendix B.)

 **Take a minute to memorize . . .**

Read the memory verse twice. Have students practice it with you two more times.

---

3 Preview

Test for knowledge of the correct spellings of these words. (See the instructions at the top right for challenge words.)

Say — I will say each word once, use the word in a sentence, then say the word again. Write the word on the lines in the Worktext.

1.	ball	Katelynn grabbed the four square **ball**.
2.	law	We must obey the **law**.
3.	all	God can help us in **all** our problems.
4.	jaw	The ball hit the boy in the **jaw**.
5.	call	Mother will **call** us when it is time to eat.
6.	fall	The box is about to **fall** off the table.
7.	saw	Sandra **saw** Katelynn in the hall.
☆	small	This is a **small** balloon.
☆	draw	Did you **draw** this picture?
☆	talk	I will **talk** to my friends.

Word Shapes

Help students form a correct image of whole words.

 Look at each word and think about its shape. Now, write the word in the correct word Shape Boxes. You may check off each word as you use it.

(In some words /ô/ is spelled with **a**, and it is often spelled this way when it is followed by **l** or **ll**. In some words /ô/ is spelled with **aw**.)

 In the word shape boxes, color the letter or letters that spell the sound of /ô/ in each word.
Circle the words which have double consonants.

 Challenge
Draw the correctly shaped box around each letter in these words.

 On a separate sheet of paper, write other words that contain the spelling patterns in the word list. See how many words you can write.

B Word Shapes   Name _____

Write each word in the correct word shape boxes. Next, in the word shape boxes, color the letter or letters that spell the sound of /ô/ in each word. Circle the words which have double consonants.

Words With /ô/
Lesson **9**

1. all
2. ball
3. fall
4. call
5. saw
6. law
7. jaw

☆ **Challenge**
Draw the correct word shape boxes around each word.

small   talk   draw

122

Answers may vary for duplicate word shapes.

Be Prepared For Fun

Check these supply lists for **Fun Ways to Spell** presented **Day 2**.
Purchase and/or gather these items ahead of time!

General
- 3 x 5 Cards (7 per child)
- 3 x 5 Cards (3 more for challenge words)
- Scissors
- Spelling List

Auditory
- Spelling List

Visual
- Dry Bar of Soap (sample size works well)
- Hand Mirror
- Strong Paper Towel or Washcloth (dry)
- Spelling List

Tactile
- Play Dough
- Spelling List

156

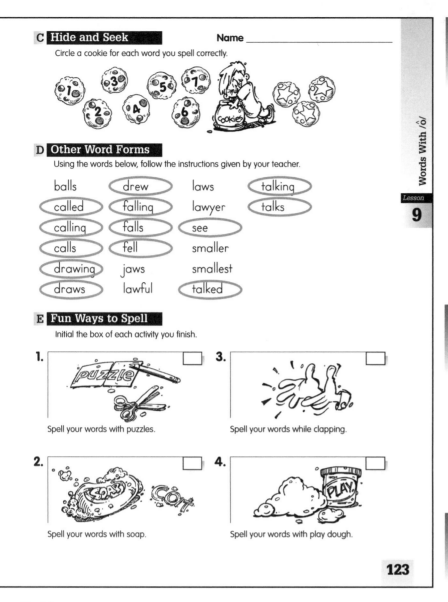

C Hide and Seek

Name _____

Circle a cookie for each word you spell correctly.

D Other Word Forms

Using the words below, follow the instructions given by your teacher.

balls   (drew)   laws   (talking)

(called)   (falling)   lawyer   (talks)

(calling)   (falls)   (see)

(calls)   (fell)   smaller

(drawing)   jaws   smallest

(draws)   lawful   (talked)

E Fun Ways to Spell

Initial the box of each activity you finish.

1. ☐
Spell your words with puzzles.

3. ☐
Spell your words while clapping.

2. ☐
Spell your words with soap.

4. ☐
Spell your words with play dough.

123

1 Hide and Seek

Reinforce spelling by using multiple styles of learning.

On a white board, Teacher writes each word—one at a time. **Have students:**

- **Look** at the word.
- **Say** the word out loud.
- **Spell** the word out loud.
- **Hide** (teacher erases word.)
- **Write** the word on their paper.
- **Seek** (teacher rewrites word.)
- **Check** spelling. If incorrect, repeat above steps.

2 Other Word Forms

This activity is optional. Have students find and circle the Other Word Forms that show action.

3 Fun Ways to Spell

Four activities are provided. Use one, two, three, or all of the activities. Have students initial the box for each activity they complete.

Options:

- assign activities to students according to their learning styles
- set up the activities in learning centers for students to do throughout the day
- divide students into four groups and assign one activity per group
- do one activity per day

General

To spell your words with puzzles…
- Write each word on a card.
- Cut each card squiggly, diagonal, or zigzag to make a puzzle.
- Mix your puzzle pieces.
- Put the puzzles together.
- Check your spelling.

Auditory

To spell your words while clapping…
- Look at a word on your spelling list.
- Close your eyes.
- Clap your hands softly while you whisper the spelling of the word.
- Open your eyes and check your spelling.

Visual

To spell your words with soap…
- Write a word on a hand mirror with a dry bar of soap.
- Check your spelling.
- Wipe the word off the mirror with a dry towel or washcloth.
- Write another word.

Tactile

To spell your words with play dough…
- Roll pieces of play dough into ropes.
- Use the ropes to make the letters of each word.
- Put them in the right order to spell each word.
- Check your spelling.

157

1 Word Find

Familiarize students with word meaning and usage.

Say Read each word in the Word Bank. Say each letter in the word, then look in the puzzle to find that same word. Circle each word you find. Write the secret word that is not in the puzzle on the lines underneath the puzzle.

Words With /ô/
Lesson **9**

F Word Find

Find and circle 9 words.

Name _____

g h k j d
t d r a w
a s a w f
l a w a a
k c a l l
s m a l l

One secret word is not used. Write it here.

ball

Word Bank

124

all	fall	saw	jaw	☆ talk
ball	call	law	☆ small	☆ draw

Take a minute to memorize...

Read the memory verse twice. Have students practice it with you two more times.

G Dictation

Listen and write the missing words.

Name _____

1. The ball hit his jaw.

2. I obey the law of God.

3. The man let us win.

H Proofreading

One word in each pair is misspelled. Fill in the oval by the misspelled word.

1. ● oll
   ○ his

2. ○ dog
   ● lov

3. ● kall
   ○ jaw

4. ○ law
   ● boll

5. ● sall
   ○ all

6. ○ call
   ● foll

☆ ● tock
   ○ back

☆ ○ still
   ● smoll

☆ ● drall
   ○ fall

125

---

1 Dictation

Reinforce correct spelling by using current and previous words in context.

Say) Listen as I read each sentence and then write it in your Worktext. (Slowly read each sentence twice. Sentences are found in the Student Worktext to the left.)

☆ Challenge

Write these incomplete sentences on the board.

___ ___ the ___ ___ ___.

___ ___ ___ to my ___ about our ___.

___ ___ ___ to ___ ___ pictures.

Say) Listen as I read each sentence. Write the sentence on your paper. (Slowly read each sentence twice.)

Mom saw the small red ball.

I will talk to my dad about our plan.

It is fun to draw funny pictures.

---

2 Proofreading

Familiarize students with standardized test format and reinforce recognizing misspelled words.

Say) Look at each set of words. One word in each set is misspelled. Fill in the oval by the misspelled word. (You may wish to pronounce each set of words to help students correctly identify them.)

159

3 Hide and Seek

Reinforce correct spelling of current spelling words. (A reproducible master is provided in Appendix A as shown on the inset page to the right.)
Write the words one at a time on a white board.
Have students:

- **Look** at the word.
- **Say** the word out loud.
- **Spell** the word out loud.
- **Hide** (teacher erases word.)
- **Write** the word on paper.
- **Seek** (teacher rewrites word.)
- **Check** spelling. If incorrect, rewrite word correctly.

4 Scrambled Words

Have your students complete this activity to strengthen spelling ability and expand vocabulary.

1 Posttest

Test mastery of the spelling words. Challenge words are starred.

 Say I will say the word once, use the word in a sentence, then say the word again. Write the word on your paper.

1.	law	It is important to obey God's **law.**
2.	all	We **all** played outside at recess.
3.	jaw	A shark has many teeth in its **jaw.**
4.	ball	Daniel ran off with the four square **ball.**
5.	fall	The leaves **fall** off the trees in autumn.
6.	saw	I **saw** some little fish in the creek.
7.	call	I'll **call** you tomorrow evening.
☆	small	The **small** dog has a very loud bark.
☆	talk	The baby is just learning to **talk.**
☆	draw	She will **draw** a picture of her family.

 Progress Chart
Students may record scores. (Reproducible master in Appendix B.)

 Personal Dictionary
Students may add any words they have misspelled to their personal dictionaries for reference when writing. (Cover in Appendix B.)

160

Appendix Lesson 9

Hide and Seek
Check a paper for each word you spell correctly.

Scrambled Words
Unscramble the letters to make a word. Write the word on the lines.

1. fslal — f a l l s
2. lalbs — b a l l s
3. rewaly — l a w y e r
4. kinglat — t a l k i n g
5. ringdaw — d r a w i n g
6. clingal — c a l l i n g

Word Bank
balls	drawing	lawyer
calling	falls	talking

370

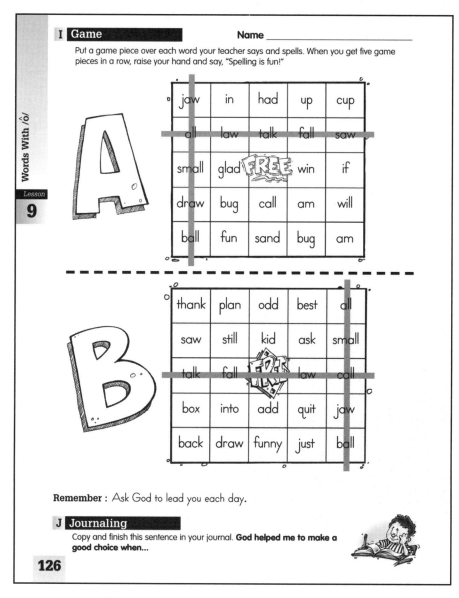

I Game

Name _____

Put a game piece over each word your teacher says and spells. When you get five game pieces in a row, raise your hand and say, "Spelling is fun!"

Card A:

jaw	in	had	up	cup
all	law	talk	fall	saw
small	glad	FREE	win	if
draw	bug	call	am	will
ball	fun	sand	bug	am

Card B:

thank	plan	odd	best	all
saw	still	kid	ask	small
talk	fall	FREE	law	call
box	into	add	quit	jaw
back	draw	funny	just	ball

Remember: Ask God to lead you each day.

J Journaling

Copy and finish this sentence in your journal. **God helped me to make a good choice when...**

126

2 Game

Reinforce spelling skills and provide motivation and interest.

Materials

- game page (from student text)
- flat buttons, dry beans, pennies, or game discs (10 per child)
- game word list
- word cards (each word from the game word list written on a card)

Game Word List

This list contains regular and challenge words.

1. **all**
2. **small**
3. **ball**
4. **talk**
5. **fall**
6. **draw**
7. **call**
☆ **saw**
☆ **law**
☆ **jaw**

3 Journaling

Provide a meaningful reason for correct spelling through personal writing.

Review the story using discussion leads provided on the following page. Encourage students to apply the Scriptural value in their journaling.

Take a minute to memorize...

Have the class say the memory verses from lessons 6, 7, 8, and 9 with you.

How to Play:

- Fold the word cards (see **Materials**) in half, and place them in a container.
- Ask your students to fold the game page in half along the dotted line.
- Have half the class use game card A, and the other half card B.
- Instructions for the students: "Cover the word **FREE** in the center of your card. (pause) I will draw a word from the container, read it aloud, then I will spell it. When you find that word on your card, put a game piece over it. When you have five game pieces in a row (up and down, across, or diagonally), raise your hand and say 'Spelling is FUN!'"
- Play as many times as you like. (As you return the word cards to the container and mix them up, remind the students to clear their game cards.)
- For variety, after playing several games, have the students turn their papers over and use the other game card.

161

Journaling (continued)

Say
- Katelynn had a big choice to make. How did she make the choice? (She asked her friend Beth. She thought about what Beth's mom had told her on the way home from the mall. She thought about the Scripture verses Miss Grant had taught her. She talked to her mom. She prayed.)
- Think about the choice Katelynn made. Do you think it was a good one?
- In your journal, write about when God helped you make a good choice.

Quotables!

"The kinds of errors that achieving children make change systematically, and each new stage reflects a logical step toward mastery of our complex spelling system."*

*Henderson, Edmund, 1985. Teaching Spelling. Boston Houghton Mifflin Company.

The Math Test

Tommy is tempted to cheat on a test.

"Good morning, Tommy!" Mother shook Tommy's shoulder gently. "Time to get up. Breakfast will be ready when you get downstairs." Tommy sat up, stretched, and yawned. He peered out the window through sleep-dimmed eyes. Sure enough, the sun was already up and shining brightly.

A few minutes later, Tommy bounced down the stairs. Mother was pouring pancake batter into a hot skillet on the stove. "Mmmm, my favorite breakfast!" Tommy gave his mother a hug. "Thanks, Mom."

"Call your sister while I make the orange juice, please, then we'll be ready to eat." Mom flipped another pancake with the spatula.

When Tommy returned to the kitchen, he noticed a small piece of paper in the middle of his plate. "What's this, Mom?" He held it up.

"Let's see . . ." Mom tilted her head as she read it aloud to Tommy.

"Dear Son," the note said, "I hope you do well on your math test today. Remember, doing your best is the important thing. I will pray for you today, and ask God to help you remember what you've practiced. I love you, Dad."

"The math test!" thought Tommy. A worried look quickly covered his face.

"Mom, does this sweater look all right with these jeans?" Tommy's sister, Lisa, took her place at the table and reached for the pitcher of orange juice.

Mrs. Rawson glanced at Lisa's red sweater and blue jeans. "They look fine together, Sweetheart." She carried the plate of pancakes to the table. "Will you say the blessing?"

"Dear Jesus," Lisa prayed as the family bowed their heads, "Thank you for this good breakfast and this sunny day. And dear Jesus, please help Tommy with his math test today. Amen."

"The math test!" Tommy frowned. "Mom," he said aloud, "What if I don't do well on my math test?" Mrs. Rawson poured maple syrup on her stack of pancakes and passed the syrup to Lisa before answering.

"Just do your best, Tommy." Mom looked thoughtfully at Tommy's serious face. "You've practiced your addition and subtraction facts every night with your dad and done your assignment every day. It will be all right."

"Yeah, Tommy, your math's not hard anyway!" Lisa said around a mouthful of pancake. "Just wait until you get to third grade. We really have tough stuff to learn in my math class!"

"Lisa, please don't talk with your mouth full." Mother shook her head. "And remember, each of us is good at different things. Math is easier for some of us than for others."

Soon they were on their way to school. As Mrs. Rawson stopped the car by the curb, she smiled and ruffled Tommy's hair. "Have a good day, son, and don't worry about that math test."

"Okay." Tommy scrambled out of the car and headed for the building. "Bye, Mom."

"Hey, Tommy! Wait for me!" Tommy's best friend James ran up the walk, his backpack and jacket flying. "Are you ready for the math test?"

"The math test!" Tommy frowned thoughtfully. "I guess so," he mumbled aloud, then added, "Let's play baseball at recess, okay?"

"Sure." James opened the door, and the boys got to their desks just in time

for class to start.

All morning Tommy worried about the math test. Math was really hard for him and it seemed to take him longer than anyone else. At recess Tommy, James, and a group of boys and girls played baseball. When it was Tommy's turn to bat, there were runners on first and third. The first pitch went wide. Tommy was ready for the second pitch, and whacked it over the right fielder's head. "Way to go, Tommy!" "Run, run!" "All right!" "What a hit!" The kids were all yelling at once as Tommy rounded the bases and slid into home. "Three runs for our team. Yea, Tommy!" Tommy grinned as his team members slapped him on the back.

But as the kids headed back to the classroom Tommy's grin faded and his steps began to lag. "The math test!" he thought to himself. "Why can't I be as good at math as I am at baseball?"

Daniel walked up beside Tommy. "Hey, I've got something for you!" he whispered. He slipped a tightly folded piece of paper into Tommy's hand just as they entered the classroom. "It's the answers to the math test! I copied them when I came in to use the bathroom during recess."

A few moments later, Miss Grant passed out the test papers, and gave directions. The room quieted quickly as the test began. Soon the ticking of the clock and scraping of pencils on paper were the only sounds in the silence.

Tommy twirled his pencil between his fingers as he read the first problem. Then he glanced down at the slip of paper in his hand. It would be so easy to open it under the edge of his desk. All the answers would be right there. He wouldn't be the last one to finish the test this time. He wouldn't have to struggle to figure out the answers to each problem. He wouldn't get any of the answers wrong if he used the paper. He would get a good grade. His mom and dad would be proud of him if he didn't miss any of the problems on the test.

Or would they? He

163

Review 10 | **Day 1**

remembered another piece of paper — the one Dad had left on his plate that morning. Dad was praying for him today. Mom wanted him to do his best. Tommy sighed and stuck the tightly folded piece of paper deep in his pocket. Then he read the first problem again.

That night, Lisa and Tommy were playing together in the back yard. "Time for supper!" Mom called out the back door.

"Race you to the porch!" Tommy yelled. He leapt to his feet, and he and Lisa ran toward the house.

"It's a tie!" Lisa laughed as they bounded up the back steps together. "You're getting pretty fast for a little brother!"

"Looks like you two are full of energy!" Dad set a bowl of spaghetti on the table as the children came in. "Did you have a good day?"

"I got to read my book report to the whole class." Lisa bubbled happily. "And Mr. Valentino said I did a really good job of writing it."

Mom carried the garlic bread to the table and sat down. "How'd the math test go, Tommy?" she asked.

"Well, it took me a long time," Tommy answered slowly. "Miss Grant let me finish it during lunch recess." Tommy paused, then smiled brightly. "But, I only missed five."

"Way to go, Tommy!" Mother beamed.

"Good job, Son!" Dad patted Tommy on the back. "That's better than you've ever done before. You practiced and did your best, and we're very proud of you."

Tommy grinned, thinking how glad he was that he hadn't cheated on the math test. Then he laughed out loud as Lisa gave him a high five, and exclaimed, "All right! Good job, Tommy!"

2 Discussion Time

Check understanding of the story and development of personal values.

- Is there something that you find very hard to do like math was very hard for Tommy?
- What choice did Tommy have to make?
- Why was it hard for Tommy to choose?
- Do you think that Tommy made the best choice? Why or why not?
- Our verse for this week says, "God blesses those who obey Him; happy the man who puts his trust in the Lord." (Proverbs 16:20) How do you think that Tommy's choice proves this Scripture?
- Did you know that when you choose to obey God in everything that you will have true happiness inside?

A | Test-Words

Name _____

Write each word as your teacher says it.

1. up
2. hug
3. had
4. and
5. in
6. if
7. saw
8. all

☆ **Test-Challenge Words**

On a sheet of paper, write each challenge word as your teacher says it.

Scripture

Proverbs 16:20

 Test-Challenge Words

On a separate sheet of paper, challenge words may be tested using the sentences below.

 Personal Dictionary

After the tests in the review unit are graded, students may add any words they have misspelled to their personal dictionaries.

Take a minute to memorize...

Have the class say the memory verses from lessons 1, 2, 3, and 4 with you.

127

---

3 | Test-Words

Test for knowledge of the correct spellings of these words. (See the instructions at the top right for challenge words.)

 (Say) I will say each word once, use the word in a sentence, then say the word again. Write the word on the lines in your Worktext.

1. up — Tommy heard someone call, "Time to get **up**."
2. hug — Mother gave Tommy a **hug**.
3. had — Tommy **had** a hard time with math.
4. and — Lisa **and** Tommy raced to the back porch.
5. in — What is **in** your cup?
6. if — Tommy wondered, "What **if** I don't do well on my math test?"
7. saw — We **saw** a rainbow in the sky!
8. all — Tommy worried about the math test **all** morning.
☆ just — "Tommy, **just** do your best," said Mrs. Rawson.
☆ plan — Did Lisa **plan** to wear her red sweater?
☆ finish — Tommy was able to **finish** his math test during recess.
☆ small — Daniel gave Tommy a **small** piece of paper.

1 Game

Materials

- game page (from student text)
- pencils or crayons (1 per child)
- game word list

Game Word List

Use of challenge words is optional.

1. **up**
2. **hug**
3. **had**
4. **and**
5. **in**
6. **if**
7. **saw**
8. **all**
☆ **just**
☆ **plan**
☆ **finish**
☆ **small**

B Game   Name _____

In the story from lesson 6, Rosa learned that the earth belongs to God and that we should take care of it. Circle one aluminum can for each review word you or your team spells correctly.

Review

Lesson **10**

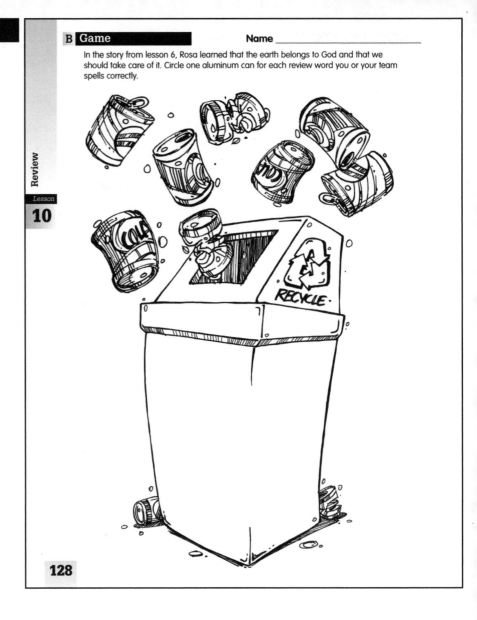

128

How to Play:

- Divide the class into two teams, and decide which team will go first.
- Have a student from team A go to the board.
- Read the spelling word two times slowly and clearly. (You may also wish to use the word in a sentence. Ex.: "cat — The cat climbed a tree. — cat")
- Have the student write the word on the board.
- If the word is spelled correctly, instruct all the members of team A to circle one aluminum can. (Note: If the word is misspelled, correct the spelling immediately before continuing the game.)
- Alternate between teams A and B as you go down the word list.
- The team with the most aluminum cans circled when you have gone through the game word list twice is the winner.

Non-Competitive Option:

At the end of the game, say: "Class, I am proud of your efforts to spell the words correctly. If you had fun and tried your best, you are all winners!"

C Test-Sentences   Name _____

The underlined word in each sentence is misspelled. Write the sentences on the lines below, spelling each underlined word correctly.

Can Tommy <u>ron</u>?

1. Can Tommy run?

Daniel put a paper in Tommy's <u>hend</u>.

2. Daniel put a paper in Tommy's hand.

D Test-Proofreading

One word in each pair is misspelled. Fill in the oval by the misspelled word.

1. ○ bug
   ● hin

2. ● jow
   ○ fun

3. ○ am
   ● fn

4. ● wil
   ○ land

5. ● foll
   ○ will

6. ○ him
   ● buq

7. ○ his
   ● em

8. ● lan
   ○ fall

9. ○ jaw
   ● hiz

☆ **Test-Challenge Words**

On a sheet of paper, write each challenge word as your teacher says it.

129

 Test-Sentences

1

Reinforce recognizing misspelled words.

 Read each sentence carefully. The underlined word in each sentence is misspelled. Write the sentences on the lines in your worktext, spelling each underlined word correctly.

2 **Test-Proofreading**

Familiarize students with standardized test format and reinforce recognition of misspelled words.

 Look at each set of words. One word in each set is misspelled. Fill in the oval by the misspelled word.

(You may wish to pronounce each pair of words to help students correctly identify them.)

 Test-Challenge Words

On a separate sheet of paper, challenge words may be tested using the sentences below.

 I will say the word once, use the word in a sentence, then say the word again. Write the word on your paper.

☆ **funny**   Lisa says **funny** things to tease Tommy.
☆ **back**   Tommy's team members slapped him on the **back** excitedly.
☆ **begin**   Miss Grant said it was time to **begin** the math test.
☆ **talk**   "Do not **talk** during the test," said Miss Grant.

167

1 Game

Materials
- game page (from student text)
- pencils or crayons (1 per child)
- game word list

Game Word List
Use of challenge words is optional.

1. **run**
2. **hand**
3. **bug**
4. **fun**
5. **am**
6. **land**
7. **will**
8. **him**
9. **his**
10. **fall**
11. **jaw**
   ☆ **funny**
   ☆ **back**
   ☆ **begin**
   ☆ **talk**

E Game

Name _____

Tommy's mom wanted to make pancakes for him the morning of his math test. Here is her list of things to buy for his favorite breakfast. Place an **X** by an item each time you or your team spells a review word correctly.

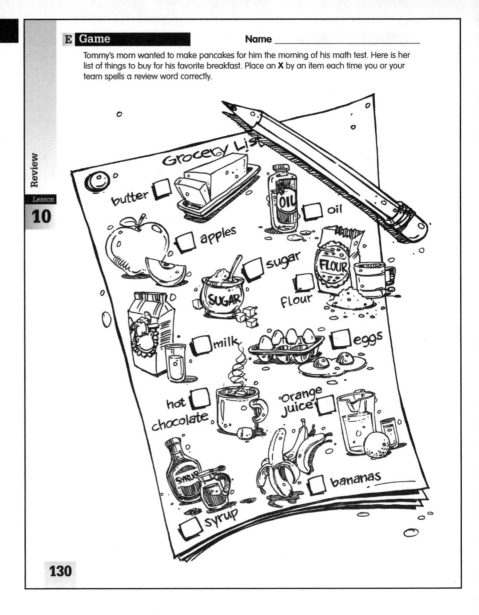

130

How to Play:

- Divide the class into two teams, and decide which team will go first.
- Have a student from team A go to the board.
- Read the spelling word two times slowly and clearly. (You may also wish to use the word in a sentence. Ex.: "cat — The cat climbed a tree. — cat")
- Have the student write the word on the board.
- If the word is spelled correctly, instruct all the members of team A to put an X in the box by one item on the grocery list. (Note: If the word is misspelled, correct the spelling immediately before continuing the game.)
- Alternate between teams A and B as you go down the word list.
- The team to have the most items checked off the grocery list when you have gone through the game word list twice is the winner.

Non-Competitive Option:
At the end of the game, say: "Class, I am proud of your efforts to spell the words correctly. If you had fun and tried your best, you are all winners!"

F Test-Sentence

Name _____

The underlined word in this sentence is misspelled. Write the sentence on the lines below, spelling the underlined word correctly.

Mother said, "<u>Coll</u> your sister."

Mother said, "Call

your sister."

G Test-Words

Write each word as your teacher says it.

1. cup   5. win

2. us   6. is

3. glad   7. ball

4. sand   8. law

☆ **Test-Challenge Words**

On a sheet of paper, write each challenge word as your teacher says it.

131

Test-Sentence

Reinforce recognizing misspelled words.

 Read this sentence carefully. The underlined word is misspelled. Write the sentence on the lines in your Worktext, spelling the underlined word correctly.

Personal Dictionary

Remind students to add any words they have misspelled to their personal dictionaries.

Test-Words

Test for knowledge of the correct spellings of these words. (Challenge words may be tested on a separate piece of paper. Challenge words are starred.)

 I will say each word once, use the word in a sentence, then say the word again. Write the word on the lines in your Worktext.

1. cup   Mother measured one **cup** of flour.
2. us   Do you want to play baseball with **us**?
3. glad   Tommy was **glad** he had not cheated.
4. sand   Let's make a castle in the **sand**.
5. win   Tommy helped his team **win** a baseball game.
6. is   It **is** important never to cheat.
7. ball   Tommy hit the **ball** over the right fielder's head.
8. law   We choose to obey God's **law**.
☆ sum   Tommy wrote the **sum** of three plus five.
☆ grand   Tommy hit a **grand** slam at recess.
☆ into   Daniel ran **into** the bathroom to write the test answers.
☆ draw   The students may **draw** pictures after the math test.

3 Writing Assessment

Assess student's spelling, grammar, and composition skills through personal writing.

(Say)

- Why is it important to obey our parents and teachers? (Because they are older; they understand what's best for us.)

- Why is it important to obey God? (He made us and knows what is best for us. We can only be truly happy and healthy by obeying His rules.)

- What did Tommy think about doing that would have been disobedient? (Cheating on the test.)

- All of us are tempted to disobey sometimes. What are some temptations you might face? (To cheat like Tommy, to lie, to take something that isn't yours, to say things that you shouldn't, etc.)

- What should we do when we are tempted? (Ask God to help us obey Him.)

- Finish the sentence in your worktext by writing what you should do when you are tempted like Tommy.

H **Writing Assessment**
Finish this sentence.

Name _____

Review Lesson **10**

When I am tempted to cheat I need to

_____

_____

_____

_____

Remember : Trust God and He will bless you.

132

A rubric for scoring is provided in Appendix B.

---

4 Action Game

Reinforce spelling skills and provide motivation and interest.

Materials
- audio player with music
- one **A Reason For Spelling®** book
- a bell (optional)
- small prizes (erasers, pencils, stickers)

How to Play:

Seat the children in a circle. Give one student the **A Reason For Spelling®** book. Have the students pass the book around the circle. When the teacher rings the bell (or says, "stop"), have the child holding the book spell a word from this review unit. If he spells it incorrectly, he remains in the circle; if he spells it correctly, he receives a prize and drops out of the game. Continue the game until every student has spelled a word correctly.

170

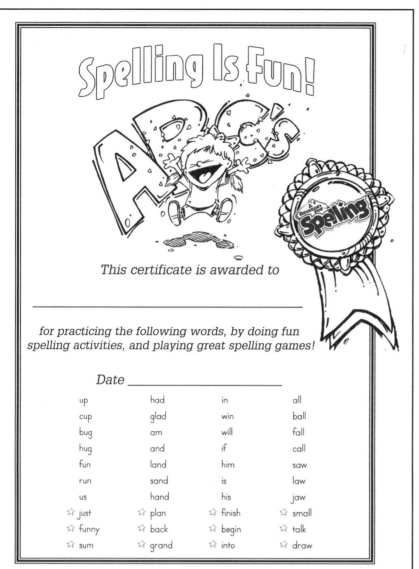

Spelling Is Fun!

This certificate is awarded to

_____

for practicing the following words, by doing fun spelling activities, and playing great spelling games!

Date _____

up	had	in	all
cup	glad	win	ball
bug	am	will	fall
hug	and	if	call
fun	land	him	saw
run	sand	is	law
us	hand	his	jaw
☆ just	☆ plan	☆ finish	☆ small
☆ funny	☆ back	☆ begin	☆ talk
☆ sum	☆ grand	☆ into	☆ draw

5 Certificate

Provide an opportunity for parents or guardians to encourage and assess their child's progress.

Say
- Write your name on the first line.
- Now I will write the date on the board for you to copy on the next line.
- Follow along as I read the certificate out loud.
- Be sure to show your parents or guardian all the words you've practiced spelling.

Take a minute to memorize...

Read the memory verse to the class twice. Have the class practice it with you two more times.

Review 10 | Day 5

Quotables!

"You may choose not to correct spelling errors if the child is not considered ready to learn a spelling pattern or concept."*

*Lutz, Elaine. 1986. ERIC/RCS Report: Invented Spelling and Spelling Development. Language Arts, Vol. 63, No. 7, November: 742-744.

6 Letter

Provide the parent or guardian with the spelling word lists for the next unit.

(Say) Show your parents or guardian this letter that tells them what your spelling words will be for the next unit. Ask them to put it in a special place where you will remember to practice them together.

Dear Parent,

We are about to begin a new spelling unit containing four weekly lessons. A set of seven words plus three challenge words will be studied each week. All the words will be reviewed in the fifth week.

Values based on the Scriptures listed below will be taught in each lesson.

Lesson 11	Lesson 12	Lesson 13	Lesson 14
he	much	may	time
she	but	day	nice
me	cut	away	ice
we	stop	play	wide
see	hop	made	side
feet	top	make	ride
eat	cot	take	hide
☆ each	☆ such	☆ grade	☆ line
☆ he's	☆ clock	☆ pray	☆ write
☆ we'll	☆ drop	☆ came	☆ kind
Psalm 13:6	Prov. 14:31	Prov. 10:22	Psalm 119:80

The Clubhouse Castle

Tommy discovers God has given him more blessings than he'd ever realized before.

"Mom! Mom! Guess what?" Tommy piled into the back seat of the car after school. "Daniel invited James and me over to his house to play in his new Clubhouse Castle! It's got a wavy slide, and swings, and a rope ladder, and a sandbox, and a trapeze-thing, and a clubhouse way up high with a red and blue tent top on it. It's even got a telescope so you can look all around! He got it for his birthday last week. Can I go? Please? Can I go?"

"Whoa, Son! Slow down a little bit," Mom laughed. "Is your seat belt buckled? Okay, now, what's this about going to Daniel's house?"

"Daniel said his mom said he could have some kids over tomorrow after school to play in his new Clubhouse Castle." Tommy bounced on the seat with excitement. "Can I go, please?"

Mom slowed the car and signaled for a left turn. "Well, Lisa has a dentist's appointment tomorrow at four, so I could probably drop you off at Daniel's house on our way and pick you up when we head home." Mrs. Rawson smiled in the rear view mirror at her wide-eyed son. "I'll call Daniel's mother tonight and make sure that it's okay with her."

"That's just great," Lisa pouted. "You get to go play, and I have to go to the dentist. It's not fair!"

"Well, you got to go to Julie's party last week," Tommy pointed out, "and I had to stay home because I was sick!"

"That's enough, kids." Mom pulled the car into a parking space at the store. Lisa and Tommy followed Mom inside and down the aisles. Mom put paper towels, laundry soap, and other household necessities in the cart.

"Look, Mom. Can I have one of these pens that writes in squiggles?" Tommy begged. "It's so cool!"

"No, dear," Mom answered. "You may save your allowance for a pen like that if you'd like."

"Oh, Mom, look!" Lisa exclaimed. "Look at these little diaries! You can even lock them with a tiny key." She pointed to a large display. "Aren't they cute? May I have one, please?"

"No, Sweetheart. But they are cute." Mrs. Rawson wheeled the cart into another aisle. As they passed the toy section, the bright displays of all the latest gadgets caught the children's eyes.

"Wow! Here's a remote control car that goes two speeds!" Tommy grabbed his mother's arm in excitement. "Mom, please, can I get it?"

"No, Son. You already have a remote control car a lot like that one," Mom answered patiently.

"Well, can I get a new matchbox car?" Tommy countered. "I don't have one like this Ferrari."

"No, Tommy."

"Why can't we get anything?" Tommy demanded. "Daniel gets new stuff all the time. We never get anything that we want!" An angry frown wrinkled his face as he placed the car back on the shelf.

"Yeah, we never get anything we want," Lisa echoed with a matching frown.

"It's true that you don't get everything you want, but it's not true that you don't get anything you want." Mom's voice remained calm, but firm. "Now, let's finish the shopping we need to do without any more complaining."

"It's just not fair," Tommy thought to himself as he and Lisa trailed behind Mrs. Rawson while she finished her shopping. *"Mom and Dad should treat us just like Daniel's parents treat him, and get us lots of toys and things, too."*

Later that night, after Dad had tucked Tommy in bed, Mom came into his room. She sat on the edge of his bed, and straightened his covers. "You know, Tommy, the Bible tells us about a man called David."

"You mean the shepherd boy?" Tommy said sleepily.

"That's right, Sweetheart." Mom rubbed Tommy's back softly. "David was a shepherd, a warrior, and a king. Sometimes, he must have been very lonely watching the sheep all day by himself. Later, the king was angry with him, and David had to flee for his life. Often he didn't even have a place to sleep. Still later, when David became king, he had many, many problems. His own son tried to take the kingdom away from him. But David loved God. And even though everything didn't go just the way he wanted it in his life, he knew that God loved him, too. David wrote, 'I will sing to the Lord because He has blessed me so richly.'" Mom paused. "Maybe you should think about that verse, Tommy. Hasn't God blessed you, too?" Mom gave Tommy a hug and a kiss. "I love you, Son. Good night."

"Good night, Mommy." Tommy snuggled deeper under the covers and closed his eyes.

When Mom pulled up after school the next afternoon, an excited Tommy ran to the car with his best friend James in tow. "Can we give James a ride to Daniel's, then take him home afterwards?" asked Tommy. His mother nodded. "Hey, where's Lisa? Isn't she coming? What's taking her so long?" Questions tumbled out as Tommy and James climbed into the back seat. Lisa came out a few minutes later, and Mom headed for Daniel's part of town.

"Here, Lisa." Mom handed her daughter a small slip of paper. "Please read me the directions Daniel's mother gave on the phone last night." Following the directions, they made two right turns, then a left. The houses seemed to grow larger and larger as they drove along. Tall fences with drive-through gates surrounded huge green lawns.

"Number 258, Stoneridge Court. There it is!" Lisa pointed to a very large, lovely-looking home. "That huge white brick house with the big columns in front!"

Mom stopped in the driveway, then walked the boys to the double front doors and rang the bell. In a moment a tall woman in an elegant black dress answered the door.

"Oh, hello. You must be the boys Daniel invited. He's in the backyard." She pointed across a spacious room with marble tile floors and peach colored furniture. "Go right through those french doors, and you can join him out there."

"I'll pick you up about 5:30," Tommy's mother reminded the boys as they headed out the french doors. Then she turned to thank Daniel's mother.

The three boys had a wonderful time. They imagined they were pirates climbing the rope ladder, soldiers building defenses in the sand box, and rangers watching for forest fires through the shiny telescope.

Soon Daniel's mother called to them from the broad patio ringed with shrubs. "Boys, you should come in now. There's hot chocolate on the kitchen counter." The boys trooped into the house and followed Daniel into the kitchen. "Daniel!" his mother shouted harshly. "Look what you've done! You've gotten sand all over my new Persian carpet!" Her voice grew louder with each word. "Just look at you! If I've told you once, I've told you a hundred times to clean up before you come in! Why can't you ever learn!" Tommy and James shrank back from the angry woman, still clutching their warm mugs of hot chocolate.

"Oh, the housekeeper will clean it up." Daniel picked up a mug.

"Don't you talk back to me like that!" his mother

shrieked. "You get right back outside this instant!" Tommy and James scurried for the door. As Daniel turned to follow them out, the mug in his hand tipped and hot chocolate splashed on the white counter and tile floor. "Now look what you've done!" Daniel's mother shook with rage. "You're such a clumsy child! Why can't you do anything right!" Her angry voice followed them into the yard.

A little later the housekeeper came out to tell them that Tommy's mother was back. "Go around the garage through the side yard," she pointed. "There's a gate over there you can use." Tommy and James thanked Daniel for inviting them, then hurried out to the warm car.

Later that night, Mom and Dad tucked Tommy into bed. "Good night, Tommy. We love you." Mom smiled as Dad gave Tommy a final good night squeeze. They turned off his light, and left the room holding hands.

Tommy snuggled deep under the covers and gazed around his room. His seashell night light cast a soft glow across the big stuffed bear with the torn ear, and his growing rock collection. Some of the cars lined up on the top shelf reflected the light; some were too old to be shiny anymore. Tommy sighed with contentment. He didn't have all the latest toys and things like Daniel, but he sure had a good home, and a mother and father who loved him.

"Thank you, God," Tommy whispered into the dark. "Thank you for all my blessings."

2 Discussion Time

Check understanding of the story and development of personal values.

- Why did Tommy wish that his parents were more like Daniel's parents?
- When Tommy was at Daniel's house, what did he learn about Daniel's mom that made him glad to have his own parents after all?
- We call the good things that God gives us our blessings. Are blessings always things that we can touch?
- Can you name some blessings that Tommy had?
- Have there been times when you have seen something that some of your friends have, or something that you want and think you just have to have?
- What do you do if your parents say no?

174

A Preview

Write each word as your teacher says it.

Name _____

1. me

2. eat

3. see

4. feet

5. she

6. we

7. he

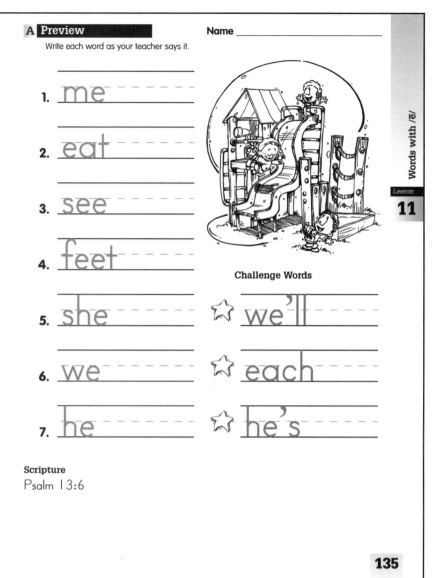

Challenge Words

 we'll

 each

 he's

Scripture
Psalm 13:6

135

Challenge

For better spellers, challenge words may be included in the weekly list. Challenge words are starred.

Correct Immediately!

Say

Let's correct our preview. I will write each word on the board. Put a dot under each letter on your preview as I spell the word out loud. If you spelled a word wrong, rewrite it correctly.

Progress Chart

Students may record scores. (Reproducible master in Appendix B.)

Take a minute to memorize . . .

Read the memory verse twice. Have students practice it with you two more times.

3 Preview

Test for knowledge of the correct spellings of these words. (See the instructions at the top right for challenge words.)

 Say

I will say each word once, use the word in a sentence, then say the word again. Write the word on the lines in the Worktext.

1.	me	God loves **me**.
2.	eat	He will **eat** an apple.
3.	see	I **see** six kittens.
4.	feet	The thick socks kept his **feet** warm.
5.	she	Did **she** give the boys some hot chocolate?
6.	we	When are **we** going to the store?
7.	he	I think **he** will share his toys with us.
☆	we'll	Then **we'll** pretend that we are firemen.
☆	each	There is one cookie for **each** of us.
☆	he's	Do you think **he's** happy to be home again?

175

4 Word Shapes

Help students form a correct image of whole words.

 Say Look at each word and think about its shape. Now, write the word in the correct word Shape Boxes. You may check off each word as you use it.

(In many words, the sound of /ē/ is spelled with **e, ee,** or **ea.**)

 Say In the word shape boxes, color the letter or letters that spell the sound of /ē/ in each word.
Circle the words that have two vowels together.
Draw a line under the words that end with the sound of /ē/.

Challenge
Draw the correctly shaped box around each letter in these words.

 Say On a separate sheet of paper, write other words that contain the spelling patterns in the word list. See how many words you can write.

 Be Prepared For Fun
Check these supply lists for **Fun Ways to Spell** presented **Day 2.**
Purchase and/or gather these items ahead of time!

B Word Shapes   **Name** _____

Write each word in the correct word shape boxes. Next, in the word shape boxes, color the letter or letters that spell the sound of /ē/ in each word. Circle the words that have two vowels together. Draw a line under the words that end with the sound of /ē/.

 Words with /ē/ — Lesson 11

1. he
2. she
3. me
4. we
5. see
6. feet
7. eat

she

see

eat

feet

me

we

he

☆ **Challenge**
Draw the correct word shape boxes around each word.

each   he's   we'll

136

Answers may vary for duplicate word shapes.

General
- Crayons
- 3 x 5 Cards cut in thirds (19 pieces per child)
- 3 x 5 Cards cut in thirds (13 more pieces for challenge words)
- Glue
- Construction Paper (about 3 pieces per child)
- Spelling List

Auditory
- Spelling List

Visual
- Sidewalk Chalk
- Spelling List

Tactile
- Damp Sand (in plastic storage box with lid)
- Spelling list

C Hide and Seek

Name _____

Circle a cookie for each word you spell correctly.

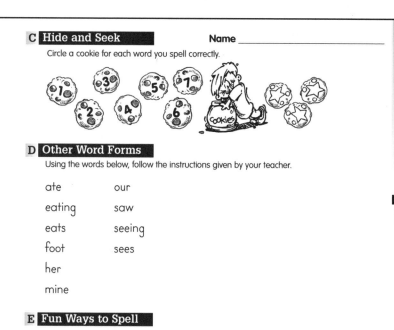

D Other Word Forms

Using the words below, follow the instructions given by your teacher.

ate	our
eating	saw
eats	seeing
foot	sees
her	
mine	

E Fun Ways to Spell

Initial the box of each activity you finish.

1.  ☐

Spell your words with crayons.

3.  ☐

Spell your words out loud.

2.  ☐

Spell your words with sidewalk chalk.

4.  ☐

Spell your words in wet sand.

137

1 Hide and Seek

Reinforce spelling by using multiple styles of learning.

On a white board, Teacher writes each word — one at a time. **Have students:**

- **Look** at the word.
- **Say** the word out loud.
- **Spell** the word out loud.
- **Hide** (teacher erases word.)
- **Write** the word on their paper.
- **Seek** (teacher rewrites word.)
- **Check** spelling. If incorrect, repeat above steps.

2 Other Word Forms

This activity is optional. Have students dictate original sentences to you using these Other Word Forms. Write them on the board.

foot   **eats**
seeing

3 Fun Ways to Spell

Four activities are provided. Use one, two, three, or all of the activities. Have students initial the box for each activity they complete.

Options:

- assign activities to students according to their learning styles
- set up the activities in learning centers for students to do throughout the day
- divide students into four groups and assign one activity per group
- do one activity per day

General

To spell your words with crayons…
- Write each letter of your spelling word on a card.
- Glue the cards on a sheet of paper in the right order to spell your words.
- Check your spelling.

Auditory

To spell your words out loud…
- Have your classmate read a spelling word.
- Say a sentence with that spelling word to your classmate.
- Spell the spelling word you used in that sentence to your classmate.
- Ask your classmate to check your spelling.
- Do this with each word on your word list.

Visual

- To spell your words with sidewalk chalk…
- Write each of your words on the sidewalk (ball court or playground).
- Check your spelling.

Tactile

To spell your words in damp sand…
- Use your finger to write a spelling word in the damp sand.
- Check your spelling.
- Smooth the sand with your finger and write another word.

1 Sentence Fun

Familiarize students with word meaning and usage. Using words from the Word Bank, write the spelling word that best completes each sentence.

Challenge

Read these incomplete sentences to your better spellers. Have them write the challenge word that best completes each sentence.

- __ a good friend. (He's)
- Give a balloon to __ child. (each)
- If we listen, __ learn a lot. (we'll)

Take a minute to memorize...

Read the memory verse twice. Have students practice it with you two more times.

Words with /ē/

Lesson **11**

F Sentence Fun

Name _____

Write the missing word in the sentence.

1. Come swing with __me__.

2. I __see__ the boy.

3. Can __she__ play with your doll?

4. __We__ like this tree.

5. My __feet__ got wet in the creek.

6. __He__ hit the ball hard.

7. It is time to __eat__.

Word Bank

he	me	see	eat
she	we	feet	

138

178

G Dictation

Listen and write the missing words.

1. He will sing songs to God.

2. We can not see two feet in this fog.

3. She will eat with me.

H Proofreading

One word in each pair is misspelled. Fill in the oval by the misspelled word.

1. ○ he ● fet

2. ● shee ○ see

3. ● eet ○ me

4. ○ we ● sae

5. ● hee ○ she

6. ○ eat ● mea

☆ ● eech ○ begin

☆ ○ talk ● wi'll

☆ ● he'z ○ each

139

Dictation

Reinforce correct spelling by using current and previous words in context.

 Say

Listen as I read each sentence and then write it in your Worktext. (Slowly read each sentence twice. Sentences are found in the Student Worktext to the left.)

☆ ## Challenge

Write these incomplete sentences on the board.

Sarah said ___ you to ___ girl.

___ ___ ___ ___ coming.

Maybe ___ ___ to ___ ___ the ___.

 Say

Listen as I read each sentence. Write the sentence on your paper. (Slowly read each sentence twice.)

Sarah said <u>thank</u> you to <u>each</u> girl.

<u>Ask</u> <u>him</u> if <u>he's</u> coming.

Maybe <u>we'll</u> <u>get</u> to <u>dig</u> <u>in</u> the <u>sand</u>.

---

2 Proofreading

Familiarize students with standardized test format and reinforce recognizing misspelled words.

Say

Look at each set of words. One word in each set is misspelled. Fill in the oval by the misspelled word. (You may wish to pronounce each set of words to help students correctly identify them.)

179

3 Hide and Seek

Reinforce correct spelling of current spelling words. (A reproducible master is provided in Appendix A as shown on the inset page to the right.)
Write the words one at a time on a white board.
Have students:

- **Look** at the word.
- **Say** the word out loud.
- **Spell** the word out loud.
- **Hide** (teacher erases word.)
- **Write** the word on paper.
- **Seek** (teacher rewrites word.)
- **Check** spelling. If incorrect, rewrite word correctly.

4 Code

Have your students complete this activity to strengthen spelling ability and expand vocabulary.

1 Posttest

Test mastery of the spelling words. Challenge words are starred.

 Say — I will say the word once, use the word in a sentence, then say the word again. Write the word on your paper.

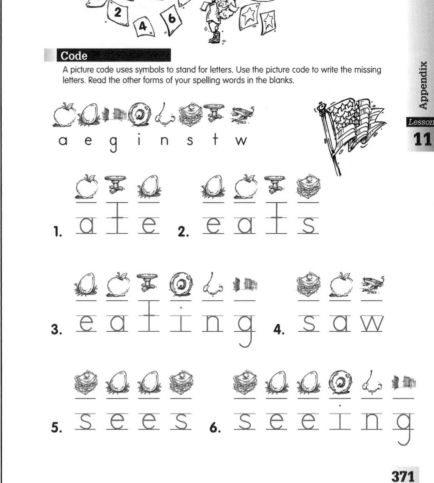

Hide and Seek
Check a paper for each word you spell correctly.

Code
A picture code uses symbols to stand for letters. Use the picture code to write the missing letters. Read the other forms of your spelling words in the blanks.

a e g i n s t w

1. a t e   2. e a t s

3. e a t i n g   4. s a w

5. s e e s   6. s e e i n g

371

1.	eat	We will **eat** pizza for supper.
2.	see	I **see** some children playing on the slide.
3.	she	Was **she** late to her dentist's appointment?
4.	me	My mother bought a new jacket for **me.**
5.	we	Daniel said **we** could come to his house.
6.	he	James said **he** will ask his dad to pick us up.
7.	feet	The boys came inside with sandy **feet.**
☆	each	It is important to wash our hands before **each** meal.
☆	we'll	Then **we'll** pretend that we are on a ship.
☆	he's	Everyone is glad that **he's** safe.

 Progress Chart
Students may record scores. (Reproducible master in Appendix B.)

 Personal Dictionary
Students may add any words they have misspelled to their personal dictionaries for reference when writing. (Cover in Appendix B.)

I Game

Name _____

Cross out each **o**, **k**, and **r** with a big **X** to find the hidden spelling words. Using one crayon, softly color the boxes you did not mark so you can see your spelling words better.

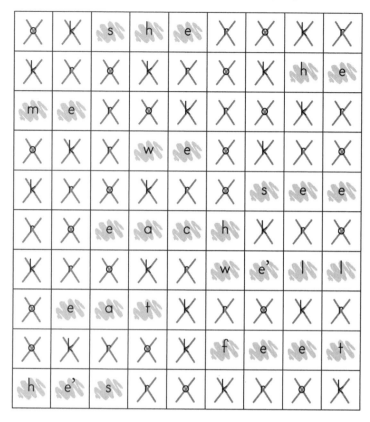

Remember : God's blessings often come through people instead of things.

J Journaling

In your journal, make a list of some blessings that God has given you.

140

---

2 Game

Reinforce spelling skills and provide motivation and interest.

Materials

- game page (from student text)
- pencils (1 per child)
- crayons or colored pencils (1 per child)

3 Journaling

Provide a meaningful reason for correct spelling through personal writing.

Review the story using discussion leads provided on the following page. Encourage students to apply the Scriptural value in their journaling.

Take a minute to memorize...

Have the class say the memory verses with you once.

How to Play:

- Have each student mark through each letter **o** found on the grid with a big **X**.
- Have each student mark through each letter **k** found on the grid with a big **X**.
- Have each student mark through each letter **r** found on the grid with a big **X**.
- Tell the students that the boxes without **X**'s contain their spelling words.
- Have the students color softly over the boxes without **X**'s so they can see their spelling words more clearly.
- Have the students follow along as you read and spell each word as it appears on the grid.

Journaling (continued)

Say

- What are blessings? (The good gifts that God gives to us.) Are blessings always things? (No.)

- What blessings did Tommy realize were his after spending the afternoon at Daniel's house? (A good home and parents that loved him and treated him kindly.)

- Just as we should say thank-you for any gift, we should thank God for His blessings. Make a list of some of your blessings in your journal. Don't forget to thank God for them!

Quotables!

Invented spelling may be encouraged in journal writing and when writing first drafts. Spelling can be edited for finished work.

Sarah's Surprise

Kristin finds a secret way to honor God.

When Kristin entered the classroom Monday morning, she went straight to Rosa's desk.

"Guess what, Rosa? We went to the store Saturday night and Mom and Dad got Christopher and me each a Risa Hank notebook with a matching pencil and stickers." Kristin plopped her new things down in front of her friend. "Christopher's have whales on them, and mine have horses!"

"Wow. These are really great!" Rosa studied the brightly-colored pony prancing on the front of Kristin's notebook and around the sides of the pencil. "I love these stickers, too." Rosa pointed to the colorful sheet. "Hey, I'll trade you one of my kitten sticker sheets for one of your horse ones!"

"Oh, Kristin, is that a new Risa Hank notebook?" Beth walked over to take a peek. "I don't think I've ever seen one with that Appaloosa horse on it before. Mine has a bunny rabbit on it." The group around Rosa's desk grew quickly.

"Hey, Christopher!" Tony called to Kristin's twin who was just starting to put his things away. "Can we see your new notebook and stuff, too?"

"Sure." Christopher's grin revealed two missing front teeth. "Come and see my whales." The group of children drifted over to Christopher's desk.

"Watch out, Tommy!" James teased. "That killer whale on Christopher's notebook might eat the dolphin on yours!"

"That old whale would have to catch my dolphin first!" Tommy swung his notebook over his head in a high arc. "Zooom!"

"Please go to your desks now, and put your things away children," Miss Grant said. As they headed to their desks to start the day, Kristin noticed that Sarah was sitting quietly at her desk all by herself.

The morning passed quickly for Kristin. She played a math game with Tommy and Beth. She read a story with two new words in it. She drew a picture of a horse standing by a big green tree. She very carefully wrote a straight row of T's with her new pencil. It seemed like no time at all before recess. The children bundled into coats, hats, and gloves. Kristin grabbed her red coat that matched Christopher's blue one and pulled her knit cap over her hair.

"Let's see if there's enough snow left by the fence to build a snowman!" The cold air made Tony's words into white puffs as he ran out onto the playground. Tony and Matthew quickly began rolling a ball of snow for the snowman's base.

"Let's make little snowmen and make a whole family," suggested Beth. Soon the children were busy working in groups of two or three on a whole village of little snowmen. As Kristin rolled a middle section over to Christopher, she glanced up at the school. "Hey, Sarah, come on and help us make this snowman!" Sarah was standing out of the wind by the window with her hands stuffed into the pockets of her thin coat.

"I can't," Sarah shrugged. "I . . . uh, I don't have any gloves or mittens here today."

When Miss Grant called the rosy-cheeked children back into the classroom, they left behind thirteen little snowmen. The littlest stood only about a foot tall; the largest about three feet

tall. Their faces were finished with pinecones, and stones, and sticks. Christopher's snowman had a crooked grin made of acorn caps — with two teeth missing in the middle. Tommy and James' snowman had brown pine-needle hair sticking up all over its snowy head.

Just before school was out, Miss Grant told a story. It was about a man who lived a long time ago. This man was very rich. He was already a ruler, even though he was still a young man. But, he wasn't happy. Something seemed to be missing in his life. He came to Jesus and asked what he could do to have eternal life. Miss Grant looked at the class. "Do you remember what Jesus' answer was, children?"

"Jesus told him to keep the commandments," Daniel said. "But the ruler told Jesus he was already keeping the commandments, didn't he?"

"That's right, Daniel. Then Jesus told the rich young man that he would have treasure in heaven if he sold his things and helped the poor." Miss Grant paused and smiled as several hands waved in the air. "Would you like to tell us what happened next, Matthew?"

"He just walked away." Matthew shook his head. "I can't believe he'd rather keep all his stuff and not have treasure in heaven!" Several heads nodded in agreement.

"Well, sometimes it's hard for us to give of the things we have," said Miss Grant. "Proverbs 14:31 says that 'to help the poor is to honor God.' Now here's something for you to think about this evening: Can children show love and honor for God in this way, or is this story just for grown-up people?"

That night, after Kristin had gone to sleep, she dreamed she was building a gigantic snowman. She rolled the snow and patted and shaped it. Then the other children came up and wanted some snow so they could build snowmen, too. "No!" Kristin yelled. "This is my snow! I need it all for my snowman. Go away! You can't have any of my snow!" And

183

Story (continued)

the children went sadly away. Kristin finished her snowman and stepped back to admire it. The giant snowman towered over her, growing taller and taller. Its crooked smile twisted into an ugly frown. Kristin backed away, but the snowman moved closer and closer. Kristin tried to run, but her feet were stuck fast in the snow. The monster snowman came closer and closer and . . .

"Wake up, Kristin." Kristin felt her mother's gentle hug, and she opened her eyes. "You were having a bad dream, dear. It's all right now." Moonlight streamed in through the bedroom window. Little Cathy sat amid the tangled covers and stared at her older sister with large round eyes.

"You just had a bad dream, Honey." Mrs. Wright smoothed her hand over Kristin's tousled brown hair. "It's all over now, girls." The children quickly settled back into their warm beds. Mom brushed Kristin's forehead with a light kiss, and she drifted back into a peaceful sleep.

At school the next day Kristin carefully wrote "p-o-o-r" in her handwriting book. She cocked her head and looked over the letters she had written. She erased a crooked "h" and carefully rewrote it. Two of the "o's" in her second "p-o-o-r" were too close together so she fixed them, too. "P-o-o-r. Poor." Kristin eyes wandered around the room. What could she do to honor God by helping the poor?

Suddenly, she noticed something. Most of the children had colorful notebooks and pencils. But Sarah didn't. Most of the children had warm coats and gloves. But Sarah didn't. Kristin remembered that Sarah's car had a mashed bumper and several places painted dull gray. Sarah's clothes were sometimes patched or a little too small. And she never talked about new toys she'd gotten. Suddenly Kristin sat up straight with a big grin on her face.

"What?" a startled Stephen whispered from his desk next

to Kristin. "What did I miss?" Kristin just shook her head and laughed quietly.

When the children burst out onto the playground for recess that day, Kristin cornered her friend Rosa. The two girls ignored the shouts and laughter of the other kids as they whispered and planned. "So, you see, Rosa, we can do this if we each use some of our allowance!" Kristin's face was flushed with excitement. "Do you want to?"

"Yes! I'll call you tonight right after I ask my dad about it." Rosa giggled. "I can't wait!"

"I can't either," Kristin grinned. "I don't want to be selfish. I had enough of that in my nightmare last night." She rolled her eyes and gave an exaggerated shudder. The two friends burst out laughing.

When Kristin entered the classroom Wednesday morning, Rosa met her at the door. "Here's my part of the money," Rosa whispered. "Did you get it?"

"Look at this." Kristin let Rosa peek into a brown paper bag. "And my mom got these, too."

"They're perfect!" Rosa exclaimed. The two girls made a quick stop at Sarah's desk, then went over to Rosa's desk to wait. A few minutes later, Sarah came in quietly. Kristin and Rosa watched as she went to her desk and sat down. They watched as she bent over and put something in her desk. Suddenly Sarah sat up with a brand-new, brightly-colored Risa Hank notebook in one hand, and warm, purple mittens in the other! Sarah laid them carefully on her desk and stared at the puppy on the front of the notebook. She gently touched the soft lining of the mittens. Finally she opened the notebook carefully. There was her own name written neatly inside the front cover!

Miss Grant had been watching, too. She stopped by Sarah's desk. "Humm. It says here, 'To Sarah Peters, from your friends,'" she read. And patting Sarah's shoulder, she moved on.

At recess that day Kristin, Rosa, AND Sarah worked on a new snowman together. As Sarah reached up with her purple-mittened hand to stick the last piece on the mouth, Kristin noticed that

the snowman looked a lot like the giant one in her dream. But this magnificent snowman was smiling.

2 Discussion Time

Check understanding of the story and development of personal values.

- What did Kristin and Christopher bring to school on Monday that most of the first graders had?
- Is there something that most of your classmates have like that?
- What did Kristin notice about Sarah?
- What was Kristin's nightmare about?
- How did Kristin and Rosa honor God?
- Did they tell Sarah who the gifts were from?
- Who do you think was happier, Sarah or Kristin and Rosa?

A Preview

Write each word as your teacher says it.

Name _____

1. cut
2. top
3. much
4. but
5. stop
6. cot
7. hop

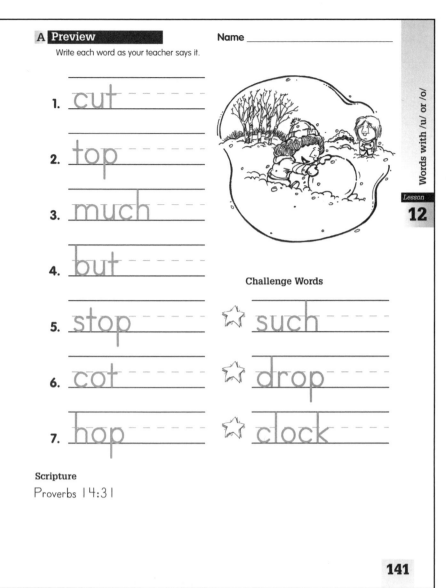

Challenge Words

⭐ such
⭐ drop
⭐ clock

Scripture
Proverbs 14:31

141

Challenge

For better spellers, challenge words may be included in the weekly list. Challenge words are starred.

Correct Immediately!

Say) Let's correct our preview. I will write each word on the board. Put a dot under each letter on your preview as I spell the word out loud. If you spelled a word wrong, rewrite it correctly.

Progress Chart

Students may record scores. (Reproducible master in Appendix B.)

Take a minute to memorize . . .

Read the memory verse twice. Have students practice it with you two more times.

---

3 ## Preview

Test for knowledge of the correct spellings of these words. (See the instructions at the top right for challenge words.)

 Say) I will say each word once, use the word in a sentence, then say the word again. Write the word on the lines in the Worktext.

1. cut — The boy **cut** out a picture.
2. top — The **top** of this snowman is not finished.
3. much — There is not **much** time before lunch.
4. but — Sarah wanted to play, **but** did not have any mittens.
5. stop — Always **stop** and look both ways before crossing the street.
6. cot — He will sleep on the **cot**.
7. hop — The rabbit can **hop** fast.
⭐ such — That was **such** a kind thing to do.
⭐ drop — Don't **drop** the jar!
⭐ clock — The **clock** tells what time it is.

Word Shapes

4

Help students form a correct image of whole words.

Day 1

Lesson 12

Say Look at each word and think about its shape. Now, write the word in the correct word Shape Boxes. You may check off each word as you use it.

(In many words **/u/** is spelled with **u** when it is at the beginning or in the middle of a word. In many words **/o/** is spelled with **o** when it is at the beginning or in the middle of a word.)

Say In the word shape boxes, color the letter that spells the sound of **/u/** or **/o/** in each word.
Circle the word that ends with the consonant digraph **ch**.

Challenge
Draw the correctly shaped box around each letter in these words.

Say On a separate sheet of paper, write other words that contain the spelling patterns in the word list. See how many words you can write.

B Word Shapes   Name _____

Write each word in the correct word shape boxes. Next, in the word shape boxes, color the letter that spells the sound of **/u/**, or **/o/** in each word. Circle the word that ends with the consonant digraph **ch**.

Words with /u/ or /o/

Lesson **12**

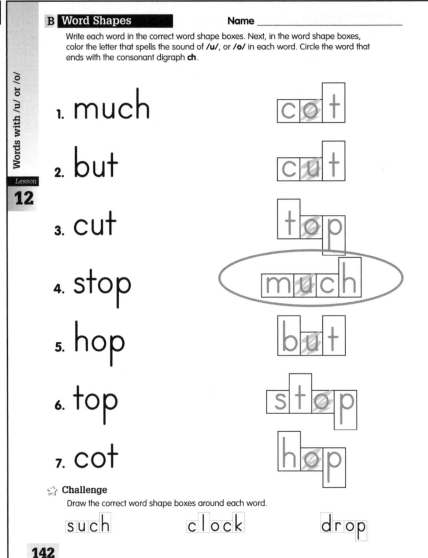

1. much
2. but
3. cut
4. stop
5. hop
6. top
7. cot

☆ **Challenge**
Draw the correct word shape boxes around each word.

such   clock   drop

142

Answers may vary for duplicate word shapes.

Be Prepared For Fun

Check these supply lists for **Fun Ways to Spell** presented **Day 2**.
Purchase and/or gather these items ahead of time!

General
- Strips of Paper 3 1/2 x 11 Inches (7 per child)
- Strips of Paper 3 1/2 x 11 Inches (3 more for challenge words)
- Crayons or Markers
- Tape
- Scissors
- Spelling List

Auditory
- Rhythm Instruments (two wooden spoons, two pan lids, maracas)
- Spelling List

Visual
- Clothespins (5 clothespins per child at the clothesline)
- b, c, h, m, o, p, s, t and u (3 x 5 cards cut in half)
- c, d, k, l and r (added for challenge words)
- Clothesline (hung up at student height)
- Spelling List

Tactile
- Shaving Cream
- Optional: Plastic Plates
- Optional: Wooden Craft Sticks
- Spelling List

186

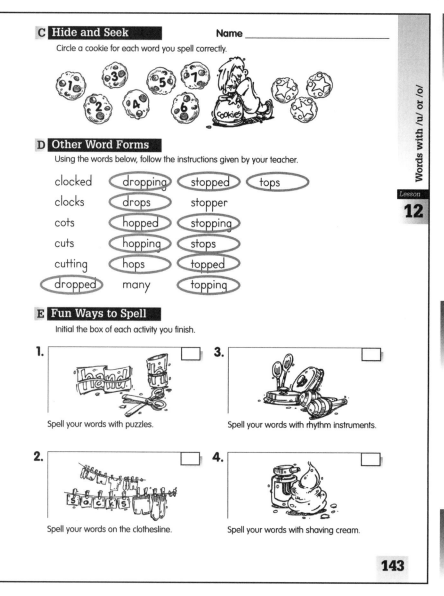

C Hide and Seek

Name _____

Circle a cookie for each word you spell correctly.

D Other Word Forms

Using the words below, follow the instructions given by your teacher.

clocked   dropping   stopped   tops

clocks   drops   stopper

cots   hopped   stopping

cuts   hopping   stops

cutting   hops   topped

dropped   many   topping

E Fun Ways to Spell

Initial the box of each activity you finish.

1.

Spell your words with puzzles.

2.

Spell your words on the clothesline.

3.

Spell your words with rhythm instruments.

4.

Spell your words with shaving cream.

143

---

1 Hide and Seek

Reinforce spelling by using multiple styles of learning.

On a white board, Teacher writes each word — one at a time. **Have students:**

- **Look** at the word.
- **Say** the word out loud.
- **Spell** the word out loud.
- **Hide** (teacher erases word.)
- **Write** the word on their paper.
- **Seek** (teacher rewrites word.)
- **Check** spelling. If incorrect, repeat above steps.

2 Other Word Forms

This activity is optional. Have students find and circle the Other Word Forms that rhyme with each other.

3 Fun Ways to Spell

Four activities are provided. Use one, two, three, or all of the activities. Have students initial the box for each activity they complete.

Options:

- assign activities to students according to their learning styles
- set up the activities in learning centers for students to do throughout the day
- divide students into four groups and assign one activity per group
- do one activity per day

General

To Spell your words with puzzles…
- Write each word on a strip of paper in big, tall letters.
- Cut your word in half lengthwise.
- Tape the ends of each strip together to make circles.
- Mix the circles together.
- Match the circles again to make your spelling words.

Auditory

To spell your words with rhythm instruments…
- Look at a word on your spelling list.
- Close your eyes.
- Play your rhythm instruments softly while you whisper the spelling of the word.
- Open your eyes and check your spelling.

Visual

To spell your words on the clothesline…
- Choose the letter cards you need to spell a word on your list.
- Clothespin the cards to the clothesline in the right order to spell the word.
- Check your spelling.
- Remove the letter cards from the clothesline and spell the next word on your list.

Tactile

To spell your words with shaving cream…
- Spread a glob of shaving cream across your desk (or on a plastic plate).
- Use your finger (or a wooden craft stick) to write a spelling word in the shaving cream.
- Check your spelling.
- Smear the word out with your finger and write another word.

187

1 Missing Letters

Familiarize students with word meaning and usage. Write **d _ c k** on the board. Say the word **duck**. Invite the children to tell you what vowel is missing.

Say

Each word is missing a letter or letters. Write the missing letters on the lines to make a spelling word.

F Missing Letters

Add the missing letters to each word.

Name _____

Words with /u/ or /o/

Lesson **12**

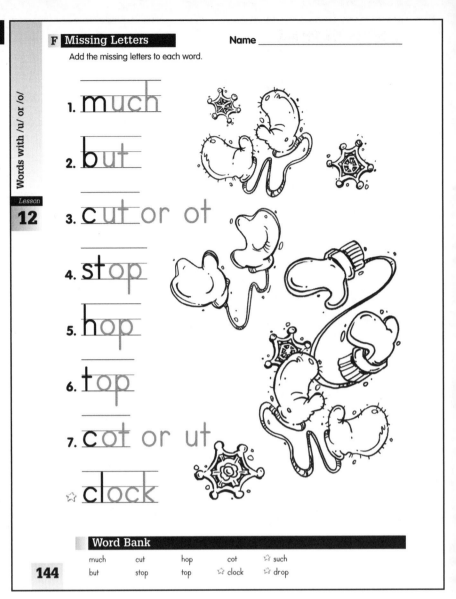

1. much
2. but
3. cut or ot
4. stop
5. hop
6. top
7. cot or ut
☆ clock

Take a minute to memorize...

Read the memory verse twice. Have students practice it with you two more times.

G Dictation
Listen and write the missing words.

1. We cannot run much.

2. The dog can see the frog hop.

3. I will stop at the top.

H Proofreading
One word in each pair is misspelled. Fill in the oval by the misspelled word.

1. ◯ much
   ● cawt

2. ● toup
   ◯ but

3. ● hoq
   ◯ cut

4. ● sotp
   ◯ hop

5. ◯ cot
   ● cutt

6. ● bot
   ◯ top

☆ ● clok
   ◯ small

☆ ◯ plan
   ● suj

☆ ● brop
   ◯ grand

145

Dictation

1

Reinforce correct spelling by using current and previous words in context.

 Listen as I read each sentence and then write it in your Worktext. (Slowly read each sentence twice. Sentences are found in the Student Worktext to the left.)

Challenge
Write these incomplete sentences on the board.

___ was ___ ___ ___ ___.

Christopher's ___ is

___ ___.

___ ___ ___ the ___ ___

the ___?

 Listen as I read each sentence. Write the sentence on your paper. (Slowly read each sentence twice.)

It was such a big dog.

Christopher's clock is not red.

Did we drop the ball on the cat?

Proofreading

2

Familiarize students with standardized test format and reinforce recognizing misspelled words.

 Look at each set of words. One word in each set is misspelled. Fill in the oval by the misspelled word. (You may wish to pronounce each set of words to help students correctly identify them.)

189

3 Hide and Seek

Reinforce correct spelling of current spelling words. (A reproducible master is provided in Appendix A as shown on the inset page to the right.)

Write the words one at a time on a white board.

Have students:

- **Look** at the word.
- **Say** the word out loud.
- **Spell** the word out loud.
- **Hide** (teacher erases word.)
- **Write** the word on paper.
- **Seek** (teacher rewrites word.)
- **Check** spelling. If incorrect, rewrite word correctly.

4 Making Words

Have your students complete this activity to strengthen spelling ability and expand vocabulary.

1 Posttest

Test mastery of the spelling words. Challenge words are starred.

 Say I will say the word once, use the word in a sentence, then say the word again. Write the word on your paper.

 **Hide and Seek**

Check a paper for each word you spell correctly.

Making Words

Add the endings to the spelling words. Write the new word on the line.
Don't forget, when a word ends with a single consonant with a vowel right before it, the final consonant is often doubled before adding endings that begin with a vowel.

1. stop + s   + ed

stops   stopped

1. hop + s   + ed

hops   hopped

1. top + s   + ed

tops   topped

☆ drop + s   + ed

drops   dropped

Appendix
Lesson **12**

372

1.	top	Let's climb to the **top** of this hill.
2.	cut	The broken glass **cut** his foot.
3.	hop	He had to **hop** on one foot.
4.	much	The cars drove slowly because there was so **much** snow on the road.
5.	but	I would play outside, **but** I am sick today.
6.	cot	Have you ever slept on a **cot**?
7.	stop	Always **stop** when the light is red.
☆	drop	Let's add a **drop** of red paint to the blue paint.
☆	clock	The **clock** chimes on every hour.
☆	such	They did **such** a good job of learning their verses.

 Progress Chart
Students may record scores. (Reproducible master in Appendix B.)

 Personal Dictionary
Students may add any words they have misspelled to their personal dictionaries for reference when writing. (Cover in Appendix B.)

190

I Game

Name _____

Color one mitten each time you or your team spells a word correctly.

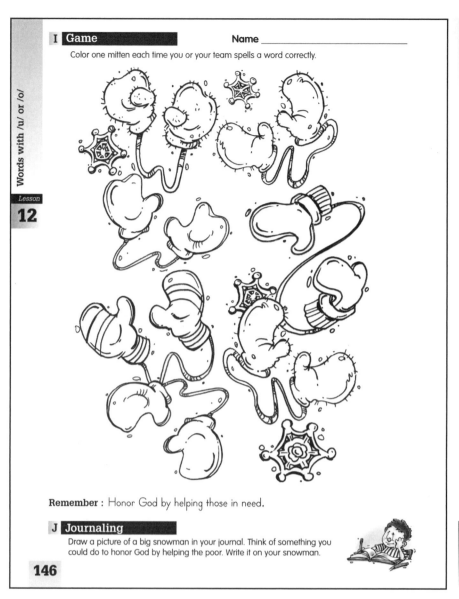

Remember : Honor God by helping those in need.

J Journaling

Draw a picture of a big snowman in your journal. Think of something you could do to honor God by helping the poor. Write it on your snowman.

146

---

2 Game

Reinforce spelling skills and provide motivation and interest.

Materials

- game page (from student text)
- crayons (1 each of blue, red, green, yellow, orange, purple, and pink - per child)
- game word list

Game Word List

Use of challenge words is optional.

1. **much**
2. **but**
3. **cut**
4. **stop**
5. **hop**
6. **top**
7. **cot**
☆ **such**
☆ **clock**
☆ **drop**

3 Journaling

Provide a meaningful reason for correct spelling through personal writing.

Review the story using discussion leads provided on the following page. Encourage students to apply the Scriptural value in their journaling.

 Take a minute to memorize...

Have the class say the memory verses from lessons 11 and 12 with you.

How to Play:

- Divide the class into two teams, and decide which team will go first.
- Have a student from team A go to the board.
- Read the spelling word two times slowly and clearly. (You may also wish to use the word in a sentence. Ex.: "cat — The cat climbed a tree. — cat")
- Have the student write the word on the board.
- If the word is spelled correctly, instruct all the members of team A to color one mitten by its match to make a pair. (Note: If the word is misspelled, correct the spelling immediately before continuing the game.)
- Alternate between teams A and B as you go down the word list.
- The team with the most mitten pairs when you have gone through the game word list twice is the winner.

Non-Competitive Option:

- At the end of the game, say: "Class, I am proud of your efforts to spell the words correctly. If you had fun and tried your best, you are all winners!"

Journaling (continued)

 Say

- Is it only grown-ups that can help the poor? (No. All of us can, even children.)

- Have you ever shared something? How did it make you feel? How do you think sharing with those who have less than you have honors God? (It is following His example of giving and kindness.)

- Kristin found that sharing with someone poorer than herself made everything, even building a snowman, more fun. Draw a big snowman in your journal. Think of a way you could help the poor and write it on your snowman.

Quotables!

You may let parents and others know you are aware of children's invented spelling by stamping papers with "Unedited," "First Draft," "Sloppy Copy," or "Work in Progress."

The Greatest Blessing

A house fire helps Rosa learn that God's greatest blessings aren't necessarily things.

"Let's take our sleds over to the hill behind the Anderson's house!" Eleven-year-old Carlos met his sisters at the front door.

"Good idea!" said Maria, his eight-year-old sister. "You're already changed, so go ask Dad if it's okay while Rosa and I get out of our school clothes. You want to go, Rosa?"

"Sure! And I'll be ready before you are." Six-year-old Rosa darted down the hall to her room.

A few minutes later the three Vasquez children were trotting down the tree-lined country road towing their tube sleds behind them. They trooped up the steps of a large old two-story home set on a hill and surrounded by snow-covered shrubs and gardens. A gray-haired lady answered the door, her wrinkled face beaming with a huge smile.

"Well, Joe," she said to the man standing behind her. "Looks like we have some sledders here."

"Will you come sledding with us, Grandpa Joe?" Rosa begged their neighbor.

"Yes, please," chimed in Maria.

"It's a lot more fun when you sled with us!" added Carlos.

"All right, all right!" Mr. Anderson's booming laugh was a funny sound that always made the children laugh, too. "You young'uns go on, and I'll be along soon as I can get my old bones movin' thet away."

Soon the Vasquez children were taking turns flying down the familiar slope. The hill began in back of the Anderson's greenhouse, and dropped down into the meadow that stretched to the river behind their farm. It was a wonderful place to sled. Mr. Anderson

and the children climbed up over and over, rushing back down with the wind in their faces. Suddenly Mr. Anderson's sled hit a pile of unpacked snow. Swoosh! The snow flew into the air and all over Mr. Anderson. "Wow!" he laughed, "that'll wake ya up!" Barkley and Digby, the two dogs, jumped up to help clean him off. Even his grey mustache was white with snow!

"What a fantastic run, Grandpa Joe!" Carlos was awestruck. "I wish I could go that f . . . oophf!" A well-tossed snowball snuffed out his words.

Rosa grinned smugly and brushed the loose snow from her mittens. "Right on target!" she laughed, then ducked as a snowball whizzed by. "I'll get you, Rosa!" Carlos shouted. "Come on, Grandpa Joe! You're on my team."

Soon the air was thick with loosely-packed snowballs. Digby ran in all directions trying to eat the snowballs that landed on the ground. Barkley was in a frenzy trying to catch each ball as it flew through the air. He looked confused when he finally caught one in midair. Grandpa Joe and the children laughed so hard that they missed more targets than they hit.

Pink and purple tinged the western sky as the tired group climbed the hill for the last time. "Hey, Dad's here!" Maria spotted the familiar blue jeep in the driveway. They parked their sleds on the back porch and clumsily shed snowsuits and boots with cold-numbed fingers.

"Hold it there, young lady." Mrs. Anderson stopped Rosa at the doorway. "Let's leave most of this snow outside." She helped Rosa clean the snow off her collar. "Now, supper's ready! Everyone get washed up and head to the table."

The delicious smell of fresh cornbread and Mrs. Anderson's homemade vegetable soup made Rosa's mouth water as she scrubbed her hands and face in the old-fashioned bathroom. She padded back into the big kitchen in her sock feet, then crawled up into her father's lap where he sat at the table.

"Grandma Ruth called and talked me into coming for supper, again." Dad grinned at the kids sheepishly. "I'm sure Grandpa Joe thinks we spend more time here than we do at home!"

"Nonsense, Rafael, you and the kids belong here! Ruthie and I wouldn't know what to do without our adopted family." Mr. Anderson looked around the packed table and smiled. "Now, let's thank the good Lord for this meal. Rosa, would you give the blessing please?"

Rosa scrambled over to her own chair, then offered prayer. The meal disappeared amidst talk and laughter as the Vasquez children and Grandpa Joe described their afternoon. It was almost bedtime when Mr. Vasquez piled tube sleds and dogs in the back of the jeep, and three sleepy children in the front. Joe and Ruth Anderson waved from their front door as the Vasquez family drove down the hill to their own front door.

Woof! Woof! Woof! Rosa's eyes popped open at the frantic barking of the dogs. It wasn't unusual for them to bark in the night. But this time they sounded different. Rosa ran down the hall to her father's room. "Daddy. Daddy," she whispered urgently into the darkness of the room. "Daddy, are you awake?"

"Whaaat? Rosa, is that you?" a sleepy voice muttered, followed by a big yawn. "I'm awake now." Father turned on his bedside lamp.

"Dad, listen!" Rosa climbed onto the bed, slipping her cold toes under the blanket. "What's wrong with the dogs?"

"They're sure upset, aren't they?" Dad sounded concerned. "I'll go check on them, Rosita. You crawl under the covers so you don't get too cold." Mr. Vasquez put on his

193

slippers, and quickly walked down the hall to the living room window. He was back in an instant and grabbed the phone by his bed. Rosa was frightened by the grim look on his face.

"911? This is Rafael Vasquez. There's a house on fire at 21341 Orchard Road . . . yes . . . 21341 Orchard Road. No, I don't know. Okay, thank you." Dad hung up the phone and threw his clothes on over his pajamas. "Rosa, you stay here! If Maria or Carlos wake up tell them to stay here, too! The Anderson's house is on fire." In a moment, he was out the door.

Rosa tiptoed into the living room. She could see the bright orange glow on the hilltop through the front window. "What's all the noise about?" Carlos rubbed his sleep-filled eyes as he stumbled into the living room. Behind him padded Maria, wrapped up in her quilt like a mummy.

Rosa pointed out the front window. "Daddy said to stay here." Maria and Carlos didn't answer. The three children curled up in quilts on the living room sofa and watched the frightening flames flicker in the night.

By dawn the firemen had the blaze under control. Ugly, black smoke billowed in the cold morning air, smudging the clear, blue sky. The children were still sitting by the living room window, gazing up the hill with tired eyes. Rosa thought the huge, burnt hole in the side of the house looked awfully dark against the snow-covered hillside.

After what seemed like forever, the fire chief's pickup stopped in front of their house. Dad climbed out and started for the door, and all three children ran out to meet him. "They're okay," Dad said before anyone could even ask the question. "Grandma Ruth's in the hospital, but she'll be fine. She just breathed too much smoke. Grandpa Joe went in the ambulance with her." He smiled tiredly at the pajama clad children standing in the snow. "As soon as we're all cleaned

up and dressed, we'll drop by the hospital and you can see for yourselves." He held up a grimy hand. "Now, I know you have a million questions, but first get ready for school, and then we'll talk on the way to the hospital. Okay, troop, let's move!"

An hour later the Vasquez family filed quietly into the hospital. It was strange to see Grandma Ruth lying in bed, and the hospital smelled kind of funny, but Grandma Ruth's smile was the same as always, and Grandpa Joe's hug was still just as comforting. Rosa cuddled up to Grandpa Joe's side and listened as the others talked about how the fire had started in the chimney of the kitchen wood stove. Big tears began to roll down her face and she couldn't hold back her sniffles.

"Why, Rosa, what's wrong, little one?" Grandpa sat down in the only chair and lifted Rosa onto his knee.

"I'm so (sniffle) scared and (sniffle) sad. Your wonderful house is all ruined. And (sniffle) Grandma Ruth got hurt!" Rosa cried harder as Grandpa Joe held her close. "How could God let this happen?"

"It's all right, Rosita," Grandma Ruth said. "We were all very scared for a little while. But I'll be fine in a day or two, and the house can be repaired. The things that we lost are not what's important." Grandma reached down and brushed away Rosa's tears. "We don't always know why bad things happen, Dear, but God has blessed us in the past, and I'm sure the blessings will continue in the future. And Grandpa and I still have each other, and that's the greatest blessing of all."

"And we still have our adopted grandparents," Carlos added.

"Hey, it looks like you'll be eating some meals at our house for a change," Dad smiled. "That is, if we can persuade you to stay with us while the repairs to your home are being made." He turned to look at his children. "After all, it's our turn to help now, isn't it kids?"

"YES!" the Vasquez children chorused. And Grandma Ruth smiled as Grandpa Joe gave out his funny, booming laugh.

2 Discussion Time

Check understanding of the story and development of personal values.

- Where did Rosa, Carlos, and Maria go after school?
- Were the Andersons the children's real grandparents?
- What awakened Rosa in the night?
- Were the Anderson's OK?
- Why do you think that Grandma Anderson said the greatest blessing was that she and Grandpa Anderson still had each other?

A Preview

Write each word as your teacher says it.

Name _____

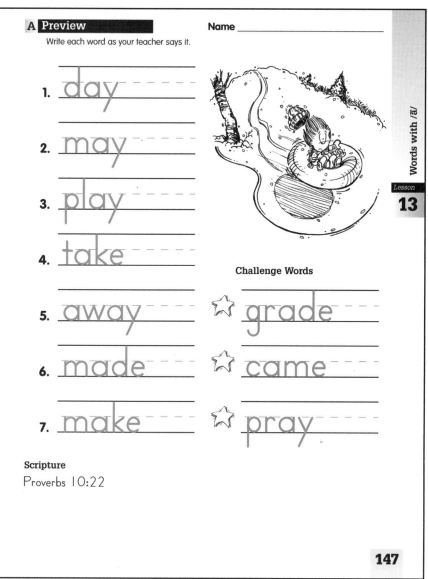

1. day
2. may
3. play
4. take
5. away
6. made
7. make

Challenge Words

 grade

came

pray

Scripture

Proverbs 10:22

147

 Challenge

For better spellers, challenge words may be included in the weekly list. Challenge words are starred.

 Correct Immediately!

Say Let's correct our preview. I will write each word on the board. Put a dot under each letter on your preview as I spell the word out loud. If you spelled a word wrong, rewrite it correctly.

Progress Chart

Students may record scores. (Reproducible master in Appendix B.)

 **Take a minute to memorize . . .**

Read the memory verse twice. Have students practice it with you two more times.

---

 3 ## Preview

Test for knowledge of the correct spellings of these words. (See the instructions at the top right for challenge words.)

Say I will say each word once, use the word in a sentence, then say the word again. Write the word on the lines in the Worktext.

1. day — It was a good **day** for sledding.
2. may — You **may** use my new finger paints.
3. play — Most children like to **play** in the snow.
4. take — It is time to **take** your medicine.
5. away — Put your toys **away** now.
6. made — Grandma Anderson **made** good soup.
7. make — Rosa will **make** a snowball.
☆ grade — You are in first **grade**.
☆ came — Mrs. Anderson **came** to the door.
☆ pray — God answers when we **pray**.

195

Word Shapes

Lesson 13 | **Day 1**

4

Help students form a correct image of whole words.

 Say Look at each word and think about its shape. Now, write the word in the correct word Shape Boxes. You may check off each word as you use it.

(In many words, the sound of /ā/ is spelled with **ay**, or with **a-consonant-e**.)

 Say In the word shape boxes, color the letters that spell the sound of /ā/ in each word. Circle the word that has two syllables.

 Challenge
Draw the correctly shaped box around each letter in these words.

 Say On a separate sheet of paper, write other words that contain the spelling patterns in the word list. See how many words you can write.

B Word Shapes

Name _____

Write each word in the correct word shape boxes. Next, in the word shape boxes, color the letters that spell the sound of /ā/ in each word. Circle the word that has two syllables.

 Words with /ā/ · Lesson **13**

1. may

2. day

3. away

4. play

5. made

6. make

7. take

☆ **Challenge**
Draw the correct word shape boxes around each word.

 grade · pray · came

148

Answers may vary for duplicate word shapes.

Be Prepared For Fun

Check these supply lists for **Fun Ways to Spell** presented **Day 2**.
Purchase and/or gather these items ahead of time!

General
- Crayons
- Piece of Paper
- Spelling List

Auditory
- Box to Store Letters
- a, a, d, e, k, l, m, p, t, w and y (written on seasonal shapes like snowmen or mittens)
- c, g and r (added for challenge words)
- Spelling List

Visual
- Eraser
- Dark Construction Paper
- Spelling List

Tactile
- Finger Paint
- Plastic Plate or Glossy Paper
- Spelling List

196

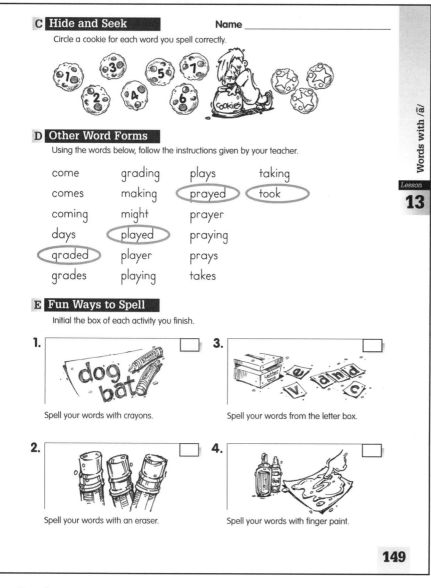

C Hide and Seek

Name _____

Circle a cookie for each word you spell correctly.

D Other Word Forms

Using the words below, follow the instructions given by your teacher.

come   grading   plays   taking

comes   making   (prayed)   (took)

coming   might   prayer

days   (played)   praying

(graded)   player   prays

grades   playing   takes

E Fun Ways to Spell

Initial the box of each activity you finish.

1. [ ]
Spell your words with crayons.

3. [ ]
Spell your words from the letter box.

2. [ ]
Spell your words with an eraser.

4. [ ]
Spell your words with finger paint.

149

Lesson **13**

1   Hide and Seek

Reinforce spelling by using multiple styles of learning.

On a white board, Teacher writes each word — one at a time. **Have students:**

- **Look** at the word.
- **Say** the word out loud.
- **Spell** the word out loud.
- **Hide** (teacher erases word.)
- **Write** the word on their paper.
- **Seek** (teacher rewrites word.)
- **Check** spelling. If incorrect, repeat above steps.

2   Other Word Forms

This activity is optional. Have students find and circle the Other Word Forms that show action that happened in the past.

3   Fun Ways to Spell

Four activities are provided. Use one, two, three, or all of the activities. Have students initial the box for each activity they complete.

Options:

- assign activities to students according to their learning styles
- set up the activities in learning centers for students to do throughout the day
- divide students into four groups and assign one activity per group
- do one activity per day

General

To spell your words with crayons…
- Write each letter of your spelling word in fat, thick letters.
- Check your spelling.

Auditory

To spell your words from the letter box…
- Spell a word from your list by putting the letters in the right order.
- Check your spelling.
- Spell your word out loud.

Visual

To spell your words with an eraser…
- Turn your pencil upside down.
- Use the eraser to write your words on a sheet of dark construction paper.
- Check your spelling.

Tactile

To spell your words with finger paint…
- Smear paint across your plate.
- Use a finger to write a spelling word in paint.
- Check your spelling.
- Smear the word out with your finger and write another word.

197

1 ABC Order

Familiarize students with word meaning and usage. Write the words **leg**, **eat**, and **go** on the board. Help the students understand that each word begins with a different letter. Write the letters **l**, **e**, and **g**. Ask the students which letter comes first in the alphabet. Ask which letter comes next. Elicit the response that the letters would come **e**, **g**, **l**. Then write the words in ABC order as **eat**, **go**, and **leg**.

Say: Write the words from each group in ABC order.

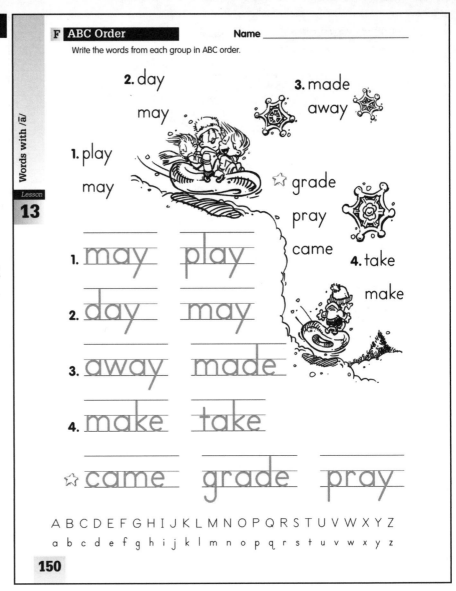

Words with /ā/

Lesson 13

F ABC Order   Name _____

Write the words from each group in ABC order.

2. day
may

1. play
may

3. made
away

☆ grade
pray
came

4. take
make

1. may   play
2. day   may
3. away   made
4. make   take
☆ came   grade   pray

A B C D E F G H I J K L M N O P Q R S T U V W X Y Z
a b c d e f g h i j k l m n o p q r s t u v w x y z

150

Take a minute to memorize...

Read the memory verse twice. Have students practice it with you two more times.

G Dictation

Listen and write the missing words.

1. Make him take his coat.

2. I may take a lunch one day.

3. The dog ran away.

H Proofreading

One word in each pair is misspelled. Fill in the oval by the misspelled word.

1. ● maa
   ○ take

2. ○ stop
   ● plae

3. ○ feet
   ● uway

4. ● dae
   ○ saw

5. ● mak
   ○ made

6. ○ play
   ● tak

☆ ● grabe
   ○ came

☆ ● prae
   ○ draw

☆ ○ finish
   ● caem

151

1 Dictation

Reinforce correct spelling by using current and previous words in context.

Say Listen as I read each sentence and then write it in your Worktext. (Slowly read each sentence twice. Sentences are found in the Student Worktext to the left.)

☆ Challenge

Write these incomplete sentences on the board.

___ are ___ the same ___.

___ says to ___ ___ ___.

The ___ ___ ___ ___ ___.

Day 4

Lesson 13

Say Listen as I read each sentence. Write the sentence on your paper. (Slowly read each sentence twice.)

We are in the same grade.

God says to pray all day.

The small cot came in a box.

2 Proofreading

Familiarize students with standardized test format and reinforce recognizing misspelled words.

Say Look at each set of words. One word in each set is misspelled. Fill in the oval by the misspelled word. (You may wish to pronounce each set of words to help students correctly identify them.)

3 Hide and Seek

Reinforce correct spelling of current spelling words. (A reproducible master is provided in Appendix A as shown on the inset page to the right.)

Write the words one at a time on a white board.

Have students:

- **Look** at the word.
- **Say** the word out loud.
- **Spell** the word out loud.
- **Hide** (teacher erases word.)
- **Write** the word on paper.
- **Seek** (teacher rewrites word.)
- **Check** spelling. If incorrect, rewrite word correctly.

4 Word Find

Have your students complete this activity to strengthen spelling ability and expand vocabulary.

1 Posttest

Test mastery of the spelling words. Challenge words are starred.

 Say I will say the word once, use the word in a sentence, then say the word again. Write the word on your paper.

1.	play	The dogs like to **play** in the snow.
2.	take	Dad will **take** us home now.
3.	day	Monday is the **day** after Sunday.
4.	away	The cat ran **away** from the dog.
5.	make	My mother will **make** a cake.
6.	may	Carlos asked, "**May** we go sledding, Dad?"
7.	made	The first graders **made** cards for their parents.
☆	came	The repairman **came** to fix the telephone.
☆	pray	I talk to my heavenly Father when I **pray**.
☆	grade	You will be in second **grade** next year.

Hide and Seek

Check a paper for each word you spell correctly.

Word Find

Find and circle these other forms of your spelling words in the puzzle.

```
p  l  a  y  i  n  g  t  p
l  p  r  a  y  e  r  a  l
a  r  y  p  s  t  a  k  a
y  a  o  t  n  a  d  m  g
e  y  a  o  g  k  i  i  r
d  s  c  o  m  i  n  g  a
i  m  a  k  i  n  g  h  d
c  o  m  e  s  g  d  t  e
g  r  a  d  e  d  a  y  s
```

Word Bank

comes	days	grades	making	played	prayer	taking
coming	graded	grading	might	playing	prays	took

373

 Progress Chart
Students may record scores. (Reproducible master in Appendix B.)

 Personal Dictionary
Students may add any words they have misspelled to their personal dictionaries for reference when writing. (Cover in Appendix B.)

200

I Game

Name _____

Cross out each **i**, **n**, and **s** with a big **X** to find the hidden spelling words. Using one crayon, softly color the boxes you did not mark so you can see your spelling words better.

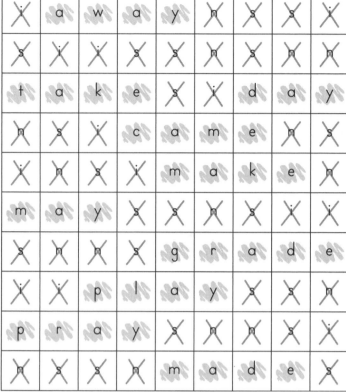

X	a	w	a	y	X	X	X	X
X	X	X	s	X	X	X	X	X
t	a	k	e	X	X	d	a	y
X	X	X	c	a	m	e	X	X
X	X	X	X	m	a	k	e	X
m	a	y	X	X	X	X	X	X
X	X	X	X	g	r	a	d	e
X	X	p	l	a	y	X	X	X
p	r	a	y	X	X	X	X	X
X	X	X	X	m	a	d	e	X

Remember : Our greatest treasure is God's love.

J Journaling

In your journal, copy and finish this thank-you note to God for a blessing He has given you.

Dear God, Thank you for...

152

How to Play:

- Have each student mark through each letter **i** found on the grid with a big **X**.
- Have each student mark through each letter **n** found on the grid with a big **X**.
- Have each student mark through each letter **s** found on the grid with a big **X**.
- Tell the students that the boxes without **X**'s contain their spelling words.
- Have the students color softly over the boxes without **X**'s so they can see their spelling words more clearly.
- Have the students follow along as you read and spell each word as it appears on the grid.

2 Game

Reinforce spelling skills and provide motivation and interest.

Materials

- game page (from student text)
- pencils (1 per child)
- crayons or colored pencils (1 per child)

3 Journaling

Provide a meaningful reason for correct spelling through personal writing.

Review the story using discussion leads provided on the following page. Encourage students to apply the Scriptural value in their journaling.

Take a minute to memorize...

Read the memory verse to the class twice. Have the class practice it with you two more times.

Journaling (continued)

Say

- Rosa, Carlos, and Maria liked to spend time with their neighbors, the Andersons. What happened to the Anderson's home? (Part of it was destroyed in a fire.)

- How did Rosa feel about that? (Scared and upset that God had let it happen.)

- What did Grandma Ruth explain to Rosa? (That the things destroyed in the fire weren't as important as the fact that both Grandma and Grandpa Anderson were O.K.)

- God gives many blessings. Can you name some of them? (Money, health, possessions, friends, family, jobs, time, etc.)

- What blessings are really the greatest? (Those that are not possessions and wealth.) Write a thank-you note in your journal for a blessing that God has given you.

Quotables!

Reading children's writing and letting them know what you think helps them learn how words are spelled.

Complaining Christopher

Christopher learns the importance of cheerful obedience.

"**M**om! Mom! Did the package come?" Christopher burst through the front door, his eyes wide with excitement. He yanked off his stocking cap, and his brown hair stuck up all over his head.

"You look like a space creature," Kristin laughed as she followed him in. She turned and waved a mittened hand at the blue jeep backing out of the driveway, then closed the door.

"Mom!" Christopher headed toward the kitchen, shedding coat and mittens on the way. "Did the package come today, Mom?" The twins rounded the corner into the kitchen, and their mother met them with a smile.

"I hope you remembered to tell Mr. Vasquez thanks for giving you two a ride home from school today," she said. "Yes, Christopher, the package did come in the mail today. But, you need to pick up your things and put them away neatly before you open it!"

Christopher rushed down the hall and into his room. There on the edge of his bed sat a box covered with brown paper and packing tape. "Christopher Wright, 715 Appleby Road," said the label. Seconds later, pieces of brown paper were scattered across the bedspread, and Christopher held a brand-new, shiny red, model airplane. He lifted the plane over his head and swooped around the room. "Vrooomm!" The bright red plane dipped and banked as Christopher supplied the sound effects. He imagined he was in the park trying out this beauty.

"Christopher!" Mom's stern voice interrupted the vision of red wings against a blue sky. Christopher gently set the plane on the bed, and headed back to the kitchen to see what Mom

wanted. Mrs. Wright held his coat up with one hand; his mittens dangled from the other. "It seems that you forgot something, young man!"

"Aw, Mom, I just had to see my plane! I've waited for three weeks now. And it's a beauty!" Christopher's eyes sparkled. "It's even better than the pictures in the catalog."

"I'm sure it is, Son, but you must learn to take care of things when I ask you to." She paused. "Since these outdoor things are still out, now would be a good time for you to shovel the snow off the front walk. Your dad took care of it after that heavy snow Monday before he left, but an inch or two of new snow has fallen since then."

"Aw, Mom . . ." Christopher protested. But Mrs. Wright shook her head, so Christopher went to the garage for the snow shovel. As he scooped the powdery white snow off the walk, his mind drifted with the fluffy white clouds. He'd saved a long time to buy the AS-6 CloudRunner. Every year Aunt Evelyn sent Christopher a birthday card with a twenty-dollar check inside. This year Christopher had put it into his savings account for the plane of his dreams. He'd also gone without buying gum or any of the small toys his sisters had bought. By the time Christopher rushed back into his room, the cold air and exercise had left his cheeks almost as red as the AS-6.

"Pwetty wed pwane!" Two-year-old Cory's eyes shone as he gazed at the airplane from the foot of Christopher's bed.

"Yeah. Isn't it great, Cory? Look, it's got an .049 engine that uses model airplane fuel so it flies all by itself! There's a wire that goes from the plane

to this control box that I use to turn it and make it go up and down," Christopher informed his little brother. "And it's made out of some stuff that's not supposed to break very easily if it crashes. But I'm not going to let this beauty crash. No way!"

"Pwetty wed pwane," Cory repeated solemnly.

"Here, you can hold it, Cory," Christopher offered generously. He carefully placed the plane in his little brother's arms. The AS-6 with its wingspan of almost two feet was quite an armful for the two-year old.

"Christopher!" Mom called. Christopher set his airplane back on the bed and with a lingering glance headed back toward the kitchen. He flew with his arms outstretched on both sides, dipping his wings as he passed Kristin and Cathy's room. Cory trailed him down the hall with his little arms outstretched, too. "R-r-r-r-r-r-r-r-r-r." The brothers flew into the kitchen.

"It's time to set the table, Christopher." Mom pointed to the silverware drawer with a spoon.

"Do I have to do it now?" Christopher whined.

"Yes, supper is almost ready," Mom said.

"Can't Kristin do it tonight?" Christopher argued. "I want to play with my new plane."

"It's your turn to help, Son." Mrs. Wright stirred the steaming vegetables and replaced the lid as Christopher began to set out placemats and plates.

After supper, Christopher looked around his room. Where would be the best place to hang the AS-6? If he hung it in the corner by the closet, the door might bump it. The corner by the window over his desk would be great in the morning when the sun shown in — kind of like a spotlight. But, he wouldn't be able to see the plane very well when he was lying in bed if it hung in that corner. Maybe he could move his bed . . .

"Christopher!" Mom called.

"What?" If he moved the dresser a little he could probably . . .

Story (continued)

"Christopher!"

"WHAT?" Christopher shouted. No, maybe it would be better to move . . .

"Christopher," Mom entered the room. "It's time for you to take your bath, Son."

"Aw, Mom . . . right now? Do I have to?" Christopher complained. "I don't want to take my bath now. Why can't Cathy or Kristin go first? I never have time to do what I want to do."

"The girls have already had their baths." Mom rubbed her finger lightly across the frown wrinkles on Christopher's forehead. "And sometimes we all feel like that, Son." Mom ruffled his hair and started out of the room, then turned at the door. "By the way, that's a fantastic CloudRunner!"

The phone rang while Christopher was still in the bathroom brushing his teeth. He tried to rinse his mouth so fast he almost swallowed the toothpaste! He ran into the kitchen in his flannel pajamas still combing his wet hair. "Is it Dad?" he whispered to Kristin. She bobbed her head up and down with a grin. Cathy danced around their mother and Cory kept trying to grab the phone from his perch in his mother's arms.

"How was your flight? Hmmm . . . well, that's better than taking a chance on having ice on the wings . . . Your business meetings may end early? That's wonderful!" Mom's smile lit up the room. The children listened to her end of the conversation anxiously. "Okay. Here's Christopher." Mom handed the phone to her oldest son.

"Hi, Dad. Guess what? My CloudRunner came today," Christopher said with a rush. ". . . Yes, it's awesome! . . . Well, I didn't have much time to play with it since I had to shovel the walk, and set the table, and take my bath and stuff . . . You didn't? . . . Oh . . . Yeah. I see . . . I love you, too, Dad."

Christopher passed the phone to Kristin and walked thoughtfully to his room. He gazed at the shiny, red AS-6 CloudRunner sitting on his desk. He hadn't had much time to play with it today, but Mom had said that no one got to do just what they liked all the time. And Dad had just told him over the phone that he hadn't wanted to go on this business trip because it took him away from his family. But then Dad had added, "Sometimes we have to do what is right or best whether we want to or not."

What was that Scripture Dad had quoted? "Help me . . ." Christopher frowned with thought. "'Help me to love Your every wish.' Yeah. That was it!"

"Dear Jesus," Christopher knelt by his bed. "Please help me to do what I need to do every day, and to do it without complaining."

2 Discussion Time

Check understanding of the story and development of personal values.

- What was Christopher expecting to come in the mail?
- What things did Christopher have to do that kept him from having very much time to play with his plane that afternoon?
- Where was Christopher's dad?
- What did Dad tell Christopher when he talked to him on the phone that night?
- Are there sometimes things that you need to do when you would really rather do something else?
- Do you do what you need to do happily?

A Preview

Write each word as your teacher says it.

Name _____

1. ice
2. side
3. ride
4. time
5. nice
6. wide
7. hide

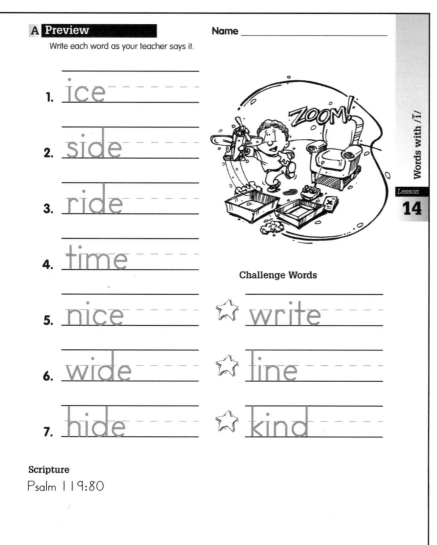

 Words with /ī/

Lesson **14**

Challenge Words

☆ write
☆ line
☆ kind

Scripture
Psalm 119:80

153

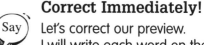

Challenge

For better spellers, challenge words may be included in the weekly list. Challenge words are starred.

Correct Immediately!

 Let's correct our preview. I will write each word on the board. Put a dot under each letter on your preview as I spell the word out loud. If you spelled a word wrong, rewrite it correctly.

Progress Chart

Students may record scores. (Reproducible master in Appendix B.)

Take a minute to memorize . . .

Read the memory verse twice. Have students practice it with you two more times.

---

3 Preview

Test for knowledge of the correct spellings of these words. (See the instructions at the top right for challenge words.)

 I will say each word once, use the word in a sentence, then say the word again. Write the word on the lines in the Worktext.

1. ice — Planes can't fly with **ice** on their wings.
2. side — Christopher shoveled the snow to the **side** of the walk.
3. ride — Mr. Vasquez gave the Wright twins a **ride** home.
4. time — What **time** will Dad's plane land?
5. nice — It is **nice** of you to help with the chores.
6. wide — The river was **wide** and swift.
7. hide — We will **hide** the present in the closet.
☆ write — Please **write** each word neatly.
☆ line — We waited in **line** at the drinking fountain.
☆ kind — It is important to always be **kind** to others.

205

4 Word Shapes

Help students form a correct image of whole words.

 Say Look at each word and think about its shape. Now, write the word in the correct word Shape Boxes. You may check off each word as you use it.

(In many words, the sound of /ī/ is spelled with **i-consonant-e**.)

 Say In the word shape boxes, color the letters that spell the sound of /ī/ in each word. Circle the **silent-e** in each word.

★ **Challenge**
Draw the correctly shaped box around each letter in these words.

 Say On a separate sheet of paper, write other words that contain the spelling patterns in the word list. See how many words you can write.

Be Prepared For Fun

Check these supply lists for **Fun Ways to Spell** presented **Day 2**. Purchase and/or gather these items ahead of time!

 B Word Shapes   Name _____

Write each word in the correct word shape boxes. Next, in the word shape boxes, color the letters that spell the sound of /ī/ in each word. Circle the silent-e in each word.

Words with /ī/ · Lesson **14**

1. nice
2. ice
3. wide
4. side
5. ride
6. hide
7. time

☆ **Challenge**
Draw the correct word shape boxes around each word.

line   write   kind

154

Answers may vary for duplicate word shapes.

General	
• 3 x 5 Cards (7 per child)
• 3 x 5 Cards (3 more for challenge words)
• Scissors
• Spelling List

Auditory	
• Spelling List

Visual	
• Dry Bar of Soap (sample size works well)
• Hand Mirror
• Strong Paper Towel or Washcloth (dry)
• Spelling List

Tactile	
• Play Dough
• Spelling List

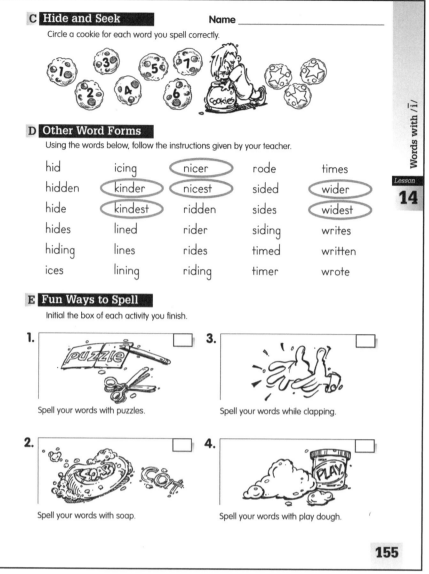

C Hide and Seek

Name _____

Circle a cookie for each word you spell correctly.

D Other Word Forms

Using the words below, follow the instructions given by your teacher.

hid	icing	nicer	rode	times
hidden	kinder	nicest	sided	wider
hide	kindest	ridden	sides	widest
hides	lined	rider	siding	writes
hiding	lines	rides	timed	written
ices	lining	riding	timer	wrote

E Fun Ways to Spell

Initial the box of each activity you finish.

1. ☐

Spell your words with puzzles.

3. ☐

Spell your words while clapping.

2. ☐

Spell your words with soap.

4. ☐

Spell your words with play dough.

Words with /ī/

Lesson **14**

155

---

1 Hide and Seek

Reinforce spelling by using multiple styles of learning.

On a white board, Teacher writes each word — one at a time. **Have students:**

- **Look** at the word.
- **Say** the word out loud.
- **Spell** the word out loud.
- **Hide** (teacher erases word.)
- **Write** the word on their paper.
- **Seek** (teacher rewrites word.)
- **Check** spelling. If incorrect, repeat above steps.

Day 2

2 Other Word Forms

This activity is optional. Have students find and circle the Other Word Forms that describe what something or someone is like.

Lesson 14

3 Fun Ways to Spell

Four activities are provided. Use one, two, three, or all of the activities. Have students initial the box for each activity they complete.

Options:

- assign activities to students according to their learning styles
- set up the activities in learning centers for students to do throughout the day
- divide students into four groups and assign one activity per group
- do one activity per day

General

To spell your words with puzzles…
- Write each word on a card.
- Cut each card squiggly, diagonal, or zigzag to make a puzzle.
- Mix your puzzle pieces.
- Put the puzzles together.
- Check your spelling.

Auditory

To spell your words while clapping…
- Look at a word on your spelling list.
- Close your eyes.
- Clap your hands softly while you whisper the spelling of the word.
- Open your eyes and check your spelling.

Visual

To spell your words with soap…
- Write a word on a hand mirror with a dry bar of soap.
- Check your spelling.
- Wipe the word off the mirror with a dry towel or washcloth.
- Write another word.

Tactile

To spell your words with play dough…
- Roll pieces of play dough into ropes.
- Use the ropes to make the letters of each word.
- Put them in the right order to spell each word.
- Check your spelling.

207

1 Word Find

Familiarize students with word meaning and usage.

(Say) Read each word in the Word Bank. Say each letter in the word, then look in the puzzle to find that same word. Circle each word you find. Write the secret word that is not in the puzzle on the lines underneath the puzzle.

F Word Find

Find and circle 9 words.

Name _____

Words with /ī/

Lesson **14**

w	r	i	t	e	s
i	m	k	i	n	d
d	l	o	m	i	v
e	a	s	e	c	b
s	l	i	n	e	d
h	i	d	e	c	e
i	c	e	f	a	b

One secret word is not used. Write it here.

ride

Word Bank

156

nice	wide	ride	time	☆ write
ice	side	hide	☆ line	☆ kind

Take a minute to memorize...

Read the memory verse twice. Have students practice it with you two more times.

208

G Dictation

Listen and write the missing words.

Name _____

1. We had a nice time at the ice rink.

2. He can go for a ride.

3. The box was too wide to fit on its side.

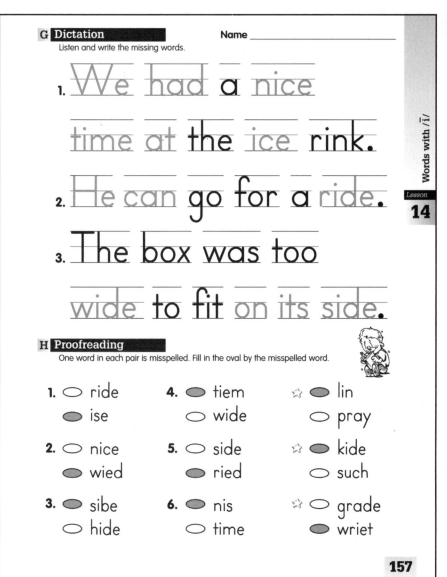

H Proofreading

One word in each pair is misspelled. Fill in the oval by the misspelled word.

1. ○ ride
   ● ise

2. ○ nice
   ● wied

3. ● sibe
   ○ hide

4. ● tiem
   ○ wide

5. ○ side
   ● ried

6. ● nis
   ○ time

☆ ● lin
   ○ pray

☆ ● kide
   ○ such

☆ ○ grade
   ● wriet

157

Dictation

Reinforce correct spelling by using current and previous words in context.

 Say

Listen as I read each sentence and then write it in your Worktext. (Slowly read each sentence twice. Sentences are found in the Student Worktext to the left.)

☆ **Challenge**

Write these incomplete sentences on the board.

James stood ___ ___ ___.

Grandpa ___ ___ to ___ ___ letter.

___ ___ ___ ___ very ___ ___.

 Say

Listen as I read each sentence. Write the sentence on your paper. (Slowly read each sentence twice.)

James stood still in line.

Grandpa has time to write a letter.

My dad is a very kind man.

Proofreading

Familiarize students with standardized test format and reinforce recognizing misspelled words.

Say

Look at each set of words. One word in each set is misspelled. Fill in the oval by the misspelled word. (You may wish to pronounce each set of words to help students correctly identify them.)

Hide and Seek

Reinforce correct spelling of current spelling words. (A reproducible master is provided in Appendix A as shown on the inset page to the right.)

Write the words one at a time on a white board.

Have students:

- **Look** at the word.
- **Say** the word out loud.
- **Spell** the word out loud.
- **Hide** (teacher erases word.)
- **Write** the word on paper.
- **Seek** (teacher rewrites word.)
- **Check** spelling. If incorrect, rewrite word correctly.

Scrambled Words

Have your students complete this activity to strengthen spelling ability and expand vocabulary.

Posttest

Test mastery of the spelling words. Challenge words are starred.

Say: I will say the word once, use the word in a sentence, then say the word again. Write the word on your paper.

1.	side	The car stopped at the **side** of the road.
2.	time	Do you know how to tell **time**?
3.	nice	It was **nice** of you to do your chores without complaining.
4.	ice	The **ice** on the pond is thick enough for skating.
5.	hide	Let's play **hide** and seek!
6.	ride	The pony was lots of fun to **ride**.
7.	wide	His mouth opened in a **wide** yawn.
☆	line	A ruler can help you draw a straight **line**.
☆	kind	What **kind** of food do you like the best?
☆	write	Please **write** your spelling words correctly on the page.

Progress Chart

Students may record scores. (Reproducible master in Appendix B.)

Personal Dictionary

Students may add any words they have misspelled to their personal dictionaries for reference when writing. (Cover in Appendix B.)

Appendix — Lesson 14

Hide and Seek

Check a paper for each word you spell correctly.

Scrambled Words

Unscramble the letters to make a word. Write the word on the lines.

1. medit   t i m e d

2. sdrei   r i d e s

3. sinel   l i n e s

4. dindeh   h i d d e n

5. redkin   k i n d e r

6. sitrew   w r i t e s

Word Bank

hidden	lines	timed
kinder	rides	writes

374

210

I Game

Name _____

Place a game piece over each word your teacher says and spells. When you get five game pieces in a row, raise your hand and say, "Spelling is fun!"

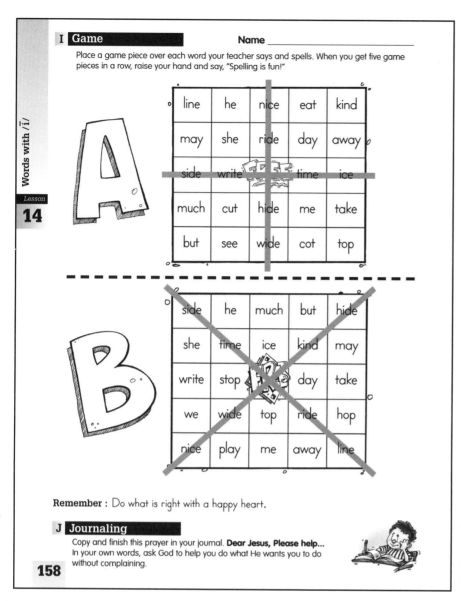

line	he	nice	eat	kind
may	she	ride	day	away
side	write	FREE	time	ice
much	cut	hide	me	take
but	see	wide	cot	top

side	he	much	but	hide
she	time	ice	kind	may
write	stop	FREE	day	take
we	wide	top	ride	hop
nice	play	me	away	line

Remember : Do what is right with a happy heart.

J Journaling

Copy and finish this prayer in your journal. **Dear Jesus, Please help...** In your own words, ask God to help you do what He wants you to do without complaining.

158

How to Play:

- Fold the word cards (see **Materials**) in half, and place them in a container.
- Ask your students to fold the game page in half along the dotted line.
- Have half the class use game card A, and the other half card B.
- Instructions for the students: "Cover the word **FREE** in the center of your card. (pause) I will draw a word from the container, read it aloud, then I will spell it. When you find that word on your card, put a game piece over it. When you have five game pieces in a row (up and down, across, or diagonally), raise your hand and say 'Spelling is FUN!'"
- Play as many times as you like. (As you return the word cards to the container and mix them up, remind the students to clear their game cards.)
- For variety, after playing several games, have the students turn their papers over and use the other game card.

---

2 Game

Reinforce spelling skills and provide motivation and interest.

Materials
- game page (from student text)
- flat buttons, dry beans, pennies, or game discs (10 per child)
- game word list
- word cards (each word from the game word list written on a card)

Game Word List
This list contains regular and challenge words.

1. **nice**
2. **line**
3. **ice**
4. **write**
5. **wide**
6. **kind**
7. **side**
☆ **ride**
☆ **hide**
☆ **time**

3 Journaling

Provide a meaningful reason for correct spelling through personal writing.

Review the story using discussion leads provided on the following page. Encourage students to apply the Scriptural value in their journaling.

Take a minute to memorize...

Have the class say the memory verse from lessons 11, 12, 13, and 14 with you.

211

Journaling (continued)

Say

- Do you have jobs or chores to do at home or at school? Name some of them.
- Are there times when you complain about doing them like Christopher did?
- How do you think those around us feel when we complain about doing our work? (Frustrated, upset, etc.)
- How do you think God feels when we complain? (Sad, disappointed.)
- How do you feel when you complain? (Unhappy, etc.)
- We please God and feel happier when we choose to do what we need to do without complaining. In your journal, ask God to help you do what He wants you to do without complaining.

*"Students will learn how to spell and will learn the value of correct spelling, if they write often for authentic purposes."**

*Scott, Jill E. 1994. Spelling for Readers and Writers. The Reading Teacher, Vol. 48, No. 2, October: 188-190.

A Safe Fort

*Matthew is glad to have Jesus as his "safe fort"
when he gets lost.*

"Okay, class! Get your coats on and line up at the door." Miss Grant smiled at the surprised faces of the children as she began spelling class Monday morning.

"Where are we going?" asked Tony.

"It's not time for recess, is it?" Katelynn looked puzzled.

"Do we need to wear our gloves?" Matthew asked.

"We're going out to the playground," Miss Grant said. "Meet under the big evergreen tree and then I'll tell you the plan." The room buzzed with happy, excited voices as the children rushed to follow Miss Grant's instructions.

Almost an hour later, the class was putting the finishing touches on their project. "Wow! You've really worked hard kids!" Miss Grant said as she helped roll the last mammoth snowball into place. "This is an incredible snow fort! I think I'm the only one who can see over the walls."

"It's so big our whole class fits inside!" said Stephen.

"Thanks for your help, Miss Grant!" Beth hugged her teacher's arm.

Tony looked a little confused. "Was this today's spelling class?"

"Only part of it, Tony," Miss Grant answered. "Let's go back inside where it's warm. Matthew's mom has a surprise waiting for us."

Matthew looked startled. "My mom? She didn't say she was coming to school today."

"I asked her to keep it a secret, Matthew." Miss Grant smiled and walked toward the classroom door. As the class rushed back inside, she heard excited voices. "Hot chocolate!" "Mmmmmm! My favorite!" "Oooooo! This should warm me up." The room continued to hum with excitement as the children returned to their desks to find a warm treat waiting.

Matthew waved at his mom. His little sister Emily toddled over and tried to climb up on his lap. "Thkool. thkool. Mathoo's thkool," she lisped as she reached for Matthew's crayons and started pulling them out of the box one by one.

"Yes, this is Matthew's school, Em." Matthew laughed and gave her a squeeze.

"You can keep drinking your hot chocolate," Miss Grant directed, "but I need your eyes looking toward the front of the room. Our Scripture verse this week for handwriting and spelling comes from Psalm 18:2. It says, 'The Lord is my fort where I can enter and be safe.'" Miss Grant wrote the text on the board, then repeated it again. "What kind of fort do you think David was talking about — a snow fort like we built this morning on the playground?"

"I don't think they had snow where David lived." Tommy frowned. "They must have used something else."

"Did they make their forts out of trees like the pilgrims?" Stephen asked.

"Palestine is a dry and very rocky place," said Miss Grant. "There are some trees, but not forests of tall, straight pines like the early settlers used to build their forts."

"They must have made them with rocks or bricks then," Rosa said. "There's nothing else you can build a fort with."

"Good thinking, Rosa! I like the way you figured out that answer."

"But how can the Lord be a fort?" Daniel asked. "God isn't a big rock or a brick or something."

As the discussion continued, Matthew noticed his mom cleaning off the counter where some hot chocolate had spilled. A stack of disposable cups sat nearby. "Mom must have bought those at the store last Friday after school," Matthew realized. He'd been surprised when they stopped at the store since Mom usually shopped for groceries when he and Alex were in school.

"That's one stop I'll never forget!" Matthew frowned to himself. The scene played back in his mind as he stared at the text on the board.

"Boys, I need to stop at the grocery store." Mrs. Schilling said as she pulled into the parking lot. "We don't have a lot of time before Mr. Wilson brings Stephen over to play, so we've got to hurry."

As she unbuckled Emily from her car seat, Matthew and Alex ran toward the door of the store. "Matthew! Alex! Please stop!" Mom said in a commanding voice. The boys froze instantly. "You know our rule boys," Mom said as she caught up with them. "You must always walk beside me in the parking lot. Drivers can't always see someone your size, and I don't want you to get run over."

"We were just trying to hurry like you said," Alex said as they walked into the store together. "I guess we forgot."

Mom started to put Emily in the seat of a grocery cart sitting right inside the door. But Emily had other ideas, and she began to wiggle and cry. "Matthew, would you hold Em's hand?" Mom asked. "I think she'd like to walk. She's tired of being buckled up, but it's not safe to let her stand up in the cart."

"Sure, Mom," Matthew took his little sister's hand. She pulled him over to a bright display of cereal boxes and tried to pick one up.

"Hi, Matthew!" Matthew's choir teacher pushed her cart down the aisle toward the Schilling family.

"Oh, Mrs. Espinoza!" Mom smiled warmly. "I've

213

been wanting to tell you what a wonderful job you did on the Christmas program. Matthew and Alex had such a good time dressing up like shepherds. I think the whole family learned the words from the CD you made for us. Where do you find such great…"

Emily pulled Matthew around the end of the aisle. Some toys were displayed just within her reach. Matthew could still hear Mom and Mrs. Espinoza talking about the program. Emily grabbed an inexpensive doll from the display. "Baby theepy," Emily said as she cuddled the little doll close to her. "So theepy."

"Yes, your baby is sleepy, Em," Matthew agreed. "See her eyes are closed. Put her back in her bed now. She needs her nap."

"No, no," Emily cried softly. "Need Mommy. Baby need Mommy."

"This baby needs to be back in her bed," Matthew said more forcefully. "Put her back now, Em."

"No! No!" Emily yelled louder as Matthew took the doll away and put it back on the shelf. Then she started to cry. Matthew tried to comfort her, but by now she was too upset. "Mommy! Mommy! I want my Mommy!"

Matthew picked her up and carried her around the corner, but Emily kicked at him and squirmed so much that he couldn't get a very good hold on her. "Mom?" Matthew rounded the corner, but Mom was nowhere in sight. Alex wasn't either.

"Em," he said in his most grown-up voice, "Mommy isn't here. Let's see if we can find her. She must have gone down the next aisle after she finished talking to Mrs. Espinoza."

Emily sensed the panic in Matthew's voice and let him pick her up. She forgot all about the doll as she clung to her big brother.

Matthew rushed down one aisle and up the next, but still didn't see Mom.

Emily was getting heavy, but he didn't want to walk slowly. He had to find Mom fast!

Where could she have gone? *"Dear Lord, keep us safe and help me to find Mom,"* Matthew prayed to himself. He remembered how Mom always said to stay beside her. "Don't go where I can't see you, Matthew," she frequently reminded when they went shopping. She'd also warned him about not talking to people he didn't know. "What if that big man on the last aisle starts to follow us?" Matthew thought. "Where should I take Em? And how am I supposed to get help? Everyone in this store is a stranger!"

As he rounded the last aisle, he saw a clerk in a blue coat putting cans on the shelf. He remembered Mom said clerks are good people to ask for help if you're ever lost in a store. He rushed up to the woman, almost dropping Emily in his panic.

"Excuse me, ma'am," he said as he fought back the tears. "I can't find my mommy. I think that m-m-maybe she left us."

"Oh, I'm sure your mommy wouldn't do that," the clerk laughed. "Let me help you find her." She led the children around the end of the aisle and started toward the courtesy desk at the front of the store. Now Matthew's tears began to flow freely — even though he felt a lot better. He tried to quit crying and rubbed his eyes with his coat sleeve.

Suddenly Mom rushed around the corner, almost knocking Emily out of his arms.

"There you two are!" She sighed with relief. "I'm so glad you are safe!" She bent down and gathered them into her arms as the smiling clerk looked on.

"And so class, what do you think?" Miss Grant continued, bringing Matthew back to Monday morning's spelling class with a jolt. "How can God be our fort?" A moment later Matthew was waving his hand back and forth frantically.

"What is it, Matthew?" Miss Grant asked. "Do you have an example of how the Lord can be our fort?"

"Yes, Miss Grant!" Matthew's face broke into a big grin. "God was my fort in the grocery store last week!" And the class listened intently as Matthew explained.

2 Discussion Time

Check understanding of the story and development of personal values.

- Have you ever made a fort?
- What did you make it out of?
- Have you ever been lost before?
- How did you feel?
- What did you do?
- Why did Matthew feel like Jesus was his fort in the middle of the store?
- Did you know that you have your very own guardian angel?
- Jesus loves to protect you. Don't forget to ask Him to be your fort next time you don't feel safe.

A Test-Words

Name _____

Write each word as your teacher says it.

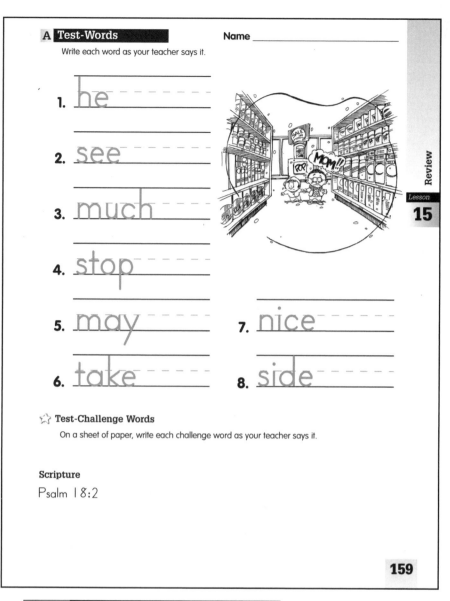

1. he

2. see

3. much

4. stop

5. may   7. nice

6. take   8. side

☆ **Test-Challenge Words**

On a sheet of paper, write each challenge word as your teacher says it.

Scripture

Psalm 18:2

159

Test-Challenge Words

On a separate sheet of paper, challenge words may be tested using the sentences below.

Personal Dictionary

After the tests in the review unit are graded, students may add any words they have misspelled to their personal dictionaries.

Take a minute to memorize...

Read the memory verse to the class twice. Have the class practice it with you two more times.

---

3 Test-Words

Test for knowledge of the correct spellings of these words.
(See the instructions at the top right for challenge words.)

Say   I will say each word once, use the word in a sentence, then say the word again. Write the word on the lines in your Worktext.

1. he   Matthew realized **he** was lost.
2. see   Matthew couldn't **see** his mother in the store.
3. much   There isn't **much** hot chocolate left.
4. stop   Mother needed to **stop** at the store.
5. may   You **may** help build a snow fort.
6. take   "Do we need to **take** our gloves?" Matthew asked.
7. nice   The clerk at the store was **nice** to Matthew.
8. side   Miss Grant was the only one who could see over the **side** of the fort.
☆ each   Matthew looked down **each** aisle for his mom.
☆ such   "The boys had **such** a good time," said Mrs. O'Brien.
☆ grade   Matthew is in the first **grade**.
☆ line   Mom got in **line** to pay for the groceries.

215

1 Game

Materials
- game page (from student text)
- crayons (1 per child)
- game word list (provided below)

Game Word List
Use of challenge words is optional.

1. he
2. see
3. much
4. stop
5. may
6. take
7. nice
8. side
☆ each
☆ such
☆ grade
☆ line

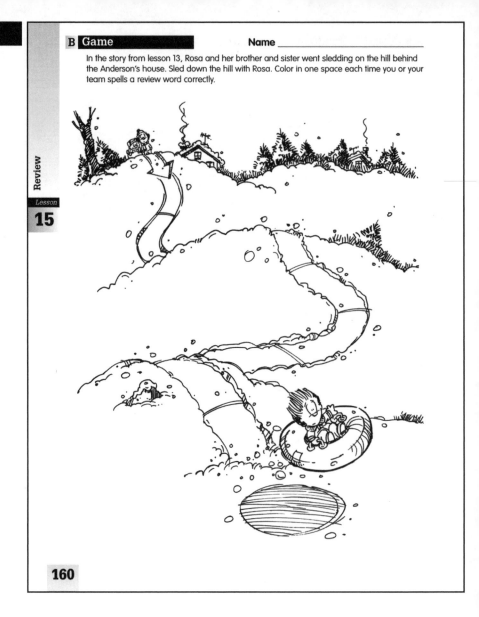

B Game   Name _____

Review
Lesson
15

In the story from lesson 13, Rosa and her brother and sister went sledding on the hill behind the Anderson's house. Sled down the hill with Rosa. Color in one space each time you or your team spells a review word correctly.

160

How to Play:

- Divide the class into two teams, and decide which team will go first.
- Have a student from team A go to the board.
- Read the spelling word two times slowly and clearly. (You may also wish to use the word in a sentence. Ex.: "cat — The cat climbed a tree. — cat")
- Have the student write the word on the board.
- If the word is spelled correctly, instruct all the members of team A to color one space, beginning at Start, on the game board. (Note: If the word is misspelled, correct the spelling immediately before continuing the game.)
- Alternate between teams A and B as you go down the word list.
- The team to reach the bottom of the hill first is the winner.

Non-Competitive Option:
At the end of the game, say: "Class, I am proud of your efforts to spell the words correctly. If you had fun and tried your best, you are all winners!"

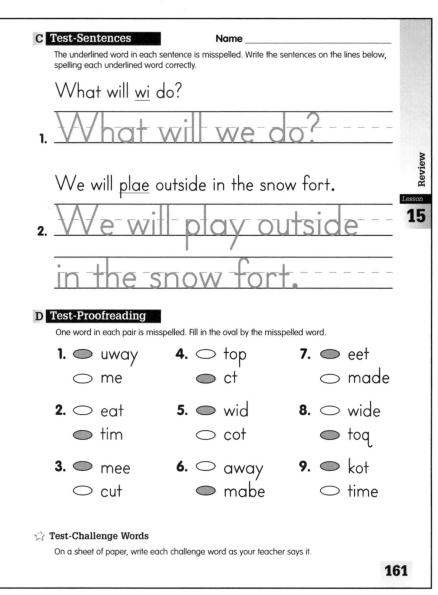

C **Test-Sentences**   Name _____

The underlined word in each sentence is misspelled. Write the sentences on the lines below, spelling each underlined word correctly.

What will <u>wi</u> do?

1. What will we do?

We will <u>plae</u> outside in the snow fort.

2. We will play outside
in the snow fort.

D **Test-Proofreading**

One word in each pair is misspelled. Fill in the oval by the misspelled word.

1. ● uway   4. ○ top   7. ● eet
   ○ me   ● ct   ○ made

2. ○ eat   5. ● wid   8. ○ wide
   ● tim   ○ cot   ● toq

3. ● mee   6. ○ away   9. ● kot
   ○ cut   ● mabe   ○ time

☆ **Test-Challenge Words**

On a sheet of paper, write each challenge word as your teacher says it.

161

Test-Sentences

Reinforce recognizing misspelled words.

Say — Read each sentence carefully. The underlined word in each sentence is misspelled. Write the sentences on the lines in your worktext, spelling each underlined word correctly.

Test-Proofreading

Familiarize students with standardized test format and reinforce recognition of misspelled words.

Say — Look at each set of words. One word in each set is misspelled. Fill in the oval by the misspelled word.

(You may wish to pronounce each pair of words to help students correctly identify them.)

Test-Challenge Words

On a separate sheet of paper, challenge words may be tested using the sentences below.

Say — I will say the word once, use the word in a sentence, then say the word again. Write the word on your paper.

☆ he's — I'm sure **he's** glad his mom brought hot chocolate.
☆ clock — Mom looked at the digital **clock** in the car.
☆ pray — Matthew stopped to **pray** for God's help.
☆ write — Miss Grant will **write** the Scripture verse on the board.

217

1 Game

Materials
- game page (from student text)
- flat buttons, dry beans, pennies, or game discs (1 per child)
- game word list

Game Word List
Use of challenge words is optional.

1. we
2. play
3. me
4. eat
5. cut
6. top
7. cot
8. away
9. made
10. wide
11. time
☆ he's
☆ clock
☆ pray
☆ write

E Game　　　　　　　　　　Name _____

Matthew and Emily got separated from their mom in the grocery store. Show Matthew the way to the friendly store clerk, who will help him and Emily find their mom. Move one space each time you or your team spells a review word correctly.

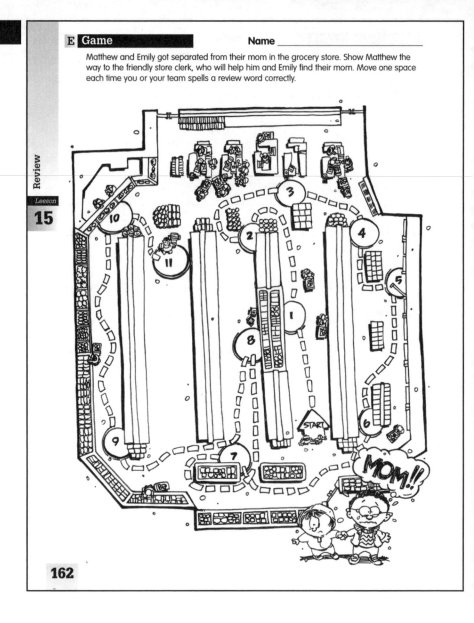

162

How to Play:

- Divide the class into two teams, and decide which team will go first.
- Have each student place his/her game piece on Start.
- Have a student from team A go to the board.
- Read the spelling word two times slowly and clearly. (You may also wish to use the word in a sentence. Ex.: "cat — The cat climbed a tree. — cat")
- Have the student write the word on the board.
- If the word is spelled correctly, instruct the members of team A to move their game pieces forward one space on the game board. (Note: If the word is misspelled, correct the spelling immediately before continuing the game.)
- Alternate between teams A and B as you go down the word list.
- The team to reach the friendly clerk first is the winner.

Non-Competitive Option:
At the end of the game, say: "Class, I am proud of your efforts to spell the words correctly. If you had fun and tried your best, you are all winners!"

F Test-Sentence Name _____

The underlined word in this sentence is misspelled. Write the sentence on the lines below, spelling the underlined word correctly.

We will <u>hibe</u> in the snow fort.

We will hide in the

snow fort.

G Test-Words

Write each word as your teacher says it.

1. she   5. day

2. feet   6. make

3. but   7. ice

4. hop   8. ride

☆ **Test-Challenge Words**
On a sheet of paper, write each challenge word as your teacher says it.

163

---

1 **Test-Sentence**

Reinforce recognizing misspelled words.

(Say) Read this sentence carefully. The underlined word is misspelled. Write the sentence on the lines in your Worktext, spelling the underlined word correctly.

 Personal Dictionary
Remind students to add any words they have misspelled to their personal dictionaries.

---

2 **Test-Words**

Test for knowledge of the correct spellings of these words. (Challenge words may be tested on a separate piece of paper. Challenge words are starred.)

 (Say) I will say each word once, use the word in a sentence, then say the word again. Write the word on the lines in your Worktext.

1. she   Matthew said, "The doll is sleepy, so **she** needs a nap."
2. feet   That wall is four **feet** high.
3. but   Matthew looked for his mother, **but** couldn't find her.
4. hop   We will **hop** like frogs.
5. day   The first graders had a fun **day**.
6. make   Do you know how to **make** a snow fort?
7. ice   The **ice** on the trees is melting.
8. ride   Emily did not want to **ride** in the cart.
☆ **we'll**   Then **we'll** build a snow fort.
☆ **drop**   Please **drop** your empty cup in the trash can.
☆ **came**   Matthew's mom **came** to his classroom.
☆ **kind**   The store clerk was very **kind**.

219

3 Writing Assessment

Assess student's spelling, grammar, and composition skills through personal writing.

(Say)
- The Scriptures say, "The Lord is my fort where I can enter and be safe." Who didn't feel safe in the story this week? (Matthew and Emily) Why? (They were lost in the grocery store.)
- Think about a time when you were lost like Matthew and Em or felt that you were not safe.
- Whenever you don't feel safe you can call on Jesus.
- Today in your worktext you are going to write about a time when you needed a safe fort.

H Writing Assessment

Finish this sentence.

Name _____

Review

Lesson **15**

I feel like I need a safe fort when

_____

_____

_____

_____

Remember : When you are afraid, call on Jesus.

164

A rubric for scoring is provided in Appendix B.

---

4 Action Game

Reinforce spelling skills and provide motivation and interest.

Materials
- blindfold
- small prizes (erasers, pencils, stickers)
- poem: Spell a word. Spell it now.
  Spell this word if you know how.

How to Play:

Choose one student to be **IT** and blindfold him. Have the other students form a circle around **IT**, holding hands. The students circle around **IT** as you say the poem, stopping on the last word. **IT** points in any direction to choose a student to spell. Give the student to whom he points a word to spell from this review unit. If he spells it correctly, give him a prize and have him return to his desk; if he spells it incorrectly, have him be **IT**. If a student has been **IT** for three turns, have him spell a word. If he spells the word correctly, give him a prize and have him return to his desk. Choose another student from the circle to be **IT**. If he does not spell the word correctly, have him join the circle and choose another student from the circle to be **IT**. Continue playing until every student has spelled a word correctly.

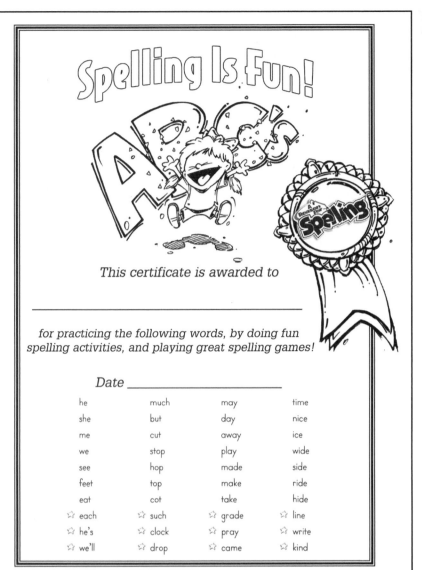

Spelling Is Fun!

ABC's

This certificate is awarded to

_____

for practicing the following words, by doing fun
spelling activities, and playing great spelling games!

Date _____

he	much	may	time
she	but	day	nice
me	cut	away	ice
we	stop	play	wide
see	hop	made	side
feet	top	make	ride
eat	cot	take	hide
☆ each	☆ such	☆ grade	☆ line
☆ he's	☆ clock	☆ pray	☆ write
☆ we'll	☆ drop	☆ came	☆ kind

5 Certificate

Provide an opportunity
for parents or guardians
to encourage and assess
their child's progress.

Say
- Write your name on the first line.
- Now I will write the date on the board for you to copy on the next line.
- Follow along as I read the certificate out loud.
- Be sure to show your parents or guardian all the words you've practiced spelling.

Take a minute to memorize...

Read the memory verse
to the class twice. Have
the class practice it with
you two more times.

Quotables!

*"The reason children learn
to spell is to be able to write.
The reason children learn to write
is to provide themselves and
others with things to read.
The reason children learn to read
is to be able to read what they
and others have written.
They all go together."*

*Harp, Bill. 1988. When the Principal Asks, "Why Are Your Kids
Giving Each Other Spelling Tests?" Reading Teacher, Vol. 41, No. 7,
March: 702-704.

6 Letter

Provide the parent or guardian with the spelling word lists for the next unit.

Say

Show your parents or guardian this letter that tells them what your spelling words will be for the next unit. Ask them to put it in a special place where you will remember to practice them together.

A Reason For Spelling

Dear Parent,

We are about to begin a new spelling unit containing four weekly lessons. A set of seven words plus three challenge words will be studied each week. All the words will be reviewed in the fifth week.

Values based on the Scriptures listed below will be taught in each lesson.

Lesson 16	Lesson 17	Lesson 18	Lesson 19
my	when	they	now
by	then	them	how
try	hen	there	down
why	ten	this	town
no	went	the	our
so	send	with	out
go	cent	thing	about
☆ going	☆ even	☆ than	☆ vowel
☆ most	☆ penny	☆ these	☆ south
☆ know	☆ sentence	☆ think	☆ round
Prov. 3:3	Psalm 119: 33, 35	Prov. 17:17	Psalm 5:11

Choosing to be Kind

A heavy snowfall gives Beth a chance to go sledding,
but tests her honesty, too.

"**B**ethy! Bethy! Wake up!"
Luke gently shook his older sister
awake.

"Go away, Luke," Beth mumbled.
"I'm still asleep!"

"Come see, Beth. Come see the
snow!"

"I saw the snow yesterday, Luke.
Let me sleep. It's only . . ." Beth opened
one eye and looked at the red numbers
on her digital clock. "It's . . . SEVEN
THIRTY! Why didn't my alarm go off?
How come no one got me up?" Beth sat
up with a jerk. "I'm going to be late for
school!" she wailed, wide awake now.
"Miss Grant reads a chapter first thing
every morning, and now I'll miss what
happens today! I hate missing the
story."

"Mommy said you don't have
school today because it snowed," Luke
said calmly.

"Luke, you aren't making sense. It
snowed yesterday, and we still had
school."

"Come look out your window,
Beth. You'll see," Luke tugged on
Beth's hand.

Beth got out of bed and walked
over to the window. "Oooooo!" Her
eyes opened wide. "It's so beautiful,
and there's so much of it. Look at those
huge flakes coming down! You can't
even see where our driveway is across
the pasture." She turned to look at
Luke. "Did Dad already go to work?
How did he know where to drive?"

"That's why you don't have
school," Luke explained. His eyes
flashed with excitement. "It's too far to
walk and Mommy can't take you in the
car. Daddy's already at work. His tracks
are all gone now."

"Oh, Luke! We can sled down our

big hill and maybe the Vasquez kids can
come over and sled with us. We can use
our new tubes Grandma got us!" Beth
slipped on her robe and ran down the
stairs into the kitchen where Mom was
fixing breakfast.

"Can we ask Carlos, Maria, and
Rosa over to go sledding down our
hill?" she asked Mom. "Their dad won't
be able to get any work done today if
they're all in the house with him."

"I don't see why not." Mom
laughed at Beth's expression. "Why
don't you give them a call and see if
they'd like to come over at 10:00?"

"We can! We can!" Beth yelled,
running back up the stairs.

At ten o'clock sharp, Mr. Vasquez
dropped off three excited children.
Their big tube sleds were already
inflated. "Thank you for inviting my
kids over this morning, Janette," Mr.
Vasquez said as he climbed back into
the jeep. "They've been wanting to play
with Beth and Luke. I'm sure I'll get
more work done this way, too!" He
laughed. "I'll pick them up around noon
if that's okay."

"No problem," said Mrs. Hill.

Just then, Beth and Luke came out
of the garage dragging their sleds.
"Look at my new tube sled, Rosa!"
Luke said. Mom walked over and
pulled his hat firmly over his ears.

"Hi, Rosa. Hi, Maria. Hi, Carlos,"
Beth yelled as she ran to greet her
friends. "See our new snow tubes
Grandma found for us? They're almost
exactly like yours."

"All right!" Carlos grinned. "Race
you to the top of the sledding hill!"

The five children took off across
the yard, dragging their tube sleds

behind them. "Have a good time!"
Mr. Vasquez shouted as he pulled
away.

"And come in if you get too
cold," Mrs. Hill added as she
hurried back into the house.

The five friends had a
wonderful time on the big hill. The
long, steep slope was perfect for
sledding. Four-year-old Luke went
only partway up the hill each time
before he jumped on his tube and
headed for the bottom. The four
older children made the long trek all
the way to the top for faster, more
exciting rides.

"Wait for me at the bottom,
Beth," Rosa yelled as Beth got
ready to jump on her new tube for
another ride.

"Okay!" Beth called back. She
gave a quick shove and slid onto the
slick, worn path down the hill.

Just as Beth crested the last
little rise near the bottom, she saw Luke
plop onto his tube right in her path.
"Watch out, Luke!" she shouted as she
bailed out and rolled off into the soft
snow. Luke looked back over his
shoulder just as Beth's tube bounced
into his, knocking him off into a snow
bank. He got up laughing, and clomped
off after his runaway tube.

"What were you thinking, Luke?"
Beth asked as she caught up with him.
"I almost hit you, Buddy. You need to
make sure no one is coming before you
jump on your tube."

"Sorry, Beth," Luke said. The two
children watched their tubes roll the rest
of the way down the hill and crash into
some bushes at the bottom. Beth
trudged through the drifted snow to
reach them. But just as she bent down
to pick up her tube, she suddenly
realized the tubes were resting on
blackberry bushes — blackberry bushes
covered with thorns!

"Oh, no! This is my brand-new
tube!" Beth thought as she checked hers
over carefully. It was already beginning
to get softer. "I'll have to use my old
plastic saucer if this loses any more air."

Beth quickly checked Luke's tube,
and realized it was okay. Then she
picked up the tube with the
hole in it, and handed it to

223

Luke. "Here you go, Luke," she said. "Be more careful. Okay, little guy?" Luke ran off laughing.

"He'll never know the difference," Beth thought, "because our tubes looks exactly alike." She began to climb the hill again, this time carrying Luke's tube. "It won't hurt him to use his old saucer — he doesn't even go to the top of the hill. It was his fault anyway."

But Beth didn't feel very good about her choice. The Scripture verse Miss Grant had taught them yesterday kept popping into her head. "Never forget to be truthful and kind."

Beth frowned. Why did she have to think of that right now?

"Never forget to be truthful and kind." She wanted to push a button in her mind, and turn off that verse! But the verse kept on playing over and over. "Never forget to be truthful and kind. Never forget . . ."

"Luke!" Beth shouted. "Hey, Buddy! You have the wrong tube."

"Oh . . . okay." Luke traded tubes with a smile, never realizing what had happened.

As Beth took back her tube with the hole in it, she smiled at the blond-haired little boy and adjusted the cap back over his ears. "Never forget to be truthful and kind." The recording in her brain played the verse again. But this time, Beth grinned. She felt good about her choice now!

Lesson 16 | **Day 1**

2 Discussion Time

Check understanding of the story and development of personal values.

- How do you think Beth felt when she knew her tube had a hole in it?
- Why did Beth take Luke's tube?
- Why was it hard for Beth to give Luke's tube back?
- What do you think the other kids will do when Beth's tube is too flat to use?
- Do you think they might share their tubes with Beth?
- Jesus knows that we will be happier if we are truthful and kind.
- Never forget He is always willing to help us when we have a hard choice to make.

224

A Preview

Write each word as your teacher says it.

Name _____

1. why
2. my
3. so
4. by
5. go
6. try
7. no

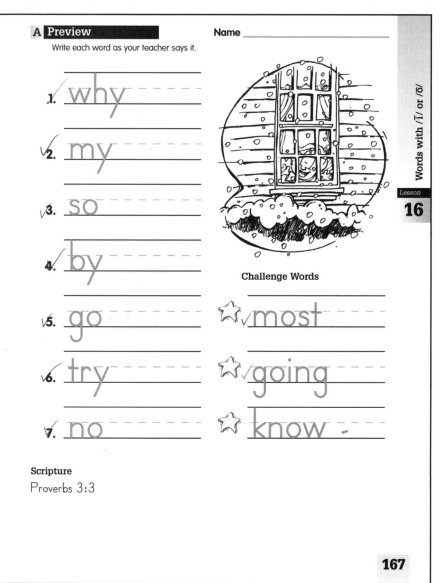

Challenge Words

☆ most
☆ going
☆ know

Scripture
Proverbs 3:3

167

Challenge

For better spellers, challenge words may be included in the weekly list. Challenge words are starred.

Correct Immediately!

Let's correct our preview. I will write each word on the board. Put a dot under each letter on your preview as I spell the word out loud. If you spelled a word wrong, rewrite it correctly.

Progress Chart

Students may record scores. (Reproducible master in Appendix B.)

Take a minute to memorize . . .

Read the memory verse twice. Have students practice it with you two more times.

---

3 Preview

Test for knowledge of the correct spellings of these words. (See the instructions at the top right for challenge words.)

 I will say each word once, use the word in a sentence, then say the word again. Write the word on the lines in the Worktext.

1. why   Do you know **why** Beth is happy?
2. my   This is **my** new tube sled.
3. so   This sled goes **so** fast down the hill!
4. by   I will slide down the hill **by** myself.
5. go   I will **go** down the hill on my sled first.
6. try   I will always **try** to do my best.
7. no   There are **no** more cookies in the cookie jar.
☆ most   The snow fell heavily during **most** of the night.
☆ going   We are **going** sledding after school!
☆ know   Do you **know** what time it is?

4 Word Shapes

Help students form a correct image of whole words.

(Say) Look at each word and think about its shape. Now, write the word in the correct word Shape Boxes. You may check off each word as you use it.

(In many words, the sound /ī/ is spelled with **y** and it is often spelled this way when it is at the end of a word. In many words, the sound of /ō/ is spelled with **o** and it is often spelled this way when it is at the end of a word.)

(Say) In the word shape boxes, color the letter that spells the sound of /ī/ or /ō/ in each word. Circle the word that begins with the digraph **wh**.

Challenge
Draw the correctly shaped box around each letter in these words.

(Say) On a separate sheet of paper, write other words that contain the spelling patterns in the word list. See how many words you can write.

Lesson 16 | **Day 1**

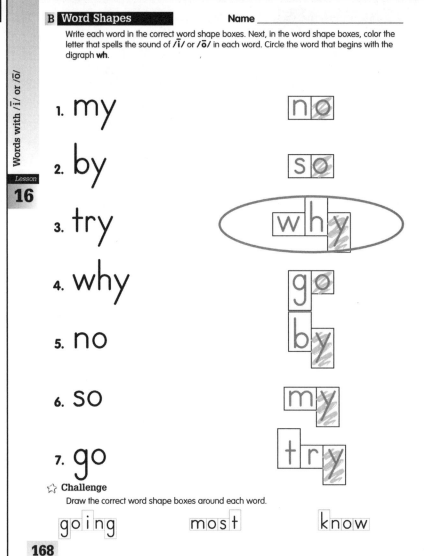

B Word Shapes   Name _____

Write each word in the correct word shape boxes. Next, in the word shape boxes, color the letter that spells the sound of /ī/ or /ō/ in each word. Circle the word that begins with the digraph **wh**.

1. my
2. by
3. try
4. why
5. no
6. so
7. go

☆ **Challenge**
Draw the correct word shape boxes around each word.

168

Answers may vary for duplicate word shapes.

Words with /ī/ or /ō/
Lesson **16**

Be Prepared For Fun

Check these supply lists for **Fun Ways to Spell** presented **Day 2**. Purchase and/or gather these items ahead of time!

General
- Crayons
- 3 x 5 Cards cut in thirds (16 pieces per child)
- 3 x 5 Cards cut in thirds (13 more pieces for challenge words)
- Glue
- Construction Paper (about 3 pieces per child)
- Spelling List

Auditory
- Spelling List

Visual
- Chalk or Whiteboard Marker
- Chalkboard or Whiteboard (could be individual boards for each child)
- Spelling List

Tactile
- Damp Sand (in plastic storage box with lid)
- Spelling List

226

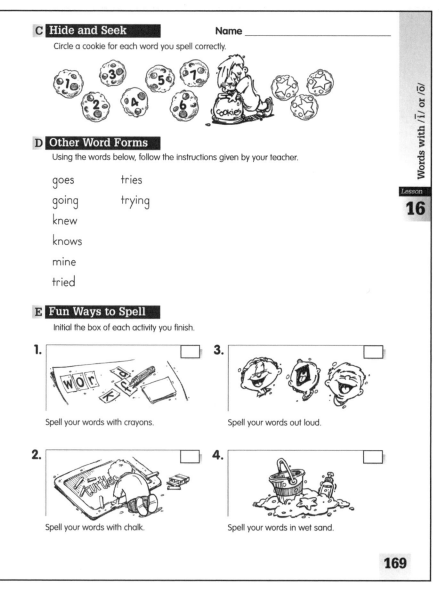

C Hide and Seek   Name _____

Circle a cookie for each word you spell correctly.

D Other Word Forms

Using the words below, follow the instructions given by your teacher.

goes   tries

going   trying

knew

knows

mine

tried

E Fun Ways to Spell

Initial the box of each activity you finish.

1. [ ]

Spell your words with crayons.

2. [ ]

Spell your words with chalk.

3. [ ]

Spell your words out loud.

4. [ ]

Spell your words in wet sand.

Words with /ī/ or /ō/

Lesson
16

169

Lesson 16 | **Day 2**

1 **Hide and Seek**

Reinforce spelling by using multiple styles of learning.

On a white board, Teacher writes each word — one at a time. **Have students:**

- **Look** at the word.
- **Say** the word out loud.
- **Spell** the word out loud.
- **Hide** (teacher erases word.)
- **Write** the word on their paper.
- **Seek** (teacher rewrites word.)
- **Check** spelling. If incorrect, repeat above steps.

2 **Other Word Forms**

This activity is optional. Have students find the Other Word Forms that best complete these sentences.

I __ to climb that tree. (tried)
Mom __ the lady's name. (knew)

3 **Fun Ways to Spell**

Four activities are provided. Use one, two, three, or all of the activities. Have students initial the box for each activity they complete.

Options:

- assign activities to students according to their learning styles
- set up the activities in learning centers for students to do throughout the day
- divide students into four groups and assign one activity per group
- do one activity per day

General

To spell your words with crayon…
- Write each letter of your spelling word on a card.
- Glue the cards on a sheet of paper in the right order to spell your words.
- Check your spelling.

Auditory

To spell your words out loud…
- Have your classmate read a spelling word.
- Say a sentence with that spelling word to your classmate.
- Spell the spelling word you used in that sentence to your classmate.
- Ask your classmate to check your spelling.
- Do this with each word on your word list.

Visual

To spell your words with chalk…
- Put your spelling list on your desk.
- Look at a word then walk to the chalkboard (or whiteboard).
- Write your spelling word on the chalkboard (or whiteboard).
- Return to your desk.
- Check your spelling.

Tactile

To spell your words in damp sand…
- Use your finger to write a spelling word in the damp sand.
- Check your spelling.
- Smooth the sand with your finger and write another word.

227

Sentence Fun

1

Familiarize students with word meaning and usage.

Say

Using words from the Word Bank, write the spelling word that best completes each sentence.

Challenge

Read these incomplete sentences to your better spellers. Have them write the challenge word that best completes each sentence.

• Where are you __? (going)

• I __ the answer to that question. (know)

• She had the __ stickers on her chart. (most)

F **Sentence Fun**   Name _____

Write the missing word in each sentence.

Words with /ī/ or /ō/

Lesson **16**

1. We want to **go** with you.

2. Please let me **try** to do it.

3. Your bike is **by** my bike.

4. This is **my** friend.

5. I always ask **why**.

6. It snowed **so** much, we went sledding.

7. It is **no** fun to be cold.

Word Bank

my	try	no	go
by	why	so	

170

Take a minute to memorize...

Read the memory verse twice. Have students practice it with you two more times.

228

G Dictation
Listen and write the missing words.

Name _____

1. I can try to ride.

2. Why did she go so fast?

3. No, it did not land by him.

H Proofreading
One word in each pair is misspelled. Fill in the oval by the misspelled word.

1. ○ try
   ● hwy

2. ○ my
   ● soe

3. ○ no
   ● bi

4. ● trie
   ○ go

5. ○ by
   ● goi

6. ○ why
   ● mie

☆ ● mosk
   ○ kind

☆ ○ pray
   ● gowing

☆ ○ clock
   ● kno

171

---

1 Dictation
Reinforce correct spelling by using current and previous words in context.

Say

Listen as I read each sentence and then write it in your Worktext. (Slowly read each sentence twice. Sentences are found in the Student Worktext to the left.)

☆ **Challenge**
Write these incomplete sentences on the board.

__ __ __ __ __ to __.

Katelynn __ the __ stickers.

__ __ __ __ __.

Say

Listen as I read each sentence. Write the sentence on your paper. (Slowly read each sentence twice.)

I am glad he's going to try.

Katelynn has the most stickers.

I do not know him.

---

2 Proofreading
Familiarize students with standardized test format and reinforce recognizing misspelled words.

Say

Look at each set of words. One word in each set is misspelled. Fill in the oval by the misspelled word. (You may wish to pronounce each set of words to help students correctly identify them.)

229

3 Hide and Seek

Reinforce correct spelling of current spelling words. (A reproducible master is provided in Appendix A as shown on the inset page to the right.)

Write the words one at a time on a white board.

Have students:

- **Look** at the word.
- **Say** the word out loud.
- **Spell** the word out loud.
- **Hide** (teacher erases word.)
- **Write** the word on paper.
- **Seek** (teacher rewrites word.)
- **Check** spelling. If incorrect, rewrite word correctly.

4 Code

Have your students complete this activity to strengthen spelling ability and expand vocabulary.

1 Posttest

Test mastery of the spelling words. Challenge words are starred.

(Say) I will say the word once, use the word in a sentence, then say the word again. Write the word on your paper.

1. so — Beth felt **so** good when she made the right choice.
2. why — Do you know **why** Beth took Luke's sled?
3. by — I will sit **by** my friends.
4. go — We will **go** to the store after school.
5. my — I am going to **my** grandparents house.
6. no — There is **no** time to play now.
7. try — Always **try** to spell every word correctly.
☆ know — Do you **know** your own phone number?
☆ most — The snow was cleared from **most** of the roads.
☆ going — The first graders are **going** on a field trip.

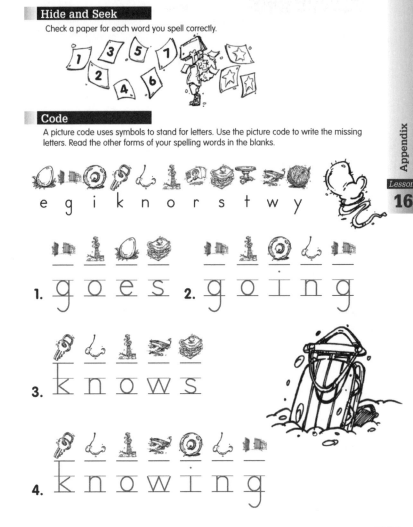

Hide and Seek
Check a paper for each word you spell correctly.

Code
A picture code uses symbols to stand for letters. Use the picture code to write the missing letters. Read the other forms of your spelling words in the blanks.

e g i k n o r s t w y

1. g o e s   2. g o i n g
3. k n o w s
4. k n o w i n g

375

Progress Chart
Students may record scores. (Reproducible master in Appendix B.)

Personal Dictionary
Students may add any words they have misspelled to their personal dictionaries for reference when writing. (Cover in Appendix B.)

I Game

Name _____

Cross out each **e**, **q**, and **z** with a big **X** to find the hidden spelling words. Using one crayon, softly color the boxes you did not mark so you can see your spelling words better.

X	X	X	X	X	X	X	b	y
X	w	h	y	X	X	X	X	X
X	X	X	X	X	X	X	n	o
g	o	X	X	X	X	X	X	X
X	X	X	X	m	y	X	X	X
X	k	n	o	w	X	X	X	X
t	r	y	X	X	X	X	s	o
X	X	X	X	X	X	X	X	X
X	X	X	g	o	i	n	g	X
m	o	s	t	X	X	X	X	X

Remember : Be kind and truthful, even when it's not easy.

J Journaling

Draw a picture in your journal of Beth taking Luke's sledding tube. Label the picture **A Bad Choice**. Draw Beth giving Luke's sledding tube back. Label it **A Good Choice**.

172

How to Play:

- Have each student mark through each letter **e** found on the grid with a big **X**.
- Have each student mark through each letter **q** found on the grid with a big **X**.
- Have each student mark through each letter **z** found on the grid with a big **X**.
- Tell the students that the boxes without **X**'s contain their spelling words.
- Have the students color softly over the boxes without **X**'s so they can see their spelling words more clearly.
- Have the students follow along as you read and spell each word as it appears on the grid.

2 Game

Reinforce spelling skills and provide motivation and interest.

Materials

- game page (from student text)
- pencils (1 per child)
- crayons or colored pencils (1 per child)

3 Journaling

Provide a meaningful reason for correct spelling through personal writing.

Review the story using discussion leads provided on the following page. Encourage students to apply the Scriptural value in their journaling.

Take a minute to memorize...

Have the class say the memory verse with you once.

Journaling (continued)

 Say

- How do you think Beth felt when she heard the air going out of her snow tube? (Sad, because she wouldn't be able to use it while it was being repaired. Angry, because Luke wasn't paying attention and caused her tube to go sailing into the blackberry bushes.)

- What thoughts were going through Beth's head as she gave Luke's good tube back to him? (Happy and content because she had made the choice to be truthful and kind even though it was not easy.)

- Draw some pictures in your journal of Beth and the way she felt.

 Quotables!

"Purposeful writing experiences are the key to cognitive growth in spelling"*

*Lutz, Elaine. 1986. ERIC/RCS Report: Invented Spelling and Spelling Development. Language Arts, Vol. 63, No. 7, November: 742-744.

Tommy's Trouble

Tommy learns the difference between "telling" and "tattling."

"Watch this!" James shouted as he ran to the swings on the playground. "I can swing as high as the top of the swing set!"

"I can swing that high faster than you can!" Daniel jumped into a swing and pushed off. Tommy and Christopher got the last two swings and each boy tried to go faster and higher than the others. Shouts and laughter filled the air as the children in Miss Grant's class enjoyed a rare break in the cold weather.

"I won," James bragged as the swings drifted to a halt.

"Did not!" Daniel shook his head. "It was a tie."

"It wasn't either! I got the highest first, didn't I, Tommy?" James looked to Tommy for support.

"Uh, yeah, I guess." Tommy shrugged. "Let's go play on the merry-go-round. There's no one using it right now." The four boys raced off.

"I got here first," Christopher panted as they climbed aboard.

"That's just because you started before the rest of us!" Daniel grabbed hold of a bar. "I'm just as fast as you are any day." The boys took turns pushing the merry-go-round as fast as they could.

"Yippee! If we go any faster, we'll take off and spin through the air!" James yelled into the wind. Tommy gave the merry-go-round a final shove, then flopped on the ground to rest.

"Let me have a turn, and it'll really fly!" Daniel hopped off.

"You always think you can do everything the best, Daniel!" James dragged his shoe in the dirt as the merry-go-round turned slower and slower. "I haven't seen you do anything better than the rest of us."

"Yeah, you're not any better than we are," Christopher agreed.

"Oh, yeah?" Daniel stuck his hands on his hips. "I can do something that none of you can do."

"What?" James demanded, as he and Christopher climbed off the merry-go-round.

"Well," Daniel glanced around the playground. "I , uh . . . I can go across the monkey bars." As James looked at Christopher and laughed, Daniel added, "I mean I can walk across the top of the monkey bars, standing up!"

"No you can't!" James exclaimed. "I don't believe it." Tommy stood up and brushed at the dirt on his jeans. Christopher stared at Daniel with his mouth open.

"I bet you're just saying that you can," James challenged. "I bet you've never done it before."

"I'll show you!" Daniel announced. "Tell your parents you'll be a little late after school Monday, then meet me on the playground. There aren't any teachers around then, and I'll walk right across the top of the monkey bars. You'll see!"

"But . . ." Tommy began to protest, but just then Miss Grant called the children back to the classroom.

As the class began to settle down, Tommy found it hard to concentrate on his math facts. Five plus six equals . . . He stared hard at the page, but kept thinking about Daniel's boast of walking across the monkey bars. That was scary! What if he fell? Sometimes Daniel was a little braggy and bossy, but he really was a nice friend most of the time.

"Let's see," he thought, trying to concentrate again, ". . . four plus seven equals twelve . . . no, that can't be right. Four plus seven equals . . ." He stopped. What if Daniel got hurt? What could he do to prevent it? What should he do?

Later that evening, the Rawsons lingered around the dinner table. "Mom, may I have another taco?" Tommy asked quietly.

"You're growing like a weed!" Mom teased. She passed the taco shells across the table. "I can't ever seem to fill you up at meal times, and your jeans are beginning to look like they belong to Matthew's little brother Alex!"

"He is a weed." Lisa grinned impishly at her little brother. "An irritating weed who shows up where you don't want him sometimes." But Tommy didn't respond to her teasing.

"Are you okay, Son?" Dad asked.

"I'm okay," Tommy answered, adding too many tomatoes to his taco. As he tried to take a bite, they scattered across his plate.

"Is there something bothering you?" Dad persisted.

"Well . . . I was just sort of wondering . . ." Tommy absently stabbed at a piece of tomato with his fork. "I don't want to be a tattle-tale, but . . . well, what should somebody do if he knows someone is going to do something and they might get hurt?"

Dad thought for a moment, then looked straight at Tommy. "Maybe your answer is right there on the 'fridge.'" He nodded at the handwriting border sheet that Tommy had brought home that afternoon. Mom had promised to mail it to Grandma Rawson tomorrow. Tommy had colored the hearts around the edge of the page red. Miss Grant had helped him write a letter in each heart so they spelled "I Love You Grandma". The verse in the middle had taken Tommy a long time to write since it was longer than most.

Dad read the verse aloud. "'Just tell me what to do and I will do it, Lord. Make me walk along the right paths.' God can always help you make the right choice, Tommy. I'm glad you don't want to tattle. Tattling is selfish. Tattling is telling on others just to get them into trouble."

Dad rubbed his finger lightly around the rim of his glass as he continued. "But telling isn't always the same as tattling. Telling can be quite different. When you care about others, you don't want them to be hurt. Telling is good when you tell about something you know may be harmful. Telling can keep other people or things from being hurt." He paused. "What do you think, Son?"

"Can you take us to school a little early on Monday, Mom?" Tommy asked. "I think I need to tell Miss Grant something."

"I'm sure we can handle that," Mom smiled. "Have you had enough to eat?" She nodded at the dishes on the table. They were all empty.

"Uh, yes, I guess so," Tommy grinned. "May I be excused, please?"

"Me, too," Lisa chimed in. At their mother's nod Lisa added, "Want to play a game of Trouble®, Tommy?"

"Not me," Tommy laughed. "I think I've had enough trouble for one day!"

Monday afternoon, as Tommy was struggling with the answer to four plus seven, he noticed Miss Grant talking quietly to Daniel. He sighed with relief. "Thank you, God, for telling me what to do," he thought. Now he knew that Daniel wouldn't get hurt.

Tommy smiled, then looking back at his paper, he wrote a very neat 11.

2 Discussion Time

Check understanding of the story and development of personal values.

- What was Daniel planning to do to show off to the other boys?
- Why was Tommy worried about Daniel doing this?
- What decision did Tommy have to make?
- Why was Tommy not sure he should tell?
- What is the difference between tattling and telling?
- Do you think Tommy made the right choice? Why or why not?
- How can God help you make right choices?

A Preview

Write each word as your teacher says it.

Name _____

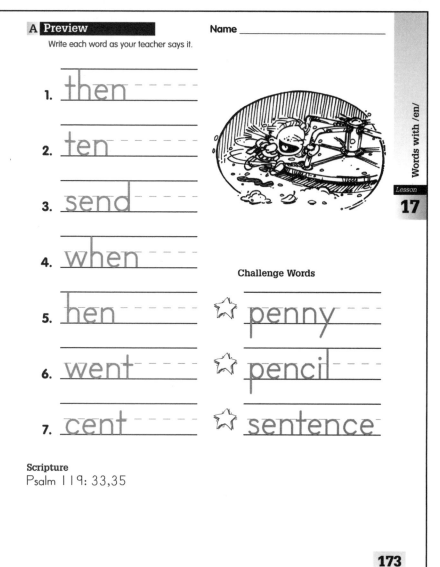

1. then
2. ten
3. send
4. when
5. hen
6. went
7. cent

Challenge Words

☆ penny
☆ pencil
☆ sentence

Scripture
Psalm 119: 33,35

173

Challenge

For better spellers, challenge words may be included in the weekly list. Challenge words are starred.

Correct Immediately!

Say

Let's correct our preview. I will write each word on the board. Put a dot under each letter on your preview as I spell the word out loud. If you spelled a word wrong, rewrite it correctly.

Progress Chart

Students may record scores. (Reproducible master in Appendix B.)

Take a minute to memorize . . .

Read the memory verse twice. Have students practice it with you two more times.

3 Preview

Test for knowledge of the correct spellings of these words. (See the instructions at the top right for challenge words.)

Say

I will say each word once, use the word in a sentence, then say the word again. Write the word on the lines in the Worktext.

1.	then	If we ask Him, **then** God will help us know what to do.
2.	ten	There were **ten** children playing on the swings and slide.
3.	send	Tommy was going to **send** a border sheet to his grandmother.
4.	when	You don't want others to be hurt **when** you care about them.
5.	hen	The **hen** laid an egg in her nest.
6.	went	The first graders **went** out to recess.
7.	cent	A penny is one **cent**.
☆	penny	There is a picture of Abraham Lincoln on each **penny**.
☆	pencil	Tommy used a **pencil** to write on his border sheet.
☆	sentence	A **sentence** always starts with a capital letter.

235

4 Word Shapes

Help students form a correct image of whole words.

Say Look at each word and think about its shape. Now, write the word in the correct word Shape Boxes. You may check off each word as you use it.

In the word shape boxes, color the letters that spell the sound of **en** in each word. Circle the words that begin with the digraphs **wh** or **th**.

 Challenge
Draw the correctly shaped box around each letter in these words.

Say On a separate sheet of paper, write other words that contain the spelling patterns in the word list. See how many words you can write.

Lesson 17 | Day 1

Words with en

Lesson 17

B Word Shapes

Name _____

Write each word in the correct word shape boxes. Next, in the word shape boxes, color the letters **en** in each word. Circle the words that begin with a digraph.

1. when

2. then

3. hen

4. ten

5. went

6. send

7. cent

☆ **Challenge**
Draw the correct word shape boxes around each word.

pencil   penny   sentence

174

Be Prepared For Fun

Check these supply lists for **Fun Ways to Spell** presented **Day 2**. Purchase and/or gather these items ahead of time!

General
- Strips of Paper 3 1/2 x 11 Inches (7 per child)
- Strips of Paper 3 1/2 x 11 Inches (3 more for challenge words)
- Crayons or Markers
- Tape
- Scissors
- Spelling List

Auditory
- Rhythm Instruments (two wooden spoons, two pan lids, maracas)
- Spelling List

Visual
- Clothespins (8 clothespins per child at the clothesline)
- c, d, e, h, n, s, t and w (written on 3 x 5 cards cut in half)
- e, e, n, p, v and y (added for challenge words)
- Clothesline (hung at student height)
- Spelling List

Tactile
- Shaving Cream
- Optional: Plastic Plates
- Optional: Wooden Craft Sticks
- Spelling List

236

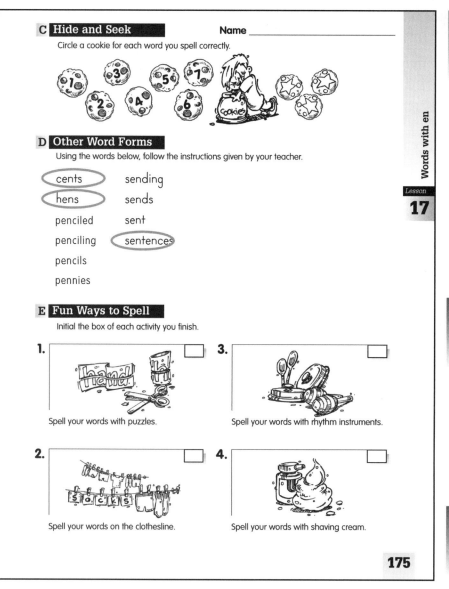

C Hide and Seek

Name _____

Circle a cookie for each word you spell correctly.

D Other Word Forms

Using the words below, follow the instructions given by your teacher.

cents   sending
hens   sends
penciled   sent
penciling   sentences
pencils
pennies

E Fun Ways to Spell

Initial the box of each activity you finish.

1. ☐

Spell your words with puzzles.

2. ☐

Spell your words on the clothesline.

3. ☐

Spell your words with rhythm instruments.

4. ☐

Spell your words with shaving cream.

175

1 Hide and Seek

Reinforce spelling by using multiple styles of learning.

On a white board, Teacher writes each word — one at a time. **Have students:**

- **Look** at the word.
- **Say** the word out loud.
- **Spell** the word out loud.
- **Hide** (teacher erases word.)
- **Write** the word on their paper.
- **Seek** (teacher rewrites word.)
- **Check** spelling. If incorrect, repeat above steps.

2 Other Word Forms

This activity is optional. Have students find and circle the Other Word Forms that name a person, place, or thing.

3 Fun Ways to Spell

Four activities are provided. Use one, two, three, or all of the activities. Have students initial the box for each activity they complete.

Options:

- assign activities to students according to their learning styles
- set up the activities in learning centers for students to do throughout the day
- divide students into four groups and assign one activity per group
- do one activity per day

General

To Spell your words with puzzles…
- Write each word on a strip of paper in big, tall letters.
- Cut your word in half lengthwise.
- Tape the ends of each strip together to make circles.
- Mix the circles together.
- Match the circles again to make your spelling words.

Auditory

To spell your words with rhythm instruments…
- Look at a word on your spelling list.
- Close your eyes.
- Play your rhythm instruments softly while you whisper the spelling of the word.
- Open your eyes and check your spelling.

Visual

To spell your words on the clothesline…
- Choose the letter cards you need to spell a word on your list.
- Clothespin the cards to the clothesline in the right order to spell the word.
- Check your spelling.
- Remove the letter cards from the clothesline and spell the next word on your list.

Tactile

To spell your words with shaving cream…
- Spread a glob of shaving cream across your desk (or on a plastic plate).
- Use your finger (or a wooden craft stick) to write a spelling word in the shaving cream.
- Check your spelling.
- Smear the word out with your finger and write another word.

237

1 ABC Order

Familiarize students with word meaning and usage. Write the words **day**, **play**, and **may** on the board. Help the students understand that each word begins with a different letter. Write the letters **d**, **p**, and **m**. Ask the students which letter comes first in the alphabet. Ask which letter comes next. Elicit the response that the letters would come **d**, **m**, **p**. Then write the words in ABC order as **day**, **may**, and **play**.

Say) Write the words from each group in ABC order.

F ABC Order

Name _____

Write the words from each group in ABC order.

2. went
   send

3. when
   then

4. send
   cent

1. hen
   ten

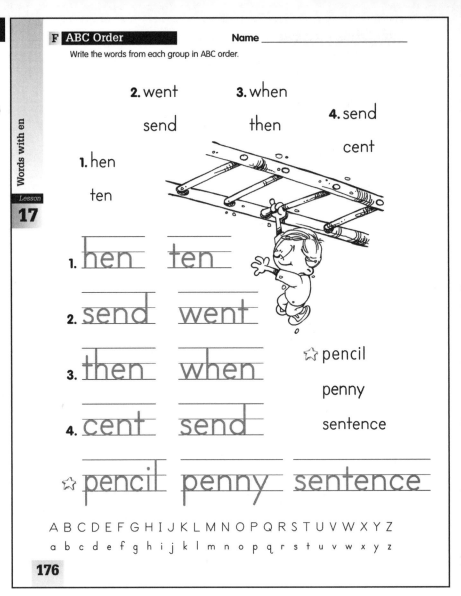

1. hen   ten
2. send   went
3. then   when
4. cent   send

☆ pencil
   penny
   sentence

☆ pencil   penny   sentence

A B C D E F G H I J K L M N O P Q R S T U V W X Y Z
a b c d e f g h i j k l m n o p q r s t u v w x y z

176

Take a minute to memorize...

Read the memory verse twice. Have students practice it with you two more times.

238

G Dictation

Name _____

Listen and write the missing words.

1. We have ten cents.

2. She went home,

   then came back.

3. Send the letter

   when you can.

H Proofreading

One word in each pair is misspelled. Fill in the oval by the misspelled word.

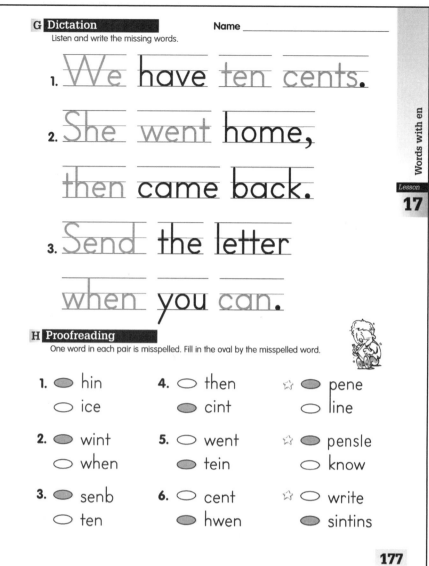

1. ● hin
   ○ ice

2. ● wint
   ○ when

3. ● senb
   ○ ten

4. ○ then
   ● cint

5. ○ went
   ● tein

6. ○ cent
   ● hwen

☆ ● pene
   ○ line

☆ ● pensle
   ○ know

☆ ○ write
   ● sintins

177

---

1 Dictation

Reinforce correct spelling by using current and previous words in context.

Say Listen as I read each sentence and then write it in your Worktext. (Slowly read each sentence twice. Sentences are found in the Student Worktext to the left.)

☆ **Challenge**

Write these incomplete sentences on the board.

__ didn't __ __ __

__ wet.

Beth __ __ the __ __ the

__.

__ __ __ to __ the __.

Say Listen as I read each sentence. Write the sentence on your paper. (Slowly read each sentence twice.)

He didn't <u>even</u> <u>get</u> <u>his</u>

<u>feet</u> wet.

Beth <u>will</u> <u>drop</u> the <u>penny</u>

<u>in</u> the <u>cup</u>.

She <u>will</u> <u>try</u> to <u>write</u>

the <u>sentence</u>.

---

2 Proofreading

Familiarize students with standardized test format and reinforce recognizing misspelled words.

Say Look at each set of words. One word in each set is misspelled. Fill in the oval by the misspelled word. (You may wish to pronounce each set of words to help students correctly identify them.)

239

3 Hide and Seek

Reinforce correct spelling of current spelling words. (A reproducible master is provided in Appendix A as shown on the inset page to the right.)

Write the words one at a time on a white board.

Have students:

- **Look** at the word.
- **Say** the word out loud.
- **Spell** the word out loud.
- **Hide** (teacher erases word.)
- **Write** the word on paper.
- **Seek** (teacher rewrites word.)
- **Check** spelling. If incorrect, rewrite word correctly.

4 Word Find

Have your students complete this activity to strengthen spelling ability and expand vocabulary.

1 Posttest

Test mastery of the spelling words. Challenge words are starred.

 Say

I will say the word once, use the word in a sentence, then say the word again. Write the word on your paper.

1. ten — The alarm clock will ring at **ten** minutes till seven.
2. send — We will **send** a picture of you to your cousin.
3. then — If it rains a whole lot, **then** the river will flood.
4. cent — How much is a **cent** worth?
5. when — Don't forget your coat **when** you go outside.
6. hen — The big white **hen** had five baby chicks.
7. went — Our family **went** to a restaurant for supper.
☆ sentence — This **sentence** ends with a period.
☆ pencil — Tommy needs to sharpen his **pencil.**
☆ penny — A **penny** is made of copper.

 Progress Chart
Students may record scores. (Reproducible master in Appendix B.)

 Personal Dictionary
Students may add any words they have misspelled to their personal dictionaries for reference when writing. (Cover in Appendix B.)

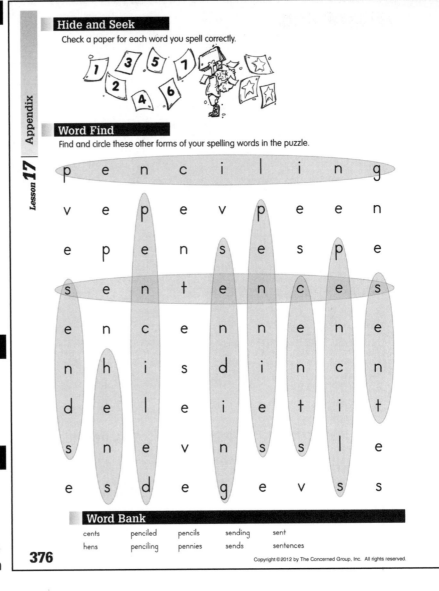

Hide and Seek
Check a paper for each word you spell correctly.

Word Find
Find and circle these other forms of your spelling words in the puzzle.

Word Bank
cents, hens, penciled, penciling, pencils, pennies, sending, sends, sent, sentences

376 Copyright ©2012 by The Concerned Group, Inc. All rights reserved.

I Game

Name _____

As he was eating tacos for dinner, Tommy's dad assured him that God would show him whether or not he should tell Miss Grant about Daniel's plan to walk across the top of the monkey bars. Color one tomato piece each time you or your team spells a word correctly from this week's word list.

Remember : *Ask God what to do, then do it!*

J Journaling

Copy and finish these sentences in your journal:
I am telling when I...
I am tattling when I...

178

2 Game

Reinforce spelling skills and provide motivation and interest.

Materials

- game page (from student text)
- red crayons (1 per child)
- game word list

Game Word List

Use of challenge words is optional.

1. **when**
2. **then**
3. **hen**
4. **ten**
5. **went**
6. **send**
7. **cent**
☆ **pencil**
☆ **penny**
☆ **sentence**

3 Journaling

Provide a meaningful reason for correct spelling through personal writing.

Review the story using discussion leads provided on the following page. Encourage students to apply the Scriptural value in their journaling.

Take a minute to memorize...

Have the class say the memory verses from lessons 16 and 17 with you.

How to Play:

- Divide the class into two teams, and decide which team will go first.
- Have a student from team A go to the board.
- Read the spelling word two times slowly and clearly. (You may also wish to use the word in a sentence. Ex.: "cat — The cat climbed a tree. — cat")
- Have the student write the word on the board.
- If the word is spelled correctly, instruct all the members of team A to color one tomato. (Note: If the word is misspelled, correct the spelling immediately before continuing the game.)
- Alternate between teams A and B as you go down the word list.
- The team with the most tomatoes colored when you have gone through the game word list twice is the winner.

Non-Competitive Option:

At the end of the game, say: "Class, I am proud of your efforts to spell the words correctly. If you had fun and tried your best, you are all winners!"

Journaling (continued)

Say

- We have choices to make everyday. What are some of the choices you make? (What to wear, what to say, what to play, how to act, etc.)

- Some choices are hard to make. How can we know which way to choose? (By asking God to help us know.)

- What tough choice did Tommy have to make in the story this week? (If he should tell about Daniel's plan to walk across the monkey bars.)

- Tattling and telling are very different. Did Tommy tattle or tell? Why? (Tell. He told because he didn't want Daniel to get hurt, not to get him into trouble.)

- In your journal, write about the difference between tattling and telling. Before you tell something you know, think about it to make sure you're not tattling!

Children learn more about writing every time they write independently.

The Measure of Friendship

Kristin proves to be a real friend when Rosa finds herself in trouble.

"Good morning, Rosa." Miss Grant smiled as she met Rosa at the classroom door. "How are you this morning?"

"Fine, Miss Grant." Rosa looked around the empty classroom. "Am I the first one here today?"

"Yes," Miss Grant smiled. "You're an early bird today." She held up a file folder. "I have to take these papers to the school office, but I'll be back in just a minute or two."

As the door closed behind her teacher, Rosa shrugged out of her coat and walked toward her desk. Dad had brought them to school earlier than usual this morning because he had an appointment. It seemed strange to be the only person in the large, quiet room.

Rosa wandered over to the windows and gazed out at the empty playground. She crossed to the board and wrote R-O-S-A in large fancy letters, then erased each letter bit by bit.

Then she spotted something new in the classroom. The table in the front of the room held several different measuring tools, but Rosa's eyes were drawn to the balance near the front of the table. A red plastic pan lay on one side of the balance, and a yellow plastic pan lay on the other. Shiny little metal weights were lined up in front of the balance.

Rosa pushed gently on the red tray with the tip of her finger. She watched the needle in the middle swing way over to the other side while the yellow tray rose up above the red one. She picked up a pencil and laid it in the red tray. Then she placed a little weight with a "2" printed on it in the yellow tray. The yellow and red pans were almost even. She added another tiny

weight to the yellow tray. There! That was a perfect match. This pencil weighed four grams. The pans were even and the needle pointed straight down the middle line. This was fun!

Rosa looked around for something else to weigh. She stretched across the table to grab a small plastic measuring cup, but as she straightened the buttons on her shirt caught the balance and pulled it right off the edge of the table!

Rosa bent to pick it up. "Oh, no! It's broken!" She set the balance back in its place and stared at the broken red pan in her hand. "Now what am I going to do?"

Rosa carefully lined up the pieces and gently put them back on the balance. "Maybe if I lay these pieces back on the balance, no one will be able to tell it's broken," she thought. Then she sat down at her own desk.

"Hi, Rosa!" Tony greeted as he came through the door. "Is today the day we get to measure stuff?" He motioned toward the things on the table. "All right! Look at this, Christopher," he added as the Wright twins entered the classroom.

"It's experiment day!" Christopher exclaimed with a grin. "When do we get to start measuring things, Miss Grant?" he asked as their teacher returned to the room.

"This afternoon," Miss Grant answered. "Tony and Christopher, would you please pass these envelopes out?" She handed a stack of long white envelopes to each boy. "Thank you, boys."

As the boys placed a single envelope on each desk, a steady stream of children arrived. The class had been

learning about measurement for several days, and were all excited to use the various tools Miss Grant had taught them about.

"What will the kids say when they find out the balance is broken and no one will be able to use it?" Rosa bit her fingernail worriedly.

When it was time for handwriting class Miss Grant said, "Yesterday you practiced writing Proverbs 17:17. Does anyone remember what it said?" She nodded toward James' waving hand.

"A true friend always helps and a brother is born to . . ." James slowed to a confused stop.

"That's very close, James," Miss Grant encouraged. "Try it again, 'A true friend is always loyal…,'" she prompted.

"A true friend is always loyal, and a brother is born to help in time of need," James finished in a triumphant rush.

"That's right, James," Miss Grant smiled. "We all want to be that kind of friend to others, don't we? After you write your verse on a border sheet today, you may put it in the envelope you were given. You may choose a special friend to send your verse to. Perhaps you know someone who has done something kind for you, someone who has helped you in a time when you really needed help."

The children busily wrote and colored their verses, but Rosa kept glancing at the experiment table as she colored her rainbow. *"What should I do? If I DON'T tell Miss Grant that I broke the balance then it's like lying."* She chewed on another fingernail. *"But if I DO tell, then everyone will know and they will all be mad at me for ruining the balance experiment."*

"Let's play freeze tag," Stephen suggested as the children ran outside into the weak winter sunshine for recess. "Who wants to be 'IT' first?"

"I will!" Tommy volunteered. The children scattered every direction as a fast-paced game of tag began. Rosa sat on a swing and watched the others run and scream as they tried to keep clear of Tommy.

Sarah stopped short with one hand outstretched and one knee slightly bent in a "frozen" position when Tommy caught her.

"What's wrong?" Kristin panted as she plunked into the swing next to Rosa. "Are you sick or something?"

"No . . . I, uh . . . Kristin, I've got a big problem," Rosa confided. The whole story of the broken balance came tumbling out. "What am I going to do?" Rosa finished in despair.

"You've got to tell Miss Grant," Kristin answered, jumping up. "I'll go with you. Come on." She dragged a reluctant Rosa out of the swing. "Let's go right now. It won't be so bad."

"Is everything okay?" Miss Grant questioned as the two girls approached with Rosa lagging behind.

"Yes. Rosa just wanted to talk to you about something," Kristin nudged Rosa, then ran back to join the game of tag. Rosa stared at a patch of bent brown grass and told the story of the broken balance in one breath.

After lunch the children enthusiastically worked in groups scattered around the room. One group measured colored water with cups and beakers and other containers. A second group used meter sticks, rulers, and tape measures to find the length of classroom items or the height of the children. Still another group worked with thermometers to measure temperatures of ice water and different colors of paper laid in the sun. The remaining group used a balance and a set of scales to measure things like heavy erasers and marbles.

"I thought you broke the balance," Kristin whispered in Rosa's ear.

"I did." Rosa grinned at the confused Kristin. "Miss Grant borrowed a balance from the third-grade teacher. She said accidents sometimes happen and she was glad I told her." Kristin returned her grin and the girls turned their attention back to their group experiment.

At the end of their fun-filled day, the children gathered their things to go home. Kristin's head was stuck halfway in her desk looking for something when Rosa tapped her on the shoulder. As Kristin sat up, Rosa held out a long white envelope. "Thank you, Kristin," Rosa said quietly. "Thank you for being such a good friend to me today."

Kristin opened the envelope, and pulled out a border sheet with a colorful rainbow. And there were the words from Proverbs: "A true friend is always loyal, and a brother is born to help in time of need."

Lesson 18 | **Day 1**

Discussion Time

2

Check understanding of the story and development of personal values.

- Why was Rosa alone in the first grade classroom?
- What were the first graders learning about?
- What happened while Rosa was all by herself in the room?
- Why was Rosa afraid to tell Miss Grant about the accident?
- What did Rosa's best friend, Kristin, do to help?
- How did Miss Grant solve the problem?
- How did Rosa show Kristin that she was glad Kristin had helped her?
- What did the border sheet say?
- How can you be a true friend?

A Preview

Write each word as your teacher says it.

Name _____

1. them
2. this
3. with
4. they
5. there
6. the
7. thing

Challenge Words

⭐ these
⭐ than
⭐ think

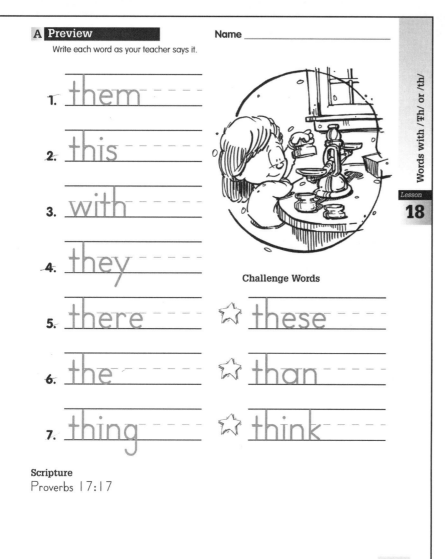

Scripture
Proverbs 17:17

179

Correct Immediately!

Say — Let's correct our preview. I will write each word on the board. Put a dot under each letter on your preview as I spell the word out loud. If you spelled a word wrong, rewrite it correctly.

Progress Chart

Students may record scores. (Reproducible master in Appendix B.)

Take a minute to memorize . . .

Read the memory verse twice. Have students practice it with you two more times.

3 Preview

Test for knowledge of the correct spellings of these words. (See the instructions at the top right for challenge words.)

Say — I will say each word once, use the word in a sentence, then say the word again. Write the word on the lines in the Worktext.

1. them — Miss Grant asked **them** to pass out the envelopes.
2. this — Look at **this** red and yellow balance.
3. with — The children measured things **with** rulers and tape measures.
4. they — Then **they** helped each other do the experiments.
5. there — Are **there** many different ways to measure?
6. the — Sometimes it is very hard to tell **the** truth.
7. thing — A thermometer is a **thing** used to measure temperature.
⭐ these — What shall we do with **these** papers?
⭐ than — It is warmer in the sun **than** in the shade.
⭐ think — Try to **think** of a way to be a good friend to someone today.

245

4 Word Shapes

Help students form a correct image of whole words.

Say

Look at each word and think about its shape. Now, write the word in the correct word Shape Boxes. You may check off each word as you use it.

(In most words, /**th**/, and /**th**/ are spelled **th** whether this digraph is in the beginning, middle or end of a word.)

Say

In the word shape boxes, color the letters that spell the sound of /**th**/, or /**th**/ in each word.
Circle the words in which you use your voice to say the sound of /**th**/.

Challenge

Draw the correctly shaped box around each letter in these words.

Say

On a separate sheet of paper, write other words that contain the spelling patterns in the word list. See how many words you can write.

B **Word Shapes**

Name _____

Write each word in the correct word shape boxes. Next, in the word shape boxes, color the letters that spell the sound of /**th**/, or /**th**/ in each word. Circle the words in which you use your voice to say the sound of /**th**/.

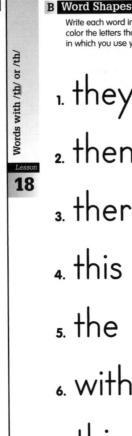

1. they
2. them
3. there
4. this
5. the
6. with
7. thing

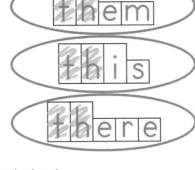

☆ **Challenge**
Draw the correct word shape boxes around each word.

than   these   think

180

Be Prepared For Fun

Check these supply lists for **Fun Ways to Spell** presented **Day 2**.
Purchase and/or gather these items ahead of time!

General
- Crayons
- Piece of Paper
- Spelling List

Auditory
- Box to Store Letters
- e, e, g, h, i, m, n, r, s, t, w and y (written on seasonal shapes like hearts or flags)
- a and k (added for challenge words)
- Spelling List

Visual
- Eraser
- Dark Construction Paper
- Spelling List

Tactile
- Finger Paint
- Plastic Plate or Glossy Paper
- Spelling List

246

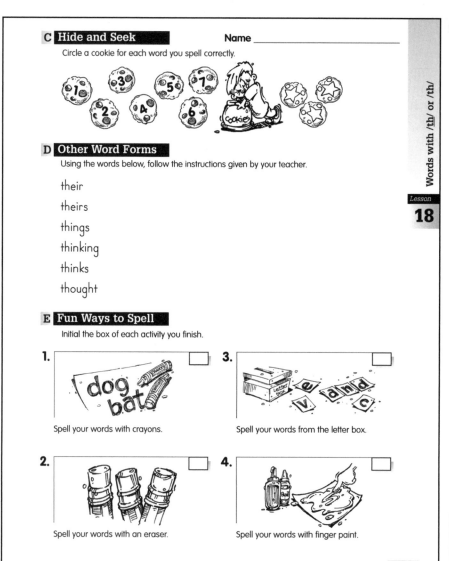

C Hide and Seek

Name _____

Circle a cookie for each word you spell correctly.

D Other Word Forms

Using the words below, follow the instructions given by your teacher.

their

theirs

things

thinking

thinks

thought

E Fun Ways to Spell

Initial the box of each activity you finish.

1. [ ]

Spell your words with crayons.

2. [ ]

Spell your words with an eraser.

3. [ ]

Spell your words from the letter box.

4. [ ]

Spell your words with finger paint.

Words with /th/ or /th/

Lesson
18

181

Hide and Seek

Reinforce spelling by using multiple styles of learning.

On a white board, Teacher writes each word — one at a time. **Have students:**

- **Look** at the word.
- **Say** the word out loud.
- **Spell** the word out loud.
- **Hide** (teacher erases word.)
- **Write** the word on their paper.
- **Seek** (teacher rewrites word.)
- **Check** spelling. If incorrect, repeat above steps.

Day 2

Lesson *18*

Other Word Forms

This activity is optional. Have students dictate original sentences to you using these Other Word Forms. Write them on the board.

theirs   things

thinking

Fun Ways to Spell

Four activities are provided. Use one, two, three, or all of the activities. Have students initial the box for each activity they complete.

Options:

- assign activities to students according to their learning styles
- set up the activities in learning centers for students to do throughout the day
- divide students into four groups and assign one activity per group
- do one activity per day

General

To spell your words with crayons…
- Write each letter of your spelling word in fat, thick letters.
- Check your spelling.

Auditory

To spell your words from the letter box…
- Spell a word from your list by putting the letters in the right order.
- Check your spelling.
- Spell your word out loud.

Visual

To spell your words with an eraser…
- Turn your pencil upside down.
- Use the eraser to write your words on a sheet of dark construction paper.
- Check your spelling.

Tactile

To spell your words with finger paint…
- Smear paint across your plate.
- Use a finger to write a spelling word in paint.
- Check your spelling.
- Smear the word out with your finger and write another word.

247

1 Word Scramble

Familiarize students with word meaning and usage.

Write the letters **gdla** on the board. Help the students understand that the scrambled letters **gdla** spell the word **glad** when they are arranged correctly. Guide the students in ordering the letters to spell **glad**.

(Say) Unscramble the letters to make a spelling word. Write the word on the line.

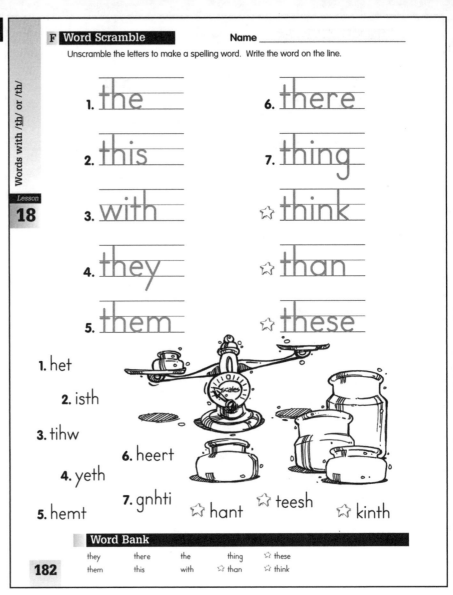

Words with /th/ or /ŧh/

Lesson **18**

F Word Scramble

Name _____

Unscramble the letters to make a spelling word. Write the word on the line.

1. the
2. this
3. with
4. they
5. them

6. there
7. thing
☆ think
☆ than
☆ these

1. het
2. isth
3. tihw
4. yeth
5. hemt
6. heert
7. gnhti
☆ hant
☆ teesh
☆ kinth

Word Bank

they	there	the	thing	☆ these
them	this	with	☆ than	☆ think

182

Take a minute to memorize...

Read the memory verse twice. Have students practice it with you two more times.

G Dictation

Name _____

Listen and write the missing words.

1. They went there this morning.

2. I hope things go well for them.

3. She will go with us.

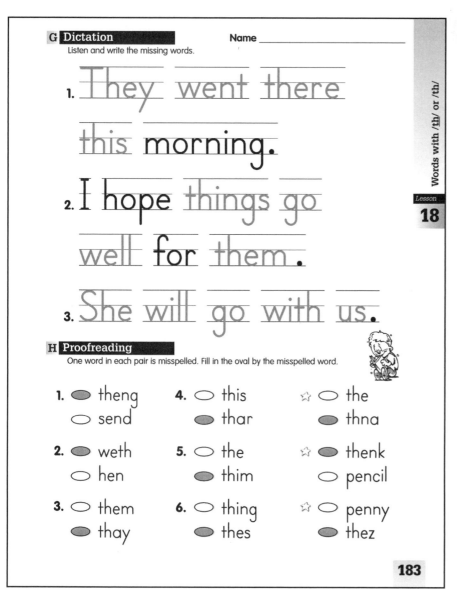

H Proofreading

One word in each pair is misspelled. Fill in the oval by the misspelled word.

1. ● theng
   ○ send

2. ● weth
   ○ hen

3. ○ them
   ● thay

4. ○ this
   ● thar

5. ○ the
   ● thim

6. ○ thing
   ● thes

☆ ○ the
   ● thna

☆ ● thenk
   ○ pencil

☆ ○ penny
   ● thez

183

---

1 Dictation

Reinforce correct spelling by using current and previous words in context.

 Say

Listen as I read each sentence and then write it in your Worktext. (Slowly read each sentence twice. Sentences are found in the Student Worktext to the left.)

 Challenge

Write these incomplete sentences on the board.

___ ___ is bigger ___
___ ___.

___ ___ to take ___ ___
cookies to ___ ___.

___ do you ___ ___ ___
___ horse?

 Say

Listen as I read each sentence. Write the sentence on your paper. (Slowly read each sentence twice.)

His dog is bigger than my dog.

Ask him to take these ten cookies to his mom.

When do you think we can ride the horse?

---

2 Proofreading

Familiarize students with standardized test format and reinforce recognizing misspelled words.

 Say

Look at each set of words. One word in each set is misspelled. Fill in the oval by the misspelled word. (You may wish to pronounce each set of words to help students correctly identify them.)

249

Hide and Seek

Reinforce correct spelling of current spelling words. (A reproducible master is provided in Appendix A as shown on the inset page to the right.)
Write the words one at a time on a white board.

Have students:

- **Look** at the word.
- **Say** the word out loud.
- **Spell** the word out loud.
- **Hide** (teacher erases word.)
- **Write** the word on paper.
- **Seek** (teacher rewrites word.)
- **Check** spelling. If incorrect, rewrite word correctly.

Scrambled Words

Have your students complete this activity to strengthen spelling ability and expand vocabulary.

Posttest

Test mastery of the spelling words. Challenge words are starred.

(Say) I will say the word once, use the word in a sentence, then say the word again. Write the word on your paper.

1. this — Miss Grant said **this** is a fun experiment to do.
2. with — Kristin went **with** Rosa to tell Miss Grant about the balance.
3. them — Rosa was afraid to tell **them** that she broke the balance.
4. there — I'm glad **there** are true friends who are always helpful.
5. thing — A beaker is a **thing** used to measure liquids.
6. they — Soon **they** were all busy learning about measurement.
7. the — All **the** children enjoyed learning about new things.
☆ think — Do you **think** it will rain today?
☆ these — Please write **these** words neatly.
☆ than — It is better to tell the truth **than** to lie.

Progress Chart
Students may record scores. (Reproducible master in Appendix B.)

Personal Dictionary
Students may add any words they have misspelled to their personal dictionaries for reference when writing. (Cover in Appendix B.)

250

Hide and Seek
Check a paper for each word you spell correctly.

Scrambled Words
Unscramble the letters to make a word. Write the word on the lines.

1. hiter — their
2. ginsth — things
3. skinth — thinks
4. stiehr — theirs
5. kertinh — thinker
6. ottghhu — thought

Word Bank
their / things / thinks
theirs / thinker / thought

377

Game

Reinforce spelling skills and provide motivation and interest.

Materials
- game page (from student text)
- pencils (1 per child)
- crayons or colored pencils (1 per child)

Day 5

Lesson **18**

Words with /th/ or /t͟h/

Lesson **18**

I Game

Name _____

Cross out each **b**, **f**, and **z** with a big **X** to find the hidden spelling words. Using one crayon, softly color the boxes you did not mark so you can see your spelling words better.

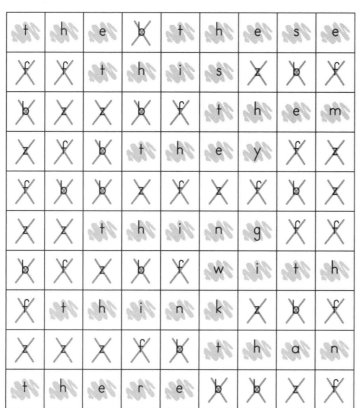

Remember : Sometimes God helps us through our friends.

J Journaling

Copy and finish this sentence in your journal:
I can be a true friend by...
Write as many ways to be a good friend as you can think of.

184

Journaling

Provide a meaningful reason for correct spelling through personal writing.

Review the story using discussion leads provided on the following page. Encourage students to apply the Scriptural value in their journaling.

 Take a minute to memorize...

Have the class say the memory verses from lessons 16, 17, and 18 with you.

How to Play:

- Have each student mark through each letter **b** found on the grid with a big **X**.
- Have each student mark through each letter **f** found on the grid with a big **X**.
- Have each student mark through each letter **z** found on the grid with a big **X**.
- Tell the students that the boxes without **X**'s contain their spelling words.
- Have the students color softly over the boxes without **X**'s so they can see their spelling words more clearly.
- Have the students follow along as you read and spell each word as it appears on the grid.

Journaling (continued)

 Say

- What kind of things do you like to do with your friends?

- Have you ever been in trouble, like Rosa, and had a friend help you?

- What should you do if other kids want to play with you but don't include your friend? (Invite your friend to play also.)

- What should you do if someone makes fun of a friend of yours? (NOT laugh. Let them know that you don't think it's kind to make fun of others.)

- Think of some other ways that you can be a good friend and write them in your journal.

"Children grow into competent writers, not when they are taught to copy someone else's writing, but when they are encouraged to write their own ideas in their own known ways."*

*Hoffman, Stevie and Nancy Knipping. 1988. Spelling Revisited: The Child's Way. Childhood Education, June: 284-287.

God's Kind of Happiness

Tony gains a new perspective after visiting the retirement center.

"Grandma! Grandma! Guess what?" Tony shouted as he ran up the steps of the duplex.

"What is it, Tony?" Mrs. Miller smiled as she opened the door for her enthusiastic grandson.

"We've been learning about a pyramid in science class, and we get to go to a place where they bake bread tomorrow! See! I have a note from Miss Grant. I need a sack lunch."

"Slow down, Tony-O," Grandma took the note from the excited boy. "What do pyramids have to do with bread?"

"Not a real pyramid, Gram. A food pyramid. Breads, grains, and pastas are on the very bottom of the pyramid. Fruits and vegetables are on the next layer. Candy bars and jelly beans are in the tiny part way up at the top."

"Oh, I see!" Grandma smiled. "A diagram of the foods you need for a healthy body, like the four food groups — that's what they called it when I was in school." Grandma turned back to the note. "It says here that you're going to a bakery in Fayetteville. You get to eat your lunch in Mason Springs Park, and then you're going on to Pleasant Valley Retirement Center to put on a program for the people who live there." Grandma looked down at Tony. "It sounds like an exciting day."

"I can hardly wait!" Tony danced around the living room. "Recess and lunch at the park!"

The next day dawned bright and clear. Warm sunshine streamed in the windows of the classroom as everyone prepared for the much-anticipated outing. Matthew's mom and two-year-old Emily greeted the kids at the door and helped them put their sack lunches in a cardboard box. Katelynn's mom collected each child's permission slip and checked his or her name off a list fastened to a clipboard. Tommy's mom was writing the names of all the kids on the board — in groups of three or four according to the list Miss Grant had given her. Daniel's mother, dressed in linen slacks and a beautiful matching blazer, sat at the back of the classroom and watched the excited children. And Miss Grant was making sure that all the props and music were ready for the program at Pleasant Valley Retirement center.

When the first bell rang, everyone scrambled to their seats and sat quietly. "Thank you for remembering our plan so well," Miss Grant said. "I like the way all of you are quietly sitting in your seats. I want to share a verse from Psalms and have prayer, then we'll be on our way." She opened the Bible on her desk. "Psalm 5:11 says, 'Fill all who love You with Your happiness.' Raise your hand if you would like to share with the class what makes you happy. Beth?"

"Playing soccer makes me happy," Beth said.

"And I love to be the striker in a soccer game," Tony added.

Miss Grant pointed to Kristin. "What do you think, Kristin?"

"I'm happy when I'm with my friends," Kristin said.

"And I like going on field trips with them," Katelynn grinned.

Miss Grant nodded at Tommy's frantically waving hand. "What makes you happy, Tommy?"

"No math class!" Tommy pointed out. His classmates laughed, knowing that Tommy really struggled with math.

"Our verse says, 'Fill all who love You with Your happiness.' David wrote it and he was talking to God. When he says, 'Your happiness,' whose happiness do you think he is talking about?"

There was a long pause as everyone thought about this. Finally, Matthew suggested an answer. "God?" he said.

"Good thinking, Matthew!" Miss Grant said. "Now, class, what do you think would make God happy?"

"Well, God is happy when we tell the truth," Beth said.

"God is happy when we help the poor." Kristin smiled at Rosa.

"God is happy when we keep our promises," Stephen said.

"I think God would be really happy about all those choices," said Miss Grant. "Jesus said we should love God with our hearts most of all. Then God wants us to love others. When we do those two things, we'll have God's happiness. Let's bow our heads and pray." Miss Grant paused. "Dear Jesus, thank you for this beautiful day. Send Your angels to watch over us and please fill us with Your happiness. Amen."

By mid-morning the children had finished their tour of the bakery. The warm, fresh smell of baking bread seemed to surround them as they stepped out the front door. Suddenly their happy chatter stopped as a gust of cold north wind hit their faces. Little drops of icy rain whipped down from the sky, scattering in all directions. "Go quickly to the car you came in and get out of the rain," Miss Grant instructed. The four mothers hurried the kids along to the parked cars and helped them get situated.

"Everybody buckled in?" Tommy's mom checked the four boys in her car.

"I can't believe it's raining!" Tony tightened his seat belt as he stared out the window.

"Where are we going to eat lunch?" Stephen asked.

"I don't know," Mrs.

Story (continued)

Rawson replied. "I'm sure Miss Grant will come and tell us. We can't go to Mason Springs Park now. We'd all be wet and freezing. That cold front must have moved in a lot quicker than anyone expected."

"Do you think we'll have math before we go to the retirement center?" Tommy asked.

"We'll just have to wait and see," his mother said.

Miss Grant came up to the window a few minutes later, a large umbrella over her head. "Let's go to the park a few blocks from here instead of ours. The one here in Fayetteville has a covered eating area where we won't get wet and we'll have some protection from the wind."

"Ahhhh! The Fayetteville park doesn't even have a playground!" Tony complained. "Papa took me there once."

The class was soon huddled under the shelter hurriedly eating their lunches. It was much too cold for a picnic. Their bags and papers kept blowing away, and the partial walls of the shelter didn't keep all the rain out. When everyone was almost finished, Miss Grant stood up. "I'm sorry that we didn't get to play at Mason Springs Park. This cold stuff wasn't supposed to get here until late tonight. I called Pleasant Valley and they said we could come early to present our program, and then we'll have some time afterward to visit with the people who live there. Let's load up into the cars again and head that direction now. Don't forget to put all your trash in the trash can!"

"Great! Instead of getting recess at the park we get to visit with a bunch of old people!" Tony kicked at a rock on the way back to the Rawson's car.

"What will we say to them?" James asked.

Tommy smiled. "At least we won't have math class!"

Later that day, Mrs. Rawson dropped Tony off at home. Grandma Miller greeted him with a warm hug. "Come into the kitchen and tell me about your day, Tony," she said as she walked in and went to the stove. "You didn't get to go to Mason Springs Park, did you?"

"No," Tony shook his head and just smiled. Grandma was surprised. She thought Tony would be upset about the rain since she knew how much he liked to play at the park. "We had fun doing our program at the retirement center instead! Those people really liked the songs. We even taught them the motions."

Tony warmed his hands on the cup of hot chocolate Grandma had set in front of him. "We all remembered the texts we were supposed to say. And this one man kept laughing at the girls' poem. I think he thought their flower costumes were funny." Tony smiled as he remembered the man's face. "The lady I gave my border sheet to cried! She said it was because she liked it so much. She said they were happy tears and that she was going to hang it on her mirror so she would see it every morning. She wants to know when we are going to come again." Tony paused and looked up at Grandma. "Do you think you could take me over there sometime, Grandma?"

"Why, I do believe Tony is starting to understand God's kind of happiness," Grandma thought to herself. Then she smiled and said, "I'd be happy to, Tony!"

2 Discussion Time

Check understanding of the story and development of personal values.

- Did Tony have a good time on the field trip?
- Do you think Tony expected to have a lot of fun at the nursing home?
- Why did Grandma think Tony was starting to understand God's kind of happiness?
- What are some things you can think of that would make God happy?

Words with /ou/

Lesson **19**

A Preview

Write each word as your teacher says it.

Name _____

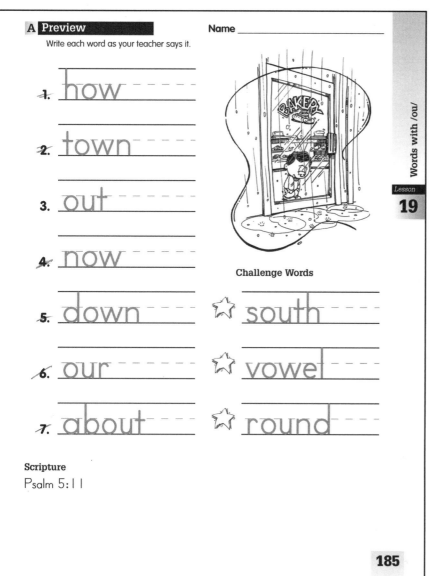

1. how
2. town
3. out
4. now
5. down
6. our
7. about

Challenge Words

⭐ south
⭐ vowel
⭐ round

Scripture
Psalm 5:11

185

For better spellers, challenge words may be included in the weekly list. Challenge words are starred.

Correct Immediately!
Say

Let's correct our preview. I will write each word on the board. Put a dot under each letter on your preview as I spell the word out loud. If you spelled a word wrong, rewrite it correctly.

Progress Chart
Students may record scores. (Reproducible master in Appendix B.)

Take a minute to memorize . . .

Read the memory verse twice. Have students practice it with you two more times.

3 Preview

Test for knowledge of the correct spellings of these words. (See the instructions at the top right for challenge words.)

Say

I will say each word once, use the word in a sentence, then say the word again. Write the word on the lines in the Worktext.

1. how — We will see **how** they make bread at the bakery.
2. town — What **town** do you live in?
3. out — The children had to get **out** of the wind and rain.
4. now — I know how to tie my own shoes **now**.
5. down — The wind blew the sign **down**.
6. our — Everyone in **our** class has learned many Scripture verses.
7. about — It is fun to learn **about** God's kind of happiness.
⭐ south — The storm blew in from the **south**.
⭐ vowel — "A" is a **vowel** that is used in many words.
⭐ round — The world is **round** like a ball.

255

4 Word Shapes

Help students form a correct image of whole words.

 Say

Look at each word and think about its shape. Now, write the word in the correct word Shape Boxes. You may check off each word as you use it.

(A diphthong is two vowels that are sounded together in the same syllable. In many words, the diphthong **/ou/** is spelled **ow** if it is at the end of a word or syllable, or comes before **l** or **n**. The **/ou/** sound is spelled **ou** everywhere else.)

 Say

In the word shape boxes, color the letters that spell the sound of **/ou/** in each word. Circle the word that has two syllables.

⭐ **Challenge**

Draw the correctly shaped box around each letter in these words.

 Say

On a separate sheet of paper, write other words that contain the spelling patterns in the word list. See how many words you can write.

B Word Shapes | Name _____

Write each word in the correct word shape boxes. Next, in the word shape boxes, color the letters that spell the sound of **/ou/** in each word. Circle the word that has two syllables.

1. now

2. how

3. down

4. town

5. our

6. out

7. about

☆ **Challenge**

Draw the correct word shape boxes around each word.

vowel   south   round

186

— Answers may vary for duplicate word shapes. —

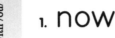 **Be Prepared For Fun**

Check these supply lists for **Fun Ways to Spell** presented **Day 2**. Purchase and/or gather these items ahead of time!

General
- 3 x 5 Cards (7 per child)
- 3 x 5 Cards (3 more for challenge words)
- Scissors
- Spelling List

Auditory
- Spelling List

Visual
- Dry Bar of Soap (sample size works well)
- Hand Mirror
- Strong Paper Towel or Washcloth (dry)
- Spelling List

Tactile
- Play Dough
- Spelling List

256

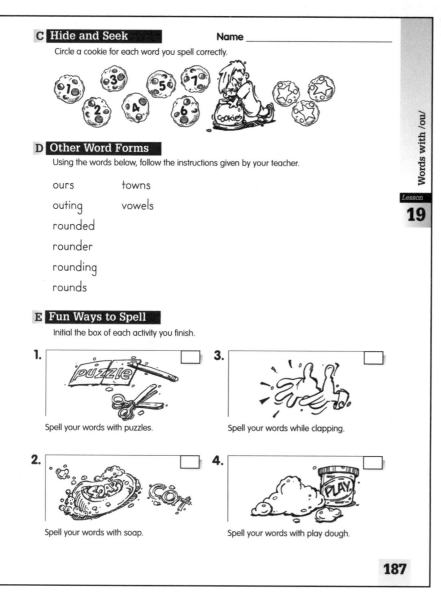

C Hide and Seek

Name _____

Circle a cookie for each word you spell correctly.

D Other Word Forms

Using the words below, follow the instructions given by your teacher.

ours   towns

outing   vowels

rounded

rounder

rounding

rounds

E Fun Ways to Spell

Initial the box of each activity you finish.

1. ☐
Spell your words with puzzles.

2. ☐
Spell your words with soap.

3. ☐
Spell your words while clapping.

4. ☐
Spell your words with play dough.

187

---

1 Hide and Seek

Reinforce spelling by using multiple styles of learning.

On a white board, Teacher writes each word — one at a time. **Have students:**

- **Look** at the word.
- **Say** the word out loud.
- **Spell** the word out loud.
- **Hide** (teacher erases word.)
- **Write** the word on their paper.
- **Seek** (teacher rewrites word.)
- **Check** spelling. If incorrect, repeat above steps.

2 Other Word Forms

This activity is optional. Have students find the Other Word Forms that best complete these sentences.

This dog is __. (ours)
We went on an __ to the park. (outing)

3 Fun Ways to Spell

Four activities are provided. Use one, two, three, or all of the activities. Have students initial the box for each activity they complete.

Options:

- assign activities to students according to their learning styles
- set up the activities in learning centers for students to do throughout the day
- divide students into four groups and assign one activity per group
- do one activity per day

General

To spell your words with puzzles…
- Write each word on a card.
- Cut each card squiggly, diagonal, or zigzag to make a puzzle.
- Mix your puzzle pieces.
- Put the puzzles together.
- Check your spelling.

Auditory

To spell your words while clapping…
- Look at a word on your spelling list.
- Close your eyes.
- Clap your hands softly while you whisper the spelling of the word.
- Open your eyes and check your spelling.

Visual

To spell your words with soap…
- Write a word on a hand mirror with a dry bar of soap.
- Check your spelling.
- Wipe the word off the mirror with a dry towel or washcloth.
- Write another word.

Tactile

To spell your words with play dough…
- Roll pieces of play dough into ropes.
- Use the ropes to make the letters of each word.
- Put them in the right order to spell each word.
- Check your spelling.

257

1 Missing Letters

Lesson 19 | Day 3

Familiarize students with word meaning and usage. Write **f _ _ t** on the board. Say the word **feet**. Invite the children to tell you what vowels are missing.

Say Each word is missing a vowel or vowels. Write the missing vowels on the lines to make a spelling word.

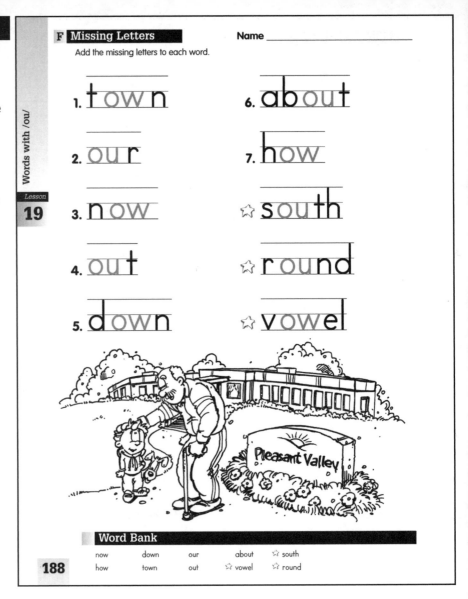

F Missing Letters

Add the missing letters to each word.

Name _____

Words with /ou/ — Lesson 19

1. town
2. our
3. now
4. out
5. down
6. about
7. how
☆ south
☆ round
☆ vowel

Word Bank

how, town, out, ☆ vowel, ☆ round

Take a minute to memorize...

Read the memory verse twice. Have students practice it with you two more times.

G Dictation

Listen and write the missing words.

Name _____

1. Will they go down to our town now?

2. How did they get this out?

3. Tell me about it.

Words with /ou/

Lesson 19

H Proofreading

One word in each pair is misspelled. Fill in the oval by the misspelled word.

1. ○ so
   ● owt

2. ○ they
   ● toun

3. ● owr
   ○ now

4. ○ how
   ● ubot

5. ● nou
   ○ out

6. ● doun
   ○ our

☆ ● sath
   ○ these

☆ ○ think
   ● rownd

☆ ● vawel
   ○ about

189

Dictation

1

Reinforce correct spelling by using current and previous words in context.

(Say) Listen as I read each sentence and then write it in your Worktext. (Slowly read each sentence twice. Sentences are found in the Student Worktext to the left.)

☆ **Challenge**

Write these incomplete sentences on the board.

Tommy practiced __ __ __ sounds.

__ birds fly ___ for __ winter.

__ __ __ __ __ circles.

Listen as I read each sentence. Write the sentence on your paper. (Slowly read each sentence twice.)

Tommy practiced <u>all the</u> <u>vowel</u> sounds.

<u>Most</u> birds fly <u>south</u> for <u>the</u> winter.

<u>I</u> <u>can</u> <u>draw</u> <u>ten</u> <u>round</u> circles.

Lesson **19** | Day 4

---

2 ## Proofreading

Familiarize students with standardized test format and reinforce recognizing misspelled words.

 Look at each set of words. One word in each set is misspelled. Fill in the oval by the misspelled word. (You may wish to pronounce each set of words to help students correctly identify them.)

259

3 Hide and Seek

Reinforce correct spelling of current spelling words. (A reproducible master is provided in Appendix A as shown on the inset page to the right.)

Write the words one at a time on a white board.

Have students:

- **Look** at the word.
- **Say** the word out loud.
- **Spell** the word out loud.
- **Hide** (teacher erases word.)
- **Write** the word on paper.
- **Seek** (teacher rewrites word.)
- **Check** spelling. If incorrect, rewrite word correctly.

4 Making Words

Have your students complete this activity to strengthen spelling ability and expand vocabulary.

1 Posttest

Test mastery of the spelling words. Challenge words are starred.

 (Say) I will say the word once, use the word in a sentence, then say the word again. Write the word on your paper.

Hide and Seek
Check a paper for each word you spell correctly.

Making Words
Add the endings to the spelling words. Write the new word on the line.

1. our + s

    ours

2. town + s

    towns

3. out + ing

    outing

☆ vowel + s

    vowels

☆ round + s

    rounds

☆ round + er

    rounder

☆ round + ing

    rounding

☆ round + ed

    rounded

378

1.	town	A **town** is a group of businesses and houses.
2.	out	Don't forget to turn **out** the light when you leave a room.
3.	now	The children couldn't play at the park **now** that it was raining.
4.	our	We all help to keep **our** classroom clean.
5.	how	Do you know **how** to spell all these words?
6.	about	What is this book **about**?
7.	down	Drops of rain dripped **down** the window.
☆	round	Pennies, dimes, quarters and nickels are **round**.
☆	south	The geese fly **south** before winter comes.
☆	vowel	Every word needs at least one **vowel** in it.

 Progress Chart
Students may record scores. (Reproducible master in Appendix B.)

 Personal Dictionary
Students may add any words they have misspelled to their personal dictionaries for reference when writing. (Cover in Appendix B.)

260

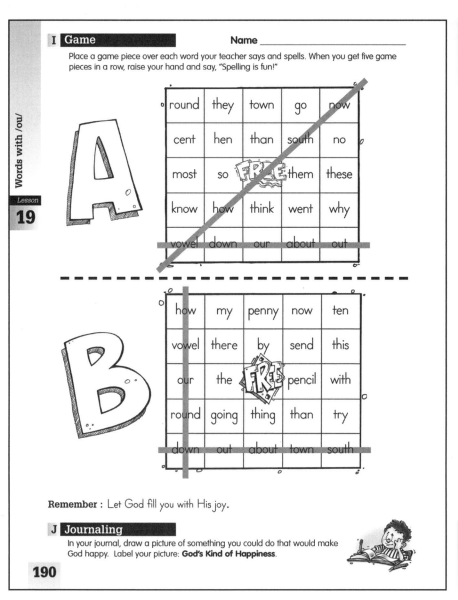

I Game

Name _____

Place a game piece over each word your teacher says and spells. When you get five game pieces in a row, raise your hand and say, "Spelling is fun!"

A

round	they	town	go	now
cent	hen	than	south	no
most	so	*FREE* them	these	
know	how	think	went	why
vowel	down	our	about	out

B

how	my	penny	now	ten
vowel	there	by	send	this
our	the	*FREE* pencil	with	
round	going	thing	than	try
down	out	about	town	south

Remember : Let God fill you with His joy.

J Journaling

In your journal, draw a picture of something you could do that would make God happy. Label your picture: **God's Kind of Happiness**.

190

How to Play:

- Fold the word cards (see **Materials**) in half, and place them in a container.
- Ask your students to fold the game page in half along the dotted line.
- Have half the class use game card A, and the other half card B.
- Instructions for the students: "Cover the word **FREE** in the center of your card. (pause) I will draw a word from the container, read it aloud, then I will spell it. When you find that word on your card, put a game piece over it. When you have five game pieces in a row (up and down, across or diagonally), raise your hand and say 'Spelling is FUN!'"
- Play as many times as you like. (As you return the word cards to the container and mix them up, remind the students to clear their game cards.)
- For variety, after playing several games, have the students turn their papers over and use the other game card.

2 ## Game

Reinforce spelling skills and provide motivation and interest.

Materials

- game page (from student text)
- flat buttons, dry beans, pennies, or game discs (10 per child)
- game word list
- word cards (each word from the game word list written on a card)

Game Word List

This list contains regular and challenge words.

1. **now**
2. **vowel**
3. **how**
4. **south**
5. **down**
6. **round**
7. **town**
☆ **our**
☆ **out**
☆ **about**

3 ## Journaling

Provide a meaningful reason for correct spelling through personal writing.

Review the story using discussion leads provided on the following page. Encourage students to apply the Scriptural value in their journaling.

Take a minute to memorize...

Have the class say the memory verses from lessons 16, 17, 18, and 19 with you.

261

Journaling (continued)

Say

- What did Tony not say when he got back from the field trip that helped Grandma Miller know he was beginning to understand God's kind of happiness? (He didn't gripe and complain about not getting to play at Mason Springs Park because of the rain.)

- What did Tony say that helped Grandma Miller know he'd found some of God's kind of happiness? (He talked about all the people he had met in the retirement center and asked to go back and visit them.)

- Think of some things you could do that would make God happy. Draw a picture in your journal of one.

Quotables!

*"Reading
is not deciphering;
writing
is not copying."*

*Ferreiro, E., and Teberosky, A. 1979. Los sistemas de escritura en el desarrollo del niño. Mexico: Siglo Veintiuno Editores, (English translation, Literacy before schooling. Exeter, NH: Heinemann, 1982.)

Bubble Gum Trouble

An impulsive theft teaches Stephen that obeying God's law is best.

"Mom, can I have a candy bar?" Stephen was waiting in the checkout line with his mom.

"No, Stephen," Mom said. "I don't want you to eat between meals. You won't want to eat the lasagna I've made for dinner if you eat that candy bar now."

"How about this pack of gum?" Stephen asked.

"All that sugar isn't good for your teeth, Stephen." Mom took the items out of the cart and put them on the counter. "I don't think so."

Mom hadn't actually said no, so Stephen tried again. "This kind doesn't have any sugar," he said, holding up another pack of gum. "Besides, I'm out of gum."

"I really don't want to spend money on gum today," Mom replied. "It isn't something you need."

"Then can I have this one piece of gum?" Stephen held up a single piece of bubble gum in a wrapper twisted on both ends. Mom didn't answer as she watched the checker scanning her purchases. "I really want some gum," Stephen begged. "I have some money at home. I'll pay you back."

Mom stopped filling out the check she was writing and looked Stephen straight in the eye. "Stephen, the answer is no," Mom said firmly. "Don't ask me again."

Stephen hung his head and started to put the gum back. He knew that was Mom's final answer — but he really wanted that gum. He could almost taste the sweet flavor in his mouth. His tongue was just itching to blow a big bubble. It didn't even cost that much. He had the money at home, and Dad had said he could choose how to spend his allowance.

Stephen looked up and saw Mom putting her sacked purchases back in the cart. He looked over and saw the checker talking to the next lady in line. He looked at the gum in his hand — then just stuck his hand in his pocket and followed Mom out of the store.

While Mom was placing the sacks in the trunk, Stephen took the gum out of his pocket and started to unwrap it. *"Oops! Mom will wonder where I got it,"* Stephen realized with a start. *"She will know I stole it. She will ask me after the very first bubble, if she doesn't notice me chewing it first."* Stephen shoved the gum back into his pocket and hopped into the car for the short trip home.

As soon as they came to a stop in their driveway he jumped out of the car and went straight into the house. He ran through the living room, back to his bedroom and shut the door. He took the gum out of his pocket and unwrapped it to put it in his mouth. *"Wait!"* he thought. *"Mom will still know I took the gum without paying for it. I told her I was out of gum!"* Frustrated, he shoved the gum back into his jacket pocket. *"A lot of good this gum does me. I can't even chew it!"* He took the gum out and looked at it again. Thoughts twirled 'round and 'round inside his head. *"I made a bad choice. I guess I could just take it back next time I go to the store. Mom never leaves me alone in the store, though. What will she do if she sees me take the gum out of my pocket and put it back? I got it into my pocket without her seeing. Maybe I could put it back the same way."* Finally, Stephen wrapped up the gum and stuck it in his top dresser drawer.

When Stephen was ready for bed that night, Dad came in for their nightly talk and prayers. "Stephen, we've been talking about God's rules for a couple weeks now," he said. "What do you remember about them?"

"The first four are about our love for God, and the last six are about how we should love others," Stephen said.

"Good job, Son!" Dad nodded. "You remember the things we've been talking about very well." He opened his Bible to Exodus 20. "Tonight we are going to learn the eighth commandment," he said. "It says here in verse 15, 'You must not steal.'"

Stephen couldn't believe it! Had Dad seen the gum in his dresser drawer? Maybe Mom had told Dad to read this verse after she'd found the gum. *"No,"* he thought, *"Dad and I have been studying the ten commandments in order, and number eight always comes after number seven."*

"Son, are you listening to me?" Dad interrupted Stephen's frantic thoughts.

"Yeah," Stephen said.

"What do you think it means then?"

"What do I think what means?"

"'You must not steal,'" Dad quoted.

"Oh." Stephen tried to focus on what Dad was saying. "Don't take something that isn't yours if you want to be happy," he said, remembering their discussions about rules five, six, and seven.

"That's right," Dad said. "God knows that if people just took what they wanted, lots of people would get angry and upset. How did you feel the other day when your new leather soccer ball wasn't in the garage and you thought someone had walked in and taken it?"

Suddenly Stephen couldn't stand it any more. "Dad, I'm tired," he said. "Can I just go to sleep now?"

"Sure, Son." Dad looked at Stephen in surprise. "I guess we can skip right to prayer. You begin."

"Why don't you do it

263

tonight, Dad," Stephen suggested. "I don't feel like it."

Dad bowed his head and began to pray, ending with, "… and thank you for my son, Stephen. Help him to love you and make the choice to follow your rules. Amen."

Dad stood up, then bent to pull the covers up under Stephen's chin. "Say, what's this?" he asked as tears began rolling down Stephen's cheeks.

Stephen buried his face in Dad's arms and began to sob. Then he told him about the gum hidden in the dresser drawer. "And the silly thing is that I can't even chew it! I have it, Dad, but I can't even chew it!"

"You know, Son, David talks about having God's law written on your heart . . ."

"Yes, I know all about David," Stephen interrupted as he tried to stop his tears. "We've been learning about him at school."

"Well," Dad continued, "he says something like 'I will be happy to do your will, God, for you've written your law in my heart.' You know, I'm glad we've been studying God's rules, because when you learn them and understand what they mean, they're much harder to break." Dad paused. "You see, Son, God has been writing them on your heart, too!"

"Dad?" Stephen asked, looking up into his father's face. "Will you go with me when I go to pay for the gum?"

"Stephen," Dad smiled, "I'd be delighted!"

2 Discussion Time

Check understanding of the story and development of personal values.

- Why did Stephen take the gum?
- How did Stephen feel as he put the gum in his dresser drawer?
- What had Stephen and his dad been studying every night?
- Why did Stephen's dad want him to learn God's rules?
- Do you think it is important to write God's law (or rules) on your heart?
- What are some of God's rules found in Exodus 20?

264

A Test-Words
Write each word as your teacher says it.

Name _____

1. my
2. no
3. when
4. send
5. they
6. thing
7. now
8. our

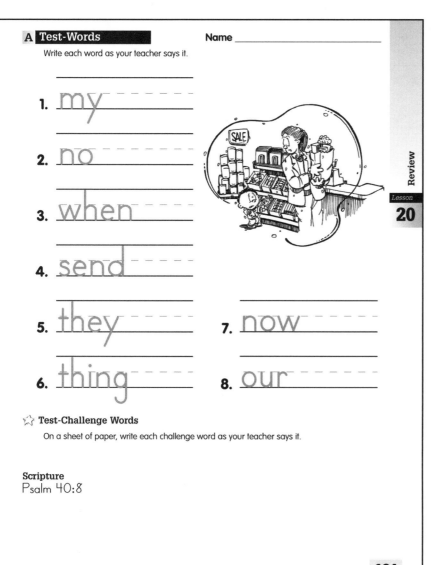

☆ **Test-Challenge Words**

On a sheet of paper, write each challenge word as your teacher says it.

Scripture
Psalm 40:8

191

Test-Challenge Words
On a separate sheet of paper, challenge words may be tested using the sentences below.

Personal Dictionary
After the tests in the review unit are graded, students may add any words they have misspelled to their personal dictionaries.

Take a minute to memorize...

Read the memory verse to the class twice. Have the class practice it with you two more times.

---

3 Test-Words

Test for knowledge of the correct spellings of these words.
(See the instructions at the top right for challenge words.)

 (Say) I will say each word once, use the word in a sentence, then say the word again. Write the word on the lines in your Worktext.

1. **my**   Dad said I could choose how to spend **my** money.
2. **no**   Mom said, "Stephen, the answer is **no.**"
3. **when**   Stephen didn't know **when** to chew the gum.
4. **send**   We can **send** messages by computer.
5. **they**   When **they** went to the grocery store, Stephen took the gum.
6. **thing**   This **thing** that looks like a TV is called a monitor.
7. **now**   It is important for you to decide **now** that you won't steal.
8. **our**   God wants us to put his law in **our** hearts.
☆ **going**   Stephen and his mom are **going** to the grocery store.
☆ **even**   He didn't **even** bring any money with him.
☆ **than**   The gum cost less **than** ten cents.
☆ **vowel**   Stephen can practice his **vowel** sounds in the car.

1 Game

Materials
- game page (from student text)
- yellow crayons (1 per child)
- game word list

Game Word List
Use of challenge words is optional.

1. my
2. no
3. when
4. send
5. they
6. thing
7. now
8. our
☆ going
☆ even
☆ than
☆ vowel

B Game   Name _____

In the story from lesson 19, Tony learned that God can fill his heart with happiness even when it's cloudy and rainy outside. Color one sun each time you or your team spells a review word correctly.

Review
Lesson
20

192

How to Play:

- Divide the class into two teams, and decide which team will go first.
- Have a student from team A go to the board.
- Read the spelling word two times slowly and clearly. (You may also wish to use the word in a sentence. Ex.: "cat — The cat climbed a tree. — cat")
- Have the student write the word on the board.
- If the word is spelled correctly, instruct all the members of team A to color one sun. (Note: If the word is misspelled, correct the spelling immediately before continuing the game.)
- Alternate between teams A and B as you go down the word list.
- The team with the most suns colored when you have gone through the game word list twice is the winner.

Non-Competitive Option:
At the end of the game, say: "Class, I am proud of your efforts to spell the words correctly. If you had fun and tried your best, you are all winners!"

C | Test-Sentences

Name _____

The underlined word in each sentence is misspelled. Write the sentences on the lines below, spelling each underlined word correctly.

Stephen stole <u>teh</u> gum.

1. Stephen stole the gum.

I would like <u>tin</u> pieces of bubble gum.

2. I would like ten pieces of bubble gum.

D | Test-Proofreading

One word in each pair is misspelled. Fill in the oval by the misspelled word.

1. ○ try
   ● doun

4. ○ hen
   ● ubout

7. ● goe
   ○ this

2. ● sint
   ○ why

5. ○ cent
   ● hin

8. ● thim
   ○ down

3. ● htis
   ○ go

6. ○ them
   ● tri

9. ○ about
   ● wy

☆ **Test-Challenge Words**

On a sheet of paper, write each challenge word as your teacher says it.

193

---

1 Test-Sentences

Reinforce recognizing misspelled words.

 Say

Read each sentence carefully. The underlined word in each sentence is misspelled. Write the sentences on the lines in your worktext, spelling each underlined word correctly.

2 Test-Proofreading

Familiarize students with standardized test format and reinforce recognition of misspelled words.

 Say

Look at each set of words. One word in each set is misspelled. Fill in the oval by the misspelled word.

(You may wish to pronounce each pair of words to help students correctly identify them.)

Test-Challenge Words

On a separate sheet of paper, challenge words may be tested using the sentences below.

 Say

I will say the word once, use the word in a sentence, then say the word again. Write the word on your paper.

☆ **most**   I like **most** of these flavors of gum.

☆ **penny**   One dime plus one **penny** equals eleven cents.

☆ **these**   God wants to write **these** laws on your heart.

☆ **south**   Their house is at the **south** end of the street.

1 Game

Materials
- game page (from student text)
- flat buttons, dry beans, pennies, or game discs (1 per child)
- game word list

Game Word List
Use of challenge words is optional.

1. ten
2. the
3. try
4. why
5. go
6. hen
7. cent
8. them
9. this
10. down
11. about
☆ most
☆ penny
☆ these
☆ south

E Game   Name _____

Stephen needs to pay for the piece of gum that he took. Lead the way to the grocery store by moving one space each time you or your team spells a review word correctly.

Review
Lesson
20

194

How to Play:

- Divide the class into two teams, and decide which team will go first.
- Have each student place his/her game piece on Start.
- Have a student from team A go to the board.
- Read the spelling word two times slowly and clearly. (You may also wish to use the word in a sentence. Ex.: "cat — The cat climbed a tree. — cat")
- Have the student write the word on the board.
- If the word is spelled correctly, instruct the members of team A to move their game pieces forward one space on the game board. (Note: If the word is misspelled, correct the spelling immediately before continuing the game.)
- Alternate between teams A and B as you go down the word list.
- The team to reach the grocery store first is the winner.

Non-Competitive Option:

At the end of the game, say: "Class, I am proud of your efforts to spell the words correctly. If you had fun and tried your best, you are all winners!"

F Test-Sentence   Name _____

The underlined word in this sentence is misspelled. Write the sentence on the lines below, spelling the underlined word correctly.

Stephen went to <u>twon</u> to pay for the gum.

Stephen went to town

to pay for the gum.

Review
Lesson
20

G Test-Words

Write each word as your teacher says it.

1. by

2. so

3. then

4. went

5. there

6. with

7. how

8. out

☆ **Test-Challenge Words**

On a sheet of paper, write each challenge word as your teacher says it.

195

---

1 Test-Sentence

Reinforce recognizing misspelled words.

(Say) Read this sentence carefully. The underlined word is misspelled. Write the sentence on the lines in your Worktext, spelling the underlined word correctly.

Personal Dictionary

Remind students to add any words they have misspelled to their personal dictionaries.

---

2 Test-Words

Test for knowledge of the correct spellings of these words. (Challenge words may be tested on a separate piece of paper. Challenge words are starred.)

(Say) I will say each word once, use the word in a sentence, then say the word again. Write the word on the lines in your Worktext.

1. by   Dad sat down **by** Stephen.
2. so   Stephen was **so** glad that he told about the stolen gum.
3. then   Stephen took the gum, but **then** couldn't chew it.
4. went   We **went** to the park yesterday.
5. there   Stephen learned that **there** are choices to be made every day.
6. with   "Will you go **with** me to pay for the gum?" Stephen asked.
7. how   The dog knows **how** to sit and beg.
8. out   Do you think the dog wants to go **out**?
☆ know   Did Stephen's dad **know** he took the gum?
☆ sentence   The **sentence** in verse 15 says, "Thou must not steal."
☆ think   "What do you **think** it means?" asked his dad.
☆ round   The piece of gum was **round**.

269

3 Writing Assessment

Assess student's spelling, grammar, and composition skills through personal writing.

(Say)

- Why was Stephen's dad studying Exodus 20 with him every night for worship? (Exodus 20 is where the Ten Commandments are found. Mr. Wilson wanted to write God's rules on his son's heart.)

- Do you think laws (or rules) are written to make us happy? (yes) Why? (Without God's rules everyone would think only of themselves and our world would be a mess.)

- In your worktext draw Stephen and his dad studying God's rules. Don't forget to label your picture!

H Writing Assessment   Name _____

Inside the heart draw a picture of Stephen and his dad studying God's rules. Write a sentence about God's rules.

Review
Lesson
20

Remember : Understanding God's laws makes them easier to follow.

196

A rubric for scoring is provided in Appendix B.

4 Action Game

Reinforce spelling skills and provide motivation and interest.

Materials

- 9 chairs
- 5 sheets of paper marked with a large **O**
- 5 sheets of paper marked with a large **X**

How to Play:

Divide the class into two teams: **X**'s and **O**'s. Place nine chairs in the front of the room in three rows of three. The chairs will form the tic-tac-toe grid. Alternate between the two teams, giving spelling words from this review unit. If a student spells a word correctly, give him an **X** or **O** sheet to hold depending on which team he represents. Allow him to sit in any one of the empty chairs to mark that spot on the grid for his team. Continue playing until all the words from this review unit have been spelled and/or the tic-tac-toe game in progress has been completed.

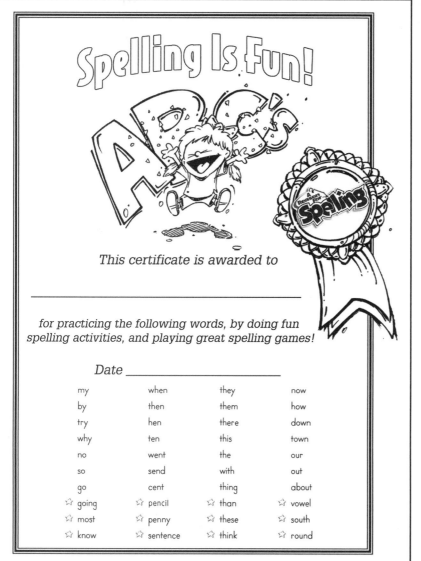

Spelling Is Fun! ABC's

This certificate is awarded to

_____

for practicing the following words, by doing fun spelling activities, and playing great spelling games!

Date _____

my	when	they	now
by	then	them	how
try	hen	there	down
why	ten	this	town
no	went	the	our
so	send	with	out
go	cent	thing	about
☆ going	☆ pencil	☆ than	☆ vowel
☆ most	☆ penny	☆ these	☆ south
☆ know	☆ sentence	☆ think	☆ round

5 Certificate

Provide an opportunity for parents or guardians to encourage and assess their child's progress.

 Say
- Write your name on the first line.
- Now I will write the date on the board for you to copy on the next line.
- Follow along as I read the certificate out loud.
- Be sure to show your parents or guardian all the words you've practiced spelling.

Take a minute to memorize...

Read the memory verse to the class twice. Have the class practice it with you two more times.

Quotables!

"When children read and write, they grow as spellers." *

*Wilde, Sandra. 1990. A Proposal for a New Spelling Curriculum. The Elementary School Journal, Vol. 90, No. 3, January: 275-289.

6 Letter

Provide the parent or guardian with the spelling word lists for the next unit.

Say Show your parents or guardian this letter that tells them what your spelling words will be for the next unit. Ask them to put it in a special place where you will remember to practice them together.

Review **20** | Day 5

Dear Parent,

We are about to begin a new spelling unit containing four weekly lessons. A set of seven words plus three challenge words will be studied each week. All the words will be reviewed in the fifth week.

Values based on the Scriptures listed below will be taught in each lesson.

Lesson 21	Lesson 22	Lesson 23	Lesson 24
do	boy	as	mother
to	joy	has	her
you	some	that	girl
school	come	happy	your
good	from	after	or
look	love	was	for
put	of	said	are
☆ tooth	☆ enjoy	☆ have	☆ Lord
☆ books	☆ above	☆ hasn't	☆ first
☆ soon	☆ none	☆ wasn't	☆ circle
Psalm 28:7	Psalm 119:73	Prov. 3:6	Prov. 29:18

272

Time with Tony

Tony learns he can praise God for lots of things, even though his parents are divorced and he doesn't see his papa very often.

"Mama! Mama! When is Papa going to get here?"

"I don't know, Tony," Mrs. Vinetti bent to straighten the rug in front of the kitchen sink. "He said he would be here to pick you up at four o'clock. That's 15 minutes from now. Do you have any homework this weekend?"

"I'm done with it," Tony pointed to the math worktext on the kitchen table.

"Come pick up your clothes in the bathroom and put them where they belong," Mama said as she walked down the hall. "And put away these blocks, too, so the living room will look nice."

"I wanted to show Papa my castle. Can I pick them up after I show him?"

"Okay, but put all the blocks you don't use back in the box."

Tony went into the bathroom and threw his pajamas in the clothes hamper, then headed toward the living room to straighten his building site. "I think I'll make this castle bigger while I wait for Papa," Tony thought. He built a wall around his castle with the long blocks, then put up another lookout tower on the back side. "I bet Papa will really like this." Tony added a road to the castle with a big gate that opened and closed. "Mama, what time is it?"

"It's 4:00 now, Tony. Papa should be here any minute. Did you put your pajamas in the dirty clothes?"

"Yes, Ma'am."

"How about the blocks?" Mom peeked around the corner in the kitchen.

"I'm working on it," Tony said.

Tony built another wall around the castle to make a moat and added a draw bridge. He built a little house for the gatekeeper, then trotted down the hall to his room to get some LEGO® people

and their horses to use in the castle. As he passed the clock beside his bed he noticed it was already 4:30. "Where is Papa?" he called to Mama as he sat down beside his castle again.

"I don't know Tony-O. I'm sure he'll be here soon."

A little later, Mama came into the living room. "Oh, Tony! What a neat castle," she said. "I like the way your LEGO® men are looking out of the towers. It makes it all look so real. Are those alligators in your moat?" Mama bent down to take a closer look.

"What time is it now, Mama?" Tony asked impatiently.

Mama looked at her watch, then out the living room window with a sigh. *"Five o'clock! I wish Marco would get here,"* she thought. *"Tony has been looking forward to this weekend with his Papa all month."* Mama bent down to work the drawbridge. "Papa should be here soon, Tony," she said. "Maybe he stopped to get some groceries or something before he picks you up."

"You know, we got this huge set of oak blocks before you were born." Tony looked up in surprise as Mama continued. "As soon as the ultrasound showed you were a boy, Papa insisted we go out and buy a set of blocks for you, because he remembered how much he'd enjoyed playing with blocks when he was a little boy. We had so much fun looking for just the right set," Mama smiled remembering a happier time.

"Where is he now, Mama? He's always late!" Tony pushed over one of the castle towers with his finger.

"His being late doesn't mean he loves you less, Tony." Mama put an arm around her son. "Say, let's build a house for the knight to ride to. Maybe he

could bring the people a secret message." She galloped a horse out the gate and across the drawbridge.

"Okay. Let's build a fence for the king's horses, too," said Tony.

Mama and Tony were so absorbed in their castle game that they both jumped when the doorbell finally rang. "Tony-O!" Papa shouted when Tony opened the door of the duplex.

There was a long moment of silence as Tony looked up at his papa. He didn't even notice the package Papa held in his arms. "Where have you been, Papa?" he demanded. "You said you'd be here at four!"

"But I brought you something, Antonio Marcus Vinetti," Papa said proudly. He handed Tony a huge, brightly-wrapped present.

Tony took it with surprise. "It's not my birthday," Tony reminded his Papa.

"Open it," Papa encouraged. Tony tore off the wrapping paper to discover a brand-new race car set! The little cars had electric motors and there was lots of track to make a huge race course. You could adjust the speed of the two cars with two separate controls. Tony was speechless as he looked in awe at the pictures on the box. He'd been begging Mama for this very set for months.

"How did you know, Papa?" asked Tony.

"Know what?"

"Know that I wanted this race track set. These are my favorite cars, too."

"Oh, I had one of these when I was a boy. It was just an oval track, though," Mr. Vinetti replied. "Let's take it over and set it up at my place, before we go out to eat. I'm going to take you to a real race track this weekend, too."

"Come see my castle, Papa," Tony pleaded. "It will just take a minute."

"That's nice, Tony," Papa said glancing at the huge castle spread across the living room floor. "Where's your suitcase? We've got to get going or we won't have time to set this up before dinner."

"It's right there by the

273

door, Marcus," Mama pointed.

Tony followed Papa out the front door and climbed in the front seat of the shiny, red sports car parked in the driveway. Mama waved from the steps of the duplex. Tony wished she were coming with them. It would be a lot more fun if they were a family again.

Papa planned such an exciting weekend that Tony didn't have much time to miss his mama. On Sunday, Papa dropped Tony off in front of the duplex on Bridge Street at 1:30 sharp, just as they had planned.

That night Tony hummed a little tune Miss Grant was teaching them as he got ready for bed. He couldn't get the catchy words out of his head.

"Only a boy named David, only a little sling . . ."

He took off his shoes and threw them in his closet.

"Only a boy named David, but he could pray and sing."

Tony found his pajamas, pulled them on slowly, then went into the bathroom to brush his teeth. *"Miss Grant said the boy David liked to write songs, too,"* he thought. *"What was the one Miss Grant wanted us to remember? Let's see, 'Joy rises in my heart until I burst out in songs of praise to God.' I didn't know I learned those words already!"* Tony smiled at his reflection in the bathroom mirror. *"She said the boy David wrote those words in Psalms. David must have felt happy like I do tonight!"* As he put his toothbrush away, Tony started to hum the second verse of the song about David. He threw his dirty clothes in the hamper and grabbed his bedtime story book and headed for the bedroom.

"And the giant came tumbling down!" Tony sang in his deepest voice, then crashed to the floor with a laugh.

Mama came in and scooped her little giant off the floor. Then she read him a story, and tucked him into bed with a hug and a kiss.

After she turned out the light Tony lay under the light cotton blanket thinking. *"I wish Papa were here to kiss me goodnight, too. Why couldn't things be like they used to be anyway? I hate it that I don't get to see my papa every day, and that Mama has to work so hard. She can't even be home to meet me after school anymore!"*

Then Tony remembered what Mama had said when he'd cried as Papa left. "We both love you very much, Tony. We can't fix everything in our sinful world, but that doesn't change our love for you at all."

And Tony thought about all the fun he'd had with Mama in Mason Springs Park. They'd had a picnic in the park and flown his kite. There'd been just the right amount of wind. He also remembered the castle they'd built together Friday afternoon. And he'd had fun with Papa, too. They'd gone out to eat three times. He'd raced cars with Papa on the new race track, then had gone to a real one.

Thinking about the wonderful weekend he'd had, Tony smiled again, then sang softly to himself. ". . . only a boy named David, but he could pray and sing . . ." And snuggling deeper in the covers, he drifted slowly off to sleep.

2 Discussion Time

Check understanding of the story and development of personal values.

- Why was Tony singing *Only A Boy named David* while he got ready for bed?
- Does everything have to go right all the time for you to be happy?
- What are some things that make you happiest?
- Have you thanked God for the happy times?

274

A Preview

Write each word as your teacher says it.

Name _____

1. to

2. school

3. look

4. do

5. you

6. good

7. put

Challenge Words

☆ books

☆ tooth

☆ soon

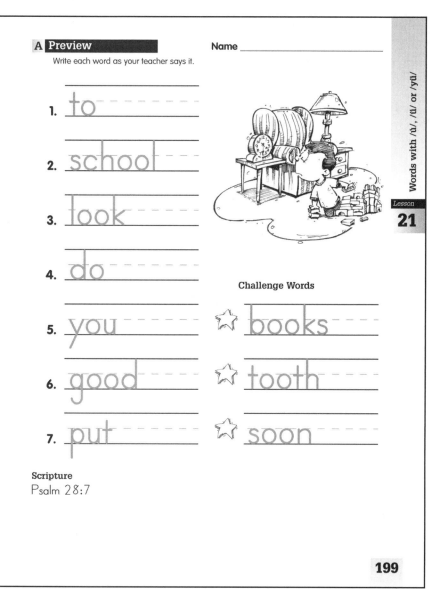

Scripture

Psalm 28:7

199

Challenge

For better spellers, challenge words may be included in the weekly list. Challenge words are starred.

Correct Immediately!

Say — Let's correct our preview. I will write each word on the board. Put a dot under each letter on your preview as I spell the word out loud. If you spelled a word wrong, rewrite it correctly.

Progress Chart

Students may record scores. (Reproducible master in Appendix B.)

Take a minute to memorize . . .

Read the memory verse twice. Have students practice it with you two more times.

---

3 Preview

Test for knowledge of the correct spellings of these words. (See the instructions at the top right for challenge words.)

 Say — I will say each word once, use the word in a sentence, then say the word again. Write the word on the lines in the Worktext.

1.	to	Tony was going **to** his papa's house.
2.	school	We learn many things at **school**.
3.	look	Tony wanted his father to **look** at the castle he made.
4.	do	What **do** you want to do after school?
5.	you	God wants **you** to have joy in your heart.
6.	good	Tony had a **good** visit with his papa.
7.	put	Mama asked Tony to **put** his pajamas in the hamper.
☆	books	The pictures in these **books** are colorful.
☆	tooth	Christopher lost his **tooth**.
☆	soon	Mama said, "I'm sure he will be here **soon**."

4 Word Shapes

Help students form a correct image of whole words.

Say ▸ Look at each word and think about its shape. Now, write the word in the correct word Shape Boxes. You may check off each word as you use it.

(In many words, the sound of /ü/, or /ū/ is spelled with **oo**. In a few words, these sounds are spelled **ou**. The sound of /u̇/ is often spelled with **u** or **oo**.)

Say ▸ In the word shape boxes, color the letter or letters that spell the sound of /ü/, /ū/, or /u̇/ in each word. Circle the words that are spelled with **oo**.

⭐ Challenge

Draw the correctly shaped box around each letter in these words.

Say ▸ On a separate sheet of paper, write other words that contain the spelling patterns in the word list. See how many words you can write.

Words with /u̇/, /ü/, or /ū/

Lesson **21**

B Word Shapes   Name _____

Write each word in the correct word shape boxes. Next, in the word shape boxes, color the letter or letters that spell the sound of /u̇/, /ü/, or /ū/ in each word. Circle the words that are spelled with **oo**.

1. do
2. to
3. you
4. school
5. good
6. look
7. put

☆ **Challenge**
Draw the correct word shape boxes around each word.

tooth   books   soon

200

Answers may vary for duplicate word shapes.

Be Prepared For Fun

Check these supply lists for **Fun Ways to Spell** presented **Day 2**. Purchase and/or gather these items ahead of time!

General
- Crayons
- 3 x 5 Cards cut in thirds (24 pieces per child)
- 3 x 5 Cards cut in thirds (14 more pieces for challenge words)
- Glue
- Construction Paper (about 3 pieces per child)
- Spelling List

Auditory
- Spelling List

Visual
- Sidewalk Chalk
- Spelling List

Tactile
- Damp Sand (in plastic storage box with lid)
- Spelling List

C Hide and Seek

Name _____

Circle a cookie for each word you spell correctly.

D Other Word Forms

Using the words below, follow the instructions given by your teacher.

(book)   done   (schools)

booked   looked   sooner

booking   looking   soonest

does   puts   (teeth)

doing   putting   teething

did   schooling your

E Fun Ways to Spell

Initial the box of each activity you finish.

1.

   Spell your words with crayons.

3.

   Spell your words out loud.

2.

   Spell your words with sidewalk chalk.

4.

   Spell your words in wet sand.

201

---

1 Hide and Seek

Reinforce spelling by using multiple styles of learning.

On a white board, Teacher writes each word — one at a time. **Have students:**

- **Look** at the word.
- **Say** the word out loud.
- **Spell** the word out loud.
- **Hide** (teacher erases word.)
- **Write** the word on their paper.
- **Seek** (teacher rewrites word.)
- **Check** spelling. If incorrect, repeat above steps.

Day 2

Lesson 21

2 Other Word Forms

This activity is optional. Have students find and circle the Other Word Forms that name a person, place, or thing.

3 Fun Ways to Spell

Four activities are provided. Use one, two, three, or all of the activities. Have students initial the box for each activity they complete.

Options:

- assign activities to students according to their learning styles
- set up the activities in learning centers for students to do throughout the day
- divide students into four groups and assign one activity per group
- do one activity per day

General

To spell your words with crayons…
- Write each letter of your spelling word on a card.
- Glue the cards on a sheet of paper in the right order to spell your words.
- Check your spelling.

Auditory

To spell your words out loud…
- Have your classmate read a spelling word.
- Say a sentence with that spelling word to your classmate.
- Spell the spelling word you used in that sentence to your classmate.
- Ask your classmate to check your spelling.
- Do this with each word on your word list.

Visual

To spell your words with sidewalk chalk…
- Write each of your words on the sidewalk (ball court or playground).
- Check your spelling.

Tactile

To spell your words in damp sand…
- Use your finger to write a spelling word in the damp sand.
- Check your spelling.
- Smooth the sand with your finger and write another word.

1 | Missing Letters

Familiarize students with word meaning and usage.

Write **c_ _k** on the board. Say the word **cook**. Invite the children to tell you what vowels are missing.

Each word is missing a vowel or vowels. Write the missing vowels on the lines to make a spelling word.

F Missing Letters

Add the missing letters to each word.

Name _____

Words with /u/, /ū/, or /ū/

Lesson
21

☆ books

1. to

2. school

☆ soon

3. good

4. look

5. do

6. you

7. put

☆ tooth

Word Bank

do	you	good	put	☆ books
to	school	look	☆ tooth	☆ soon

202

Take a minute to memorize...

Read the memory verse twice. Have students practice it with you two more times.

G Dictation

Listen and write the missing words.

Name _____

1. Do you go to school?

2. This will look good on you.

3. Put your books away.

H Proofreading

One word in each pair is misspelled. Fill in the oval by the misspelled word.

1. ⬤ yuw
   ○ put

2. ⬤ skool
   ○ good

3. ○ look
   ⬤ tuo

4. ○ town
   ⬤ luuk

5. ○ school
   ⬤ guud

6. ○ down
   ⬤ dou

☆ ⬤ sune
   ○ south

☆ ⬤ tuth
   ○ with

☆ ○ most
   ⬤ bux

203

Dictation

Reinforce correct spelling by using current and previous words in context.

 (Say)

Listen as I read each sentence and then write it in your Worktext. (Slowly read each sentence twice. Sentences are found in the Student Worktext to the left.)

☆ **Challenge**

Write these incomplete sentences on the board.

__ __ lost __ __ __ .

__ __ __ __ __ on __ shelf.

__ __ __ home __ .

 (Say)

Listen as I read each sentence. Write the sentence on your paper. (Slowly read each sentence twice.)

The dog lost a small tooth.

We can put the books on the shelf.

He will go home soon.

---

2 Proofreading

Familiarize students with standardized test format and reinforce recognizing misspelled words.

(Say)

Look at each set of words. One word in each set is misspelled. Fill in the oval by the misspelled word. (You may wish to pronounce each set of words to help students correctly identify them.)

279

3 Hide and Seek

Reinforce correct spelling of current spelling words. (A reproducible master is provided in Appendix A as shown on the inset page to the right.)

Write the words one at a time on a white board.

Have students:

- **Look** at the word.
- **Say** the word out loud.
- **Spell** the word out loud.
- **Hide** (teacher erases word.)
- **Write** the word on paper.
- **Seek** (teacher rewrites word.)
- **Check** spelling. If incorrect, rewrite word correctly.

4 Making Words

Have your students complete this activity to strengthen spelling ability and expand vocabulary.

1 Posttest

Test mastery of the spelling words. Challenge words are starred.

Say I will say the word once, use the word in a sentence, then say the word again. Write the word on your paper.

Hide and Seek

Check a paper for each word you spell correctly.

Making Words

Add the endings to the spelling words. Write the new word on the line.

1. put + s   + t + ing
    puts    putting

2. school + s   + ing
    schools   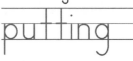 schooling

3. look + s   + ing
    looks    looking

4. do + e + s   + ing
    does    doing

☆ tooth – oo + ee
    teeth

379

1.	school	We can make new friends at **school**.
2.	look	She wanted to **look** at all the pictures.
3.	do	Let's **do** something different with these blocks.
4.	you	God loves **you** so much.
5.	put	Always **put** your things away neatly.
6.	to	Tony's father took him **to** a real race track.
7.	good	This is a very **good** lunch.
☆	soon	We will **soon** be finished with this test.
☆	books	I like the **books** about sea creatures best.
☆	tooth	The girl's new **tooth** is coming in.

 Progress Chart
Students may record scores. (Reproducible master in Appendix B.)

 Personal Dictionary
Students may add any words they have misspelled to their personal dictionaries for reference when writing. (Cover in Appendix B.)

280

I Game

Name _____

Tony got a new race track and cars from his papa. Choose one of the cars at the starting line to race. Color in one section of the race track in front of that car for each word you or your team spells correctly from this week's word list.

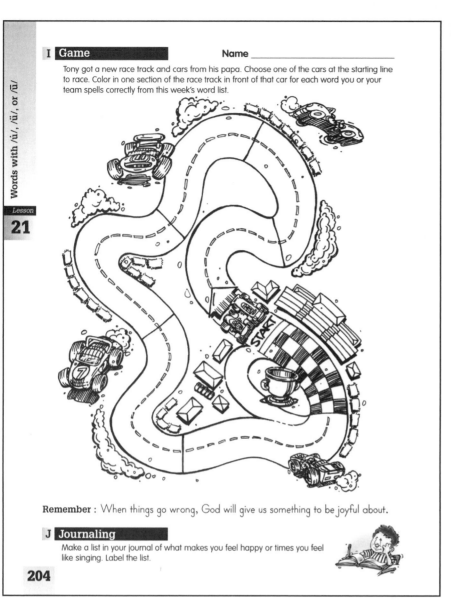

Remember : When things go wrong, God will give us something to be joyful about.

J Journaling

Make a list in your journal of what makes you feel happy or times you feel like singing. Label the list.

How to Play:

- Divide the class into two teams, assign each team a car to race, and decide which team will go first.
- Optional: If you have an even number of students, you may wish to pair students from opposing teams and have them share a game page, each coloring the spaces in front of their team's car, on that page.
- Have a student from team A go to the board.
- Read the spelling word two times slowly and clearly. (You may also wish to use the word in a sentence. Ex.: "cat — The cat climbed a tree. — cat")
- Have the student write the word on the board.
- If the word is spelled correctly, instruct all the members of team A to color one space in front of their team car, beginning at Start, on the game board. (Note: If the word is misspelled, correct the spelling immediately before continuing the game.)
- Alternate between teams A and B as you go down the word list.
- The team to reach the finish line first is the winner.

Non-Competitive Option:

At the end of the game, say: "Class, I am proud of your efforts to spell the words correctly. If you had fun and tried your best, you are all winners!"

2 Game

Reinforce spelling skills and provide motivation and interest.

Materials

- game page (from student text)
- crayons or colored pencils (1 per child)
- game word list

Game Word List

Use of challenge words is optional.

1. **do**
2. **to**
3. **you**
4. **school**
5. **good**
6. **look**
7. **put**
☆ **tooth**
☆ **books**
☆ **soon**

3 Journaling

Provide a meaningful reason for correct spelling through personal writing.

Review the story using discussion leads provided on the following page. Encourage students to apply the Scriptural value in their journaling.

Take a minute to memorize...

Have the class say the memory verse with you once.

Journaling (continued)

Say

- Our story this week was called "Time With Tony."

- Do you remember how Tony felt at the beginning of the story? (Tony was frustrated that Papa was so late coming to pick him up for their weekend together.)

- Why did Tony feel so happy by the end of our story? (He realized that even though he didn't have a perfect family he had a lot to praise God for.)

- Think of some things you feel happy about. Make a list of them in your journal.

Quotables!

Command of oral language is the foundation for success in reading and writing.

Too Rushed To Brush

Tommy learns why it's important to brush his teeth.

"May I be excused?" Tommy set his empty glass down on the breakfast table.

"Yes, Son. Carry your dishes over to the sink, please." Mom began putting things away in the refrigerator. "We need to leave for school in 10 minutes, so make sure you get your teeth brushed and your things together quickly."

"Better wash your face, too, Tommy," Lisa giggled. "You look like a walrus with a huge white milk mustache!" Tommy made a face at his older sister behind his mother's back, then escaped up the stairs. Behind him he heard Lisa complaining. "Mom! Tommy just . . ."

In his room, Tommy grabbed his backpack and stuffed his math book inside. Glancing out the window, he decided it would be a good day to take his baseball glove. The sun was shining in a clear blue sky without a cloud in sight. "Now, where is that glove?" he thought, beginning to search his room. Just as he finally spotted it, he heard his mother call. "Time to go, kids."

"Oh, well. No time to brush my teeth this morning," Tommy thought. "No one's gonna notice, anyway." He stopped by the bathroom long enough to quickly swipe a washcloth across his face, then ran out the door to the car.

Later that evening, Dad stood up and stretched. "Very good, son. You were able to get the answers to your addition facts much faster than you could a few weeks ago." He patted Tommy on the back. "I'm really proud of you!" Dad gathered the stack of flash cards and snapped a rubber band around them. "You've really worked hard on these, so how about a quick game of

catch before it gets too dark to see?"

"All right!" Tommy jumped up so fast the kitchen chair he'd been sitting on almost fell over backwards. "I'll be right back, Dad!" he flung over his shoulder as he headed upstairs for his glove.

In the backyard, Mr. Rawson tossed some different kinds of pitches to Tommy. He even threw a couple of curve balls. The sun slowly drifted down the western sky and the shadows grew thicker. "Okay, Dad. Throw another one like that last one!" Tommy stood with his glove ready.

"I already did, Son," Dad laughed. "It's so dark now it sailed right past you, and you never even saw it! I guess we'd better call it quits for tonight." Tommy and Dad were still chuckling as they came in the back door, and almost bumped into Lisa. "You kids run up and get ready for bed, then we'll read another chapter in our book." Brother and sister raced off, and Tommy was the first one back downstairs. "Whoa!" Dad held up a hand as Tommy charged through the living room door. "That was fast! Did you already brush your teeth?"

"Well, uh, no." Tommy scuffed his bare toes into the carpet. He turned and retraced his steps to the bathroom. *Brushing my teeth seems like such a waste of time.*" Tommy thought as he squirted toothpaste onto his toothbrush. He opened his mouth and peered in the mirror at his teeth. *They look fine to me. I don't know why I have to brush them so often.*" With a shrug Tommy stuck the toothbrush in his mouth and brushed halfheartedly. When he returned to the living room Lisa was curled up next to Dad on the couch and Mom was sitting in her favorite chair.

Tommy hopped up by Dad and made himself comfortable while Dad began the story.

"'And so they weren't curious about anything at all.'" Dad read the final words of the story and Tommy stretched. "We'll stop there tonight."

"Aw, Dad," Tommy whined, "We want to know what happened."

"Read just a little more, Dad, please." Lisa tugged on his sleeve.

"Not tonight, kids. It's your bedtime and you need your sleep." Dad grinned. "And so do Mom and I."

"Mom! I can't find my jean jacket," Lisa called downstairs the next morning as they were getting ready to leave for school.

"Did you leave it in the car yesterday?" Mom asked. Lisa ran out to check.

"Tommy, do you have all your things for school?" Mom picked up her purse, and looked for her car keys. "Did you brush your teeth?" Tommy looked down and shook his head. "Thomas Nathaniel Rawson!" Mom frowned and shook her finger at Tommy. "You go brush your teeth right now, young man!"

As Tommy and Lisa snuggled next to Dad on the couch that night, he opened his Bible. "Before we read our story tonight, I want to show you something." Dad read Psalm 119:73. "'You made my body, Lord; now give me sense to heed Your laws.' What do you think that means, Lisa?"

"Well, God made us and we need to take care of our bodies," Lisa said.

"That's right, Lisa. The word 'heed' means to 'pay attention' to God's laws of health. Tommy, what would happen if you jumped off a cliff?" Dad turned to look at Tommy.

Tommy stood his hand up straight on Dad's shoulder, then made it dive off and crash against his other hand lying on the couch. "Sh-h-h-h-h-h-oom, BOOM!! I'd get smashed."

"That's true." Dad nodded. "God made certain physical laws that always work. Like the

283

Day 1

Lesson 22

one that says you'll fall if you jump off a cliff. There are also laws or rules about taking care of our bodies. We call these the laws of health. If we obey these laws then our bodies will be in better shape. We need to eat good food, get plenty of rest, drink lots of water, get exercise and fresh air, and keep our bodies clean. Can you think of ways that you do these things?" Dad challenged.

"We get plenty of sleep because we go to bed every night by eight o'clock." Lisa tucked her feet under her on the couch. "And we take baths every day to keep clean."

"We eat good food because Mom cooks good stuff, and she won't let us eat too much candy and things like that." Tommy flashed a smile at his mother.

"And we drink milk," Lisa added. "But Tommy always gets more on his face than inside of him," she teased. "We also get exercise and a lot of fresh air when we play outside — like last night when you guys played catch practically in the dark!" Lisa laughed and reached across Dad to poke Tommy.

Dad held up a hand when Tommy reached back to tickle Lisa, and both children settled down. "What about keeping the inside of our bodies clean?" Dad questioned.

"Well, we drink lots of water every day." Lisa wrinkled her forehead as she thought about that one.

"Good answer, Lisa. We also brush our teeth to keep them healthy and clean," Dad commented.

"Yeah," Tommy grumbled, "It seems like we're always brushing our teeth. Why do we have to brush them so often?"

"Well, Tommy," Dad said, "every time we eat a meal our teeth need to be cleaned. That way we won't get cavities or have problems with our gums or even lose our teeth. God designed you, and wants you to be your very best. It's your job to obey God's laws and take good care of your body," Dad tapped Tommy's chest, "And

your mind." Dad turned and patted Lisa's head.

"'You made my body, Lord; now give me sense to heed your laws.'" Dad read the Scripture again thoughtfully and then opened the story book.

The next morning Tommy stuck a finger in each side of his mouth and studied his teeth in the bathroom mirror. "I really like you guys," he said as he squeezed toothpaste onto his toothbrush. "And I want to keep you around for a long, long time!" And with that, he stuck his toothbrush in his mouth, and went to work.

2 Discussion Time

Check understanding of the story and development of personal values.

- What did Tommy not want to take time to do?
- Why is it important to brush your teeth?
- What are the "Laws of Health?"
- How did Tommy's family keep these laws?
- How do you keep these laws of health?
- Don't you think that since God made you, He knows the best way for you to take care of the incredible body He gave you?

284

A Preview

Write each word as your teacher says it.

Name _____

1. joy
2. come
3. love
4. boy
5. some
6. from
7. of

Challenge Words

☆ above
☆ enjoy
☆ none

Scripture
Psalm 119:73

205

Challenge

For better spellers, challenge words may be included in the weekly list. Challenge words are starred.

Correct Immediately!

Let's correct our preview. I will write each word on the board. Put a dot under each letter on your preview as I spell the word out loud. If you spelled a word wrong, rewrite it correctly.

Progress Chart

Students may record scores. (Reproducible master in Appendix B.)

Take a minute to memorize . . .

Read the memory verse twice. Have students practice it with you two more times.

---

3 Preview

Test for knowledge of the correct spellings of these words. (See the instructions at the top right for challenge words.)

 I will say each word once, use the word in a sentence, then say the word again. Write the word on the lines in the Worktext.

1.	joy	When we are kind to others it gives us **joy**.
2.	come	Will you **come** to my birthday party?
3.	love	We show our parents that we **love** them by obeying them.
4.	boy	The **boy** played catch with his dad.
5.	some	It is important to drink **some** water every day.
6.	from	Bodies grow stronger **from** eating healthy food.
7.	of	Let's all obey the laws **of** health.
☆	above	The plane flew **above** the clouds.
☆	enjoy	They will **enjoy** reading this story.
☆	none	We will have **none** left if we do not save some paint now.

4 Word Shapes

Help students form a correct image of whole words.

 Say Look at each word and think about its shape. Now, write the word in the correct word Shape Boxes. You may check off each word as you use it.

(In many words, the sound of **/oi/** is spelled with the diphthong **oy**. Some words have the sound of **/u/** spelled with **o** or **o-consonant-e**.)

 Say In the word shape boxes, color the letter or letters that spell the sound of **/oi/** or **/u/** in each word. Circle the words that end with **silent-e**.

 Challenge
Draw the correctly shaped box around each letter in these words.

 Say On a separate sheet of paper, write other words that contain the spelling patterns in the word list. See how many words you can write.

 Be Prepared For Fun
Check these supply lists for **Fun Ways to Spell** presented **Day 2**. Purchase and/or gather these items ahead of time!

Words with /oi/ or /u/

Lesson **22**

B Word Shapes

Name _____

Write each word in the correct word shape boxes. Next, in the word shape boxes, color the letter or letters that spell the sound of **/oi/** or **/u/** in each word. Circle the words that end with silent-**e**.

1. boy
2. joy
3. some
4. come
5. from
6. love
7. of

☆ **Challenge**
Draw the correct word shape boxes around each word.

enjoy   above   none

206

Answers may vary for duplicate word shapes.

General
- Strips of Paper 3 1/2 x 11 Inches (7 per child)
- Strips of Paper 3 1/2 x 11 Inches (3 more for challenge words)
- Crayons or Markers
- Tape
- Scissors
- Spelling List

Auditory
- Rhythm Instruments (two wooden spoons, two pan lids, maracas)
- Spelling List

Visual
- Clothespins (about 5 clothespins for each child at the clothesline)
- b, c, e, f, j, l, m, o, r, s, v and y (written on 3 x 5 card cut in half)
- a, b, n and n (added for challenge words)
- Clothesline (hung at student height)
- Spelling List

Tactile
- Shaving Cream
- Optional: Plastic Plates
- Optional: Wooden Craft Sticks
- Spelling List

286

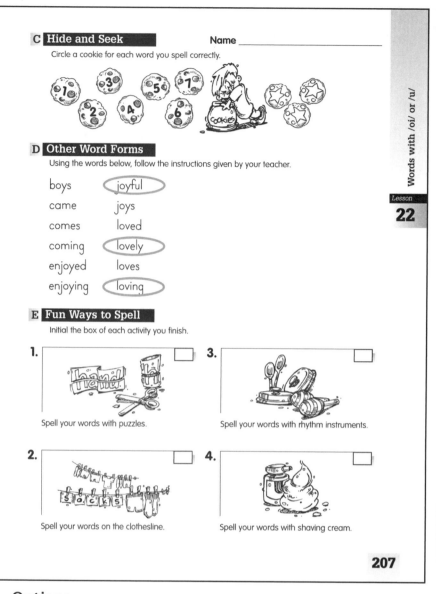

C Hide and Seek   Name _____

Circle a cookie for each word you spell correctly.

D Other Word Forms

Using the words below, follow the instructions given by your teacher.

boys   (joyful)

came   joys

comes   loved

coming   (lovely)

enjoyed   loves

enjoying   (loving)

E Fun Ways to Spell

Initial the box of each activity you finish.

1. ☐
Spell your words with puzzles.

3. ☐
Spell your words with rhythm instruments.

2. ☐
Spell your words on the clothesline.

4. ☐
Spell your words with shaving cream.

207

1 Hide and Seek

Reinforce spelling by using multiple styles of learning.

On a white board, Teacher writes each word — one at a time. **Have students:**

- **Look** at the word.
- **Say** the word out loud.
- **Spell** the word out loud.
- **Hide** (teacher erases word.)
- **Write** the word on their paper.
- **Seek** (teacher rewrites word.)
- **Check** spelling. If incorrect, repeat above steps.

2 Other Word Forms

This activity is optional. Have students find and circle the Other Word Forms that describe what something or someone is like.

3 Fun Ways to Spell

Four activities are provided. Use one, two, three, or all of the activities. Have students initial the box for each activity they complete.

Options:

- assign activities to students according to their learning styles
- set up the activities in learning centers for students to do throughout the day
- divide students into four groups and assign one activity per group
- do one activity per day

General

To Spell your words with puzzles…
- Write each word on a strip of paper in big, tall letters.
- Cut your word in half lengthwise.
- Tape the ends of each strip together to make circles.
- Mix the circles together.
- Match the circles again to make your spelling words.

Auditory

To spell your words with rhythm instruments…
- Look at a word on your spelling list.
- Close your eyes.
- Play your rhythm instruments softly while you whisper the spelling of the word.
- Open your eyes and check your spelling.

Visual

To spell your words on the clothesline…
- Choose the letter cards you need to spell a word on your list.
- Clothespin the cards to the clothesline in the right order to spell the word.
- Check your spelling.
- Remove the letter cards from the clothesline and spell the next word on your list.

Tactile

To spell your words with shaving cream…
- Spread a glob of shaving cream across your desk (or on a plastic plate).
- Use your finger (or a wooden craft stick) to write a spelling word in the shaving cream.
- Check your spelling.
- Smear the word out with your finger and write another word.

Word Maze

 Say

Familiarize students with word meaning and usage. The current spelling words are written on the tooth maze. Color all the spelling words, then trace the path through the maze by drawing a line connecting the words you colored. Note: The maze can be completed with or without using the challenge words.

☆ Challenge

Color all the spelling words, including the challenge words, then trace the path through the maze by drawing a line connecting the words you colored.

F **Word Maze**   Name _____

Color each spelling word. Trace the path from start to finish.

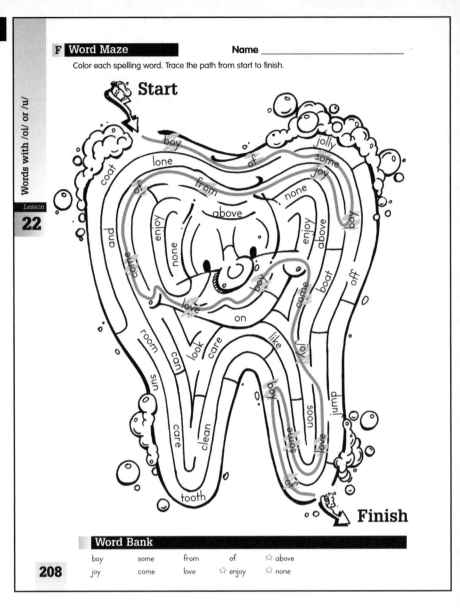

Start

Finish

Word Bank

boy	some	from	of	☆ above
joy	come	love	☆ enjoy	☆ none

208

 ## Take a minute to memorize...

Read the memory verse twice. Have students practice it with you two more times.

G Dictation

Listen and write the missing words.

Name _____

1. The boy had a box
of new toys.

2. Love and joy come
from God.

3. I had some raisins.

Words with /oi/ or /u/

Lesson **22**

H Proofreading

One word in each pair is misspelled. Fill in the oval by the misspelled word.

1. ○ boy ● jowe
2. ○ from ● som
3. ● lov ○ of
4. ● frum ○ come
5. ○ love ● ov
6. ○ some ● bowe

☆ ● abuv ○ round
☆ ○ books ● injoy
☆ ● nune ○ you

209

Familiarize students with standardized test format and reinforce recognizing misspelled words.

Say: Look at each set of words. One word in each set is misspelled. Fill in the oval by the misspelled word. (You may wish to pronounce each set of words to help students correctly identify them.)

1 Dictation

Reinforce correct spelling by using current and previous words in context.

Say: Listen as I read each sentence and then write it in your Worktext. (Slowly read each sentence twice. Sentences are found in the Student Worktext to the left.)

☆ Challenge

Write these incomplete sentences on the board.

__ __ __ __ __.
__ __ __ raise __ arms
__ __ head.
Daniel __ __ __ __ __
of __ __ ready.

Say: Listen as I read each sentence. Write the sentence on your paper. (Slowly read each sentence twice.)

You enjoy going to town.
The boy can raise his arms above his head.
Daniel will tell us if none of them are ready.

Day 4

Lesson **22**

Copyright ©2012 by The Concerned Group, Inc. All rights reserved.

289

3 Hide and Seek

Reinforce correct spelling of current spelling words. (A reproducible master is provided in Appendix A as shown on the inset page to the right.)

Write the words one at a time on a white board.

Have students:

- **Look** at the word.
- **Say** the word out loud.
- **Spell** the word out loud.
- **Hide** (teacher erases word.)
- **Write** the word on paper.
- **Seek** (teacher rewrites word.)
- **Check** spelling. If incorrect, rewrite word correctly.

4 Code

Have your students complete this activity to strengthen spelling ability and expand vocabulary.

1 Posttest

Test mastery of the spelling words. Challenge words are starred.

 Say

I will say the word once, use the word in a sentence, then say the word again. Write the word on your paper.

Appendix

Lesson **22**

Hide and Seek

Check a paper for each word you spell correctly.

Code

A picture code uses symbols to stand for letters. Use the picture code to write the missing letters. Read the other forms of your spelling words in the blanks.

e d f g i j l n o s u v y

1. e n j o y e d

2. e n j o y i n g

3. j o y s   4. j o y f u l

380

1. come	The bus will **come** in five minutes.
2. love	Tell your parents that you **love** them.
3. boy	The **boy** didn't like to brush his teeth.
4. some	There are **some** foods that are not good for our bodies.
5. of	Let's drink plenty **of** water.
6. joy	God gives us **joy** in our hearts when we are kind to others.
7. from	Muscles get stronger **from** exercise.
☆ none	There are **none** of the blue tooth brushes left.
☆ above	The flag waved **above** the school.
☆ enjoy	Do you **enjoy** stories about animals?

 Progress Chart

Students may record scores. (Reproducible master in Appendix B.)

 Personal Dictionary

Students may add any words they have misspelled to their personal dictionaries for reference when writing. (Cover in Appendix B.)

I **Game**

Name _____

Help Tommy take care of his teeth. Color in one blob of toothpaste on a toothbrush for each word you or your team spells correctly from this week's word list.

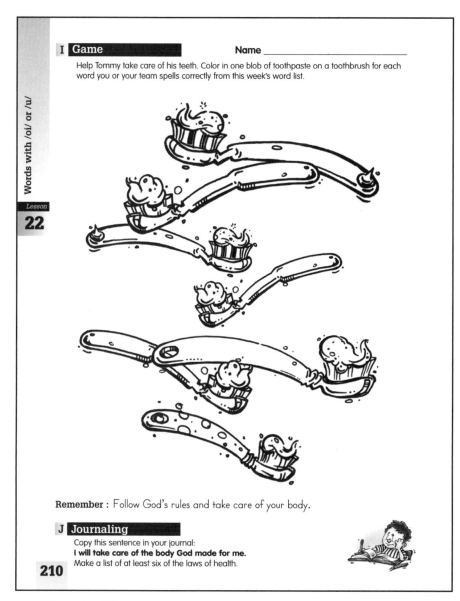

Remember : Follow God's rules and take care of your body.

J **Journaling**

Copy this sentence in your journal:
I will take care of the body God made for me.
Make a list of at least six of the laws of health.

210

2 **Game**

Reinforce spelling skills and provide motivation and interest.

Materials

- game page (from student text)
- crayons or colored pencils (1 per child)
- game word list

Game Word List

Use of challenge words is optional.

1. **boy**
2. **joy**
3. **some**
4. **come**
5. **from**
6. **love**
7. **of**
☆ **enjoy**
☆ **above**
☆ **none**

3 **Journaling**

Provide a meaningful reason for correct spelling through personal writing.

Review the story using discussion leads provided on the following page. Encourage students to apply the Scriptural value in their journaling.

Take a minute to memorize...

Have the class say the memory verses from lessons 21 and 22 with you.

How to Play:

- Divide the class into two teams, and decide which team will go first.
- Have a student from team A go to the board.
- Read the spelling word two times slowly and clearly. (You may also wish to use the word in a sentence. Ex.: "cat — The cat climbed a tree. — cat")
- Have the student write the word on the board.
- If the word is spelled correctly, instruct all the members of team A to color in one blob of toothpaste on a toothbrush. (Note: If the word is misspelled, correct the spelling immediately before continuing the game.)
- Alternate between teams A and B as you go down the word list.
- The team to have the most colored blobs of toothpaste on their toothbrushes when you have gone through the game word list twice is the winner.

Non-Competitive Option:

At the end of the game, say: "Class, I am proud of your efforts to spell the words correctly. If you had fun and tried your best, you are all winners!"

Journaling (continued)

 Say

- God made our bodies and knows exactly how they should be cared for to be the healthiest. God made certain rules that always work and some of these rules are about taking care of our bodies. What do we call the rules? (The Laws of Health)

- Tommy learned that it was important to brush his teeth so that they wouldn't get cavities or other serious problems. Can you name some of the other Laws of Health? (Sleep, fresh air, exercise, bathing/washing, healthy food, drinking water)

- What would happen if you never slept? (You'd get sick, very tired, etc.)

- What if you never took a bath? (Get sick, sores or problems with skin, etc.)

- List six laws of health in your journal.

 Quotables!

Children will write like the authors they read.

Putting God First

Rosa makes a new friend when she follows the good Samaritan's example.

Rosa put her elbow on the edge of the table and rested her chin in her hand as she waited for Maria to come to breakfast. "Dad, I really miss Grandma and Grandpa Anderson, don't you?" She gave a little sigh.

"Sure, I do, Rosita," Dad poured milk over her cereal. "It was really nice sharing our home with them for a while. But, you know, Rosa, I'm sure they're glad to be back in their own home now that the fire damage is all repaired. We can still visit them often." Dad turned to look at Rosa's brother. "Aren't you going over to help Grandpa Joe with something after school today, Carlos?"

"Yes, he asked me to help do some work in his greenhouse. We're going to get things ready for some special tomato plants he has ordered." The dark-eyed 11-year-old sat proud and straight in his chair. "Grandpa Joe says I'm a big help to him."

"May I go over after school, too, Dad?" Rosa begged. "Maybe Grandma Ruth needs me."

Dad smiled at his youngest daughter and winked. "She might have something that only my little Rosita can do. I'll call her this morning and we'll see."

"Aghhhhhh!" Mr. Vasquez jumped as Maria snuck up behind him and gave him a surprise hug. Everyone laughed as Dad tickled Maria before returning her hug. When they were all settled at the table, Dad picked up his Bible. "'In everything you do, put God first, and He will direct you,'" he read. "That advice was from Proverbs 3:6. Let's remember to put God first in our choices today." Dad prayed for each of his children by name. He asked God to watch over them that day, and to help

them make wise decisions. He also thanked God for their home, good health, fine friends, and the food they were about to eat.

Later that morning, Rosa sat at a table in the classroom with Sarah and Beth. The girls each wore headphones as they listened to a Scripture story, and turned the pages of a picture book that went with the tape.

The story was about a man who was traveling alone to Jericho. As he walked along, a band of robbers attacked him and took everything that he had. The robbers hurt the man, then left him beside the road. A traveler from his same country came along and saw him lying there, but did nothing to help. A second traveler passed by and also ignored the hurt man. Finally, a man from a different country came by. The man from the different country stopped and helped the man right there by the road. He put the man on his own donkey, took him to a safe place, and even paid for the hurt man to be cared for.

While the three girls listened to the Scripture story, the other children were busy working on different activities around the room. Suddenly the classroom door opened. The school secretary, Mrs. Bentley, entered the room followed by a little girl who looked very scared. Mrs. Bentley talked to Miss Grant for several minutes while all the children stared at the new girl. She had dark black hair like Rosa's, but her face looked a lot more like Katelynn's. She wore a dress that was made of pink checked material with a blue sweater and red socks. Rosa heard Daniel snicker and whisper something

to Tommy.

As Mrs. Bentley turned to leave, Miss Grant placed her arm around the little girl's shoulders and spoke quietly with her for a moment. Then she led her to a chair at the table where Rosa and the other girls sat.

Facing the class Miss Grant said, "I'm sure you're all wondering about our newest student. Her name is Setsuko [pronounced set-soo¹-koh] Noma." She turned to the table where the little girl now sat. "Setsuko, we're really glad to have you in our class."

"Now, everyone, please get out your spelling books." The classroom was noisy for a few moments as the children that were scattered around the room returned to their desks and pulled out their spelling books. Two eighth-grade boys came in carrying another desk. Miss Grant showed them where to place it, and helped Setsuko get settled. A few minutes later, the classroom had calmed back into its normal routine.

At recess time, some children played on the swings while others kicked a soccer ball around. Daniel, James, Rosa, and Kristin tried to catch the balls Tommy batted to them. Rosa glanced up and noticed Setsuko standing by the slide all alone.

"I've caught more balls than you have!" Daniel bragged.

"You've caught three and Rosa's caught three," James objected. "And I've caught two, so you're not that far ahead."

"You'll see," Daniel pounded his fist into his baseball glove. "I'll catch more than Rosa. I can catch more than a girl any day!"

"O-o-o-o-o, I want to show that Daniel I can catch as well as he can — maybe even better. Playing with Carlos has helped me learn to catch pretty well." The thoughts chased each other around in Rosa's head. *"But Setsuko is over there all by herself. I really ought to go and play with her. She's probably feeling left out and lonely."*

"Hey, Rosa! Where you going?" Daniel shouted as

she walked away. As Rosa neared the slide, she heard Daniel laugh. "She knows there's no way she can beat me, so she's just giving up." Rosa ignored him and smiled at Setsuko.

After school was out for the day, Rosa ran eagerly up the hill to the Anderson's house. Early spring flowers were already in bloom. As the afternoon shadows lengthened into evening, Rosa threw another clump of weeds into the red wheelbarrow sitting by Grandma Ruth's flower bed. "It's takes lots of work to get the ground ready for flowers, doesn't it?" Rosa brushed the hair out of her face leaving a smudge of brown dirt across her forehead.

"Yes, Rosa." Grandma Ruth stood and stretched with her hands on her back. "But, then, anything that is worth doing takes work. How was school today?"

"We have a new girl in our class," Rosa bubbled. "She's really nice. She was born in America, but her mom and dad came here from Japan not long before that. She calls her mom, 'Okasan' [pronounced oh-kaaᴵ-sahn], instead of Mom, and her dad, 'Otosan' [oh-toeᴵ-sahn]. I talked to her at recess."

"She sounds like an interesting friend to have." Grandma Ruth smiled as she moved the wheelbarrow a little farther down the bed.

The two worked in silence for a while, then Rosa added in a small voice, "I almost didn't go over and talk to her, Grandma Ruth." She explained how Setsuko was standing all alone. She told about the game of catch and about Daniel. "Then I remembered the story we listened to on the tape today about the traveler who stopped and helped the man who was hurt. And I remembered the Scripture Dad read at breakfast this morning. So I decided to put God first — and then I knew what to do!"

Grandma Ruth slipped off her gardening gloves and gave Rosa a tight hug. "I'm very proud of you, Rosa," she said. "We all

need to remember to put God first every day!"

Check understanding of the story and development of personal values.

- What story from the Scriptures did Rosa, Sarah, and Beth listen to at school?
- Who came into the first grade room that morning?
- Do you think it was easy for Setsuko to go to this new school? Why or why not?
- What did Rosa do when she saw Setsuko standing by the slide all alone at recess?
- Was it easy for Rosa to do this? Why or why not?
- What made Rosa decide to go over to Setsuko?
- How was Rosa like the good Samaritan in the Scriptures?

294

A Preview

Write each word as your teacher says it.

Name _____

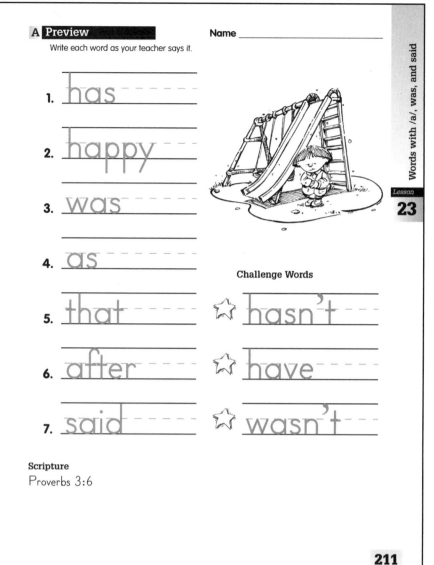

1. has
2. happy
3. was
4. as
5. that
6. after
7. said

Challenge Words

☆ hasn't
☆ have
☆ wasn't

Scripture
Proverbs 3:6

211

Challenge

For better spellers, challenge words may be included in the weekly list. Challenge words are starred.

Correct Immediately!

 Say

Let's correct our preview. I will write each word on the board. Put a dot under each letter on your preview as I spell the word out loud. If you spelled a word wrong, rewrite it correctly.

Progress Chart

Students may record scores. (Reproducible master in Appendix B.)

Take a minute to memorize . . .

Read the memory verse twice. Have students practice it with you two more times.

3 Preview

Test for knowledge of the correct spellings of these words. (See the instructions at the top right for challenge words.)

 Say

I will say each word once, use the word in a sentence, then say the word again. Write the word on the lines in the Worktext.

1.	has	This garden **has** a lot of weeds in it.
2.	happy	Rosa was **happy** to make a new friend.
3.	was	It **was** hard for Rosa to leave the game and go talk to Setsuko.
4.	as	Rosa talked to Grandma Ruth **as** they worked.
5.	that	Put the weeds in **that** wheelbarrow.
6.	after	Carlos will help Grandpa Joe **after** school.
7.	said	Grandma Ruth **said**, "We need to put God first every day."
☆	hasn't	She **hasn't** been skiing before.
☆	have	We **have** a new girl at school.
☆	wasn't	There **wasn't** a desk for Setsuko, so the older boys brought one in.

295

4 Word Shapes

Help students form a correct image of whole words.

(Say) Look at each word and think about its shape. Now, write the word in the correct word Shape Boxes. You may check off each word as you use it.

(In many words /a/ is spelled with **a**, and it is often spelled this way when it is at the beginning or in the middle of a word.)

(Say) In the word shape boxes, color the letter that spells the sound of /a/ in each word, except **was** and **said**. Circle the words in which the letter **a** has the sound of /u/ or /e/.

⭐ Challenge

Draw the correctly shaped box around each letter in these words.

(Say) On a separate sheet of paper, write other words that contain the spelling patterns in the word list. See how many words you can write.

📝 Be Prepared For Fun

Check these supply lists for **Fun Ways to Spell** presented **Day 2**. Purchase and/or gather these items ahead of time!

B Word Shapes   Name _____

Write each word in the correct word shape boxes. Next, in the word shape boxes, color the letter that spells the sound of /a/ in each word, except was and said. Circle the words in which the letter **a** has the sound of /u/ or /e/.

1. as
2. has
3. that
4. happy
5. after
6. was
7. said

was

said

after

that

as

happy

has

☆ Challenge

Draw the correct word shape boxes around each word.

have   hasn't   wasn't

212

Answers may vary for duplicate word shapes.

General	**Auditory**
• Crayons • Piece of Paper • Spelling List	• Box to Store Letters • a, d, e, f, h, i, p, p, r, s, t, t, w and y (written on seasonal shapes like kites, sheep or shamrocks) • v and n (added for challenge words) • Spelling List
Visual	**Tactile**
• Eraser • Dark Construction Paper • Spelling List	• Finger Paint • Plastic Plate or Glossy Paper • Spelling List

C Hide and Seek

Name _____

Circle a cookie for each word you spell correctly.

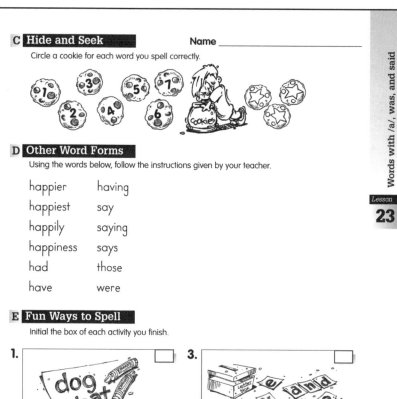

D Other Word Forms

Using the words below, follow the instructions given by your teacher.

happier	having
happiest	say
happily	saying
happiness	says
had	those
have	were

E Fun Ways to Spell

Initial the box of each activity you finish.

1.

Spell your words with crayons.

3.

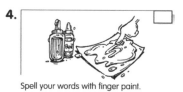

Spell your words from the letter box.

2.

Spell your words with an eraser.

4.

Spell your words with finger paint.

213

Day 2

Lesson 23

1 Hide and Seek

Reinforce spelling by using multiple styles of learning.

On a white board, Teacher writes each word — one at a time. **Have students:**

- **Look** at the word.
- **Say** the word out loud.
- **Spell** the word out loud.
- **Hide** (teacher erases word.)
- **Write** the word on their paper.
- **Seek** (teacher rewrites word.)
- **Check** spelling. If incorrect, repeat above steps.

2 Other Word Forms

This activity is optional. Have students dictate original sentences to you using these Other Word Forms. Write them on the board.

happiness   saying those

3 Fun Ways to Spell

Four activities are provided. Use one, two, three, or all of the activities. Have students initial the box for each activity they complete.

Options:

- assign activities to students according to their learning styles
- set up the activities in learning centers for students to do throughout the day
- divide students into four groups and assign one activity per group
- do one activity per day

General

To spell your words with crayons…
- Write each letter of your spelling word in fat, thick letters.
- Check your spelling.

Auditory

To spell your words from the letter box…
- Spell a word from your list by putting the letters in the right order.
- Check your spelling.
- Spell your word out loud.

Visual

To spell your words with an eraser…
- Turn your pencil upside down.
- Use the eraser to write your words on a sheet of dark construction paper.
- Check your spelling.

Tactile

To spell your words with finger paint…
- Smear paint across your plate.
- Use a finger to write a spelling word in paint.
- Check your spelling.
- Smear the word out with your finger and write another word.

1 Word Scramble

Familiarize students with word meaning and usage. Write the letters **efet** on the board. Help the students understand that the scrambled letters **efet** spell the word **feet** when they are arranged correctly. Guide the students in ordering the letters to spell **feet**.

 Say

Unscramble the letters to make a spelling word. Write the word on the line.

Words with /a/, was, and said

Lesson
23

F Word Scramble   Name _____

Unscramble the letters to make a spelling word. Write the word on the line.

2. dsia
1. sa
4. refat
5. tath
3. sha
7. phapy
6. saw
☆ n'atsw
☆ htnsa'
☆ veha

1. as
2. said
3. has
4. after
5. that

6. was
7. happy
☆ hasn't
☆ wasn't
☆ have

Word Bank

as	that	after	said	☆ hasn't
has	happy	was	☆ have	☆ wasn't

214

 Take a minute to memorize...

Read the memory verse twice. Have students practice it with you two more times.

G Dictation
Listen and write the missing words.

Name _____

1. Are you as happy as I am?

2. He said he was going after lunch.

3. He has a red dog.

H Proofreading
One word in each pair is misspelled. Fill in the oval by the misspelled word.

1. ● hapy
   ○ said

2. ○ has
   ● aftr

3. ○ as
   ● wuz

4. ● sed
   ○ that

5. ● haz
   ○ happy

6. ○ after
   ● thet

☆ ● wuzn't
   ○ vowel

☆ ○ above
   ● hazn't

☆ ○ soon
   ● hav

215

---

2 Proofreading
Familiarize students with standardized test format and reinforce recognizing misspelled words.

Say

Look at each set of words. One word in each set is misspelled. Fill in the oval by the misspelled word. (You may wish to pronounce each set of words to help students correctly identify them.)

---

1 Dictation
Reinforce correct spelling by using current and previous words in context.

Say

Listen as I read each sentence and then write it in your Worktext. (Slowly read each sentence twice. Sentences are found in the Student Worktext to the left.)

☆ Challenge
Write these incomplete sentences on the board.

__ __ __ __ __ heart.

Rosa __ __ __ __
  house yet.

__ __ __ very soft.

Lesson 23 | Day 4

Say

Listen as I read each sentence. Write the sentence on your paper. (Slowly read each sentence twice.)

I have joy in my heart.

Rosa hasn't come to our
  house yet.

His bed wasn't very soft.

---

3 Hide and Seek

Reinforce correct spelling of current spelling words. (A reproducible master is provided in Appendix A as shown on the inset page to the right.)

Write the words one at a time on a white board.

Have students:

- **Look** at the word.
- **Say** the word out loud.
- **Spell** the word out loud.
- **Hide** (teacher erases word.)
- **Write** the word on paper.
- **Seek** (teacher rewrites word.)
- **Check** spelling. If incorrect, rewrite word correctly.

4 Word Find

Have your students complete this activity to strengthen spelling ability and expand vocabulary.

1 Posttest

Test mastery of the spelling words. Challenge words are starred.

Say I will say the word once, use the word in a sentence, then say the word again. Write the word on your paper.

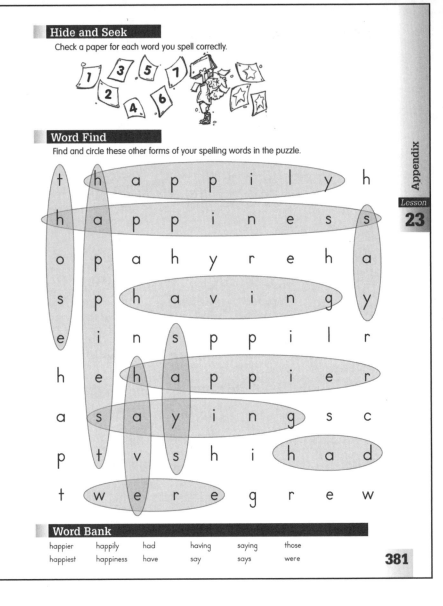

Hide and Seek
Check a paper for each word you spell correctly.

Word Find
Find and circle these other forms of your spelling words in the puzzle.

t	h	a	p	p	i	l	y	h
h	a	p	p	i	n	e	s	s
o	p	a	h	y	r	e	h	a
s	p	h	a	v	i	n	g	y
e	i	n	s	p	p	i	l	r
h	e	h	a	p	p	i	e	r
a	s	a	y	i	n	g	s	c
p	t	v	s	h	i	h	a	d
t	w	e	r	e	g	r	e	w

Word Bank

| happier | happily | had | having | saying | those |
| happiest | happiness | have | say | says | were |

381

1.	happy	Carlos is **happy** to help Grandpa Joe in his greenhouse.
2.	was	There **was** a lot of work to do in the flower bed.
3.	as	It was noisy **as** the children returned to their desks.
4.	that	Can you hear **that** train whistle?
5.	said	Rosa **said**, "I asked God to help me put Him first!"
6.	has	Rosa **has** a brother named Carlos.
7.	after	Spring comes **after** winter.
☆	wasn't	That **wasn't** the fire alarm, was it?
☆	hasn't	This dog **hasn't** had a bath in a long time.
☆	have	They **have** a tree house in their back yard.

 Progress Chart
Students may record scores. (Reproducible master in Appendix B.)

 Personal Dictionary
Students may add any words they have misspelled to their personal dictionaries for reference when writing. (Cover in Appendix B.)

300

I Game

Name _____

Cross out each **c**, **k**, and **o** with a big **X** to find the hidden spelling words. Using one crayon, softly color the boxes you did not mark so you can see your spelling words better.

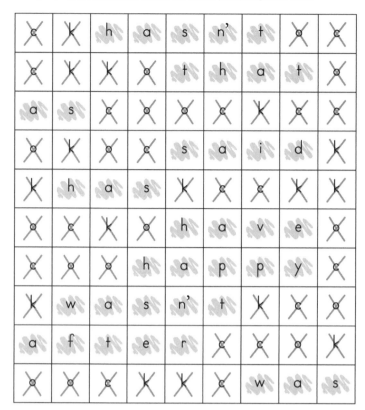

c	k	h	a	s	n'	t	o	c
X	X	X	X	t	h	a	t	o
a	s	c	X	o	X	X	c	c
X	X	o	c	s	a	i	d	k
k	h	a	s	X	X	c	X	k
o	c	X	o	h	a	v	e	X
c	o	X	h	a	p	p	y	c
k	w	a	s	n'	t	X	X	c
a	f	t	e	r	X	c	o	k
o	o	c	X	X	X	w	a	s

Remember : Always put God first in everything you do!

J Journaling

In your journal, write as many ways as you can think of to put others first. (Remember the good Samaritan in the Bible story.)

216

Reinforce spelling skills and provide motivation and interest.

Materials

• game page (from student text)
• pencils (1 per child)
• crayons or colored pencils (1 per child)

Journaling

3

Provide a meaningful reason for correct spelling through personal writing.

Review the story using discussion leads provided on the following page. Encourage students to apply the Scriptural value in their journaling.

 Take a minute to memorize...

Have the class say the memory verses from lessons 21, 22, and 23 with you.

How to Play:

• Have each student mark through each letter **c** found on the grid with a big **X**.
• Have each student mark through each letter **k** found on the grid with a big **X**.
• Have each student mark through each letter **o** found on the grid with a big **X**.
• Tell the students that the boxes without **X**'s contain their spelling words.
• Have the students color softly over the boxes without **X**'s so they can see their spelling words more clearly.
• Have the students follow along as you read and spell each word as it appears on the grid.

(Say)

- Rosa found that it's not always easy to do the right thing. She saw Setsuko, the new girl in class, standing all alone. Rosa didn't really want to leave the game she was playing to go and talk to Setsuko. What helped Rosa make up her mind to do it anyway? (She remembered what her dad had read from the Bible that morning. It said to always put God first, in everything you do.)

- How did the Good Samaritan, told about in the Bible, put God first? (He stopped and helped the injured man beside the road.)

- How can you, like the Good Samaritan and Rosa, put God first in everything you do? Write your ideas down in your journal.

"Anytime a child pays close attention to what's written, spelling awareness increases."*

*Scott, Jill E. 1994. Spelling for Readers and Writers. The Reading Teacher, Vol. 48, No. 2, October: 188-190.

"I Led the Pigeons"

Christopher is surprised to find out what the pledge of allegiance really says.

"*I* pledge allegiance to the flag…" Miss Grant's class at Knowlton Elementary School faced the front of their classroom as they repeated the pledge of allegiance. Early morning sunshine slanted through the windows, highlighting the flag's brilliant red, white, and blue. "…with liberty and justice for all," they concluded.

"Miss Grant," asked James as the children sat down at their desks, "Why do we put our hands on our chests when we say that every morning?"

"That's a good question, James." Miss Grant leaned against the edge of her desk. "Does anyone have an idea?"

Instead of an answer, Christopher had another question. "Who's Richard Stands?"

Miss Grant looked puzzled. "Richard Stands? Why do you ask that, Christopher?"

"Well," Christopher shrugged. "We always say 'I led the pigeons to the flag of the United States of America and to the republic for Richard Stands, one nation under God, invisible, with liberty and justice for all.' I just wondered who this Richard Stands was."

Miss Grant chuckled. "Maybe we should start from the beginning. First of all, we say 'I pledge allegiance to the flag of the United States of America.' Allegiance is a really big word. Can anyone tell me what it means to pledge allegiance? Sarah?"

"It means that we'll be loyal to our own country, doesn't it?" Sarah asked timidly.

"That's right, Sarah." Miss Grant nodded.

"You mean there aren't any pigeons?" Christopher interrupted.

"No, no pigeons," Miss Grant smiled. "How can we be loyal to our country, Beth?"

"Well, we can obey our country's rules," Beth answered.

"Very good answer, Beth. We show allegiance to our country by obeying the rules, or laws. Rosa, what is one way that children can do that?"

"We can buckle our seat belts!"

"That's a very important law to obey." Miss Grant nodded approvingly. "Now the next thing we say is 'and to the republic for which it stands.'" She said the last few words very slowly and clearly. "It does sound a lot like 'Richard Stands,' but it really means that this flag…" Miss Grant pointed to the flag at the front of the room, "…stands for, or represents, our country. So, when we stand and say the pledge to the flag, it shows that we honor our country, the United States of America."

"I know what the next part is," Daniel said smugly. "It's 'one nation under God, indivisible.' It's not 'invisible,' Christopher." Daniel put his fingers around his eyes like glasses and peered around the room. "Can't you see anything?"

Miss Grant shook her head slightly as many of the children started to laugh. "And what does 'indivisible' mean, Daniel?" she asked.

"Uh, well, it means…" Daniel drifted to an embarrassed stop and slid lower in his chair.

Miss Grant walked to the shelves at the side of the room and picked up a puzzle that fit inside a cardboard frame. "We are all different like the pieces of this puzzle are different. Our country is made of many states, or parts, that are different from each other, too. But together we make a nation, or country, that is strong. 'Indivisible' means that all the states will stay together to make our country, like these pieces all together make a picture."

"The last part, 'with liberty and justice for all,' means that everyone in our country is free to make their own choices if he or she doesn't hurt others," Miss Grant finished. "Now, the Scripture that you will practice for handwriting today fits right in with what we've been talking about." Miss Grant turned and wrote Proverbs 29:18 on the board. "It says, 'What a wonderful thing it is for a nation to know and keep God's laws!' God expects us to honor our country by keeping its laws."

At home that evening, Christopher found his dad working on the computer. "Well, hello, young man." Dad moved away from the desk a little bit and lifted Christopher up on his knee. "Did you learn anything new in school today?"

"There aren't any pigeons in the pledge to our flag!" Christopher paused at the look on Dad's face and thought, *"Dad sure looks surprised, so he must not have known that."* "Miss Grant told us all about it," Christopher began to share all the things he'd learned about the pledge that day.

"That last part, 'with liberty and justice for all,' is one of the best parts," Dad commented when Christopher finished. "Let me show you something." Dad reached into one of the desk drawers and pulled out some coins. "The man on this coin was the very first leader, or president, of our country. His name was George Washington." Dad handed a quarter to Christopher.

"He sure had funny looking hair," Christopher giggled.

Dad pointed to some tiny little words on the quarter. "These words say 'In God We Trust'. George Washington and the other men who started our country believed in God. They made sure each of us would be free to worship and serve God in the way we feel is right. That's a

303

Lesson 24 | Day 1

liberty, or freedom, that's very important."

"Hey!" Christopher was examining a penny, a nickel, and a shiny, new dime. "Those words are on these other coins, too!"

"Sharp eyes, Son!" Dad grinned and suddenly swooped Christopher right up into the air over his head. Christopher was almost touching the ceiling when Kristin stuck her head around the door.

"It's time to eat," she announced. Then seeing her brother high in the air, she begged, "Hold me up, too, Daddy. Please?" Dad laughed as he picked her up and headed for the kitchen with a twin tucked under each arm.

On the way to school the next day Christopher asked, "Are you driving the speed limit, Mom?"

"Yes," Mom glanced at the gauges in front of her. "Why do you ask?"

"I want to make sure that we honor our country by keeping its laws," Christopher explained. "We have a great country! I'm so glad we live in America!"

2 Discussion Time

Check understanding of the story and development of personal values.

- Why do you think that Christopher didn't understand all the words to the pledge to the flag correctly?
- What does "I pledge allegiance" to the flag mean?
- Why do we put our hand over our heart when we say the pledge?
- What does "indivisible" mean?
- What does "with liberty and justice for all" mean?
- What did Christopher find written on the penny, nickel, dime, and quarter?
- Why are those words important?
- Does God want us to obey the laws of our country?

A Preview

Write each word as your teacher says it.

Name _____

1. her
2. your
3. for
4. mother
5. girl
6. or
7. are

Challenge Words

☆ first

☆ Lord

☆ circle

Scripture
Proverbs 29:18

217

 Challenge

For better spellers, challenge words may be included in the weekly list. Challenge words are starred.

 Correct Immediately!

Say — Let's correct our preview. I will write each word on the board. Put a dot under each letter on your preview as I spell the word out loud. If you spelled a word wrong, rewrite it correctly.

Progress Chart

Students may record scores. (Reproducible master in Appendix B.)

 **Take a minute to memorize . . .**

Read the memory verse twice. Have students practice it with you two more times.

3 Preview

Test for knowledge of the correct spellings of these words. (See the instructions at the top right for challenge words.)

 Say — I will say each word once, use the word in a sentence, then say the word again. Write the word on the lines in the Worktext.

1.	her	The girl took **her** dog for a walk.
2.	your	Hang **your** coat up in the closet.
3.	for	Let's thank God **for** our country.
4.	mother	My **mother** made spaghetti for supper.
5.	girl	The **girl** said the pledge to the flag.
6.	or	You may have milk **or** orange juice to drink.
7.	are	We **are** learning more about our country.
☆	first	The **first** graders said the pledge to the flag.
☆	Lord	We sometimes say "**Lord**" when we talk to, or about, God.
☆	circle	I can draw a large **circle** on this paper.

305

4 Word Shapes

Help students form a correct image of whole words.

 Say Look at each word and think about its shape. Now, write the word in the correct word Shape Boxes. You may check off each word as you use it.

(In many words a vowel or vowels are followed by the letter **r**, producing an **r**-controlled vowel sound.)

Say In the word shape boxes, color the letter **r** and the vowel or vowels that come before **r** to give the **r**-controlled vowel sound. Circle the word that contains the sound /**th**/.

 Challenge
Draw the correctly shaped box around each letter in these words.

 Say On a separate sheet of paper, write other words that contain the spelling patterns in the word list. See how many words you can write.

B Word Shapes   Name _____

Write each word in the correct word shape boxes. Next, in the word shape boxes, color the letter **r** and the vowel or vowels that come before **r** to give the r-controlled vowel sound. Circle the word that contains a digraph.

1. mother

2. her

3. girl

4. your

5. or

6. for

7. are

☆ **Challenge**
Draw the correct word shape boxes around each word.

218

Answers may vary for duplicate word shapes.

 Be Prepared For Fun

Check these supply lists for **Fun Ways to Spell** presented **Day 2**. Purchase and/or gather these items ahead of time!

General
- 3 x 5 Cards (7 per child)
- 3 x 5 Cards (3 more for challenge words)
- Scissors
- Spelling List

Auditory
- Spelling List

Visual
- Dry Bar of Soap (sample size works well)
- Hand Mirror
- Strong Paper Towel or Washcloth (dry)
- Spelling List

Tactile
- Play Dough
- Spelling List

306

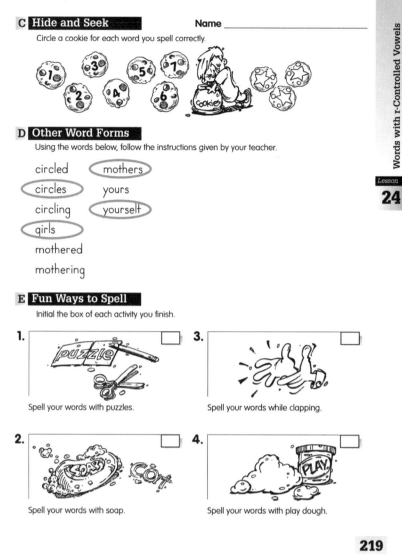

C Hide and Seek

Name _____

Circle a cookie for each word you spell correctly.

D Other Word Forms

Using the words below, follow the instructions given by your teacher.

circled   (mothers)

(circles)   yours

circling   (yourself)

(girls)

mothered

mothering

E Fun Ways to Spell

Initial the box of each activity you finish.

1.

Spell your words with puzzles.

3.

Spell your words while clapping.

2.

Spell your words with soap.

4.

Spell your words with play dough.

219

1 Hide and Seek

Reinforce spelling by using multiple styles of learning.

On a white board, Teacher writes each word — one at a time. **Have students:**

- **Look** at the word.
- **Say** the word out loud.
- **Spell** the word out loud.
- **Hide** (teacher erases word.)
- **Write** the word on their paper.
- **Seek** (teacher rewrites word.)
- **Check** spelling. If incorrect, repeat above steps.

2 Other Word Forms

This activity is optional. Have students find and circle the Other Word Forms that name a person, place, or thing.

3 Fun Ways to Spell

Four activities are provided. Use one, two, three, or all of the activities. Have students initial the box for each activity they complete.

Options:

- assign activities to students according to their learning styles
- set up the activities in learning centers for students to do throughout the day
- divide students into four groups and assign one activity per group
- do one activity per day

General

To spell your words with puzzles…
- Write each word on a card.
- Cut each card squiggly, diagonal, or zigzag to make a puzzle.
- Mix your puzzle pieces.
- Put the puzzles together.
- Check your spelling.

Auditory

To spell your words while clapping…
- Look at a word on your spelling list.
- Close your eyes.
- Clap your hands softly while you whisper the spelling of the word.
- Open your eyes and check your spelling.

Visual

To spell your words with soap…
- Write a word on a hand mirror with a dry bar of soap.
- Check your spelling.
- Wipe the word off the mirror with a dry towel or washcloth.
- Write another word.

Tactile

To spell your words with play dough…
- Roll pieces of play dough into ropes.
- Use the ropes to make the letters of each word.
- Put them in the right order to spell each word.
- Check your spelling.

307

Word Maze

Familiarize students with word meaning and usage.

The current spelling words are written on the star maze. Color each spelling word, then trace the path through the maze by drawing a line to connect the words you colored. Note: The maze can be completed with or without using the challenge words.

Challenge

Color all the spelling words, including the challenge words, then trace the path through the maze by drawing a line connecting the words you colored.

Lesson 24 | Day 3

Words with r-Controlled Vowels

Lesson 24

F Word Maze

Name _____

Color each spelling word. Trace the path from start to finish.

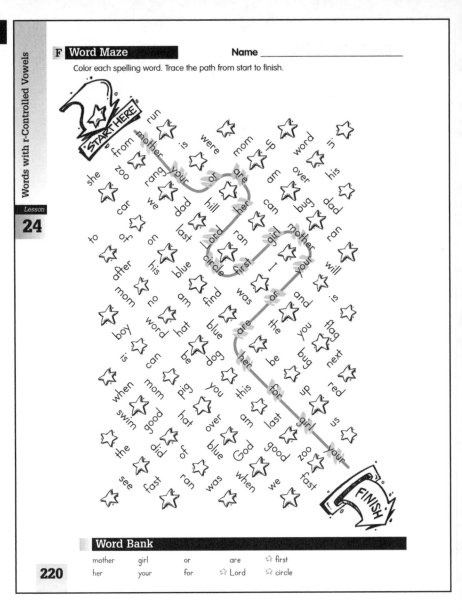

Word Bank

mother	girl	or	are	☆ first	
her	your	for	☆ Lord	☆ circle	

220

Take a minute to memorize...

Read the memory verse twice. Have students practice it with you two more times.

G Dictation

Listen and write the missing words.

1. The girl looks like her mother.

2. Is this for you or me?

3. They are with you.

H Proofreading

One word in each pair is misspelled. Fill in the oval by the misspelled word.

1. ● arr
   ○ her

2. ○ girl
   ● farr

3. ○ your
   ● hur

4. ● muthr
   ○ are

5. ● yur
   ○ for

6. ○ are
   ● orr

☆ ● ferst
   ○ hasn't

☆ ○ Lord
   ● surkl

☆ ○ tooth
   ● lored

221

Dictation

1

Reinforce correct spelling by using current and previous words in context.

 Say

Listen as I read each sentence and then write it in your Worktext. (Slowly read each sentence twice. Sentences are found in the Student Worktext to the left.)

Challenge

Write these incomplete sentences on the board.

__ __ __ __.

T ony __ __ __.

__ __ __ __ __ __ __

__ __.

 Say

Listen as I read each sentence. Write the sentence on your paper. (Slowly read each sentence twice.)

The Lord is God.

Tony will hide first.

I can draw a circle in the sand.

Proofreading

2

Familiarize students with standardized test format and reinforce recognizing misspelled words.

 Say

Look at each set of words. One word in each set is misspelled. Fill in the oval by the misspelled word. (You may wish to pronounce each set of words to help students correctly identify them.)

3 Hide and Seek

Reinforce correct spelling of current spelling words. (A reproducible master is provided in Appendix A as shown on the inset page to the right.)

Write the words one at a time on a white board.

Have students:

- **Look** at the word.
- **Say** the word out loud.
- **Spell** the word out loud.
- **Hide** (teacher erases word.)
- **Write** the word on paper.
- **Seek** (teacher rewrites word.)
- **Check** spelling. If incorrect, rewrite word correctly.

4 Scrambled Words

Have your students complete this activity to strengthen spelling ability and expand vocabulary.

1 Posttest

Test mastery of the spelling words. Challenge words are starred.

Say I will say the word once, use the word in a sentence, then say the word again. Write the word on your paper.

1.	your	Please write **your** words neatly.
2.	for	It is time **for** supper.
3.	mother	Christopher's **mother** is not home from the store yet.
4.	girl	The **girl** drew a picture of the flag.
5.	are	There **are** lots of things to learn.
6.	her	She cleaned up **her** room.
7.	or	Do you want toast **or** cereal?
☆	circle	The campfire burned inside a **circle** of stones.
☆	first	We learn to spell new words in **first** grade.
☆	Lord	The word **Lord** is another name for God.

Progress Chart

Students may record scores. (Reproducible master in Appendix B.)

Personal Dictionary

Students may add any words they have misspelled to their personal dictionaries for reference when writing. (Cover in Appendix B.)

Appendix | **Lesson 24**

Hide and Seek

Check a paper for each word you spell correctly.

Scrambled Words

Unscramble the letters to make a word. Write the word on the lines.

1. lirgs — g i r l s
2. soyur — y o u r s
3. slirecc — c i r c l e s
4. ricclde — c i r c l e d
5. rsothem — m o t h e r s
6. foyrelsu — y o u r s e l f

Word Bank

circled	girls	yours
circles	mothers	yourself

382

310

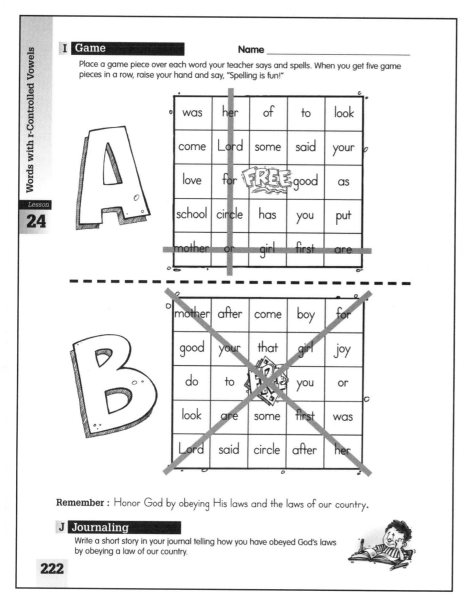

Words with r-Controlled Vowels

Lesson 24

I   Game

Name _____

Place a game piece over each word your teacher says and spells. When you get five game pieces in a row, raise your hand and say, "Spelling is fun!"

Card A

was	her	of	to	look
come	Lord	some	said	your
love	for	FREE	good	as
school	circle	has	you	put
mother	or	girl	first	are

Card B

mother	after	come	boy	for
good	your	that	girl	joy
do	to	FREE	you	or
look	are	some	first	was
Lord	said	circle	after	her

Remember : Honor God by obeying His laws and the laws of our country.

J   Journaling

Write a short story in your journal telling how you have obeyed God's laws by obeying a law of our country.

222

---

2 Game

Reinforce spelling skills and provide motivation and interest.

Materials

- game page (from student text)
- flat buttons, dry beans, pennies, or game discs (10 per child)
- game word list
- word cards (each word from the game word list written on a card)

Game Word List

This list contains regular and challenge words.

1. **mother**
2. **Lord**
3. **her**
4. **first**
5. **girl**
6. **circle**
7. **your**
☆ **or**
☆ **for**
☆ **are**

Day 5

Lesson 24

3 Journaling

Provide a meaningful reason for correct spelling through personal writing.

Review the story using discussion leads provided on the following page. Encourage students to apply the Scriptural value in their journaling.

Take a minute to memorize...

Have the class say the memory verses from lessons 21, 22, 23, and 24 with you.

How to Play:

- Fold the word cards (see **Materials**) in half, and place them in a container.
- Ask your students to fold the game page in half along the dotted line.
- Have half the class use game card A, and the other half card B.
- Instructions for the students: "Cover the word **FREE** in the center of your card. (pause) I will draw a word from the container, read it aloud, then I will spell it. When you find that word on your card, put a game piece over it. When you have five game pieces in a row (up and down, across or diagonally), raise your hand and say 'Spelling is FUN!'"
- Play as many times as you like. (As you return the word cards to the container and mix them up, remind the students to clear their game cards.)
- For variety, after playing several games, have the students turn their papers over and use the other game card.

311

Journaling (continued)

 Say

- In the story this week Christopher learned what the pledge to the flag really says and what the words mean. Why is it important to obey the laws of our country?

- Why is it important to obey God's laws?

- What are some of the laws of our country that you keep? (Not stealing, buckling seat belt, using crosswalks correctly, reminding the driver to go the speed limit, etc.)

- Write a story in your journal telling how you have kept God's laws by obeying a law of our country.

 Quotables!

*"Standard spelling is the result of writing and reading — not the way to it."**

*Scott, Jill E. 1994. Spelling for Readers and Writers. The Reading Teacher, Vol. 48, No. 2, October: 188-190.

Words Like Honey

Rachel's first day at Knowlton Elementary is made easier by Rosa's kind words.

"Well, here we are," Father said as he drove the van down Main Street late Thursday afternoon. "That's the office building where I'll be working. Our house is not far from here. I should be able to walk to work."

Mrs. Jacobson turned to look at the four kids squeezed in among their possessions in the back of the van. "What do you think, girls?"

"Neat!" said eight-year-old Vanessa.

"Which way to our new house?" Natalie asked.

Mrs. Jacobson smiled and pointed ahead toward a side street. "Up there and to the right." She turned to look out the front window again.

"I can't believe we had to move to this dumpy old town!" Rachel whispered to Rebecca. "It's out in the middle of nowhere, and I'll never get to see my friends at home again."

"You know that Father wants to practice law in a small town, Sis," Rebecca whispered back. "That way he'll have more time to spend with his family. After all," she added with a little chuckle, "it did just double in size!"

"You mean he wants to spend more time with Helen Arkusinski," griped Rachel.

"She's Helen Jacobson, now," corrected 11-year-old Rebecca. "Rache, you might as well get used to the idea that Father loves Helen. It doesn't mean he loves us any less!"

"I wish Mom hadn't died when we were little," Rachel whispered fiercely. "Why did Father have to marry again, anyway? I sure didn't need a new stepmother!"

"Your new school is just down that road, girls!" Father pointed as he turned off Main Street.

Moments later they stopped in front of a large, two-story house with a huge front yard. "Well, what do you think?" Father turned to smile at the cluster of kids in the back. "Mother and I looked a long time to find a house with something special for everyone. This one is close to my job and not far from the school we'd like to send you to. And I'll be able to come home often for lunch and see you and Mom, Natalie." Father reached back to tickle the blue-eyed four year old directly behind him.

"See, I told you we moved here so Father could spend more time with Helen." Rachel frowned as she whispered to Rebecca. "All he ever did before they were married was work, work, work!"

"And Rachel," Father interrupted his daughters' whispered conversation, "Mother and I thought you and Vanessa would like being close to Mason Springs Park. It's right there across the street." Mr. Jacobson pointed out his window at the huge trees and blooming flowers. "It has a big slide and swings on the other side of those trees. And the city is almost done building a new swimming pool, too. It's supposed to be open by the middle of this summer." The children were suddenly all ears. "The woman at the Chamber of Commerce told me they have a swim team with a really good coach," Dad continued. "I'm sure they'd love to have Rebecca with her terrific back crawl. The pool is supposed to have two water slides, a diving board, even a spouting whale in the kiddy pool! And all of you can take swimming lessons this summer."

The girls looked out the windows excitedly as they started to unbuckle their seat belts. Even Rachel forgot her anger and frustration for a minute. "Do you think I could be on the swim team this year too, Father? I'll be seven in July?"

"Depends how much you remember from last summer, Kiddo." Father stepped around the van. "Not many six-year-olds can do the butterfly stroke as well as you do!" he bragged. Rachel smiled at the unexpected praise, then ran to catch up with the rest of the excited Jacobson clan as they went inside to explore their new house.

But Rachel was a lot less excited Monday morning as they drove to their new school.

"Mom, do you know who our teachers are?" asked Vanessa.

"Yes, Father and I met them on our second trip house hunting. They all seemed very nice, and they're expecting you this morning." She slowed as she neared the school. "Your teacher is a man, I think, Vanessa. Rachel's teacher is Miss Grant. And . . . well, I can't remember what the fifth-grade teacher's name is, Rebecca. I guess there've been too many new things in my life lately." Mrs. Jacobson parked in a space marked visitors and opened her car door. "I'll go with you this morning, help you each find your classroom, and we'll meet your new teachers."

Rachel followed Helen into the school. She wouldn't admit it to anyone else, but she was really relieved. Helen would be going with her! She'd worried about coming to this new school ever since Father had told them they were moving. *I hate places where I don't know anyone,* she thought to herself, *"And I'm afraid I'm going to cry when Helen leaves. At least I know Helen."* Rachel followed her sister down the hall. *"I wish I were still at my old school in Dallas where I know everyone in my whole class."*

Then she remembered something Mommy had told her over and over. "Rache, you can always talk to Jesus about any problem, any

313

time. He's always willing to help you." And so Rachel offered a silent prayer. *"Dear Jesus, please help me! I need you today."*

As Rachel neared her classroom, she noticed there weren't very many kids in the hall yet. "We must be early," she thought. "I'm glad. There's only one thing worse than not knowing anybody in the room — that's not knowing anybody and being late! Everyone always stares and whispers."

"This way," Helen said, interrupting her thoughts. "Your classroom is the first door on the right. See, it has a big number one on the door." Helen patted Rachel's shoulder. "Rebecca will come and get you here after school today, then you both can meet me where I parked the van."

"Okay," Rachel nodded.

"You must be Rachel!" A tall lady with bright red hair met them at the door. "I'm Miss Grant, and right over here is your desk." She paused as a fluffy ball of fur bounced up. "And this is our puppy, Muffy. She loves to play with this little ball. Would you like to roll it to her?"

"She's so little." Rachel bent down to take a closer look at the puppy.

"Bye, Rachel," Helen waved from the door. "See you this afternoon after school."

Rachel was so busy playing with the puppy that she scarcely noticed the room filling up with kids she didn't know. When the bell rang her new classmates scurried to their desks. Rachel wasn't sure what to do with Muffy, so she picked her up and carried her to the desk Miss Grant had assigned her and sat down.

She looked at Rosa sitting next to her but didn't smile. *"I just hate this,"* she thought. *"Everyone is staring at me!"* Rachel was about to burst into tears when Rosa turned to her. "Hi, my name is Rosa," she said. "Miss Grant said you are Rachel from Dallas. You'll like our class. Miss Grant's a lot of fun." Rachel just

nodded. She was afraid she would cry if she said anything at all.

Rosa didn't say any more because Miss Grant was starting to read this week's story from their spelling book. "'Kind words are like honey — enjoyable and healthful.'"

"That's what Grandma Ruth is always telling us," thought Rosa. *"It didn't work on this new girl though. She isn't nice. I tried to be kind to her but she won't even speak."* Rosa frowned to herself. *"At least Setsuko Noma smiled at us when she came. This Rachel girl just looks mad."*

When Miss Grant finished reading Rosa decided to try again. "Do you want to jump rope and play 'Teddy Bear, Teddy Bear' with us at recess, Rache?"

Rachel looked at Rosa in surprise, then took a deep breath — only her Mommy and Becka had ever called her Rache. "Sure, but you'll have to teach me how," she smiled shyly. "I don't know the 'Teddy Bear, Teddy Bear' verse."

"Kind words ARE like honey," thought Rosa. *"It took two tries, but Rachel is smiling now."*

Rosa gave Rachel a big smile back. "It goes like this," she said. "Teddy bear, Teddy Bear climb the stairs. Teddy Bear, Teddy Bear say your prayers . . ."

"Wow," thought Rachel. *"My Mommy was right! Jesus heard my prayers for help. And He sent Miss Grant and Rosa with kind words!"*

2 Discussion Time

Check understanding of the story and development of personal values.

- Why was Rachel scared about the first day of school?
- Have you ever felt scared to do something new like Rachel did?
- What did you do?
- Would it have helped you feel more comfortable if someone had talked kindly to you?
- Let's make a list of kind words you would enjoy hearing.

314

A Test-Words

Write each word as your teacher says it.

Name _____

1. do

2. school

3. boy

4. come

5. as

6. happy

7. mother

8. or

☆ **Test-Challenge Words**

On a sheet of paper, write each challenge word as your teacher says it.

Scripture
Proverbs 16:24

Test-Challenge Words

On a separate sheet of paper, challenge words may be tested using the sentences below.

Personal Dictionary

After the tests in the review unit are graded, students may add any words they have misspelled to their personal dictionaries.

Take a minute to memorize...

Read the memory verse to the class twice. Have the class practice it with you two more times.

223

Test-Words

Test for knowledge of the correct spellings of these words.
(See the instructions at the top right for challenge words.)

Say I will say each word once, use the word in a sentence, then say the word again. Write the word on the lines in your Worktext.

1. do   Think of something kind to **do** for someone else.
2. school   Rachel was worried about going to a new **school**.
3. boy   The **boy** picked up the little puppy.
4. come   Dad might be able to **come** home for lunch.
5. as   Rachel could swim **as** well **as** many older children.
6. happy   Rachel was **happy** that Rosa spoke to her.
7. mother   Helen Jacobson was Rachel's new **mother**.
8. or   Do you want to play Teddy Bear, Teddy Bear **or** something else?
☆ books   Rachel will need new **books** for school.
☆ above   Miss Grant got the flashcards from the shelf **above** the puzzles.
☆ hasn't   Mr. Jacobson **hasn't** shown them the pool yet.
☆ first   There was a number one on the **first** grade door.

315

1 Game

Materials
- game page (from student text)
- yellow crayons (1 per child)
- game word list

Game Word List
Use of challenge words is optional.

1. do
2. school
3. boy
4. come
5. as
6. happy
7. mother
8. or
☆ books
☆ above
☆ hasn't
☆ first

Review **25** | Day 2

B Game

Review

Lesson
25

Name _____

In the story from Lesson 24, Christopher learned that we obey God by obeying the laws of our country. Color one star for each review word you or your team spell correctly.

224

How to Play:

- Divide the class into two teams, and decide which team will go first.
- Have a student from team A go to the board.
- Read the spelling word two times slowly and clearly. (You may also wish to use the word in a sentence. Ex.: "cat — The cat climbed a tree. — cat")
- Have the student write the word on the board.
- If the word is spelled correctly, instruct all the members of team A to color one star on the flag. (Note: If the word is misspelled, correct the spelling immediately before continuing the game.)
- Alternate between teams A and B as you go down the word list.
- The team with the most stars colored when you have gone through the game word list twice is the winner.

Non-Competitive Option:
At the end of the game, say: "Class, I am proud of your efforts to spell the words correctly. If you had fun and tried your best, you are all winners!"

316

C Test-Sentences   Name _____

The underlined word in each sentence is misspelled. Write the sentences on the lines below, spelling each underlined word correctly.

Rosa <u>sed</u>, "Hello."

1. Rosa said, "Hello."

God wants us to <u>luv</u> one another.

2. God wants us to love one another.

D Test-Proofreading

One word in each pair is misspelled. Fill in the oval by the misspelled word.

1. ● gurl
   ○ you

2. ○ look
   ● sume

3. ● htat
   ○ put

4. ○ some
   ● ar

5. ○ of
   ● luk

6. ● yu
   ○ that

7. ○ was
   ● uf

8. ○ girl
   ● pt

9. ● wuz
   ○ are

☆ **Test-Challenge Words**

On a sheet of paper, write each challenge word as your teacher says it.

225

---

1 **Test-Sentences**

Reinforce recognizing misspelled words.

(Say) Read each sentence carefully. The underlined word in each sentence is misspelled. Write the sentences on the lines in your worktext, spelling each underlined word correctly.

2 **Test-Proofreading**

Familiarize students with standardized test format and reinforce recognition of misspelled words.

(Say) Look at each set of words. One word in each set is misspelled. Fill in the oval by the misspelled word.

(You may wish to pronounce each pair of words to help students correctly identify them.)

Test-Challenge Words

On a separate sheet of paper, challenge words may be tested using the sentences below.

(Say) I will say the word once, use the word in a sentence, then say the word again. Write the word on your paper.

☆	soon	Rachel and Rebecca will leave for school **soon.**
☆	none	Rachel knew **none** of the kids in her class.
☆	wasn't	She **wasn't** excited about moving to a new town.
☆	circle	The puppy ran in a **circle** chasing his tail.

317

1 Game

Materials

- game page (from student text)
- crayons (1 per child)
- game word list

Game Word List

Use of challenge words is optional.

1. **love**
2. **said**
3. **girl**
4. **some**
5. **that**
6. **are**
7. **look**
8. **you**
9. **of**
10. **put**
11. **was**
☆ **soon**
☆ **none**
☆ **wasn't**
☆ **circle**

E Game   Name _____

Rosa's kind words helped Rachel feel welcome on her first day at school. Lead Rachel to the play ground to jump rope with Rosa by moving one space each time you or your team spells a review word correctly.

Review

Lesson

25

start

226

How to Play:

- Divide the class into two teams, and decide which team will go first.
- Optional: If you have an even number of students, you may wish to pair students from opposing teams and have them share a game page, each coloring the spaces for his/her own team on that page.
- Have a student from team A go to the board.
- Read the spelling word two times slowly and clearly. (You may also wish to use the word in a sentence. Ex.: "cat — The cat climbed a tree. — cat")
- Have the student write the word on the board.
- If the word is spelled correctly, instruct all the members of team A to color one space, beginning at Start, on the game board. (Note: If the word is misspelled, correct the spelling immediately before continuing the game.)
- Alternate between teams A and B as you go down the word list.
- The team to reach Rachel first is the winner.

Non-Competitive Option:

At the end of the game, say: "Class, I am proud of your efforts to spell the words correctly. If you had fun and tried your best, you are all winners!"

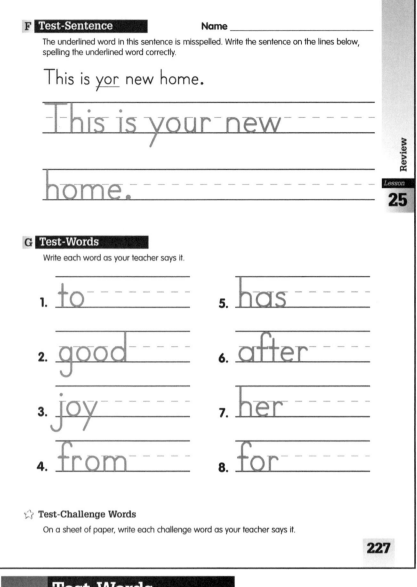

F Test-Sentence   Name _____

The underlined word in this sentence is misspelled. Write the sentence on the lines below, spelling the underlined word correctly.

This is <u>yor</u> new home.

This is your new
home.

Review
Lesson **25**

G Test-Words

Write each word as your teacher says it.

1. to   5. has
2. good   6. after
3. joy   7. her
4. from   8. for

☆ **Test-Challenge Words**

On a sheet of paper, write each challenge word as your teacher says it.

227

Test-Sentence

Reinforce recognizing misspelled words.

 Say — Read this sentence carefully. The underlined word is misspelled. Write the sentence on the lines in your Worktext, spelling the underlined word correctly.

Personal Dictionary

Remind students to add any words they have misspelled to their personal dictionaries.

2 Test-Words

Test for knowledge of the correct spellings of these words. (Challenge words may be tested on a separate piece of paper. Challenge words are starred.)

Say — I will say each word once, use the word in a sentence, then say the word again. Write the word on the lines in your Worktext.

1. to	The Jacobson family moved **to** a new town.
2. good	That was a very **good** story.
3. joy	You can have **joy** in your heart when you say kind things.
4. from	It was not far **from** their house to the school.
5. has	The puppy **has** long hair.
6. after	We will go to the park **after** school.
7. her	Rachel missed **her** mother.
8. for	Thank you, God, **for** answering my prayer.
☆ tooth	Every **tooth** in the puppy's mouth was tiny and sharp.
☆ enjoy	Rosa told Rachel that she would **enjoy** Miss Grant's class.
☆ have	"The team would love to **have** you," said Mrs. Jacobson.
☆ Lord	The **Lord** answered Rachel's prayer.

319

3 Writing Assessment

Assess student's spelling, grammar, and composition skills through personal writing.

(Say)

- Do you remember who made the new first grade girl feel welcome in our story this week? (Miss Grant, Muffy the class dog, and Rosa)

- What kind words did Rosa say to Rachel? (She introduced herself to Rachel and tried to get her to talk. Later she asked her if she would like to jump rope with them at recess.) Let's think of some ways to remind kids how important kind words are. (Spend some time brainstorming. Make a list on the board.)

- Today in your worktext you are going to design a sign.

Review

Lesson **25**

H Writing Assessment   Name _____

Design a sign that reminds people to use kind words. You may use words and pictures.

Remember : Saying kind things to someone is like giving them delicious food to eat!

228

A rubric for scoring is provided in Appendix B.

4 Action Game

Reinforce spelling skills and provide motivation and interest.

Materials

- construction paper (all the same color) cut in half lengthwise
- marker
- scissors

How to Play:

Print a spelling word from this review unit on each half; then, cut each half crosswise into two pieces dividing the spelling word approximately in half and creating two puzzle pieces. Give each student a puzzle piece, face down. At your signal, have each student turn over his puzzle piece and move about to find the player whose puzzle piece fits with his to form a word.

Instruct the students to run to you when they think they have a correct match. If they have a match, have them write the word neatly on the board and return to their seats; if they do not, have them return to the group to continue the hunt for their match. Continue the game until all the word puzzles are completed.

Spelling Is Fun!

ABC's

This certificate is awarded to

_____

for practicing the following words, by doing fun spelling activities, and playing great spelling games!

Date _____

do	boy	as	mother
to	joy	has	her
you	some	that	girl
school	come	happy	your
good	from	after	or
look	love	was	for
put	of	said	are
☆ tooth	☆ enjoy	☆ have	☆ Lord
☆ books	☆ above	☆ hasn't	☆ first
☆ soon	☆ none	☆ wasn't	☆ circle

5 Certificate

Provide an opportunity for parents or guardians to encourage and assess their child's progress.

Say
- Write your name on the first line.
- Now I will write the date on the board for you to copy on the next line.
- Follow along as I read the certificate out loud.
- Be sure to show your parents or guardian all the words you've practiced spelling.

Take a minute to memorize...

Read the memory verse to the class twice. Have the class practice it with you two more times.

Quotables!

> "Teaching a child to be a good speller involves both mental and verbal processes and needs to include the active participation of the child."*

---

*Downing, John, Robert M. Coughlin and Gene Rich. 1986. Children's Invented Spellings in the Classroom. The Elementary School Journal, Vol. 86: No. 3, January: 295-303.

6 Letter

Provide the parent or guardian with the spelling word lists for the next unit.

Say Show your parents or guardian this letter that tells them what your spelling words will be for the next unit. Ask them to put it in a special place where you will remember to practice them together.

Dear Parent,

We are about to begin the last spelling unit containing three weekly lessons. A set of seven words plus three challenge words will be studied each week. All the words will be reviewed in the fourth week.

Values based on the Scriptures listed below will be taught in each lesson.

Lesson 26	Lesson 27	Lesson 28
one	blue	little
two	black	tall
three	brown	short
four	green	long
five	yellow	few
six	white	many
seven	pink	more
☆ zero	☆ orange	☆ thin
☆ count	☆ purple	☆ thick
☆ number	☆ color	☆ digit
Psalm 96:1, 2	Prov. 14:14	Prov. 10:4

The Swimming Lesson

Rachel gains new insights into salvation after being saved from drowning.

"I can't believe Daniel invited the whole class!" Tommy carried the soccer ball out the classroom door for recess.

"Even the girls!" Stephen grinned, then snatched the ball away.

Matthew ran up to join the group of children headed for the playground. "The water will be freezing, you know! It still gets cold at night."

"No, it won't," Tommy shot back over his shoulder as he chased after Stephen. "I've been swimming in Daniel's pool when the air was cold, but the water was nice and warm." He grabbed Stephen for a good-natured tussle. "Besides, Daniel has that big bathtub-thing-a-ma-jig that's full of hot water. You can jump in that if you get cold."

"There's a button you can press that makes the water in the bathtub thing all bubbly!" James' eyes lit up with excitement. "If you push another button it feels like someone's squirting you with a hose under the water."

"You must mean a hot tub," said Matthew.

"Yeah, but they call it something else," said Tommy. "Besides, we never stay in the hot tub thing-a-ma-jig very long because Daniel has a basketball hoop hooked to the side of the pool, and lots of rings you can dive for. He even has a slide that goes right into the water!"

"Wow!" said Stephen. "I can hardly wait for Thursday!"

Thursday was sunny and warm. Miss Grant tried to keep her students busy and focused on reading, spelling, and handwriting before lunch, but everyone was full of energy and thinking more about swimming than reading and writing. Miss Grant decided today was not the best day to introduce double-digit addition like she'd planned! She looked around the room and smiled. "Okay, everyone outside for a story under the big pine tree, and a game of math tag!" She didn't have to tell them twice this time.

Finally the school day was over. Daniel's mom had arranged for all the students to be picked up in a big van and driven directly to the DeVores' home. As soon as Miss Grant finished the dismissal prayer, the children rushed out to the waiting van. "Hey, Daniel, what do you call your hot tub?" asked Matthew.

"A Jacuzzi."

"How far away do you live, Daniel?" Rachel looked out the window at the passing cars.

"Just a few miles."

"I already have my swimming suit on," whispered Rachel in Rosa's ear.

"So do I," Rosa giggled. "Let's try to be the first ones in the pool."

When the van arrived, Mrs. DeVore came out the front door and down the curved sidewalk to meet her son's classmates, and welcome them to her home. She took the class through a massive iron gate beside the house, and pointed to dressing rooms in a lovely bath house beside the pool.

"Ever been here before, Rosa?" whispered Rachel in awe.

"No. Just look at that pool. It's huge, and there's a diving board too! Tommy didn't tell us about that."

The two girls entered the dressing room together and looked around. Bright towels and matching washcloths were neatly folded on the counter by the mirror. A little bottle of shampoo, another of cream rinse, and a bar of soap in the shape of a bunny were nestled on top of each washcloth.

"One, two, three, four, five, six, seven," counted Rosa. "There's a stack for each girl in our class. Neat! I wonder if we get to keep this stuff?" She picked up a bunny soap. "Can you swim, Rache?"

"Sure. I took swimming lessons all last summer at the pool near our house in Dallas." Rachel put her pile of clothes on the bench in one of the private changing rooms. "I hope I can join the swim team this summer." She paused. "How about you? Can you swim?"

"Si, señorita!" said Rosa happily. She danced off toward the pool with one of the DeVores' green towels draped over her shoulder. "This is going to be so much fun!" Rachel grabbed a large red towel and followed her out the door.

"Race you to the other end of the pool!" Daniel shouted from the shallow end as Rosa and Rachel walked out. The girls looked around to see if he was talking to someone else.

"Guess we won't be the first ones in the pool! He's such a show off!" whispered Rosa. "Let's race him. He doesn't know you're going to be on the swim team this summer." Out loud she said, "Okay, Daniel! You're on!" The girls joined Daniel on the edge of the pool, and curled their toes around the deck's edge.

"On your mark! Get set! Go!" yelled Daniel.

Rachel started with a long, shallow dive. She glided smoothly through the water with strong steady strokes and a smooth kick with hardly a splash. She passed Rosa, then Daniel. She looked up to see how much farther she had to go. "This pool's a lot bigger than what I'm used to," she thought. Her stroke began to get sloppy and she began weaving a little bit, breathing fast and hard. "I must be almost there. Just another stroke or two." She lifted her head to make sure she didn't hit the end of the pool, and

323

took a deep breath — but got a mouthful of water instead! Gasping and coughing, Rachel quickly flipped her feet down so she could stand up and fill her lungs. But she couldn't touch the bottom! She was in the deepest part of the pool!

Terrified, Rachel kicked hard toward the surface and tried to flip onto her back to catch her breath like she'd been taught. She sputtered and coughed, but only got a small gulp of air before she started sinking again. Her scream let out the small amount of air she'd managed to get in! *"I'm going to drown!"* she thought, her body going limp with panic. *"There's nothing I can do!"*

Suddenly she felt a strong hand grab her right wrist and whip her around, and an arm reached over her shoulder from behind and held her firmly. Her body was supported from underneath, and she was pushed toward the surface quickly by a powerful scissors kick.

That night, as Rachel snuggled safely in her own bed across from Rebecca, Father came in and sat down beside her. "You learned a different kind of swimming lesson today, Little Lady — and it's one I want you to always remember. Even though you're a good swimmer, you got in trouble and couldn't save yourself." Father paused, his voice tight with emotion. "I don't even want to think about what would have happened if Mr. DeVore hadn't come home early from work today!"

Father bent over and gave Rachel a big hug. "Mr. DeVore saved your life, Rachel. And that's what Jesus did for us, too. Our world is drowning in sin. But when we believe in Jesus, He has promised He will save us." He tucked the covers snugly under her chin. "I love you, Rachel Jacobson. We have a lot to be thankful for tonight!"

2 Discussion Time

Check understanding of the story and development of personal values.

- How did Rachel feel when she thought she was going to drown?
- Who rescued Rachel from the pool?
- We have all sinned and need to be rescued from this world. Who will save us?
- Jesus loves to hear you tell others that He saves! How can you do that?

A Preview

Name _____

Write each word as your teacher says it.

1. two
2. four
3. six
4. one
5. three
6. five
7. seven

Challenge Words

 count
zero
number

Scripture
Psalm 96:1, 2

Number Words

Lesson **26**

231

 Challenge

For better spellers, challenge words may be included in the weekly list. Challenge words are starred.

Correct Immediately!

Let's correct our preview. I will write each word on the board. Put a dot under each letter on your preview as I spell the word out loud. If you spelled a word wrong, rewrite it correctly.

Progress Chart

Students may record scores. (Reproducible master in Appendix B.)

Lesson **26** | **Day 1**

Take a minute to memorize . . .

Read the memory verse twice. Have students practice it with you two more times.

---

3 Preview

Test for knowledge of the correct spellings of these words. (See the instructions at the top right for challenge words.)

 I will say each word once, use the word in a sentence, then say the word again. Write the word on the lines in the Worktext.

1. two — Rosa and Rachel were the first **two** girls in the pool.
2. four — We will go to Daniel's pool in **four** days.
3. six — The pool is **six** feet deep right here.
4. one — Daniel was the first **one** into the water.
5. three — Choose **three** pieces of candy each.
6. five — Dad gets off work at **five** o'clock each day.
7. seven — At least **seven** birds came to the feeder.
☆ count — Can you **count** to 1 000?
☆ zero — A one and then a **zero** makes a ten.
☆ number — His favorite **number** is twelve.

4 Word Shapes

Help students form a correct image of whole words.

Say Look at each word and think about its shape. Now, write the word in the correct word Shape Boxes. You may check off each word as you use it.

(This lesson contains spelling patterns for the sounds of /ü/, /u/, /ē/, /or/, /ī/, /i/, and /e/. A few students may continue to have difficulty spelling some of these patterns.)

Challenge

Draw the correctly shaped box around each letter in these words.

Say On a separate sheet of paper, write other words that contain the spelling patterns in the word list. See how many words you can write.

B Word Shapes

Name _____

Write each word in the correct word shape boxes.

Number Words

Lesson **26**

1. one

2. two

3. three

4. four

5. five

6. six

7. seven

☆ **Challenge**

Draw the correct word shape boxes around each word.

z e r o   c o u n t   n u m b e r

232

Answers may vary for duplicate word shapes.

Be Prepared For Fun

Check these supply lists for **Fun Ways to Spell** presented **Day 2**. Purchase and/or gather these items ahead of time!

General
- Crayons
- 3 x 5 Cards cut in thirds (27 pieces per child)
- 3 x 5 Cards cut in thirds (15 more pieces for challenge words)
- Glue
- Construction Paper (about 3 pieces per child)
- Spelling List

Visual
- Chalk or Whiteboard Marker
- Chalkboard or Whiteboard (could be individual boards for each child)
- Spelling List

Auditory
- Spelling List

Tactile
- Damp Sand (in plastic storage box with lid)
- Spelling List

Lesson 26 | Day 1

326

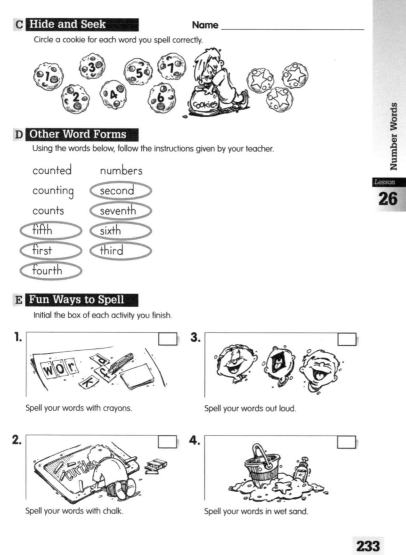

C **Hide and Seek**   Name _____

Circle a cookie for each word you spell correctly.

D **Other Word Forms**

Using the words below, follow the instructions given by your teacher.

counted   numbers

counting   (second)

counts   (seventh)

(fifth)   (sixth)

(first)   (third)

(fourth)

E **Fun Ways to Spell**

Initial the box of each activity you finish.

1. ☐

Spell your words with crayons.

2. ☐

Spell your words with chalk.

3. ☐

Spell your words out loud.

4. ☐

Spell your words in wet sand.

233

Number Words

Lesson
26

Lesson 26   **Day 2**

1 Hide and Seek

Reinforce spelling by using multiple styles of learning.

On a white board, Teacher writes each word — one at a time. **Have students:**

- **Look** at the word.
- **Say** the word out loud.
- **Spell** the word out loud.
- **Hide** (teacher erases word.)
- **Write** the word on their paper.
- **Seek** (teacher rewrites word.)
- **Check** spelling. If incorrect, repeat above steps.

2 Other Word Forms

This activity is optional. Have students circle each ordinal number word.

3 Fun Ways to Spell

Four activities are provided. Use one, two, three, or all of the activities. Have students initial the box for each activity they complete.

Options:

- assign activities to students according to their learning styles
- set up the activities in learning centers for students to do throughout the day
- divide students into four groups and assign one activity per group
- do one activity per day

General

To spell your words with crayons…
- Write each letter of your spelling word on a card.
- Glue the cards on a sheet of paper in the right order to spell your words.
- Check your spelling.

Auditory

To spell your words out loud…
- Have your classmate read a spelling word.
- Say a sentence with that spelling word to your classmate.
- Spell the spelling word you used in that sentence to your classmate.
- Ask your classmate to check your spelling.
- Do this with each word on your word list.

Visual

To spell your words with chalk…
- Put your spelling list on your desk.
- Look at a word then walk to the chalkboard (or whiteboard).
- Write your spelling word on the chalkboard (or whiteboard).
- Return to your desk.
- Check your spelling.

Tactile

To spell your words in damp sand…
- Use your finger to write a spelling word in the damp sand.
- Check your spelling.
- Smooth the sand with your finger and write another word.

1 Crossword Clues

Familiarize students with word meaning and usage.

(Say) Count the number of objects shown in each picture clue. Write the number word in the row of boxes with the correct number of spaces. (Do the first one on the board.)

F **Crossword Clues**   Name _____

Use the clues to write the number words in each puzzle.

1. Across

1. | t | h | r | e | e |

| w |
| o |

3. Down

1. Down

2. Across

3. | f |

3. | o | n | e |

2. | s | i | x |

| e |

| u |

4. | f | i | v | e |

| r |

| e |

2. Down

| n |

3. Across

4. Across

■ **Word Bank**

| one | three | five | seven |
| two | four | six |

234

 Take a minute to memorize...

Read the memory verse twice. Have students practice it with you two more times.

1. One and six are seven.

2. There are four cats.

3. Two and three are five.

H **Proofreading**
One word in each pair is misspelled. Fill in the oval by the misspelled word.

1. ◯ three   4. ⬤ fiv   ☆ ⬤ numbr
   ⬤ fuor   ◯ four   ◯ seven

2. ⬤ sevin   5. ◯ one   ☆ ⬤ cownt
   ◯ two   ⬤ siks   ◯ first

3. ⬤ wun   6. ⬤ thre   ☆ ◯ have
   ◯ six   ◯ five   ⬤ zeero

235

Reinforce correct spelling by using current and previous words in context.

 (Say) Listen as I read each sentence and then write it in your Worktext. (Slowly read each sentence twice. Sentences are found in the Student Worktext to the left.)

☆ **Challenge**
Write these incomplete sentences on the board.

___ comes before ___.

Rachel ___ learn ___ ___ ___ ___ hundred.

___ ___ ___ your phone ___.

 (Say) Listen as I read each sentence. Write the sentence on your paper. (Slowly read each sentence twice.)

<u>Zero</u> comes before <u>one</u>.

Rachel <u>will</u> learn <u>to</u> <u>count</u> <u>to</u> <u>five</u> hundred.

<u>The</u> <u>girl</u> <u>has</u> your phone <u>number</u>.

---

 2 **Proofreading**

Familiarize students with standardized test format and reinforce recognizing misspelled words.

 (Say) Look at each set of words. One word in each set is misspelled. Fill in the oval by the misspelled word. (You may wish to pronounce each set of words to help students correctly identify them.)

3 Hide and Seek

Reinforce correct spelling of current spelling words. (A reproducible master is provided in Appendix A as shown on the inset page to the right.)

Write the words one at a time on a white board.

Have students:

- **Look** at the word.
- **Say** the word out loud.
- **Spell** the word out loud.
- **Hide** (teacher erases word.)
- **Write** the word on paper.
- **Seek** (teacher rewrites word.)
- **Check** spelling. If incorrect, rewrite word correctly.

4 Code

Have your students complete this activity to strengthen spelling ability and expand vocabulary.

1 Posttest

Test mastery of the spelling words. Challenge words are starred.

 Say

I will say the word once, use the word in a sentence, then say the word again. Write the word on your paper.

1. **four** — Your doctor's appointment is at **four** o'clock.
2. **six** — She has saved **six** dollars and seventy-two cents.
3. **one** — Which **one** of you would like to say the verse first?
4. **three** — The **three** children started to race across the pool.
5. **seven** — There were **seven** towels, one for each girl.
6. **two** — We have **two** dogs.
7. **five** — Rachel was **five** last year.
☆ **number** — The **number** on the sign says fifty-five.
☆ **count** — It is fun to **count** by fives.
☆ **zero** — A **zero** means none.

 Progress Chart
Students may record scores. (Reproducible master in Appendix B.)

 Personal Dictionary
Students may add any words they have misspelled to their personal dictionaries for reference when writing. (Cover in Appendix B.)

Appendix · Lesson **26**

 **Hide and Seek**
Check a paper for each word you spell correctly.

 **Code**
A picture code uses symbols to stand for letters. Use the picture code to write the missing letters. Read the other forms of your spelling words in the blanks.

c d e g h i k n o s t u

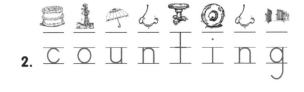
1. c o u n t e d

2. c o u n t i n g

3. c o u n t s

383

330

I Game

Name _____

Cross out each **a**, **g**, and **p** with a big **X** to find the hidden spelling words. Using one crayon, softly color the boxes you did not mark so you can see your spelling words better.

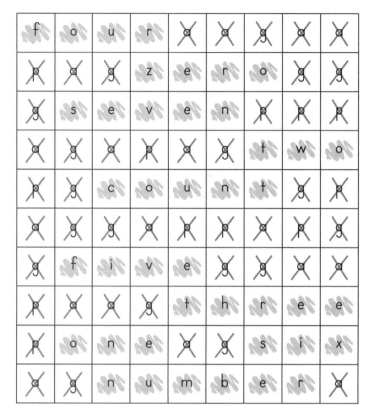

f	o	u	r	X	X	X	X	X
X	X	X	z	e	r	o	X	X
X	s	e	v	e	n	X	X	X
X	X	X	X	X	X	t	w	o
X	X	c	o	u	n	t	X	X
X	X	X	X	X	X	X	X	X
X	f	i	v	e	X	X	X	X
X	X	X	X	t	h	r	e	e
X	o	n	e	X	X	s	i	x
X	X	n	u	m	b	e	r	X

Remember : Praise God every day for sending His Son to save you.

J Journaling

Copy and finish one of these sentences in your journal:
It is easy for me to tell someone about my friend Jesus when...
I like to talk about Jesus to...

236

2 Game

Reinforce spelling skills and provide motivation and interest.

Materials

- game page (from student text)
- pencils (1 per child)
- crayons or colored pencils (1 per child)

3 Journaling

Provide a meaningful reason for correct spelling through personal writing.

Review the story using discussion leads provided on the following page. Encourage students to apply the Scriptural value in their journaling.

 Take a minute to memorize...

Have the class say the memory verse with you once.

How to Play:

- Have each student mark through each letter **a** found on the grid with a big **X**.
- Have each student mark through each letter **g** found on the grid with a big **X**.
- Have each student mark through each letter **p** found on the grid with a big **X**.
- Tell the students that the boxes without **X**'s contain their spelling words.
- Have the students color softly over the boxes without **X**'s so they can see their spelling words more clearly.
- Have the students follow along as you read and spell each word as it appears on the grid.

Journaling (continued)

Say
- Daniel's dad saved Rachel's life in our story this week. Do you think she would want to tell people about what happened? (yes) Why? (She would have drowned in the pool if he hadn't been there to save her.)
- What has Jesus done for our world? (He died on the cross because He loved us.)
- Think about a time when you really wanted to tell someone about your friend Jesus. Write about that time in your journal.

Quotables!

*"Mastering spelling is a complex intellectual achievement, not a low-order memory task."**

*Watson, Alan J. 1988. Developmental Spelling: A Word Categorizing Instructional Experiment. Journal of Educational Research, Vol. 82, No. 2, November/December: 82-88.

Camping with Daniel

Daniel is surprised at how fun a simple camping trip can be!

"*So* you're certain it would be acceptable?" asked Mrs. DeVore hopefully. "I don't wish to impose, but my housekeeper, Helen, feels she must be available for her family this weekend. Her aunt has been ill, and has recently taken a turn for the worse." Sandra DeVore's face wore an unaccustomed look of concern. "Helen usually stays with Daniel, you know, when I accompany Donald on these business trips . . . Yes, yes, of course, but Daniel has never been camping before . . . No, hiking isn't something we do as a family. What equipment will be required?" She paused for a moment. "Certainly. I can arrange for him to have those items. I am so grateful for your willingness to help in this emergency. Good-bye." Daniel's mother flipped her cell phone closed and turned the big luxury sedan toward Fayetteville. She would need to do some serious shopping in order for Daniel to have the appropriate equipment for a camping trip, and surely he would need more than the few items Mrs. Schilling had suggested! She really hadn't planned on shopping today, but . . .

"Who's going on our camping trip with us, Mom?" Matthew looked up as Mrs. Schilling hung up the phone.

"Daniel DeVore, Champ," Mom said.

"Daniel?" Matthew wrinkled his nose with disgust. "Why can't we invite someone like Tony or Stephen? They love nature stuff and camping. Daniel will probably think it's boring without his computer and video games along."

"Mr. and Mrs. DeVore have to go out of town this weekend, and Daniel needs a place to stay," Mom answered patiently. "His family asked for help

and I think we should be willing to give it."

"But Daniel doesn't have any camping stuff, and I bet he'll be mean to Alex," Matthew whined. "Does he have to come?"

Mom looked Matthew firmly in the eye. "I've already told Mrs. DeVore that Daniel can stay with us this weekend."

Matthew shrugged and walked slowly out of the kitchen. "Our weekend is doomed!" he mumbled to himself.

The next morning at school, Daniel met Matthew at their classroom door. "Matthew, Matthew, guess what my mom bought me yesterday." He didn't wait for an answer. "I've got all kinds of cool camping things! I've got a day pack with lots of pockets on it, a water bottle, and a new down sleeping bag. She even bought me a red pocket knife! It has a spoon, a can opener, and scissors on it!"

"And it's not even his birthday!" thought Matthew. *"I don't have a pocket knife, and we go camping all the time!"*

"And check out these new boots," Daniel continued. He lifted his foot and pointed to a pair of expensive hiking boots. "They aren't heavy at all and they're waterproof, too. I'm supposed to break them in today before we leave on our trip." Daniel punched Matthew's arm playfully. "Mom even picked up a huge bag of candy for us to munch on while we play my little video games and listen to CDs all night." He paused. "Hey, Alex won't sleep in our tent, will he?"

Before Matthew could explain, the bell rang and ended the one-sided conversation. *"Oh great,"* thought

Matthew to himself as he took his seat. *"He's going to think that the things our family likes to do are boring!"*

Later that afternoon Daniel scrunched in beside Matthew in the back seat of the Schilling's Suburban. Gear was packed in every available space around them. "Which of these bags has our tent in it?" Daniel pushed a canvas duffle out of his way.

"Dear Jesus," Matthew prayed silently. *"Daniel thinks camping means playing video games, eating candy, and listening to CDs in a tent! Please help him not to think the stuff we do is boring."*

"We all stay in the same tent, Daniel." Matthew rushed on before he lost his courage. "But since we camp a lot, we have a big tent with two sections. One is for Mom, Dad, and Emily. The other is where Alex and I sleep with the stove, pots, and pans."

"Is the food in our side too?" asked Daniel eagerly.

"You can't keep food in a tent, Daniel," Matthew explained. "The wild animals might smell it and tear up the tent to get it. We keep the food locked up in the Suburban until meal time."

"Oh." Daniel shrugged and pulled a video game out of his bright new day pack. Matthew picked up his nature magazine to look at an article about crows and ravens. The two boys rode in silence for the next hour.

"Here we are gang!" Dad nodded to the State Park sign as he turned off the highway.

"Look at that field!" Mom pointed out the side window. "It looks pink!"

Alex leaned forward for a better look. "Spring Beauties! Just like the ones in our yard at home!"

"Good job, Son! This should be a great weekend for learning about wild flowers." Mother scanned the passing scenery as Father drove even slower. "Look at all those little Johnny-jump-ups on that rocky bank over there! Did anyone remember to bring the wild flower b . . ."

"Where do you want to camp this time?" interrupted

Mr. Schilling.

"By the creek!" Alex said.

"Cweek! Cweek!" echoed Emily.

Moments later Dad pulled into one of the family's favorite campsites, a quiet corner beside the big creek running through the park. After everyone helped unload the Suburban, Mom and Dad began setting up the tent. Dad sent the three boys to look for dead branches to start a fire.

When the boys returned, the tent was set up. "I want you to get settled in the tent now, gentlemen. Daniel, put your sleeping bag on the left side with Alex and Matthew's," Dad directed. "We'll store our cooking gear in the back of the Suburban with the food this time."

"Do we have to sleep with Alex?" Daniel complained to Matthew as he lugged his new sleeping bag and day pack to the tent. "I can't believe it!"

"Get everything where you want it because it will be dark soon," Dad called. "When you get done come back out, and we'll see if we can start a fire with no paper or lighter fluid — using only one match!"

"One match!" Daniel was amazed. "You can't do that."

"Sure I can. And I'll teach you how, too," promised Mr. Schilling.

The boys hurried to put their things away. When they were finished, Mr. Schilling showed them how to arrange tiny twigs in a teepee shape, gradually adding bigger and bigger ones. They left a little hole in the bottom, just big enough to poke in a match. When they were through, Mr. Schilling let Daniel strike the match. The small, dry twigs caught fire quickly when Daniel put the match in the hole. Dad blew gently on the flame, which leapt up to catch the bigger sticks on fire.

The campfire was soon burning brightly, and Mom brought Emily over to enjoy the warmth before she started supper. "Anyone like to roast hot dogs and marshmallows?"

"I would. I would. I

would," chorused the three boys.

Mom gave the boys bananas to snack on while she got the food ready. "Here you go boys." Dad handed them coat hangers bent into roasting sticks with hot dogs poked on the ends. "Squat down like this, and roast your hot dogs over the bright, orange coals."

After supper, Dad lit the big lantern. Then the Schilling family taught Daniel how to play Bible Charades. He learned quickly, and no one could guess the one he and Matthew did. It was King Solomon building the temple after his father, King David, died. Alex thought they were building the Ark. Even Mom and Dad didn't guess this one before the timer went off. All too soon Dad announced bedtime.

"Tomorrow we're going to hike down to Sheep Falls." Dad zipped the three boys into their sleeping bags. "On the way we'll see how many different wild flowers we can find. We'll take our lunch in the day packs so we can eat when we get there. You guys get some sleep now so you can keep up with me and Emily!"

"Okay," the boys agreed sleepily.

"Daniel," whispered Matthew a few minutes later. "Daniel."

"I think he's all worn out from building the temple," giggled Alex. "He's already asleep."

"Shhhh!" Dad said from his seat beside the fire. "We have a long hike tomorrow, boys."

Late Sunday afternoon, the weary campers returned home. Matthew tossed Daniel's day pack on his pile of gear in the Schilling's garage. Two video games, several CDs, and a bag of candy slid out onto the garage floor. The two boys looked at each other and burst out laughing. "We never did play those games after we went to bed, did we?" said Daniel.

"That's because you were too tired to keep your eyes open once your head hit the pillow," laughed Matthew. "And you should see your hair! It's sticking straight up on top. Did you ever comb it on our trip?" Daniel made a silly face and shook his head no.

"I think that's Friday night's supper holding it up!" giggled Matthew patting Daniel's head. "Kind of a marshmallow mousse!"

"And we both smell like a campfire," teased Daniel, who had never gone a day in his life without a bath. "Hey, can I borrow your wildflower book?" He walked over to the big pile of camping gear, and lifted the colorful volume from the floor. "We can't let Alex win the next wildflower contest! He sure doesn't seem like he's just five. You're really lucky to have a brother to play with."

"You mean you didn't mind sleeping in the tent with him?" asked Matthew.

"No, and I had a really nice time with your family this weekend." Daniel turned as the housekeeper pulled into the driveway to pick him up. "And you know what?" he added with a grin. "It wasn't boring at all!"

2 Discussion Time

Check understanding of the story and development of personal values.

- Does your family ever go camping?
- Do you sleep in a tent?
- Why did Matthew not want Daniel to go on the camping trip?
- Why was he worried Daniel would think camping was boring?
- How did Daniel feel about the camping trip when he got back Sunday afternoon?
- Do you think the boys had an exciting weekend?

A Preview

Write each word as your teacher says it.

Name _____

1. black
2. green
3. white
4. blue
5. brown
6. yellow
7. pink

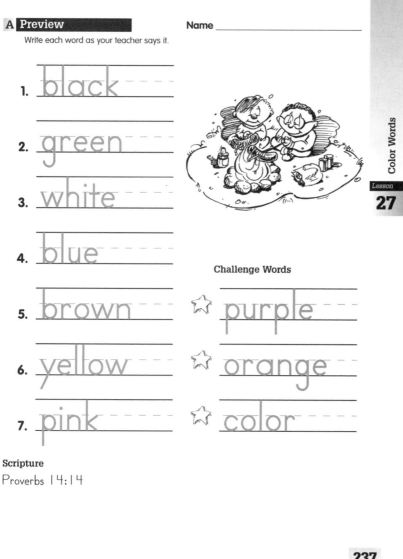

Challenge Words

☆ purple
☆ orange
☆ color

Scripture
Proverbs 14:14

237

Challenge

For better spellers, challenge words may be included in the weekly list. Challenge words are starred.

Correct Immediately!

Say Let's correct our preview. I will write each word on the board. Put a dot under each letter on your preview as I spell the word out loud. If you spelled a word wrong, rewrite it correctly.

Progress Chart

Students may record scores. (Reproducible master in Appendix B.)

Take a minute to memorize . . .

Read the memory verse twice. Have students practice it with you two more times.

---

3 Preview

Test for knowledge of the correct spellings of these words. (See the instructions at the top right for challenge words.)

 Say I will say each word once, use the word in a sentence, then say the word again. Write the word on the lines in the Worktext.

1. black — The crow has **black** feathers.
2. green — Many **green** leaves cover the trees.
3. white — Fluffy **white** clouds float through the sky.
4. blue — The creek reflects the **blue** sky.
5. brown — Can you spot a light **brown** deer?
6. yellow — The buttercups are a brilliant **yellow**.
7. pink — Some spring flowers are light **pink**.
☆ purple — This is a **purple** hyacinth.
☆ orange — We will share this **orange**.
☆ color — God made this world filled with **color**.

Word Shapes

4

Help students form a correct image of whole words.

Say Look at each word and think about its shape. Now, write the word in the correct word Shape Boxes. You may check off each word as you use it.

(A cluster is two or more consonant sounds said together and spelled with more than one letter.)

Say In the word shape boxes, color the letters that spell a consonant cluster or digraph in each word. Circle the word that does not contain a cluster or digraph.

Lesson 27 | Day 1

Challenge
Draw the correctly shaped box around each letter in these words.

Say On a separate sheet of paper, write other words that contain the spelling patterns in the word list. See how many words you can write.

B Word Shapes   Name _____

Write each word in the correct word shape boxes. Next, in the word shape boxes, color the letters that spell a consonant cluster or digraph in each word. Circle the word that does not contain a cluster or digraph.

Color Words

Lesson **27**

1. blue

2. black

3. brown

4. green

5. yellow

6. white

7. pink

☆ **Challenge**
Draw the correct word shape boxes around each word.

238

Answers may vary for duplicate word shapes.

Be Prepared For Fun

Check these supply lists for **Fun Ways to Spell** presented **Day 2**. Purchase and/or gather these items ahead of time!

General
- Strips of Paper 3 1/2 x 11 Inches (7 per child)
- Strips of Paper 3 1/2 x 11 Inches (3 more for challenge words)
- Crayons or Markers
- Tape
- Scissors
- Spelling List

Auditory
- Rhythm Instruments (two wooden spoons, two pan lids, maracas)
- Spelling List

Visual
- Clothespins (6 clothespins per child at the clothesline)
- a, b, c, e, e, g, h, i, k, l, l, n, o p, r, t, u, w and y (written on 3 x 5 card cut in half)
- o and p (added for challenge words)
- Clothesline (hung at student height)
- Spelling List

Tactile
- Shaving Cream
- Optional: Plastic Plates
- Optional: Wooden Craft Sticks
- Spelling List

336

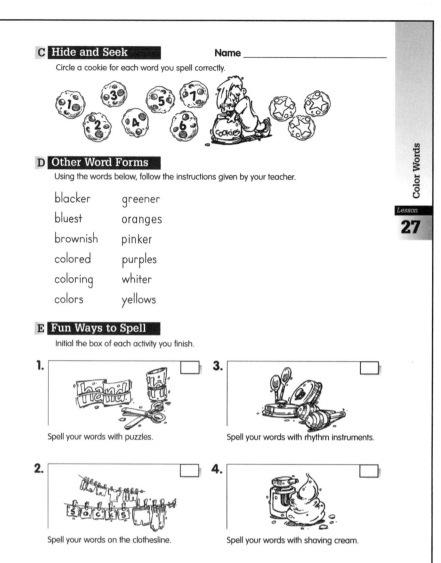

C Hide and Seek

Name _____

Circle a cookie for each word you spell correctly.

D Other Word Forms

Using the words below, follow the instructions given by your teacher.

blacker	greener
bluest	oranges
brownish	pinker
colored	purples
coloring	whiter
colors	yellows

E Fun Ways to Spell

Initial the box of each activity you finish.

1. ☐

Spell your words with puzzles.

2. ☐

Spell your words on the clothesline.

3. ☐

Spell your words with rhythm instruments.

4. ☐

Spell your words with shaving cream.

239

1 Hide and Seek

Reinforce spelling by using multiple styles of learning.

On a white board, Teacher writes each word — one at a time. **Have students:**

- **Look** at the word.
- **Say** the word out loud.
- **Spell** the word out loud.
- **Hide** (teacher erases word.)
- **Write** the word on their paper.
- **Seek** (teacher rewrites word.)
- **Check** spelling. If incorrect, repeat above steps.

2 Other Word Forms

This activity is optional. Have students name some nouns that these Other Word Forms might describe.

bluest
brownish
greener

3 Fun Ways to Spell

Four activities are provided. Use one, two, three, or all of the activities. Have students initial the box for each activity they complete.

Options:

- assign activities to students according to their learning styles
- set up the activities in learning centers for students to do throughout the day
- divide students into four groups and assign one activity per group
- do one activity per day

General

To Spell your words with puzzles…
- Write each word on a strip of paper in big, tall letters.
- Cut your word in half lengthwise.
- Tape the ends of each strip together to make circles.
- Mix the circles together.
- Match the circles again to make your spelling words.

Auditory

To spell your words with rhythm instruments…
- Look at a word on your spelling list.
- Close your eyes.
- Play your rhythm instruments softly while you whisper the spelling of the word.
- Open your eyes and check your spelling.

Visual

To spell your words on the clothesline…
- Choose the letter cards you need to spell a word on your list.
- Clothespin the cards to the clothesline in the right order to spell the word.
- Check your spelling.
- Remove the letter cards from the clothesline and spell the next word on your list.

Tactile

To spell your words with shaving cream…
- Spread a glob of shaving cream across your desk (or on a plastic plate).
- Use your finger (or a wooden craft stick) to write a spelling word in the shaving cream.
- Check your spelling.
- Smear the word out with your finger and write another word.

337

1

Crossword Clues

Familiarize students with word meaning and usage.

Invite the students to identify each picture. Talk about what color they think of as they name each one.

Say

Write the correct color word in the box beside each object.

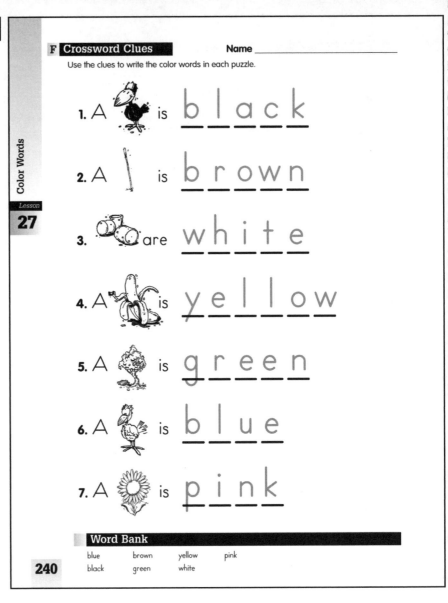

F **Crossword Clues**   Name _____

Use the clues to write the color words in each puzzle.

Color Words

Lesson **27**

1. A 🐦 is b l a c k

2. A ⫾ is b r o w n

3. 🥛 are w h i t e

4. A 🍌 is y e l l o w

5. A 🌳 is g r e e n

6. A 🐦 is b l u e

7. A 🌻 is p i n k

Word Bank

blue	brown	yellow	pink
black	green	white	

240

Take a minute to memorize...

Read the memory verse twice. Have students practice it with you two more times.

338

G Dictation
Listen and write the missing words.

Name _____

1. White clouds are in the blue sky.

2. The sunset is pink.

3. Green leaves turn brown in the fall.

H Proofreading
One word in each pair is misspelled. Fill in the oval by the misspelled word.

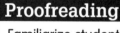

1. ○ pink
   ● grene

2. ● blak
   ○ blue

3. ● yello
   ○ white

4. ○ brown
   ● blu

5. ● penk
   ○ black

6. ● bronw
   ○ green

☆ ● colur
   ○ zero

☆ ○ circle
   ● pirple

☆ ● aranj
   ○ count

241

---

1 Dictation

Reinforce correct spelling by using current and previous words in context.

(Say) Listen as I read each sentence and then write it in your Worktext. (Slowly read each sentence twice. Sentences are found in the Student Worktext to the left.)

 Challenge
Write these incomplete sentences on the board.

Sarah painted ___ ___ ___.

___ ___ likes ___ ___

___ plums.

___ ___ ___ what ___

___ ___?

 (Say) Listen as I read each sentence. Write the sentence on your paper. (Slowly read each sentence twice.)

Sarah painted the ball orange.

My mother likes to eat

 purple plums.

Do you know what color it is?

---

2 Proofreading

Familiarize students with standardized test format and reinforce recognizing misspelled words.

 (Say) Look at each set of words. One word in each set is misspelled. Fill in the oval by the misspelled word. (You may wish to pronounce each set of words to help students correctly identify them.)

3 Hide and Seek

Reinforce correct spelling of current spelling words. (A reproducible master is provided in Appendix A as shown on the inset page to the right.)

Write the words one at a time on a white board.

Have students:

- **Look** at the word.
- **Say** the word out loud.
- **Spell** the word out loud.
- **Hide** (teacher erases word.)
- **Write** the word on paper.
- **Seek** (teacher rewrites word.)
- **Check** spelling. If incorrect, rewrite word correctly.

4 Word Find

Have your students complete this activity to strengthen spelling ability and expand vocabulary.

1 Posttest

Test mastery of the spelling words. Challenge words are starred.

 Say

I will say the word once, use the word in a sentence, then say the word again. Write the word on your paper.

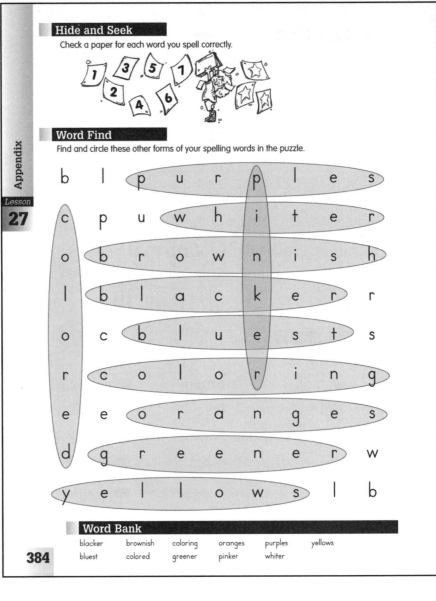

Hide and Seek

Check a paper for each word you spell correctly.

Word Find

Find and circle these other forms of your spelling words in the puzzle.

```
b  l  p  u  r  p  l  e  s
c  p  u  w  h  i  t  e  r
o  b  r  o  w  n  i  s  h
l  b  l  a  c  k  e  r  r
o  c  b  l  u  e  s  t  s
r  c  o  l  o  r  i  n  g
e  e  o  r  a  n  g  e  s
d  g  r  e  e  n  e  r  w
y  e  l  l  o  w  s  l  b
```

Word Bank

blacker	brownish	coloring	oranges	purples	yellows
bluest	colored	greener	pinker	whiter	

384

1. green — The new spring grass was light **green.**
2. white — Look at this tiny **white** flower.
3. blue — The **blue** jay wants some of our supper.
4. brown — The little **brown** striped chipmunk is begging for some crumbs.
5. pink — The sky turns light **pink** as the sun begins to rise in the morning.
6. black — Smoke from the campfire turned the stones around it **black.**
7. yellow — The flames in the campfire dance **yellow** and orange.
☆ color — I'm so glad that everything is not the same **color.**
☆ purple — My sleeping bag is **purple.**
☆ orange — The sunset turns the sky a vivid **orange** and gold.

 Progress Chart

Students may record scores. (Reproducible master in Appendix B.)

 Personal Dictionary

Students may add any words they have misspelled to their personal dictionaries for reference when writing. (Cover in Appendix B.)

340

I Game

Name _____

Daniel had an exciting camping trip with Matthew and his family. Color a campfire next to a tent each time you or your team spells a word correctly from this week's word list.

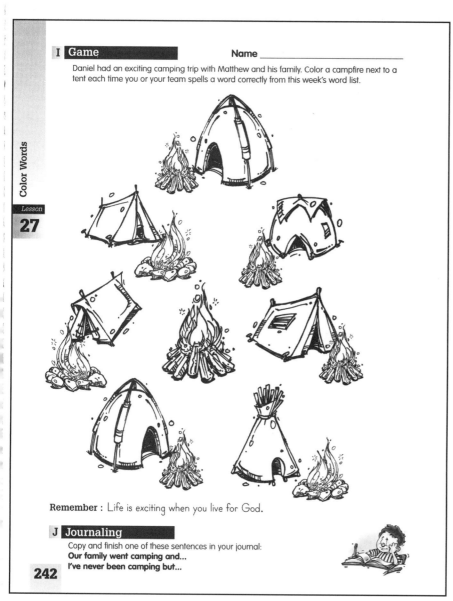

Lesson
27

Remember : Life is exciting when you live for God.

J Journaling

Copy and finish one of these sentences in your journal:
Our family went camping and...
I've never been camping but...

242

2 Game

Reinforce spelling skills and provide motivation and interest.

Materials

- game page (from student text)
- orange crayons (1 per child)
- game word list

Game Word List

Use of challenge words is optional.

1. **blue**
2. **black**
3. **brown**
4. **green**
5. **yellow**
6. **white**
7. **pink**
☆ **orange**
☆ **purple**
☆ **color**

3 Journaling

Provide a meaningful reason for correct spelling through personal writing.

Review the story using discussion leads provided on the following page. Encourage students to apply the Scriptural value in their journaling.

Take a minute to memorize...

Have the class say the memory verses from lessons 26 and 27 with you.

How to Play:

- Divide the class into two teams, and decide which team will go first.
- Have a student from team A go to the board.
- Read the spelling word two times slowly and clearly. (You may also wish to use the word in a sentence. Ex.: "cat — The cat climbed a tree. — cat")
- Have the student write the word on the board.
- If the word is spelled correctly, instruct all the members of team A to color one campfire. (Note: If the word is misspelled, correct the spelling immediately before continuing the game.)
- Alternate between teams A and B as you go down the word list.
- The team with the most campfires colored when you have gone through the game word list twice is the winner.

Non-Competitive Option:

At the end of the game, say: "Class, I am proud of your efforts to spell the words correctly. If you had fun and tried your best, you are all winners!"

Journaling (continued)

 Say

- What does your family enjoy doing on the weekend? (Write comments on the board.)
- Daniel and Matthew had an exciting weekend in this week's story. What did they do? (They went camping with the Schilling family.)
- In your journal, write about what your family likes to do.

Quotables!

*"Spelling correctly is a courtesy to the reader."**

*Scott, Jill E. 1994. Spelling for Readers and Writers. The Reading Teacher, Vol. 48, No. 2, October: 188-190.

Treasure for Mom

Christopher and his sisters learn how to work hard and stick to the job, even when it's difficult.

"Whatcha doing?" Cathy crawled around the corner into Christopher's room, pushing a truck loaded with toy horses in front of her.

"Counting my money," Christopher answered importantly. Dollar bills and coins were spread on the carpet in the middle of his room.

"How much do you have?" Cathy took the horses out of the truck and stood them in a half-circle around Christopher's money like they were looking at it, or getting ready to eat it.

"I don't know yet," Christopher's voice rose. "You keep making me lose track of what I've counted!" He picked up a bill and laid it aside as he counted, "One, . . ."

Kristin came in and plopped down on Christopher's plaid bedspread. "What're you guys doing?"

"I'm TRYING to count my money," Christopher growled as he flung the dollar back into the pile with the others.

"What's wrong with counting your money?" Kristin looked innocent. "Why are you so upset about it?" She flopped over on her stomach on his bed with her knees bent and her feet sticking up in the air.

"Aaargh!!" Christopher squeezed both eyes shut and pressed his hands to his head. "I can't count it when my sisters keep interrupting me," he explained.

"Oh." Kristin reached one hand down and moved a grey mare closer to the coins while Cathy mimicked Christopher's actions and giggled. "Why don't you ask Mom to help you count all this?" Kristin ran her finger through the pile of coins.

"Because I want to buy a surprise present for Mom's birthday. I heard Dad teasing her about being as old as he is on her birthday next month." Christopher frowned and dropped the coins he was trying to count. "I'm mixed up again!" he exclaimed in despair.

"Well, why don't you ask Dad to help when he gets home," Kristin suggested. "Now, what are you going to get for Mom?"

"I don't know . . . something really nice," Christopher thought aloud. "What would she like a lot?"

The three children sat in silence for a moment, then Cathy bounced up on her knees sending her ponytail flying. "I know! She always talks about the canary she had when she was a little girl! Remember? She says it sang and sat on her finger and she called it 'Joy!'"

"A canary is probably a lot of money." Christopher sounded doubtful.

"We'll help, too, won't we, Kristin?" Cathy offered for both of the girls and Kristin nodded enthusiastically as she climbed down off the bed and joined the other two on the floor.

"All right!" Christopher concluded with shining eyes. "We'll ask Dad to count all our money when he gets home to make sure we have enough, okay?"

"Okay," the sisters chorused.

After supper that evening the three children cornered their father and led him to Christopher's room. They excitedly showed him their three piles of money and explained their plan. Dad listened carefully and looked very thoughtful after he counted the money. He rubbed his hand over his hair and studied the eager faces in front of him.

Finally, he spoke slowly. "You have $15.68 here. A canary is quite a bit more than that and it would need a cage and food. You'll get another $12 in allowance between the three of you before Mom's birthday." He looked at the three of them. "How would you get the rest of the money you'd need?"

"I would do some job or something to make some more money," Christopher slumped against the wall in discouragement. "But what could I do?"

Dad didn't answer Christopher's question right away. Instead he asked, "What about you girls? Would you be willing to work for the rest of the money it would take to get Mom a canary for her birthday?"

"Yes, but I don't know what I could do either," Kristin sighed.

"There's got to be something kids can do, isn't there, Dad?" Cathy gazed into Dad's face in earnest.

"I think I can help you with that part." Dad chuckled and playfully tugged Cathy's ponytail. "But you'll have to stick with it, okay? Now let's make some plans. Our next door neighbor, Mr. Peterson, just mentioned to me the other day that he needs some help."

During the next four weeks, Christopher spent quite a few afternoons after school in Mr. Peterson's backyard. A spring storm had brought down a huge old maple tree near the back fence. One thick limb had smashed right through the boards of the wooden fence. Mr. Peterson had already cut up the main part of the tree and replaced the broken boards, but didn't have time to finish the job. Christopher picked up many small branches and twigs scattered all over the rest of the yard. The new part of the back fence also needed to be painted.

"I never knew trees held so much stuff up in the air all the time," he mused as he bent to pick up another armful of small branches. "There must have been a zillion limbs on this one tree! I'm surprised it didn't fall down a long time ago.

343

Story (continued)

I'm sure ready to!"

The day he picked up the very last twig, Christopher never wanted to see another stick and was ready to start painting the new boards. Surely painting would be more fun! And it was, for a while, until he got a blister on the palm of his hand. Dad put medicine on the sore place and lent Christopher some thick gloves for the next day. As the fence was slowly covered with white paint, so was Christopher.

Meanwhile, Kristin was busy across the street feeding the Jefferson's three cats while they were out of town, sweeping Miss Koehn's screened porch and scrubbing out Mr. Thompson's bird bath. Three times a week she held the Thompson's cocker spaniel, Gypsy, still long enough to give her a good brushing, whether she wanted it or not, which she didn't.

"There, you're beautiful again," an exhausted Kristin told the dog one afternoon. Before taking Gypsy back inside, she sat back on her heels and admired the dog's shiny long black hair that she'd worked so hard to untangle. With a "WOOF," the energetic cocker jerked free and bounded happily around the yard, always just out of Kristin's reach. After she found a mud puddle and plunked herself in it, rolled in some leaves and chased a squirrel through some bushes, Gypsy returned to Kristin wagging her stubby tail and looking very proud of herself. With a groan Kristin picked up the brush and started over again.

Cathy spent her afternoons watering Miss Koehn's flower bed, Mr. Jefferson's fruit trees, and Mr. Peterson's vegetable garden. She got so good with the hose that she even watered Christopher!

When Mom's birthday finally arrived, Kristin, Christopher, and Cathy were ready. Dad kept Mom busy in the study while the three children slipped next door. The Petersons had kept the canary at their house after Dad had helped the children pick it out a few days ago. Christopher carried the cage and Kristin carried the canary's food while Cathy opened doors for them. They sneaked into their own house and quietly set up the cage on a little table in the bay window, trying hard not to giggle. They were about to burst with excitement by the time Cathy walked by the study door and gave Dad the signal that they were ready. When Mom entered the room the whole family yelled, "Surprise! Happy Birthday!" Mom stopped and stared at the bay window. She walked over and opened the cage door. The vivid, colorful little bird inside willingly hopped up on her offered finger.

Christopher's grin almost split his face until he noticed that Mom was crying. His grin slipped and he turned to Dad. "It's okay, Son," Dad smiled at the confused look on his son's face. "Sometimes your mom does this. When she's really, really happy, she cries." He shrugged his shoulders and shifted Cory to his other arm. Christopher wasn't sure about that until his mom replaced the canary and whirled around. Before she scooped him along with his sisters into a huge bear hug, he could see that she was smiling and laughing through her tears. Mom had a million questions and the kids all tried to answer at once. Dad stood there grinning while Cory kept clapping his little hands and repeating, "Suppise! Suppise!"

That evening Mom sat on the couch with Cathy in her lap and a twin snuggled up close on each side. Dad held a sleepy Cory against his chest. "I love you all so much." Mom squeezed them all together. "I'm going to name this canary 'Treasure,' and every time he sings it will tell everyone what a wonderful gift of love you've given."

"Mom and I are very proud of you," Dad added. "You've learned something that some people never learn in a lifetime." At their quizzical looks he picked up his Bible with his free hand and placing it on his knee, turned to Proverbs 10:4 and read, "'Lazy men are soon poor; hard workers get rich.'" Dad rubbed Cory's back in little circles and smiled at his other three children. "Not only have you learned how to work and stick with a job even when it's hard, you've learned that the best riches, the ones that make us the happiest, are those we give."

2 Discussion Time

Check understanding of the story and development of personal values.

- Why was Christopher trying to count his money?
- What kinds of jobs did the twins and Cathy do to earn money for the gift?
- Do you think these jobs were easy for the children to stick with? Why or why not?
- When the children presented the canary to their mother, do you think that they felt all their hard work was worth it?
- When you work hard for something, do you appreciate it or value it more?
- How do you feel when you give a gift to someone else?
- Why do you think that the best riches, the ones that make us the happiest, are those we give?

344

A Preview

Write each word as your teacher says it.

Name _____

1. tall

2. long

3. many

4. little

5. short

6. few

7. more

Challenge Words

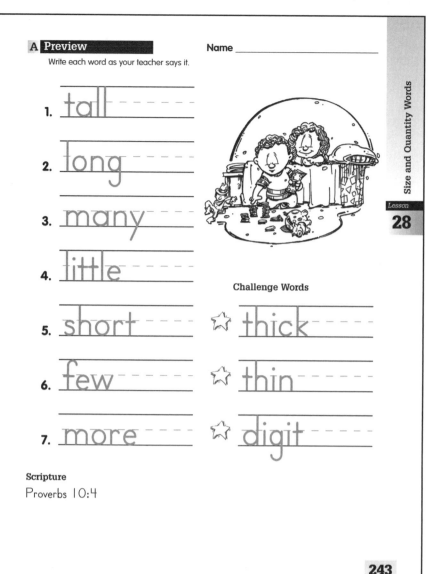

☆ thick

☆ thin

☆ digit

Scripture
Proverbs 10:4

243

Challenge

For better spellers, challenge words may be included in the weekly list. Challenge words are starred.

Correct Immediately!

Say — Let's correct our preview. I will write each word on the board. Put a dot under each letter on your preview as I spell the word out loud. If you spelled a word wrong, rewrite it correctly.

Progress Chart

Students may record scores. (Reproducible master in Appendix B.)

Take a minute to memorize . . .

Read the memory verse twice. Have students practice it with you two more times.

---

3 Preview

Test for knowledge of the correct spellings of these words. (See the instructions at the top right for challenge words.)

 Say — I will say each word once, use the word in a sentence, then say the word again. Write the word on the lines in the Worktext.

1.	tall	The spring storm knocked the **tall** old maple tree down.
2.	long	It took Christopher a **long** time to pick up all the sticks and twigs.
3.	many	The children worked **many** days to earn enough money for the canary.
4.	little	The **little** dog ran away from Kristin.
5.	short	Zacchaeus was a **short** man.
6.	few	It will take a **few** minutes to set up the cage.
7.	more	Would you like **more** applesauce?
☆	thick	Christopher wore **thick** gloves to protect his hands.
☆	thin	The sick man is **thin** and weak.
☆	digit	A **digit** is a single number.

345

4 Word Shapes

Help students form a correct image of whole words.

(Say) Look at each word and think about its shape. Now, write the word in the correct word Shape Boxes. You may check off each word as you use it.

(This lesson contains spelling patterns for the sounds of /ȯ/, /or/, /o/, /ü/, /i/, and /ē/. A few students may continue to have difficulty spelling some of these patterns.

Challenge

Draw the correctly shaped box around each letter in these words.

(Say) On a separate sheet of paper, write other words that contain the spelling patterns in the word list. See how many words you can write.

Be Prepared For Fun

Check these supply lists for **Fun Ways to Spell** presented **Day 2**. Purchase and/or gather these items ahead of time!

General
- Crayons
- Piece of Paper
- Spelling List

Auditory
- Box to Store Letters
- a, e, f, g, h, i, l, l, m, n, o, r, s, t, t, w and y (written on seasonal shapes like flowers or baseballs)
- c, d, i and k (added for challenge words)
- Spelling List

Visual
- Eraser
- Dark Construction Paper
- Spelling List

Tactile
- Finger Paint
- Plastic Plate or Glossy Paper
- Spelling List

B Word Shapes

Write each word in the correct word shape boxes.

Name _____

Size and Quantity Words

Lesson **28**

1. little
2. tall
3. short
4. long
5. few
6. many
7. more

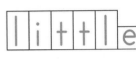

☆ **Challenge**
Draw the correct word shape boxes around each word.

thin　　　thick　　　digit

244

Answers may vary for duplicate word shapes.

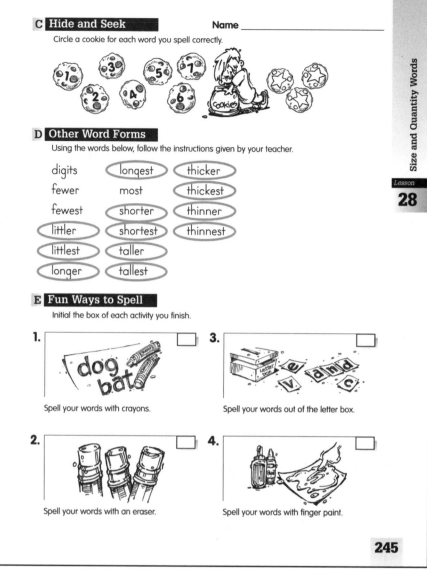

C Hide and Seek

Name _____

Circle a cookie for each word you spell correctly.

D Other Word Forms

Using the words below, follow the instructions given by your teacher.

digits   (longest)   (thicker)

fewer   most   (thickest)

fewest   (shorter)   (thinner)

(littler)   (shortest)   (thinnest)

(littlest)   taller

(longer)   tallest

E Fun Ways to Spell

Initial the box of each activity you finish.

1. Spell your words with crayons.

3. Spell your words out of the letter box.

2. Spell your words with an eraser.

4. Spell your words with finger paint.

245

Reinforce spelling by using multiple styles of learning.

On a white board, Teacher writes each word — one at a time. **Have students:**

- **Look** at the word.
- **Say** the word out loud.
- **Spell** the word out loud.
- **Hide** (teacher erases word.)
- **Write** the word on their paper.
- **Seek** (teacher rewrites word.)
- **Check** spelling. If incorrect, repeat above steps.

2 Other Word Forms

This activity is optional. Have students find and circle the Other Word Forms that describe what something or someone is like.

3 Fun Ways to Spell

Four activities are provided. Use one, two, three, or all of the activities. Have students initial the box for each activity they complete.

Options:

- assign activities to students according to their learning styles
- set up the activities in learning centers for students to do throughout the day
- divide students into four groups and assign one activity per group
- do one activity per day

General

To spell your words with crayons…
- Write each letter of your spelling word in fat, thick letters.
- Check your spelling.

Auditory

To spell your words from the letter box…
- Spell a word from your list by putting the letters in the right order.
- Check your spelling.
- Spell your word out loud.

Visual

To spell your words with an eraser…
- Turn your pencil upside down.
- Use the eraser to write your words on a sheet of dark construction paper.
- Check your spelling.

Tactile

To spell your words with finger paint…
- Smear paint across your plate.
- Use a finger to write a spelling word in paint.
- Check your spelling.
- Smear the word out with your finger and write another word.

347

Word Find

1

Familiarize students with word meaning and usage.

(Say) Read each word in the Word Bank. Say each letter in the word, then look in the puzzle to find that same word. Circle each word you find.

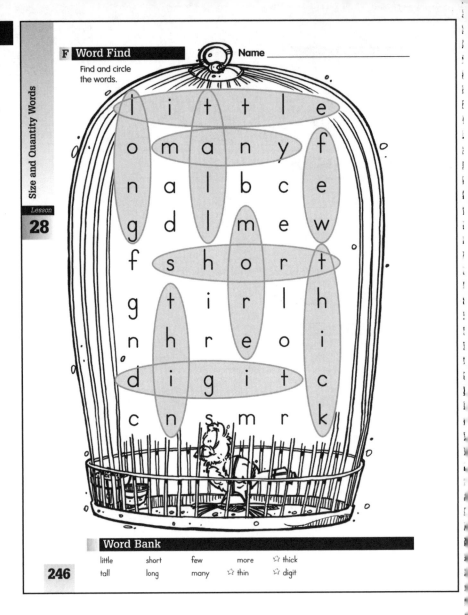

F Word Find

Find and circle the words.

Name _____

Size and Quantity Words

Lesson **28**

```
l  i  t  t  l  e
o  m  a  n  y  f
n  a  l  b  c  e
g  d  l  m  e  w
f  s  h  o  r  t
g  t  i  r  l  h
n  h  r  e  o  i
d  i  g  i  t  c
c  n  s  m  r  k
```

Word Bank

little	short	few	more	☆ thick
tall	long	many	☆ thin	☆ digit

246

Take a minute to memorize...

Read the memory verse twice. Have students practice it with you two more times.

Lesson 28 | **Day 3**

348

G Dictation

Name _____

Listen and write the missing words.

1. A little ant came, then many more.

2. He ran a short time.

3. His long legs make him tall.

H Proofreading

One word in each pair is misspelled. Fill in the oval by the misspelled word.

1. ○ tall
   ● shurt

2. ● liddl
   ○ long

3. ○ more
   ● miny

4. ● fue
   ○ short

5. ○ little
   ● tol

6. ○ many
   ● mor

☆ ● dijit
   ○ orange

☆ ○ color
   ● thik

☆ ○ none
   ● htin

247

2 Proofreading

Familiarize students with standardized test format and reinforce recognizing misspelled words.

 Say

Look at each set of words. One word in each set is misspelled. Fill in the oval by the misspelled word. (You may wish to pronounce each set of words to help students correctly identify them.)

 1 **Dictation**

Reinforce correct spelling by using current and previous words in context.

 Say

Listen as I read each sentence and then write it in your Worktext. (Slowly read each sentence twice. Sentences are found in the Student Worktext to the left.)

☆ **Challenge**

Write these incomplete sentences on the board.

___ ___ ___ bread ___
___ slices.

Tommy ___ ___ ___ ___
___ paint.

___ secret ___ ___ ___ ___ .

Say

Listen as I read each sentence. Write the sentence on your paper. (Slowly read each sentence twice.)

Mom cut the bread in thin slices.

Tommy will stir the thick green paint.

The secret number has one digit.

Day 4 **Lesson 28**

349

3 Hide and Seek

Reinforce correct spelling of current spelling words. (A reproducible master is provided in Appendix A as shown on the inset page to the right.)

Write the words one at a time on a white board.

Have students:

- **Look** at the word.
- **Say** the word out loud.
- **Spell** the word out loud.
- **Hide** (teacher erases word.)
- **Write** the word on paper.
- **Seek** (teacher rewrites word.)
- **Check** spelling. If incorrect, rewrite word correctly.

4 Making Words

Have your students complete this activity to strengthen spelling ability and expand vocabulary.

1 Posttest

Test mastery of the spelling words. Challenge words are starred.

Say I will say the word once, use the word in a sentence, then say the word again. Write the word on your paper.

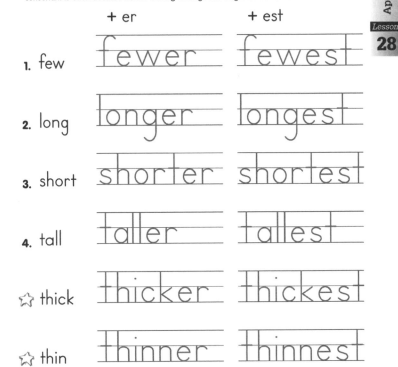

Hide and Seek
Check a paper for each word you spell correctly.

Making Words
Add the endings to the spelling words. Write the new word on the line.
Don't forget, when a word ends with a single consonant with a vowel right before it, the final consonant is often doubled before adding endings that begin with a vowel.

		+ er	+ est
1.	few	fewer	fewest
2.	long	longer	longest
3.	short	shorter	shortest
4.	tall	taller	tallest
☆	thick	thicker	thickest
☆	thin	thinner	thinnest

385

1.	long	The dog had **long** black hair.
2.	many	There are **many** limbs and twigs in a tree.
3.	little	The **little** canary hopped onto Mother's finger.
4.	short	This is a **short** piece of hose.
5.	more	It is **more** fun to give than to get.
6.	tall	That is a very **tall** building.
7.	few	Dad had a **few** ideas of jobs the children could do.
☆	digit	Another name for your finger is **digit**.
☆	thick	A **thick** coat of paint will cover the wooden fence.
☆	thin	Cathy aimed a **thin** stream of water at the flower bed.

Progress Chart
Students may record scores. (Reproducible master in Appendix B.)

Personal Dictionary
Students may add any words they have misspelled to their personal dictionaries for reference when writing. (Cover in Appendix B.)

350

I Game

Name _____

Place a game piece over each word your teacher says and spells. When you get five game pieces in a row, raise your hand and say, "Spelling is fun!"

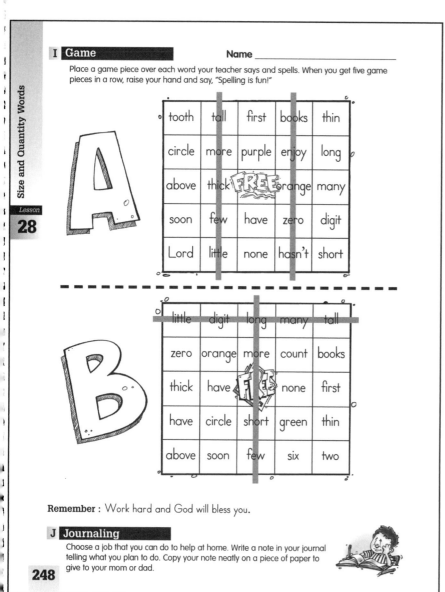

tooth	tall	first	books	thin
circle	more	purple	enjoy	long
above	thick	FREE	orange	many
soon	few	have	zero	digit
Lord	little	none	hasn't	short

little	digit	long	many	tall
zero	orange	more	count	books
thick	have	FREE	none	first
have	circle	short	green	thin
above	soon	few	six	two

Remember : Work hard and God will bless you.

J Journaling

Choose a job that you can do to help at home. Write a note in your journal telling what you plan to do. Copy your note neatly on a piece of paper to give to your mom or dad.

248

How to Play:

- Fold the word cards (see **Materials**) in half, and place them in a container.
- Ask your students to fold the game page in half along the dotted line.
- Have half the class use game card A, and the other half card B.
- Instructions for the students: "Cover the word **FREE** in the center of your card. (pause) I will draw a word from the container, read it aloud, then I will spell it. When you find that word on your card, put a game piece over it. When you have five game pieces in a row (up and down, across or diagonally), raise your hand and say 'Spelling is FUN!'"
- Play as many times as you like. (As you return the word cards to the container and mix them up, remind the students to clear their game cards.)
- For variety, after playing several games, have the students turn their papers over and use the other game card.

2 Game

Reinforce spelling skills and provide motivation and interest.

Materials

- game page (from student text)
- flat buttons, dry beans, pennies, or game discs (10 per child)
- game word list
- word cards (each word from the game word list written on a card)

Game Word List

This list contains regular and challenge words.

1. **little**
2. **thin**
3. **tall**
4. **thick**
5. **short**
6. **digit**
7. **long**
☆ **few**
☆ **many**
☆ **more**

3 Journaling

Provide a meaningful reason for correct spelling through personal writing.

Review the story using discussion leads provided on the following page. Encourage students to apply the Scriptural value in their journaling.

 Take a minute to memorize...

Read the memory verse to the class twice. Have the class practice it with you two more times.

Journaling (continued)

Say

- Christopher and his sisters worked very hard to earn enough money to get a special birthday present for their mother. They found out that it isn't easy to stick with a difficult job. Have you done a difficult job that was hard to keep at and finish?

- What kind of job was it?

- Why do you think Dad said that the best riches, the ones that make us the happiest, are those we give away? (Because working hard and giving to others makes a person feel really good inside. Giving helps us become less selfish.)

- Think of a job you can do to help at home. (For example: Setting the table, feeding the pet, making your bed every day if you're not already doing so, putting away clothes, watering plants, etc.)

- Write a note telling what job you plan to do. Write the first draft in your journal. Write an edited version on a piece of paper and take it home with you to give to your mom or dad.

Quotables!

> *"Capitalize on students' strengths, encourage risk taking, and celebrate progress!"* *

*Scott, Jill E. 1994. Spelling for Readers and Writers. The Reading Teacher, Vol. 48, No. 2, October: 188-190.

352

Successful Symphony

Tommy deals with disappointment and learns the value of teamwork.

*I*t was a fine day in May and everyone in the Rawson family was busy. Lisa was creating a masterpiece in chalk on the sidewalk. Dad was leaning over the lawn mower checking the oil and getting it ready to cut the grass. Tommy could hear the hum of the vacuum cleaner Mom was using on the living room carpet. And Tommy, well, he was very busy feeling sorry for himself. He sat on the back steps, chin in hand, gazing into the yard.

"Tommy," Dad lifted his head to call. "Come here, please." When Tommy reluctantly arrived by the mower Dad continued. "Please go get my wrench set out of the big red toolbox, son. If it's not there, check my workbench."

Tommy ambled off without a reply and returned in a minute or two with the wrenches Dad needed. As he approached, Dad stood up wiping his hands on an old rag and studied Tommy's face. "You look like you've lost your last friend, Tommy. What's up? Want to tell me about it?"

Tommy bent over and picked a long blade of grass. He concentrated on pulling it apart straight down the middle as he muttered, "We're having a special program to end the school year."

"Hey, that sounds great!" Dad exclaimed. Dad didn't seem to get the point, so Tommy continued.

"I don't have any special part at all. I never got a special part in any play or program we did all year." He glanced up as he finished and saw that Dad looked much more serious.

"That bothers you," Dad stated. Tommy nodded and hung his head. "Take a look at this lawn mower, Tommy," Dad requested. Tommy jerked his head up in surprise.

"What does the lawn mower have to do with the program? Dad must be trying to get me to just think about something else and forget all about the end-of-the-year program," Tommy thought. *"I guess I'll just go along with him and listen,"* he decided.

"Now, Son, these are the spark plugs." Dad gave Tommy a quick lesson on lawn mower parts and then slammed the hood down over the riding mower's engine. He brushed his hands off and turned to Tommy. "Can you see the spark plugs now, Tommy?" When Tommy shook his head, Dad questioned, "What about the carburetor?" Tommy was getting dizzy from shaking his head back and forth. Dad put his hand on Tommy's shoulder and bent down so he could look his son straight in the eye. "What do you think would happen if I tried to start this mower and mow the grass without the spark plugs? Or the battery? Would it work?" Tommy shook his head again. "Son, every part of this lawn mower is very important, even if we can't see the part. Every person who helps in a program at school is very important, whether they have a special part or not. Without each one of you children doing your part to the best of your ability, the program wouldn't be the same." Dad stood up and handed the wrench set to Tommy. "Will you put this back in the tool box for me? Thanks for your help, Son."

As Dad began mowing the frontyard, Tommy wandered back to the swing set in the backyard. He sat in a swing and swayed slowly back and forth. Out of the corner of his eye he saw something move in the grass.

Tommy got down on his knees to investigate. There, winding along through the grass, was a little path covered with big black ants. One ant was carrying a large piece of something. Hundreds more crawled along on ant business. Tommy crawled beside the trail to see where it went. He crawled under the legs of the swing set, around the base of the large oak tree and along the edge of the storage building. Then he had to follow the trail on foot as it wound through the fence and out into the pasture. Finally, in some tall grass he spotted the anthill, alive with busy black ants.

Tommy returned to the yard and plopped down under the oak tree. He picked up a twig and laid it across the ant highway to see what the ants would do. They marched over it. He placed a rock on the trail, making sure he didn't smash any traveling ant underneath it. They walked around it. He dug a trench through their trail. They traipsed through it. Tommy lay on his stomach with his elbows bent, head resting on hands and watched the traffic go by.

A memory tickled his brain. At school, Miss Grant had taught the children that all of the Scriptures they had practiced writing that year had been written by two people: either King David, or his son, King Solomon. The program the children were preparing to present was about these men. David had been a shepherd and then a mighty warrior. Solomon was known as one of the wisest men who had ever lived. And, Tommy remembered, Miss Grant had said something about Solomon and the ants.

The back door slammed and Mom came out in the yard. She held a throw rug out and shook it in the breeze. Dust drifted and settled over Tommy where he lay on the grass. "Mom!" Tommy called.

"E-e-e-e!" Mom shrieked and jumped back. "Oh, Tommy, you scared me! I didn't see you there! What on earth are you doing down there on the ground?" Mom put her hand over her heart and walked

353

Review 29 | **Day 1**

over to Tommy's shady spot under the oak tree.

"Mom, look at these awesome ants!" Tommy invited.

Mrs. Rawson crouched by her son to look at the ant trail. "They surely are busy," she commented. "It's wonderful that they all work together so well to make their colony a success." As she stood, she looked a little worried. "Their anthill isn't in the yard, is it?"

"It's out there," Tommy waved one hand toward the pasture. Mom smiled and returned to her rug.

"Working together. Every part important." The thoughts repeated themselves in Tommy's head over and over. *"Working together to make a success. Every part important, whether a special part or not."*

"Hey, Terrible Tommy, where are you?" Lisa's call came from the front yard. "Tommy, come play with me!" she yelled again. Tommy jumped up and trotted around the house to the driveway.

"Hey, Loud Lisa, here I am!" He dodged as Lisa threw her chalk his way.

The night after the end-of-the-year program Tommy snuggled down in his bed as his mom rubbed his back just the way he liked. Dad surprised them both when he came in carrying a big book that Tommy recognized as the dictionary. Mom looked up with a question on her face as Dad sat on the edge of Tommy's bed and opened the huge book. "This book says that 'symphony' means something that has a lot of parts that all work together in harmony or sound good together. That is just how your program was, Tommy. Everyone in your class did their part, whether big or little, and the whole program was beautiful." Dad smiled down at his son. He plunked the big dictionary down and tickled Tommy's foot before giving him a hug and a goodnight kiss. "I'm

very proud of you, son, for doing your part so willingly and so well."

As Tommy drifted into dreams, he remembered standing with his classmates and singing, "Only a boy named David . . ." He remembered repeating with the others, "Make a joyful symphony before the Lord, the King!" In his dreams Tommy felt the warmth of his heavenly Father's loving smile.

2 Discussion Time

Check understanding of the story and development of personal values.

- How did Dad know that Tommy was feeling upset about something?
- What was bothering Tommy?
- How did Dad use the mower to explain to Tommy that everyone in the program was important?
- What did Tommy learn from the ants?
- What is a symphony?
- How did Tommy help to make his class program a symphony?
- Do you think God is happy when we choose to do our best, even in little things that others might not notice, like Tommy did?
- Is it important to work together? Is it important to work together even if you don't get to be the leader?

A | Test-Words

Write each word as your teacher says it.

Name _____

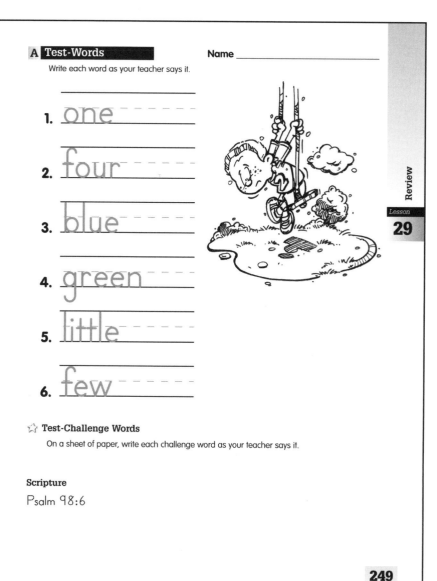

1. one

2. four

3. blue

4. green

5. little

6. few

☆ **Test-Challenge Words**

On a sheet of paper, write each challenge word as your teacher says it.

Scripture

Psalm 98:6

249

Test-Challenge Words

On a separate sheet of paper, challenge words may be tested using the sentences below.

Personal Dictionary

After the tests in the review unit are graded, students may add any words they have misspelled to their personal dictionaries.

Take a minute to memorize...

Read the memory verse to the class twice. Have the class practice it with you two more times.

---

3 Test-Words

Test for knowledge of the correct spellings of these words.
(See the instructions at the top right for challenge words.)

 I will say each word once, use the word in a sentence, then say the word again. Write the word on the lines in your Worktext.

1. one   Which **one** of the kittens would you choose?
2. four   There are **four** long–haired kittens in the box.
3. blue   Clouds float through the **blue** sky.
4. green   Dad needed to mow the tall, **green** grass.
5. little   The **little** ants scurried about their business.
6. few   There are a **few** ants climbing on this twig.
☆ zero   Tommy's class counts from **zero** to one hundred.
☆ orange   Dad's wrench was in an **orange** pouch.
☆ thin   The blade of grass was long and **thin**.

355

Game

1

Materials
- game page (from student text)
- pencils or crayons (1 per child)
- game word list

Game Word List
Use of challenge words is optional.

1. **one**
2. **four**
3. **blue**
4. **green**
5. **little**
6. **few**
☆ **zero**
☆ **orange**
☆ **thin**

B Game   Name _____

In the story from lesson 29, as Tommy watched the ants make their way across the backyard, he understood what his dad had meant. He could make a joyful symphony to the Lord no matter how small his part in the school program. Circle one ant for each review word you or your team spells correctly.

250

How to Play:

- Divide the class into two teams, and decide which team will go first.
- Have a student from team A go to the board.
- Read the spelling word two times slowly and clearly. (You may also wish to use the word in a sentence. Ex.: "cat — The cat climbed a tree. — cat")
- Have the student write the word on the board.
- If the word is spelled correctly, instruct all the members of team A to circle one ant on the trail to the ant hill. (Note: If the word is misspelled, correct the spelling immediately before continuing the game.)
- Alternate between teams A and B as you go down the word list.
- The team with the most ants circled when you have gone through the game word list twice is the winner.

Non-Competitive Option:
At the end of the game, say: "Class, I am proud of your efforts to spell the words correctly. If you had fun and tried your best, you are all winners!"

356

C Test-Sentences

Name _____

The underlined word in each sentence is misspelled. Write the sentences on the lines below, spelling each underlined word correctly.

I like the <u>wite</u> kitten.

1. I like the white kitten.

Tommy was <u>siks</u> years old.

2. Tommy was six years old.

D Test-Proofreading

One word in each pair is misspelled. Fill in the oval by the misspelled word.

1. ● hsort
   ○ three

4. ● bron
   ○ short

2. ● mor
   ○ seven

5. ● pinc
   ○ long

3. ○ brown
   ● thre

6. ○ more
   ● sevn

☆ **Test-Challenge Words**

On a sheet of paper, write each challenge word as your teacher says it.

251

1 Test-Sentences

Reinforce recognizing misspelled words.

 Say — Read each sentence carefully. The underlined word in each sentence is misspelled. Write the sentences on the lines in your worktext, spelling each underlined word correctly.

2 Test-Proofreading

Familiarize students with standardized test format and reinforce recognition of misspelled words.

 Say — Look at each set of words. One word in each set is misspelled. Fill in the oval by the misspelled word.

(You may wish to pronounce each pair of words to help students correctly identify them.)

Test-Challenge Words

 On a separate sheet of paper, challenge words may be tested using the sentences below.

 Say — I will say the word once, use the word in a sentence, then say the word again. Write the word on your paper.

☆ count — Tommy could not **count** all the ants on the anthill.
☆ purple — There are **purple** flowers in the pasture.
☆ thick — Tommy's dad mowed the **thick** grass.

Game

Materials
- game page (from student text)
- flat buttons, dry beans, pennies, or game discs (1 per child)
- game word list

Game Word List
Use of challenge words is optional.

1. six
2. white
3. three
4. seven
5. brown
6. pink
7. short
8. long
9. more
☆ count
☆ purple
☆ thick

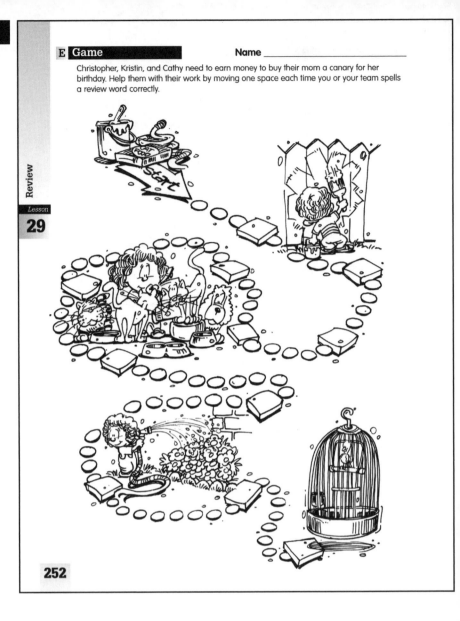

E **Game**   Name _____

Christopher, Kristin, and Cathy need to earn money to buy their mom a canary for her birthday. Help them with their work by moving one space each time you or your team spells a review word correctly.

Review
Lesson
29

252

How to Play:

- Divide the class into two teams, and decide which team will go first.
- Have each student place his/her game piece on Start.
- Have a student from team A go to the board.
- Read the spelling word two times slowly and clearly. (You may also wish to use the word in a sentence. Ex.: "cat — The cat climbed a tree. — cat")
- Have the student write the word on the board.
- If the word is spelled correctly, instruct all the members of team A to move forward one space on the game board. (Note: If the word is misspelled, correct the spelling immediately before continuing the game.)
- Alternate between teams A and B as you go down the word list.
- The team to reach the canary in the cage first is the winner.

Non-Competitive Option:

At the end of the game, say: "Class, I am proud of your efforts to spell the words correctly. If you had fun and tried your best, you are all winners!"

358

F **Test-Sentence**

Name _____

The underlined word in this sentence is misspelled. Write the sentence on the lines below, spelling the underlined word correctly.

The ants crawled in a <u>lawng</u> line.

The ants crawled in a

long line.

G **Test-Words**

Write each word as your teacher says it.

1. two
2. five
3. black
4. yellow

5. tall
6. many

☆ **Test-Challenge Words**

On a sheet of paper, write each challenge word as your teacher says it.

253

---

1 **Test-Sentence**

Reinforce recognizing misspelled words.

(Say) Read this sentence carefully. The underlined word is misspelled. Write the sentence on the lines in your Worktext, spelling the underlined word correctly.

Personal Dictionary

Remind students to add any words they have misspelled to their personal dictionaries.

2 **Test-Words**

Test for knowledge of the correct spellings of these words. (Challenge words may be tested on a separate piece of paper. Challenge words are starred.)

(Say) I will say each word once, use the word in a sentence, then say the word again. Write the word on the lines in your Worktext.

1. two — There are **two** days before the program.
2. five — There are **five** houses on this street.
3. black — The big **black** ants crawled along their path.
4. yellow — A **yellow** dandelion must seem huge to an ant.
5. tall — How **tall** are you?
6. many — The **many** children working together made a nice program.
☆ number — There were a **number** of small parts in the program.
☆ color — What **color** was Tommy's dad's tool box?
☆ digit — What is the first **digit** in the number one hundred?

359

3 Writing Assessment

Assess student's spelling, grammar, and composition skills through personal writing.

Say • A symphony is something with a lot of parts that all work together in harmony and sound good together. Dad helped Tommy understand that each person's part is important by showing him that each part of the lawn mower had to work or the mower wouldn't mow. Can you think of other things that have lots of parts that all must work together? (Airplane, watch/clock, computer, car, etc.)

• What are some things that people have to work together to get done? (Choir, programs, games, sailing ships, etc.)

• What would happen if the captain of a football team tried to play the game all by himself?

• Think of a time when you worked with a group to do something important. Write about it in your worktext.

H Writing Assessment   Name _____

Write about a time when you worked with a group to do something important.

Review
Lesson
29

_____

- - - - - - - - - - - - - - - - - - -

_____

- - - - - - - - - - - - - - - - - - -

_____

- - - - - - - - - - - - - - - - - - -

_____

- - - - - - - - - - - - - - - - - - -

_____

Remember : Even little things done for God become great.

254

A rubric for scoring is provided in Appendix B.

4 Action Game

Reinforce spelling skills and provide motivation and interest.

Materials

• audio player with music

How to Play:

Choose two students to hold up their hands to form a bridge. Have all other students line up to march under the bridge. Have the students march to the music. Instruct the students forming the bridge that they are to lower the bridge over a student when the music stops. Have that student spell a word from this review unit. If he misspells the word, have him continue marching; if he spells the word correctly, have him take the place of one of the students forming the bridge. If either one of the students forming the bridge has not been replaced in three turns, have him march and replace him with a student who has spelled a word correctly at some point during the game. Continue playing until every student has spelled a word correctly. Note: Having some students who have correctly spelled a word or words return to their desks toward the end of the game will ensure that each of the remaining students has an opportunity to get "caught" by the lowered bridge.

360

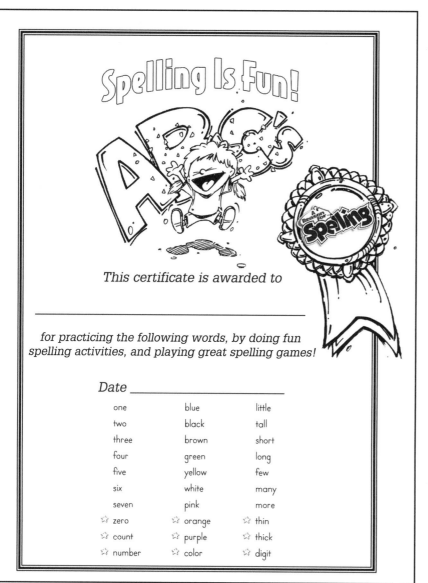

Spelling Is Fun!

This certificate is awarded to

_____

for practicing the following words, by doing fun spelling activities, and playing great spelling games!

Date _____

one	blue	little
two	black	tall
three	brown	short
four	green	long
five	yellow	few
six	white	many
seven	pink	more
☆ zero	☆ orange	☆ thin
☆ count	☆ purple	☆ thick
☆ number	☆ color	☆ digit

5 Certificate

Provide an opportunity for parents or guardians to encourage and assess their child's progress.

 Say

- Write your name on the first line.
- Now I will write the date on the board for you to copy on the next line.
- Follow along as I read the certificate out loud.
- Be sure to show your parents or guardian all the words you've practiced spelling.

 Take a minute to memorize...

Have the class say the memory verses from lessons 26, 27, 28, and 29 with you.

Quotables!

"Spelling consciousness — not expert spelling — is more closely tied to success."*

*Gentry, J. Richard. 1997. My Kid Can't Spell. Portsmouth, NH: Heinemann Educational Books.

PLEASE
PHOTOCOPY!*

The following pages contain Black Line Masters for use with the *A Reason For Spelling*® Student Worktext.

*Photocopy privileges extend only to the material in this section, and permission is granted only for those classrooms or homeschools using *A Reason For Spelling*® Student Worktexts. Any other use of this material is expressly forbidden and all copyright laws apply.

Hide and Seek

Check a paper for each word you spell correctly.

Making Words

Add the endings to the spelling words. Write the new word on the line.

1. can + s

☆ thank + s

2. dad + s

☆ add + ed

3. cat + s

☆ ask + ed

☆ ask + s

☆ thank + ed

363

Hide and Seek

Check a paper for each word you spell correctly.

Code

A picture code uses symbols to stand for letters. Use the picture code to write the missing letters. Read the other forms of your spelling words in the blanks.

b   d   g   l   n   s   t

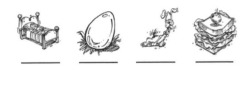

1. __ e __ __

2. __ e __ __ i __ __

3. __ e __ __

4. __ e __ __ i __ __

364

Hide and Seek

Check a paper for each word you spell correctly.

Word Find

Find and circle these other forms of your spelling words in the puzzle.

f r o g s o r f g

b o x e d x s o b

o m o t h e r m o

k g e t t o f o x

b o x i n g o d e

o m r n d g b d x

x o t g o t t e n

e h e r g b x s o

s o d d s g o t m

Word Bank

| boxed | boxing | frogs | getting | mother | odds |
| boxes | dogs | get | gotten | oddest | |

Hide and Seek

Check a paper for each word you spell correctly.

Scrambled Words

Unscramble the letters to make a word. Write the word on the lines.

1. dehi ___ ___ ___ ___

2. gids ___ ___ ___ ___

3. rigbeg ___ ___ ___ ___ ___ ___

4. dikidgn ___ ___ ___ ___ ___ ___ ___

5. gibsteg ___ ___ ___ ___ ___ ___ ___

6. stingit ___ ___ ___ ___ ___ ___ ___

Word Bank

bigger	digs	kidding
biggest	hide	sitting

Hide and Seek

Check a paper for each word you spell correctly.

Making Words

Add the endings to the spelling words. Write the new word on the line.

1. hug + s
_____

2. bug + s
_____

3. cup + s
_____

4. sum + s
_____

5. hug + g + ed
_____

6. bug + g + ed
_____

☆ cup + p + ed
_____

☆ sum + m + ed
_____

367

Hide and Seek

Check a paper for each word you spell correctly.

Code

A picture code uses symbols to stand for letters. Use the picture code to write the missing letters. Read the other forms of your spelling words in the blanks.

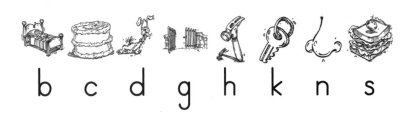

b   c   d   g   h   k   n   s

1. __ a __ __ __

2. __ a __ __ e __

3. __ a __ __ i __ __

Hide and Seek

Check a paper for each word you spell correctly.

Word Find

Find and circle these other forms of your spelling words in the puzzle.

f i n i s h h i n g
i f i n i s h e s
w i l l i n g w b
n n l i w h i i e
w i n n i n g n h
i s w o n a g n e
s h i i s n n e w
b e g a n l l r i
h d w f w i l n f

Word Bank

began	finishes	he	winner	wins
finished	finishing	willing	winning	won

Hide and Seek

Check a paper for each word you spell correctly.

Scrambled Words

Unscramble the letters to make a word. Write the word on the lines.

1. fslal

   ___ ___ ___ ___ ___

2. lalbs

   ___ ___ ___ ___ ___

3. rewaly

   ___ ___ ___ ___ ___ ___

4. kinglat

   ___ ___ ___ ___ ___ ___ ___

5. ringdaw

   ___ ___ ___ ___ ___ ___ ___

6. clingal

   ___ ___ ___ ___ ___ ___ ___

Word Bank

| balls | drawing | lawyer |
| calling | falls | talking |

370

Hide and Seek

Check a paper for each word you spell correctly.

Code

A picture code uses symbols to stand for letters. Use the picture code to write the missing letters. Read the other forms of your spelling words in the blanks.

a e g i n s t w

1. — — —   2. — — — —

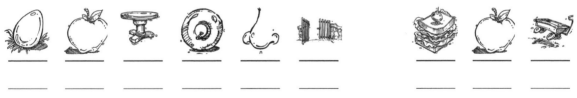

3. — — — — — —   4. — — —

5. — — — —   6. — — — — — —

Hide and Seek

Check a paper for each word you spell correctly.

Making Words

Add the endings to the spelling words. Write the new word on the line. Don't forget, when a word ends with a single consonant with a vowel right before it, the final consonant is often doubled before adding endings that begin with a vowel.

1. stop + s

+ ed

1. hop + s

+ ed

1. top + s

+ ed

☆ drop + s

+ ed

372

Hide and Seek

Check a paper for each word you spell correctly.

Word Find

Find and circle these other forms of your spelling words in the puzzle.

p l a y i n g t p
l p r a y e r a l
a r y p s t a k a
y a o t n a d m g
e y a o g k i i r
d s c o m i n g a
i m a k i n g h d
c o m e s g d t e
g r a d e d a y s

Word Bank

| comes | days | grades | making | played | prayer | taking |
| coming | graded | grading | might | playing | prays | took |

Hide and Seek

Check a paper for each word you spell correctly.

Scrambled Words

Unscramble the letters to make a word. Write the word on the lines.

1. medit

___ ___ ___ ___ ___

2. sdrei

___ ___ ___ ___ ___

3. sinel

___ ___ ___ ___ ___

4. dindeh

___ ___ ___ ___ ___ ___

5. redkin

___ ___ ___ ___ ___ ___

6. sitrew

___ ___ ___ ___ ___ ___

Word Bank

hidden	lines	timed
kinder	rides	writes

Hide and Seek

Check a paper for each word you spell correctly.

Code

A picture code uses symbols to stand for letters. Use the picture code to write the missing letters. Read the other forms of your spelling words in the blanks.

e   g   i   k   n   o   r   s   t   w   y

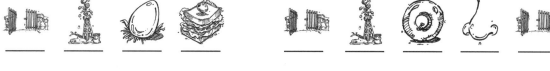

1. __ __ __ __ __ __ __ __ __ __ __ __

2. __ __ __ __ __ __ __ __ __ __ __ __

3. __ __ __ __ __ __ __ __ __ __ __ __

4. __ __ __ __ __ __ __ __ __ __ __ __

375

Hide and Seek

Check a paper for each word you spell correctly.

Word Find

Find and circle these other forms of your spelling words in the puzzle.

p e n c i l i n g

v e p e v p e e n

e p e n s e s p e

s e n t e n c e s

e n c e n n e n e

n h i s d i n c n

d e l e i e t i t

s n e v n s s l e

e s d e g e v s s

Word Bank

cents	penciled	pencils	sending	sent
hens	penciling	pennies	sends	sentences

376

Hide and Seek

Check a paper for each word you spell correctly.

Scrambled Words

Unscramble the letters to make a word. Write the word on the lines.

1. hiter _ _ _ _ _

2. ginsth _ _ _ _ _ _

3. skinth _ _ _ _ _ _

4. stiehr _ _ _ _ _ _

5. kertinh _ _ _ _ _ _ _

6. ottghhu _ _ _ _ _ _ _

Word Bank

their	things	thinks
theirs	thinker	thought

Hide and Seek

Check a paper for each word you spell correctly.

Making Words

Add the endings to the spelling words. Write the new word on the line.

1. our + s

_____

_____

_____

2. town + s

_____

_____

_____

3. out + ing

_____

_____

_____

☆ vowel + s

_____

_____

_____

☆ round + s

_____

_____

_____

☆ round + er

_____

_____

_____

☆ round + ing

_____

_____

_____

☆ round + ed

_____

_____

_____

378

Hide and Seek

Check a paper for each word you spell correctly.

Making Words

Add the endings to the spelling words. Write the new word on the line.

1. put + s   + t + ing

_____   _____

_____   _____

2. school + s   + ing

_____   _____

_____   _____

3. look + s   + ing

_____   _____

_____   _____

4. do + e + s   + ing

_____   _____

_____   _____

☆ tooth − oo + ee

_____

_____

_____

Hide and Seek

Check a paper for each word you spell correctly.

Code

A picture code uses symbols to stand for letters. Use the picture code to write the missing letters. Read the other forms of your spelling words in the blanks.

e d f g i j l n o s u v y

1. ___ ___ ___ ___ ___ ___ ___

2. ___ ___ ___ ___ ___ ___ ___ ___

3. ___ ___ ___ ___   4. ___ ___ ___ ___ ___ ___

380

Hide and Seek

Check a paper for each word you spell correctly.

Word Find

Find and circle these other forms of your spelling words in the puzzle.

```
t  h  a  p  p  i  l  y  h
h  a  p  p  i  n  e  s  s
o  p  a  h  y  r  e  h  a
s  p  h  a  v  i  n  g  y
e  i  n  s  p  p  i  l  r
h  e  h  a  p  p  i  e  r
a  s  a  y  i  n  g  s  c
p  t  v  s  h  i  h  a  d
t  w  e  r  e  g  r  e  w
```

Word Bank

happier	happily	had	having	saying	those
happiest	happiness	have	say	says	were

Hide and Seek

Check a paper for each word you spell correctly.

Scrambled Words

Unscramble the letters to make a word. Write the word on the lines.

1. lirgs — — — — —

2. soyur — — — — —

3. slirecc — — — — — — —

4. ricclde — — — — — — —

5. rsothem — — — — — — —

6. foyrelsu — — — — — — — —

Word Bank

circled	girls	yours
circles	mothers	yourself

Hide and Seek

Check a paper for each word you spell correctly.

Code

A picture code uses symbols to stand for letters. Use the picture code to write the missing letters. Read the other forms of your spelling words in the blanks.

c d e g h i k n o s t u

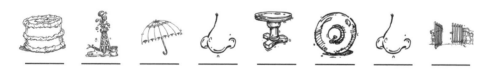

1. __ __ __ __ __ __ __

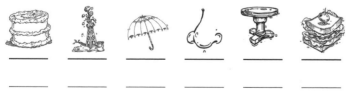

2. __ __ __ __ __ __ __ __ __

3. __ __ __ __ __ __

Hide and Seek

Check a paper for each word you spell correctly.

Word Find

Find and circle these other forms of your spelling words in the puzzle.

```
b  l  p  u  r  p  l  e  s
c  p  u  w  h  i  t  e  r
o  b  r  o  w  n  i  s  h
l  b  l  a  c  k  e  r  r
o  c  b  l  u  e  s  t  s
r  c  o  l  o  r  i  n  g
e  e  o  r  a  n  g  e  s
d  g  r  e  e  n  e  r  w
y  e  l  l  o  w  s  l  b
```

Word Bank

blacker	brownish	coloring	oranges	purples	yellows
bluest	colored	greener	pinker	whiter	

Hide and Seek

Check a paper for each word you spell correctly.

Making Words

Add the endings to the spelling words. Write the new word on the line. Don't forget, when a word ends with a single consonant with a vowel right before it, the final consonant is often doubled before adding endings that begin with a vowel.

	+ er	+ est
1. few		
2. long		
3. short		
4. tall		
☆ thick		
☆ thin		

PLEASE PHOTOCOPY!*

The following pages contain Black Line Masters for use with the *A Reason For Spelling®* Student Worktext.

*Photocopy privileges extend only to the material in this section, and permission is granted only for those classrooms or homeschools using *A Reason For Spelling®* Student Worktexts. Any other use of this material is expressly forbidden and all copyright laws apply.

The Months of the Year

January lies white and bare.
February breathes crispy air.
March winds chase away the snow
So April's first shy flowers can grow.
May opens blossoms on the trees.
June stirs summer's gentle breeze.
July ripens melons, peaches.
August calls with sandy beaches.
September smells of apple pies.
October, pumpkin, corn, and spice.
November's prayers of thanks we lift.
December celebrates God's gift
Of Jesus — to a world God knew
Would need His love the whole year through!

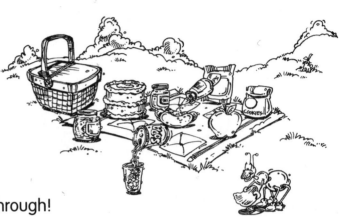

Look at the picnic items on your page. Write the beginning letter for each month on the line, remembering to use capital letters.

Now, color each picnic item, cut it out, and paste it on another sheet of paper to complete the picture.

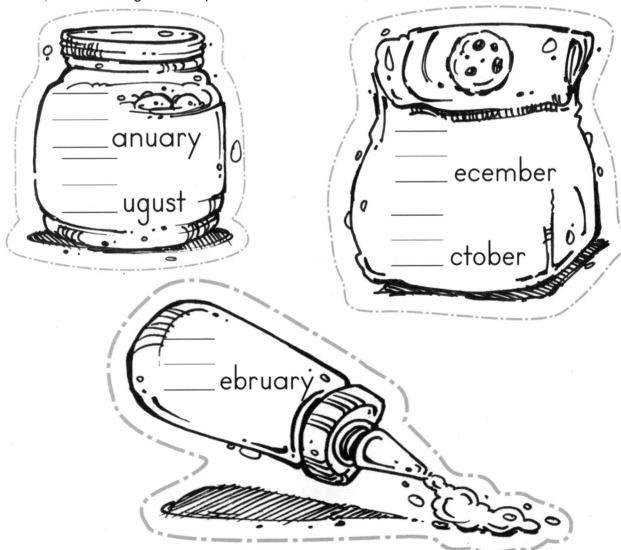

_____ anuary

_____ ugust

_____ ecember

_____ ctober

_____ ebruary

388

Name _____

____eptember

____uly

____pril

____ay

____ovember

____arch

____une

Spelling Progress Chart

Fill in the four lesson numbers for the unit in the first row of blocks. Use the first half of the column under each block to record the score for the Preview, and the second half of the column for the Posttest. To record the score, begin at the bottom of the column and color the blanks to show the number of words spelled correctly. Use one color for Preview and another for Posttest.

Lesson Numbers							
Preview	Posttest	Preview	Posttest	Preview	Posttest	Preview	Posttest
☆							
☆							
☆							
7.							
6.							
5.							
4.							
3.							
2.							
1.							

Words Spelled Correctly

Rubric for Scoring

You may wish to use this rubric at the end of each unit to track student progress.

	Standard	Usually	Sometimes	Not Yet
1.	Writes all letters correctly and legibly (upper and lower case)			
2.	Uses correct spelling on words from current and previous lessons			
3.	Invented spellings are phonetically correct			
4.	Writes in response to a prompt			
5.	Uses appropriate end punctuation			
6.	Uses capital letters correctly			
7.	Includes some descriptive language			
8.	Uses simple sentence structure			
9.	Uses a logical sequence of events			

391

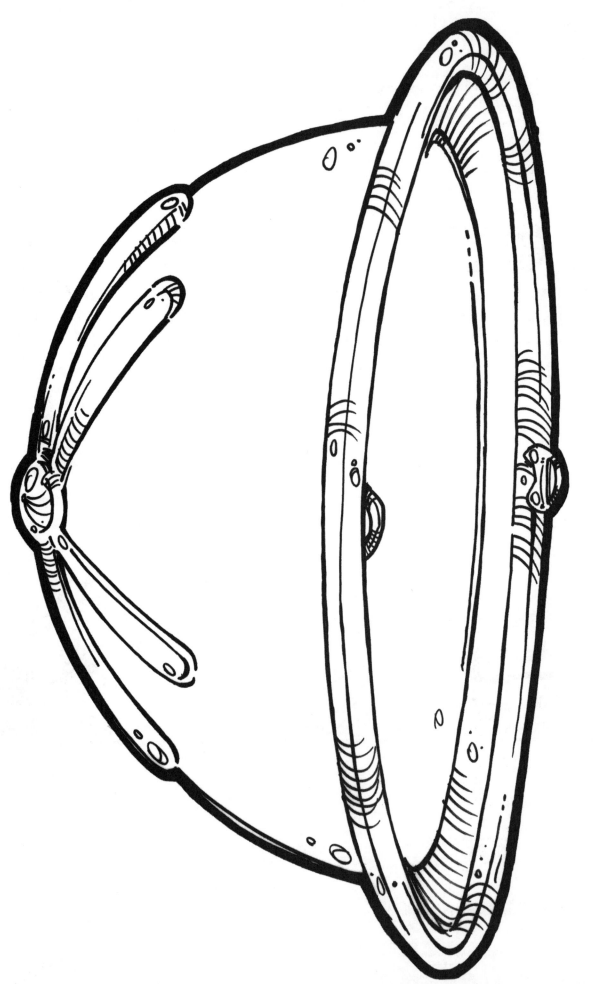

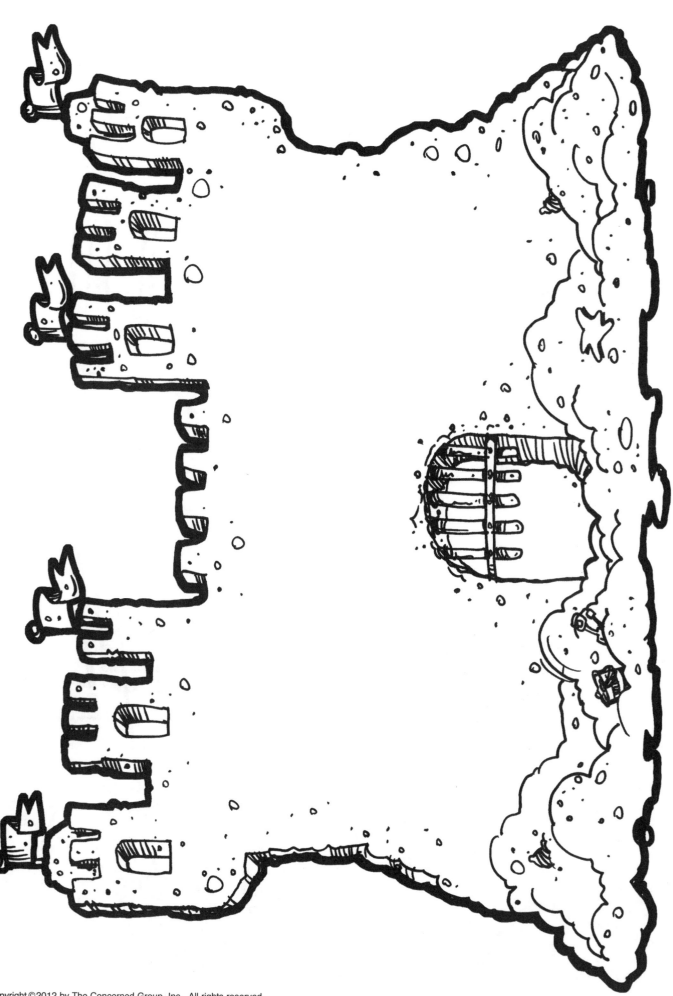

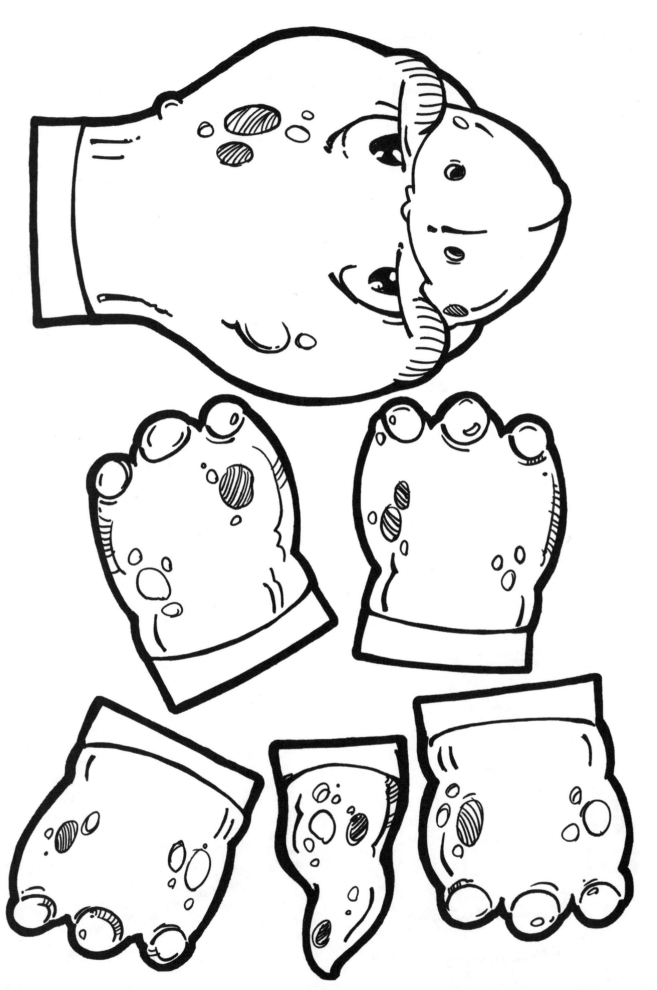